AMERICAN DIVA

~

Rosa Ponselle

AMERICAN DIVA

Mary Jane Phillips-Matz

WITH A FOREWORD BY BEVERLY SILLS

NORTHEASTERN UNIVERSITY PRESS
Boston

Advisor in music to Northeastern University Press

GUNTHER SCHULLER

FRONTISPIECE

Ponselle in the title role of Bellini's *Norma,* her greatest accomplishment. This production opened at the Metropolitan Opera in November 1927.
Courtesy of the Metropolitan Opera Archives

Library of Congress Cataloging-in-Publication Data

Phillips-Matz, Mary Jane.

Rosa Ponselle : American diva / Mary Jane Phillips-Matz.

p.   cm.

Includes bibliographical references, discography, and index.

ISBN 1-55553-317-5 (cloth : alk. paper)

1. Ponselle, Rosa, 1897–1981.   2. Sopranos (Singers)—United States—Biography.   I. Title.

ML420.P825P5   1997

782.1′092—dc21

[B]   97-19825

MN

Designed by Brian Hotchkiss/Vernon Press

Composed in Minion by Coghill Composition, Richmond, Virginia. Printed and bound by Thomson-Shore, Inc., Dexter, Michigan. The paper is Glatfelter Supple Opaque Recycled, an acid-free stock.

MANUFACTURED IN THE UNITED STATES OF AMERICA

01   00   99   98   97   5   4   3   2   1

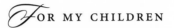FOR MY CHILDREN

Mary Ann

Catherine Eleanor

Margaret Spencer

Clare Ann

Carlino

~

Contents

Illustrations

Foreword

My singing teacher, Estelle Liebling, was a great pal of Rosa Ponselle. In 1953 Rosa, who was artistic director of the Baltimore Civic Opera, announced that Massenet's *Manon* would be part of her company's repertoire. Ms. Liebling arranged for me to go to Villa Pace, Rosa's home in Stevenson, Maryland, and audition for her. I had heard that Rosa was dieting and cranky. I bought her two pounds of dietetic breadsticks, ten calories each, and after tripping over 101 minute poodles that greeted me at the door, was ushered up to her bedroom. It was, after all, only 2 P.M. and Rosa was having breakfast. I offered her the breadsticks. We became friends for life. She immediately insisted I stay with her for "a few days" and work on *Manon*. "Don't you want to hear me sing it first?" "No," she said, "I want to *teach* you how to sing it." A few days turned into six weeks of exhilarating arguments about the difference between the Puccini heroine and the French one.

Two other arguments dominated our conversations. One was her efforts to get my voice in the "mask." Alas, not all of us had that incredible Ponselle mask. Would that we did. The other was her insatiable desire to find me a rich man to "sponsor" me. As a matchmaker her talent and determination were second only to that voice. Whether the man was married meant nothing. All that mattered was that I should be "sponsored"—and *never* marry. Her own experience with marriage was tragic. When I called to tell her a few years later that I was getting married, all she said was "Why?"

I loved Rosa Ponselle. And in my entire life I have never, ever, at any time heard a voice like that. Not *ever*. One evening at 2 A.M. she sang, unaccompanied, wandering around in a beautiful black velvet robe. I heard the "Liebestod" sung in a heartbreaking, passionate, and beautiful voice the likes of which I know I shall never hear again. She was complex, moody, noisily teary, hilariously funny, warm, encouraging, relentlessly critical, and very,

very easily hurt. Rosa, the woman, was quite a lot like the rest of us. Rosa, the artist, was unlike any other I have ever known.

BEVERLY SILLS

February 15, 1997

Acknowledgments

I should like to thank Miss Elayne Duke, President of the Rosa Ponselle Charitable Foundation, Inc., for her dedication to Ponselle and her support for this book. Having asked me to write it, she also helped with information as I conducted research in many archival sources. She provided the names of many people who contributed to my understanding of the life and career of the great dramatic soprano. Music lovers owe a debt of gratitude to Miss Duke for taking care to preserve the soprano's personal papers, scrapbooks, photographs, account books, costumes, and memorabilia. Beyond that, she was also responsible for saving many of the personal papers, scrapbooks, and photographs of Carmela Ponselle. After the two sisters' deaths, the trustees of the Ponselle Foundation placed most of this collection in the New York Public Library for the Performing Arts at Lincoln Center, where it is found in the Music Division's Special Collections and in the Archive of Recorded Sound. Costumes and other items of memorabilia were also donated to the Metropolitan Opera Archives and the Rosa Ponselle Fund of Meriden, Connecticut.

Beverly Sills needs no introduction to my readers, who are already familiar with the events of a career that now spans nearly fifty years. I have never ceased to admire her for her commitment to theater, especially to the Metropolitan, where she sits on the Managing Board of Directors, and to the Lincoln Center for the Performing Arts, where she is Chairman of the Board. I am truly grateful to her for writing the foreword to this biography of Rosa Ponselle, with whom she studied *Manon*.

This book could never have been published without the support of William Frohlich and his staff at Northeastern University Press, all of whom I thank for their help on this project. To Gunther Schuller, who read the typescript, I owe thanks for his kind words about it.

The entire staff of the Music Division and the Theater Collection of the New York Public Library for the Performing Arts at Lincoln Center contributed time and effort to this book. I want especially to thank Jean Bowen, former Chief of the Music Division (now Director of the Center for the Humanities of the New York Public

Library); Susan Sommer, Charles Eubanks, Linda Fairtile, John Shepard, and Frances Barulich. George Boziwick, who catalogued the Ponselle Collection, was particularly helpful.

At the New York Public Library Map Division I was guided by Alice Hudson, Chief, and Nancy Kandoian, Librarian, through the maze of real estate registers and atlases as I was identifying the buildings where the Ponzillo/Ponselle sisters lived and appeared in vaudeville.

As I have done through my entire professional life, I turned to my colleagues at the Metropolitan Opera Guild, Inc., and *Opera News* for information, advice, and moral support. I am particularly grateful to Rudoloph S. Rauch, Director of the Guild, for giving me a tape of David Grozier's Radio Free Europe interview with Ponselle. At *Opera News* I had unfailing support from Patrick J. Smith, Editor; Jane Poole, Senior Editor; Brian Kellow, Managing Editor; John Freeman, Marylis Sevilla-Gonzaga, and Jennifer Melick, Associate Editors; Lorraine Rosenfeld, Editorial Assistant; Gregory Downer, Art Director; Elaine Kones, Advertising Director; and Louise Guinther, the Assistant Editor of the magazine. The whole staff was responsible for the generous coverage *Opera News* gave to my 1997 article on the Ponzillo sisters in vaudeville. In addition to these dear colleagues, I owe heartfelt thanks to Paul Gruber, Director of Program Development at the Metropolitan Opera Guild, for advice all along the way and for generously lending his recordings of Ponselle. Geoff Peterson set aside his own concerns to rush me his *Custom Chronology* of Ponselle, drawn from the *Annals of the Metropolitan Opera*. C. J. Luten, the former Advertising Director and now a contributor to *Opera News,* offered his analysis of Ponselle's technique and commentary on her recordings. My thanks also go to Jerome Hines and Lucia Evangelista Hines for help in understanding Ponselle's technique, to Patricia Brown for research on it, and to Mr. Luten's colleague and friend Anne J. O'Donnell, the Artistic Consultant for the Sarasota Opera Guild, for information about many figures associated with Ponselle, among them the heirs of Anna Ryan. Louis Snyder, former director of the Met's Press Office, contributed his recollections.

No words could adequately express my gratitude to James Ryan Mulvey, a descendant of the family of Anna Ryan, who was the Ponzillo sisters' teacher, mentor, sponsor, advisor, and friend for nearly forty years. By lending me the Ryan family scrapbooks and other loose clippings inherited from James Edgar Ryan, he made it easy for me to confirm data on dozens of events in Carmela's and Rosa's careers in vaudeville and opera.

Robert Tuggle, Archivist, and John Pennino, Assistant Archivist of the Metropolitan Opera Archives, were generous with their time and advice, particularly in choosing illustrations for this book; I owe special thanks to Bob for also letting me use photographs from his private collection and to John for providing the complete box office figures for Ponselle's last two seasons at the Metropolitan. Richard Wandel, archivist of the New York Philharmonic, gave me the correct dates for Ponselle's Carnegie Hall and Brooklyn concerts with that orchestra.

Aldo Mancusi, Founder and President of the Enrico Caruso Museum of America, went miles out of his way, literally, to visit Caiazzo, the southern Italian town from which the Ponzillos and Contes emigrated. The documentation he brought back included certificates of baptism and birth records from the civil registry, photographs, and absolute confirmation that Caruso's ancestors came from a large town just a few miles from the Ponzillos' home. Other documents were provided by Mancusi's friend Enrico Caruso. His friend Nino Pantano offered valuable Caruso and Ponselle material.

Licia Albanese contributed her recollections of Ponselle, as did Rose Bampton, who made her Metropolitan Opera debut in *La Gioconda* when Ponselle sang the title role. Ninety-two-year-old Michael Sisca, who attended Ponselle's debut in 1918, was always ready to answer my questions and bring forth his precious personal recollections of Caruso, Gatti-Casazza, Ponselle, Romani, and dozens of other figures from the opera business, many of whom were personal friends of the Sisca family. Charles Mintzer corrected biographical data on the careers of Rosa Raisa and Tullio Serafin, while Thomas G. Kaufman provided many exact dates and casts of operas.

One descendant of Ponselle's mother's family, Cynthia Di Tallo Starks, has been tireless in her pursuit of civil records and other historical material in Connecticut. In Meriden assistance was provided by Valerie Bubon and Robert Cyr of the Rosa Ponselle Fund, the librarians of the public library, and the staffs of the City Clerk's office, the Probate Court, and the Registry of Deeds. I owe particular thanks to Christine Boganski for help in the City Clerk's office.

In the Italian Government Travel Office I relied on Robert Talignani for information about present-day Caiazzo and Josephine Inzerillo, now retired, for her knowledge of Italian culture in Italy and New York City. The staff of the Italian Cultural Institute assisted with research on the Risorgimento battles in the Terra di Lavoro. I owe particular thanks to the Consul General, Franco Mistretta, to Mrs. Nives Mutti, who directs music programs at the Institute, and to Dr. Gioacchino Lanza Tomasi, its Director.

Help in finding census and immigration documents was given by my longtime colleague Robert Morris, Director, and Joel Buchman, Assistant Archivist of the National Archives Branch in New York City.

Ponselle's trusted friend and collaborator, Igor Chichagov, recalled for me the years at Villa Pace after 1951 and particularly of Ponselle's recording and coaching sessions in her home. I have often turned to Enrico Aloi, an early admirer of the soprano and author of books about her, for confirmation of scattered facts about her life. Leigh Martinet, whom I first met in Baltimore decades ago, and Anthony and Yolanda Stivanello provided information on early performances of opera in Baltimore and on the Baltimore Civic Opera. Alan Coleridge brought his knowledge of the theater to this project, directing me to valuable research resources for the vaudeville era. David Alexander Terry deserves my special thanks for giving up his time to this project. William Crawford III has been unfailingly generous with information about scores and performance practice. Edgar Vincent helped me tie up loose ends and offered help in matters concerning Ponselle's colleagues. I thank Edward Downes for his father's review of Ponselle's debut.

Mrs. Elaine Troostwyck Toscanini and Walfredo Toscanini contributed their own and their families' recollections of Rosa Ponzillo's life in New Haven. Ginger Dreyfus Karren kindly lent me books by her grandmother Marie Volpe on her own career and that of her husband, Arnold Volpe, and their friendship with William Thorner and the Ponzillos.

Difficult research on Villa Platani and Ponselle's summers on Lake Como was done at the site by two dear friends, Florence and Ralph Postiglione, and their acquaintances there. I am also grateful to another much-loved associate, Dr. Giuseppe Pugliese, former Director of Public Relations for the Teatro La Fenice in Venice, for his generous sharing of his friendship with Tullio Serafin. The Banca Nazionale di Lavoro made available *Campania,* its ambitious study of the history and art of that province.

Emelise Aleandri's study of Italian-American vaudeville and her stage presentation of "Frizzi e lazzi," with its recreation of the art of Farfariello (Eduardo Migliaccio), opened the doors to an understanding of why the Ponzillo sisters got booked into Mrs. Mary Marino's nickelodeon on First Avenue and the old Star Theatre on Lexington Avenue in Manhattan.

Also of special interest are the Ponselle interviews conducted by Dr. James A. Drake for the Ithaca College Archives and Special Collections, Ithaca, New York. I am grateful to Keith D. Eiten, Music Librarian of Ithaca College, for permission to use this material. William Ashbrook, Editor, *Opera Quarterly,* and Kay Robin Alexander, Permissions Specialist, Duke University Press, have generously given permission for use of Dr. Drake's two articles about Rosa Ponselle in *Opera Quarterly.* Dr. Drake has also generously shared information on the Ponzillos' early years in vaudeville as well as other data relevant to their opera careers.

Personal observations on Ponselle's art were offered by Harold C. Schonberg, David Hamilton, Will Crutchfield, William Weaver, and Frank Bradley. Hugh Johns, Thomas Brown, and George Bernard shared their recollections of the soprano, as did Joseph Puglisi, Blanche Thebom, William Warfield, and Paul Hume. Dr. James Bailey of Petersburg, Virginia, recalled his friendship with Ponselle in the years after World War II.

Robert Tollett, my respected colleague, lent several unusual pictures of Ponselle, for which he has my deepest gratitude.

To Michael Bronson, the Metropolitan Opera, and Texaco, I owe thanks for permission to use excerpts from Ponselle's broadcasts during the Saturday afternoon intermissions and from Francis Robinson's biographical study of her.

William Park and James Drake are responsible for helping with the discography. Mr. Park's compilation of Ponselle's recordings appeared in her autobiography, written with Dr. Drake, and more recently, in Dr. Drake's centennial biography of the soprano, published by Amadeus Press in 1997. I also thank the Rosa Ponselle Charitable Foundation, Inc., for its permission for use of the discography.

I owe sincere thanks to several people who are no longer living, among them the Very Reverend Monsignor Dante Del Fiorentino, a beloved friend who baptized all but one of my children; Giuseppe Bamboschek, perhaps the Ponzillo sisters' earliest trusted colleague in New York, and the man who introduced me to Carmela in the mid-1940s; Hans Busch, Earle Lewis, Francis Robinson, Boris Goldovsky, Gerald Fitzgerald, William Seward, and Ida and Louise Cook.

Finally, to my dearly loved children: Clare helped to compile the acknowledgments and bibliography and read the completed manuscript; she, Margaret, and Carlino chose the illustrations and helped with editorial matters. As they have always done, they gave me unfaltering moral support.

A NOTE ABOUT THE
ANNA RYAN—JAMES E. RYAN SCRAPBOOKS

As I was working on the research for this book, one question remained unanswered: Who was Anna Ryan?

I became convinced that solid information about her was essential for any study about her three best pupils, Carmela, Anthony, and Rosa Ponzillo. Apart from her name, however, little was known about her. In many of Carmela's and Rosa's interviews—when they were still known as the Ponzillo sisters and, later, when they had both taken the name Ponselle—Anna Ryan was acknowledged generously by both sisters as the organist and choir director of the Church of Our Lady of Mount Carmel in Meriden, Connecticut, the woman who had first taught them piano, voice, and sight-reading.

When we construct a chronology of the Ponzillos' childhood and youth, we see at once that all three children of Ben and Maddalena Ponzillo left school in or just after sixth grade. In several interviews Carmela said that she left school when she was twelve to work in the five-and-ten, then in a millinery shop. Tony told James E. Drake that his father took him out of school to help in the family's bakery and coal business. And Rosa said in several interviews that her formal schooling was "nil or next to nothing."

From the day they left school, then, the Ponzillo children's sole education came from catechism classes and from Anna Ryan. Carmela, eight and a half years older than Rosa, and Tony, six years older, became the first beneficiaries of Anna Ryan's teaching. She was their music teacher, beginning just after the turn of the century— between 1903 and 1910—when Rosa was still a small child. According to several of Carmela's accounts, theirs was a household where the only musical instrument was their father's accordion, which Carmela learned to play. Not until Carmela was a teenager did her father buy the upright piano that the Ponzillo parents showed to the truant officer when he went to their house to track down Rosa when she was absent from school. When Tony was old enough, he belonged to the parish band and the town band; then he brought in the instruments that Rosa remembered his storing in his room.

Out of that house on Springdale Avenue came three children who grew up to have careers in music. Carmela's and Rosa's were long, while Tony's was brief. All three acknowledged their debt to the parish organist. Anna M. Ryan, born in Meriden in May 1874, had been the organist at Saint Rose's Church before she came to Our Lady of Mount Carmel. She was in her twenties when she first heard Carmela's voice ring out in the children's choir. Like the Ponzillos, Anna Ryan was the child of immigrant parents. Patrick F. Ryan and his wife, Katherine Degnan, were both born in Ireland. They had a son, Joseph P. Ryan, and two daughters, Anna and Kitty. Anna, the Ponzillo children's teacher, remained single.

Anna Ryan was responsible for perceiving Carmela's talent and encouraging it. Two years after she first heard Carmela, she then had Tony to deal with. Anna Ryan got Carmela to New York City and to a reputable voice teacher. Through a church placement bureau she found jobs for herself as organist and Carmela as soloist at Saint Patrick's Church in Long Island City. From dozens of interviews and from Rosa Ponselle's financial records we learn that she lived with Carmela in the McCabe family rooming house on West Sixty-fourth Street in New York. It seems likely that she commuted back and forth to Meriden for part of this period, for we know she was there when Rosa was about ten or twelve, in 1907 or 1910.

She was certainly in New York, though, when Rosa came to live there in 1915, to join Carmela in the dinner concerts at Adolph Lorber's restaurant and in vaudeville, for Carmela, in an interview at that time, described their rooms on Sixty-fourth Street, "where Anna Ryan was always with me and still is." Ryan also moved with Carmela and Rosa to 307 West Ninety-seventh Street, then to the larger apartment one block away, in the building at 260 Riverside Drive, and finally to Rosa's luxury penthouse at 90 Riverside. Rosa was paying Anna Ryan for "house" (household expenses) and "music lessons" long after she became famous. She continued to support her former teacher through the last years of Ryan's life. After Ryan died in New York in 1943, she left some of her possessions to her cousin, James E. Ryan, who was by then living at 415 East Fifty-second Street, "near Greta Garbo," as he told his family. (Garbo then lived in River House, at the end of the block.) To James Ryan, an officer of the J. P. Morgan Company, came the two scrapbooks that I have referred to in this book as the "Ryan Scrapbooks" or the "Anna Ryan–James E. Ryan Scrapbooks." They were begun when he was a child.

Given Anna Ryan's long association with the Ponzillo children—from when Rosa was a small child through her entire career—any object from her estate relating to the Ponselle sisters' careers would be valuable. The two scrapbooks, which were left by James E. Ryan to his own cousin and godson, James Ryan Mulvey, contain material gathered from day to day, including items from someone who had access to the sisters themselves and to their managers. They reach from Carmela's and Rosa's career in vaudeville through the end of Carmela's life and beyond. There are "reminiscence" interviews, in which every reference to Anna Ryan is underlined in red. Then come hundreds of tiny clipped items from reviews. Many are raves, but some are balanced assessments of a given performance, a concert, recital, or opera. After Anna Ryan's death other material was added, including the *Opera News* obituary of Carmela and accounts of Rosa's marriage, divorce, and life at Villa Pace.

Introduction

Rosa Ponselle, born Rosa Ponzillo in 1897, belonged to my parents' generation. She began her career in her native Connecticut, first as a "song slide
girl" in silent film houses, then as a dinner concert singer. She and her sister
and brother had all learned piano and the rudiments of vocal technique
from their parish church's organist and choir director, Anna M. Ryan. In
1915 Rosa moved to vaudeville in a duo with her older sister, Carmela. The
Ponzillos first presented their act in Mrs. Mary Marino's tiny theater on
First Avenue in Italian Harlem, then, as Carmela said in an early interview,
in the "old Star Theatre on the Upper East Side," both in New York City.

Both sisters eventually got into opera. One of the most improbable debuts in operatic history took place in 1918, when Rosa Ponzillo, rechristened
Ponselle, first appeared at the Metropolitan Opera House in Giuseppe Verdi's *La forza del destino*, partnered by Enrico Caruso. Here was a twenty-
one-year-old with no extensive vocal training in America or Europe, with
no experience singing opera anywhere and almost no real knowledge of it,
bursting on the scene in a difficult Verdi opera, at the side of the world's
most famous and beloved tenor. Ponselle made her mark at first because she
possessed one of the most glorious and distinctive voices of her century.
With her musicianship and mastery of technique, control, and art, she won
a phenomenal success that sustained her through nearly two decades as a
Metropolitan Opera artist and as a concert, recital, and recording artist.

Over the years, as Rosa Ponselle sang all over the United States, she
became this country's best-loved prima donna. Critics hailed her with thousands of favorable reviews; she was truly "Our American Rose," as one reviewer dubbed her. Between 1929 and 1933 Ponselle's European engagements
with the Royal Opera at Covent Garden in London and the first Florence
May Festival in Italy proved her mettle on foreign soil, where she was greeted
as a diva in the grandest traditions of her art.

After her retirement from the Metropolitan and the concert stage in the late 1930s, Ponselle lived in style in her home, Villa Pace, just outside Baltimore. At first she came to the city as the wife of the mayor's son; after their divorce she remained there. Past fifty, Ponselle found yet another career coaching young singers—both famous and yet to be discovered—and shaping the success of the Baltimore Civic Opera, where she worked as artistic director until 1979. Hers was a lifetime of dedication to music.

I was a child when I first heard Ponselle's voice on the old wind-up Victrola in the living room of my grandmother, Evelyn Osborn Spencer. Stacked with Ponselle's old, black wax platters were Caruso's "La donna è mobile" and the quartet from *Rigoletto,* a noisy "Marching through Georgia," and Vernon Dalhart's "The Wreck of the Old 97" and "The Prisoner's Song." Yet another star of that peculiar collection was Al Jolson, who, as I later learned, had studied voice with William Thorner, the man who acted as a manager and agent for Carmela and Rosa Ponzillo and got auditions for both of them at the Metropolitan Opera. From those auditions their careers were born.

Having been raised in Ohio on concerts by the Dayton Philharmonic and performances by touring opera companies that came regularly, I had heard a lot of music even before my teen years. But the most important musical influence in my youth was the open-air Cincinnati Summer Opera at the Zoo.

As a "Zoo regular," I had also interviewed many famous singers and had met scores of them long before I moved to New York. And in the early 1950s, when I was a writer and assistant editor of *Opera News,* I was asked to interview Geraldine Farrar and Rosa Ponselle, among other singers and conductors, active and retired. "Dear Gerry," who was then living in Ridgefield, Connecticut, proved to be rather remote and cool. But Ponselle, whom I had met earlier in Baltimore, was another matter. Living in luxury in the white stucco mansion she had built on a hilltop in the country outside the city, she won me in a moment with her fire and spirit. She was as opulent of character as her house was of style, the perfect embodiment of everything I loved as "Italian" and "operatic." Tall, bold, dramatic, and grand of gesture, she remained the generous prima donna of earlier years. But Ponselle also had something else: to her "operatic" nature was matched a healthy, American-girl manner, suggestive of Helen Wills Moody and Amelia Earhart. Ponselle never lost her Connecticut accent; she occasionally tossed out a slang word or phrase. This was an utterly modern woman: "our American Rose."

The day with her was a refreshing change from hours I had spent in the suffocating apartments of retired singers, listening to them lament the passing of the grand old days, long gone. Ponselle had found a new life, a new world, with the just-organized Baltimore Civic Opera. Although we spoke of the "old Met" and her reverence for Caruso, because that was what I was commissioned to do, Ponselle ended my visit by having me hear some of her students as she rehearsed them. She was looking to the future, not to the past.

My 1952 interview with Ponselle, originally published in *Opera News*, served as the starting point for my research for this biography. Almost all other sources for this book are documents from public and private collections in the United States and abroad. As I worked through them, I discovered not just the diva but also the rich personality of the sportswoman—swimming, sledding on Long Island and in Riverside Park, playing tennis in Hollywood with David O. Selznick and Fanny Brice, mountain climbing in the Alps, golfing in Atlanta, biking in New York City, fishing in the Atlantic off the Connecticut shore, watching the races from the royal enclosure at Ascot in England or from the members' suite at Pimlico. Ponselle's screen test of October 13, 1936, showed (as the clack board described her) a woman who was five feet seven inches tall, weighing 139 pounds, with light brown eyes and black hair. The snapshots of her in California show a lithe player on the tennis courts. This was a diva with a difference.

Even some sixteen years later, when I interviewed her in Baltimore, Ponselle was beautiful by any standard, bursting with the energy that powered one of the most fascinating careers of all time: from the parish church children's choir to the "slide singer" to half of a sister act in "vaude," and from there to the Metropolitan Opera, as star, and to the Baltimore Civic Opera, as artistic director.

AMERICAN DIVA

~

CHAPTER 1

Italy, Fortunate Campania, and the Terra di Lavoro

The soprano known as Rosa Ponselle was born Rosa Ponzillo to first-genera-
tion Italian immigrant parents in the New England factory city of Meriden,
Connecticut, on January 22, 1897. Their third child, she was also the third
born in this country. Over the previous seventeen years a large contingent
of Ponselle's close relatives had come to the United States, most from the
area northeast of Naples. In 1881 some of her family emigrated; others followed later. Like members of the group who had preceded them, they declared to the Immigration Service that they were "cultivators," "farmers,"
or "peasants." In this country, through their own industry, they created a
small empire in the grocery and coal business, and as tailors, dressmakers,
and owners of saloons and boarding houses in New York City, Schenectady,
and later Connecticut. This set them apart from the millions of immigrants
who became day laborers and factory hands.

From her simple origins Ponselle rose to become one of the greatest
sopranos in the history of music. Like her voice, her career has no real
parallel in theater, for it began not on the opera or concert stage but in that
familiar, homey American emporium the five-and-ten, the dime store,
where she played the piano and sang, demonstrating sheet music for pro-

spective buyers. As a teenager she sang in motion picture houses, popular restaurants, and in 1915 on the vaudeville stage, where her sister had already made a name for herself. Ponselle made her debut at the Metropolitan Opera in November 1918, just after World War I ended, as Leonora in Verdi's *La forza del destino,* with Enrico Caruso as her tenor. The twenty-one-year-old soprano, with no previous experience in opera, became a celebrity with interviewers at the door, contracts with the Metropolitan and a recording company, and a full calendar of lucrative concert and recital engagements. Ponselle's operatic career reached across the years of "the Peace between the Wars," from 1918 until 1937, when she left the Metropolitan. But even after she had married and officially retired, she continued to work, teaching and later assuming the title of artistic director of the Baltimore Civic Opera.

The critic David Hamilton calls this an operatic "Cinderella story"; but it is also the saga of a clan, the Ponzillo family and their relatives, who swam in the stream of immigration but rose above it, powered by their pride, courage, and fierce spirit of independence. After they left Italy, these strengths brought them into the ranks of American entrepreneurs and transformed the three Ponzillo children into adventurers. These qualities gave us a peerless artist, Rosa Ponselle.

THE TERRA DI LAVORO ⁓

Of all the wonders of Italy, perhaps none is more recognizable than the image of the Bay of Naples, with its azure sky, the port, the teeming city itself, and Vesuvius looming in the background. Like Venice with its gondolas, like Rome with Saint Peter's and the Colosseum, the Bay of Naples suggests ancient mysteries beyond what the eye can see. Unlike those other, equally famous cities, Naples also has a heart that sings, for dozens of the most familiar "Italian folk songs" are actually the voice of emigration, evoking the much-loved places or people from that cherished sea and strand. From " 'O Sole Mio" and "Torna a Surriento" to "Funiculì, Funiculà," "Santa Lucia," and "Addio, mia bella Napoli," this repertory brings back memories of things loved and lost. Italians, particularly those from the south, possess a kind of spirit of place that they never surrender. Theirs is the world that was left behind by millions of Italian emigrants who came to the United States, for Naples was the "capital of the south" for nearly two thousand years and the point of departure for most who left Italy in the last century. Because Naples was the closing door on an old life for generations of emigrants, the city and Vesuvius were the last Italian sights the departing passengers saw. Small wonder, then, that they never lost their nostalgia for the world they left behind.

Naples itself began as two small settlements of Greek and Italic peoples on the hills above the bay. The first of these, Parthenope, founded between 800 and 700 B.C., was followed sometime after the year 524 B.C. by Neapolis, peopled mostly by Greeks from their original seat at Cuma, just beyond the northernmost reach of the bay. About a century later the prosperity of this "New City" aroused the envy of the warlike Samnites, who lived in the hilly region to the north and east. Over the centuries Naples was the seat of rude tribes and Roman masters, of powerful dukes and bishops, and later, of the rulers from the houses of the Normans, Hohenstaufen and Brunswick, Anjou, Aragon, and Bourbon, of the Bonapartes, and after 1815, of the last Bourbons of Naples, the sovereigns of the Kingdom of the Two Sicilies. With its royal residences, some in medieval fortresses and others in more recent structures, its magnificent churches and the Royal San Carlo Theater, Naples once surpassed Rome, Milan, and Venice in population.

The Neapolitans could never have amassed their riches without the natural wealth that came from the agricultural Eden north of the bay. In this crescent-shaped hinterland above Naples is the plain of "Fortunate Campania," or Campania Felix, as the Romans called it. Through it the Volturno River flows to the sea, describing a great arc northeast of Naples and through the farm country around Caserta and Capua. This area is the Terra di Lavoro, the Land of Work, and it is the home soil of the Ponzillos and their collateral families. As the Italian essayist Roberto Mainardi observes, "The economic and cultural life of the region, even that of the coastal strip, is only moderately influenced by the sea and sea activities. . . . Even Naples itself is not really a maritime center; most Neapolitans belong to the countryside or to the hills and are more inclined toward agriculture and the typical service industries of a center with a rural hinterland than toward maritime activity. The pervading rural character of the region can be seen in the very names Campania [countryside] and Terra di Lavoro [land of work]." This entire region benefited from the radial pattern of roads leading to Naples. "Of the various nuclei that went to make up Campania, the Terra di Lavoro has always had the strongest agricultural tradition," Mainardi goes on. "The presence of trees (poplars, elms, vines) is a characteristic of this countryside. . . . Mediterranean polyculture flourishes, with the mixed farming of olive trees and vines, fruit trees and fodder crops."

All this might have changed when Italy became a nation after 1860 and the Second War of Italian Independence, which brought new blood and ideas to the south; but it did not. Unification was achieved in the battles of 1859 and 1860; the sovereign, Vittorio Emanuele II, reigned in Turin, the capital. Lombardy, Emilia-Romagna, and Tuscany had been freed before March 1860; by October of that year Garibaldi's victories in the south added Naples and the entire Kingdom of the Two Sicilies to the new country. In this struggle Garibaldi's campaign along the Volturno River was decisive in defeating the Neapolitan army. George Martin, in *Verdi: His Music, Life and Times,* states that the Battle of the Volturno was "possibly the most important of the war."

This battle was fought where the Ponzillo and Conte families lived; and the ruin it brought—then and in the decades that followed—was one factor in inducing them and others in their area to leave Italy. Had Garibaldi not won the Battle of the Volturno, the Neapolitan army would have restored the king, Francesco II, to his throne. With that, Naples, Sicily, and the whole of southern Italy would have been lost. As King Vittorio Emanuele II and his recently seated parliament discovered, progress in the south would not be swift, for the traditional ways of feudalism remained in place in the former Kingdom of the Two Sicilies, no matter how many well-meaning, modern, educated bureaucrats and teachers were sent down from the north to drag this ancient culture into the circle of European nations. Massimo D'Azeglio, the son-in-law of the novelist Alessandro Manzoni and one of the most powerful and respected figures in Italy, had been a minister in the government of Vittorio Emanuele II before unification. Deploring the condition of the new nation-state in the autumn of 1861, he even questioned whether "the Neapolitans" really wanted to be part of Italy, given their massive resistance to the influence of the north.

When the early revolts in Campania and a major uprising in Sicily erupted, Vittorio Emanuele II sent his troops to prevent further violence because the aroused populace threatened the very existence of Italy. In Turin, Milan, Venice, and Florence these "new Italians" of the south were perceived as a threat to public order. Considered poor, backward, superstitious, sick, illiterate, and too religious in the eyes of the secular government of Italy, they appeared to have no interest in the idea of progress. Keeping their children out of public schools so they could work in the family shop or in the fields, refusing vaccination, suspecting the reclamation and draining of marshlands, and despising developments in agriculture, they also often supported the very landlords and overseers who oppressed them rather than show allegiance to Vittorio Emanuele II. The ancient culture of the south—the culture that produced a Rosa Ponselle—was dismissed as "pagan," and southerners were thought of as dangerous, fractious children.

This was a struggle no one could win, and soon there emerged a new generation of southerners so disaffected that they were disposed to leave everything they knew and seek a new life on the other side of the Atlantic. This was the situation of the Ponzillos and their relatives in their towns and villages of the Terra di Lavoro.

THE PONZILLOS AND THEIR CLAN IN THE VOLTURNO VALLEY ⌒

Far from being a backwater, the Terra di Lavoro was the very heart of Campania, a world that could boast thousands of years of history and culture. It was also a hotbed of disturbance after 1859. When Rosa Ponselle's ancestors lived there, the capital of the Volturno Valley was the twin community of Santa Maria Capua Vetere, which attracts tourists today, and the newer

Capua. Now the nearest large, modern city is Caserta, the present capital of the province that bears its name. Its recent reputation as a tourist attraction is owed to the royal palace built there in 1752 for Charles III of Bourbon.

The road that meanders north and east from Capua leads to several villages and small market towns that lie on the way to the next important commercial and administrative center. On hillsides along the winding Volturno stand these towns, some scattered precariously on rough terrain, others nestled near the foot of valleys leading down to the river. The first is Caiazzo, the home of the Ponzillos; next come Alvignano and Dragoni, the original towns of the Faraone family, who were relatives and godparents of Rosa Ponselle's mother. Each of these towns is about five miles from the next. About five miles beyond Dragoni, in plain sight, perched on a steep slope on the north side of the river, stands Piedimonte d'Alife, now called Piedimonte Matese, the home of Enrico Caruso's parents, Marcellino Caruso and Anna Baldini.

After the unification of Italy, Caiazzo and these other villages fell under the jurisdiction of Piedimonte d'Alife. This meant that when the Ponzillos and their closest relatives, the Contes, Giannellis, and Faraones, had to transact official business, it had to be done in the Carusos' town. In Piedimonte they paid taxes, registered tenant contracts and deeds, got permission to travel, and took care of all legal disputes and matters relating to the new universal military service.

Caiazzo, the Ponzillos' home, now has just over five thousand people in the town itself and another eight hundred in the hamlets around it. The largest of these is Piana di Caiazzo, on the banks of the Volturno. Here is the bridge built by Hannibal of Carthage to facilitate his march on Capua. The ancient monuments of Piana are Roman ruins, the parish church of Santa Maria a Marciano, built in the 1300s on the foundations of a far older sanctuary, and on one wall of the transept of the church, a Roman milestone from Caiatia. Looming above the valley of Piana di Caiazzo is Monte Santa Croce, where a medieval monastery stood. At Castel Morrone the ruins of a huge fortress from the 1200s are surrounded by farmhouses. The site of battles in the thirty-year war between Emperor Frederick II and the papacy, this hamlet also saw an engagement in the Second War of Italian Independence in September and October 1860, when Garibaldi's men were fighting the troops of the Kingdom of the Two Sicilies in one of the crucial battles along the Volturno. Rosa Ponselle's father, Bernardino Ponzillo, was less than one year old when this furious engagement tore through the area.

Caiazzo, where he was born, stands above Piana, on a hillside dominated by a massive medieval fortress. The town is surrounded by fields, groves of fruit and olive trees, and woodlands with stands of holm oaks, with their twisted trunks, black bark, and thick canopy overhead, all inviolable and sacred to pagan worshipers. In such forests stone altars were built for religious rites; inscriptions carved on their bases warned that anyone who cut down a tree would be killed. Because this area was inhabited by Italic peoples in prehistoric times, we have every reason to believe that these woods were holy sites, like the sacred forest in the opera *Norma*. The town of Caiazzo was probably founded by the Oscans, but like so much of the Terra di Lavoro, it was overrun by the warrior Samnites from the east. With the coming of the Romans down the Via Appia, Caiazzo became Caiatia. Its other masters over the centuries were the abbot of the monastery of Montecassino, the dukes of Benevento, the counts of Capua, Ferdinand of Aragon, and a noble family from Florence, its feudal lords. Nobles here possessed huge estates, or *latifondi*, the source of the peasants' misery.

Caiazzo was not without great historical figures, among them a Roman consul, Aulo Attilio Caiatino, and Pier delle Vigne, who began his career as a minister of state for Frederick II. Born about 1190 in Caiazzo, Pier reached the apex of his power when he was named chancellor to the emperor, soon after the balance between the popes and the Western Empire was tipped in favor of the papacy. In his capacity as Frederick's chancellor, Pier rewrote the laws of this realm and became his most trusted counsellor. He remained in a position of almost absolute power until 1247; then he was suspected of treason and committed suicide after being imprisoned and tortured. More than 250 years after Pier's death, his genius was revealed when his collected letters, poetry, and account of his life were published. One of the streets of Caiazzo is named for this brilliant courtier, whose house is marked with a coat of arms.

Like most Italian towns, Caiazzo has changed over the centuries, and particularly since World War II, as new buildings have been added around the historic center; but within it many of its old monuments remain. Except for the street names, much of Caiazzo's center is unchanged from the days when Rosa Ponselle's parents were living there. Along the Via Attilio Caiatino is the Church of San Francesco, built in the 1300s. Near to it is the city hall, the *municipio* established after 1860, occupying the building that was once a monastery belonging to the Franciscans. Further on, a votive chapel boasts a fine Renaissance doorway. The town square, Piazza Giuseppe Verdi, stands over the ruins of the old Roman forum; it, in turn, was built where the center of the primitive community was originally located. A Roman cistern, with six huge basins for water, is hidden beneath the square; it was fed by a reservoir constructed by the Romans in the nearby hamlet of San Giovanni e Paolo. On market day this picturesque piazza is crowded with vendors from surrounding towns, selling all kinds of hard and soft goods, and with local farmers who bring in their produce. In the nineteenth century, when the Ponzillos lived here, this meant that Caiazzo was a center for the exchange of information by word of mouth, the medium that was crucial to the people, more than 80 percent of whom could not read or write. The market was their place of learning, and the culture of this place was the baggage the Ponzillos, Contes, and Faraones brought with them to America.

The most important religious structure in the town is the Church of Maria Santissima Assunta, for Caiazzo was the seat of a bishop from about A.D. 800 until the see was suppressed in 1818. A new bishopric was founded there in 1849, after the uprisings, and the present diocese is Alife-Caiazzo. Beyond Maria Santissima is the small Church of the Annunciation, with a fine Renaissance doorway. At the top of the hill stands the castle originally built by the Lombards.

This, then, is Caiazzo, the home of Rosa Ponselle's antecedents, the Ponzillos, Contes, Giannellis, and Espositos. Several respected artists were born here during the last four centuries, and in the 1700s and early 1800s the town was the birthplace of two scientists, one of whom was the physician Niccolo Giannelli, who may have come from the family of Carmela Giannelli, Rosa Ponselle's grandmother. As its history shows, Caiazzo was fortunate in having a certain level of education and culture that reached everyone who lived there. In this it is superior to other rural towns where all knowledge is kept within the four walls of the landlord's villa, where the parish church has one or two insignificant paintings and perhaps a decaying fresco. In the churches of Caiazzo are many fine works of art, which were called "the Bible of the poor." The very civic order and architecture of the place distinguish it from many of its drastically impoverished neighbors. Because there was a cathedral, there was also a rich tradition of music. Rosa Ponselle was told by someone in her family that one of the Ponzillos, a prelate of the church, had a fine baritone voice. If this is true, it is beyond doubt that he sang in the Church of Maria Santissima Assunta, for this was the Ponzillos' home parish; it is here that their records are found in the parish registers. As we know from Rosa Ponselle's later interviews and from evidence gathered from a cousin of Rosa's, Cynthia Di Tallo Starks, the Contes also had a family musical tradition.

In Caiazzo in the mid-nineteenth century two branches of the Ponzillos lived in the center of the town. Two first cousins, Francesco and Antonio, were having children at the same time; the baptism and civil records show a small difference in status between them, for one tilled the soil and the other had a trade.

Bernardino Ponzillo, Rosa Ponselle's father, was born on December 1, 1859. The son of Antonio Ponzillo and Carmela Giannelli, he was baptized in the cathedral on December 2. The godparents were Antonio Mondrone and Stefana Di Giglio, both from that parish. On that same day, just after having his son baptized, Antonio Ponzillo presented himself at the city hall and declared his son's birth before the constituted official of the civil registry of the province of the Terra di Lavoro. This was, of course, still in the old Kingdom of the Two Sicilies. Antonio Ponzillo, "by profession a coachman," swore that the infant had been born the day before in his house on Strada San Felice. Although we do not know who employed him, it is safe to say that it was either a prelate, the bishop or one of the monsignors, or a noble or aristocratic family, for only they could afford horses and a carriage. Antonio said that he was the son of Giuseppe Ponzillo, who was still living, and that he and his wife were both thirty-six years of age. His witnesses, who accompanied him to the civil registry office, were both tailors, one being Nicola Bernardo, living on the Ponzillos' street, and the other, Stefano Petrucci, living on Strada Tasso.

Bernardino Ponzillo was just eleven when Rosa Ponselle's mother, Maddalena Conte, was born on the same Strada Tasso, in another parish of Caiazzo, San Nicola de Figulis. Born on December 20, 1870, she was the daughter of Antonio Conte and Fortunata Esposito. Her godparents, Giovanni Battista Faraone and his sister Filomena, figured so heavily in the child's life that the family later believed that Maddalena's mother was a Faraone rather than an Esposito. Maddalena's father, Antonio Conte, took her for baptism, then registered her birth at the city hall, where he stated that he and his wife were both peasants. One of his witnesses, Giacinto Di Carlo, was a servant; the other, Luigi Squegli, was a tailor. One lived on Strada San Francesco, the other on Strada Tasso. Like Antonio Ponzillo, Antonio Conte could neither read nor write.

We know nothing of the childhood of Rosa Ponselle's parents, save that conditions in towns like Caiazzo were considerably better than those in country villages, where farmers often slept on the ground floor with their animals or, if they were better off, slept on the top floor and kept the animals below. Townspeople were healthier and better fed than those in the hamlets. Of Ponselle's parents, we know that Bernardino Ponzillo could read and write; Maddalena could not.

When Bernardino Ponzillo turned twenty, he was conscripted into the army of Vittorio Emanuele II, where he became a *bersagliere,* or sharpshooter, wearing the splendid plumed hat that was the crown of his uniform. Of all the troops, these were the most beloved, and a repertory of patriotic songs grew up around them. The hat was the hallmark of Luciano Manara, the boy-general of the First War of Italian Independence, who was killed in 1849 outside Rome, and his myth, enshrined, sanctified his uniform. The *bersaglieri* were a veritable synonym for patriotism; the black-green feathers from the *gallo cedrone,* a huge rooster, became an icon of manhood and liberty. As Bernardino Ponzillo began his military service, the dangerous five-year war against the brigands was largely over, at least in the Terra di Lavoro, although it continued for decades in Calabria and Sicily, and a far more risky venture had been accomplished: the conquest of Rome. Venetia and Venice had become united with Italy in October 1866. The Italy we know was virtually complete.

Because so many of the *bersaglieri* had been called in the campaign to take Rome, Bernardino Ponzillo became an heir to their exploits. It is a family tradition that Maddalena Conte, his future wife, was impressed by his dashing appearance in this uniform, with its cargo of romance and history. Because he was eleven years older than she, Bernardino was performing his military service just in the years when her childhood ended. The year he came of age and became a *bersagliere,* 1880, was also marked by the effects of the first decade of emigration, particularly in the south, for in 1876 the Italian government lifted some of its early restrictions. Between 1876 and 1886 about 134,000 people emigrated each year.

As many historians have shown, poverty was not the sole motive driving people to leave. Many who had emigrated had earned enough to be able to return to their hometowns and villages and talk about the new status they had acquired abroad, by which they usually meant North or South America. Although critics of the southern way of life believed that the lack of entrepreneurial spirit was the dominant character trait and the greatest shortcoming in those who lived south of Rome, many families there had great independence of spirit and a desire to rise above the traditional laborers' role and establish small businesses in their own names. From what we know about the Ponzillos' life in New York State and Connecticut, it is clear that they had this spirit.

THE CARUSOS OF PIEDIMONTE D'ALIFE ⟶

Although Enrico Caruso was born in Naples in 1873, his entire family, paternal and maternal, came from Piedimonte d'Alife, just three towns to the north of Caiazzo. The tenor's grandfathers, Vincenzo Baldini and Giovanni

Caruso, grew up and found wives in Piedimonte. His father, Marcellino Caruso, had one brother, Salvatore, whose descendant still lives there and teaches music. True to tradition, this present representative of the family is also named Enrico Caruso. He and Cav. Aldo Mancusi, founder of the Enrico Caruso Museum of America in New York City, located many of the documents relating to the Ponzillos' life in the diocese of Caiazzo and contributed invaluable help in this research; they were helped by the clergy of the cathedral of Caiazzo.

The Carusos were firmly grounded in Piedimonte; the tenor's grandparents never moved from there. Enrico Caruso's father, Marcellino, was born in Piedimonte, as were the several generations before him. He married Anna Baldini (whose mother was a d'Onofrio) in August 1866 in the Church of the Annunciation there and remained in the town for several years after marriage, living in a house at Via Sorgente 10. Apparently they had no children born there.

Sometime before 1869 Marcellino and Anna Baldini Caruso moved to Naples, as hundreds of families from the country were doing from all over the south, in their mass flight from the fields. Enrico Caruso was baptized in the Church of San Giovanni e Paolo on February 26, 1873, having been born one day earlier. In Naples Caruso grew up, studied singing, and began his career, first in a choir, then as a soloist for weddings and other ceremonies and for evening concerts in restaurants and small theaters. He made his opera debut in 1895, in a work called *L'amico Francesco* at the Teatro Nuovo in Naples, and went on to perform in several Italian cities and in Cairo before reaching Milan in the winter of 1897–98. Caruso's first engagement in America was in Buenos Aires in 1899, the same year that he first went to Russia. He made his first appearance at the Teatro alla Scala in Milan in 1900–1901, under its director, Giulio Gatti-Casazza, who had taken over the theater two years earlier.

Caruso's later career is described in another chapter, but here it is enough to say that he was engaged by the Metropolitan Opera in New York for the 1903–04 season and made his debut as the Duke in *Rigoletto* on November 23. Gatti-Casazza and Arturo Toscanini did not join the Metropolitan until several years later, arriving there together at the beginning of the 1908–09 season, at the invitation of Otto Kahn and members of the board. Once in office, Gatti presided over and helped to shape Caruso's sensational career in America. These two men, Caruso and Gatti-Casazza, had the sole responsibility for launching Rosa Ponzillo's operatic career, for it was Caruso who heard her sing in her teacher's studio and asked Gatti-Casazza to give her an audition, and it was Gatti, as general manager of the company, who wrote her first contract with it, engaging her to make her debut at the Metropolitan Opera in 1918.

DEPARTURES: THE PONZILLOS AND THEIR RELATIVES LEAVE ITALY ∾

The first member of the Ponzillo family to emigrate in the 1880s from the Terra di Lavoro to the United States was Vittorio, who left in 1881, at the age of thirty-eight, on the steamship *Château Léoville*. Like his traveling companion, twenty-six-year-old Pietro Faraone, Vittorio Ponzillo was described on the passenger list as a laborer. The two men were in the first wave of the huge emigration movement of 1876–86, as were several other members of the Faraone family who left through the port of Naples in 1883 and 1884; all males, they ranged in age from fourteen to forty, and like those who had gone before them, they embarked for New York. Two of the Giannellis also left; one stated that he was a carpenter, the other that he was a cultivator. Later in the decade three more Ponzillos and a group of nine relatives from Alvignano and Dragoni (including some of the Faraones) joined other members of their families on their journey to the New World.

Early in June 1886, when he was twenty-eight, Bernardino Ponzillo set off from Caiazzo for America. With him went his fiancée's sister, Filomena Conte, who was eighteen, and Alfonso Faraone, at thirty-eight the oldest of the three. These travelers made their way to Naples and, with about five hundred other passengers and crew, boarded the steamship *Burgundia*. The passenger list, like many similar lists from this period, shows utter indifference to the individual histories of the emigrants, for with the exception of those designated "infant" or "child," everyone in the lower classes was identified as "peasant." Beyond that, everyone is identified as coming from "Italy"; no more-specific places of origin are mentioned. Bernardino, Alfonso, and Filomena had packed their possessions in two suitcases, both of which were tagged in Bernardino's name. Those two suitcases are a clue to their relative prosperity, compared to that of the other passengers, most of whom tied their belongings in great scarves or blankets. And unlike hundreds of thousands of desperate emigrants from southern Italian villages and farms, this little party of adventurers possessed the confidence that comes from growing up in a town such as Caiazzo, where a certain level of culture, civility, experience, education, and even sophistication penetrates the whole social body.

Maddalena Conte, Bernardino's fiancée, found herself in a rather awkward situation, for she had recently broken an earlier pledge to another suitor, a cooper in Caiazzo to whom her family had promised her. According to the Ponzillo-Conte family tradition, Maddalena had fallen in love with Bernardino instead, had become engaged to him, and had decided to marry in America to avoid a scandal at home. When she saw him off on the *Burgundia,* she could be sure that he would prepare the way for her own departure and for their eventual marriage in New York State. This plan and the fact that they had a fixed destination raised their expectations far above those of emigrants who knew no one in the United States and were without a base there. On that June day, then, the little group that would become Rosa Ponzillo's core family had reasonable hope for the future as they sailed out of the Bay of Naples, bound for America.

CHAPTER 2

America and the Immigrant Experience

When Bernardino Ponzillo and his two compatriots from Caiazzo reached New York City, the Statue of Liberty was new, having been raised on its pedestal in 1885, the year before the *Burgundia* sailed into the Lower Bay with them on board. They may not have seen it, though, for many steerage class passengers were not allowed on deck until after others in first, second, and third had been cleared. Among the tens of thousands of Italian immigrants, some hopeful, some skeptical or desperate, Ponzillo was particularly lucky in having successful relatives who had come to America before him. In addition to those who had come from Alvignano and Dragoni, three of the older Faraones and Vittorio Ponzillo had landed in 1881, to be followed by several more relatives in 1882 and 1883, when Antonio and Giuseppe Conte and their neighbor Antonio Coppola, all "farmers from Caiazzo," arrived on the *Burgundia* in June. Newcomers who could profit from their predecessors' sponsorship, moral support, and knowledge (however meager) of American ways were often saved from being cheated, robbed, or sold into virtual wage slavery with illegal work contracts. So far as we know, the members of the Ponzillo-Conte clan were spared that. When the three travelers arrived, they went directly to Schenectady, where Bernardino Ponzillo would wait for his fiancée to join him.

 HE PONZILLO-CONTE CLAN IN SCHENECTADY

The area that is now New York State began welcoming immigrants, with more grace or less, in the 1600s, when the first Dutch settlers established a colony on the Hudson River where Albany now stands. Among the most numerous and prominent early arrivals upstate were the English and the Germans. A scattering of Canadian French was followed by waves of Irish, but until the 1870s and 1880s only a few natives of Mediterranean countries had settled around the Tri-Cities area of Albany, Troy, and Schenectady. Not until around 1880 did the Italian population begin to reach up the Hudson and out into the Mohawk Valley, settling chiefly in Albany, Rochester, Utica, and Syracuse before finally reaching Buffalo. Many of these upstate immigrants were drawn by the promise of finding work on the railroads.

Because of its geographical position, the city of Schenectady became a major transportation hub where the New York Central joined the Troy and Schenectady Railroad and other lines. Apart from small machine shops, the first major industry there was the Westinghouse Company, founded in 1856 to manufacture agricultural implements. In 1886, the year that Bernardino Ponzillo arrived, this became the Westinghouse Illuminating Company. Four years earlier, the New York Central had built a new train station in the city; at that time the largest employer was the Schenectady Locomotive Works, which stood near the river at the end of Fonda and Romeyn Streets.

This was the beginning of the era of Schenectady's rapid expansion. The historian Joel H. Monroe, in his *Schenectady, Ancient and Modern,* describes the waves of arriving foreigners, many of whom worshiped at Saint John's Catholic Church, erected on Liberty Street in 1873, or the other Catholic parish, Saint Anthony of Padua, where only Italian was spoken. The attraction of what Monroe calls "one of the greatest manufacturing industries in the world," General Electric, and the Schenectady Locomotive Works even-

tually proved irresistible to many Italian families who had originally settled
in New York City's Little Italy.

When Bernardino Ponzillo landed in the United States in 1886 with
Filomena Conte and Alfonso Faraone, and went to live in Schenectady, there
were relatively few Italians in that city. Among them was Vittorio Ponzillo,
who was just Bernardino's age and who, with his son, Vincenzo, and his
wife, Vita, appears to be the first of this family to settle there. The most
prominent Italian residents by far were the Bernardis. Joseph Bernardi
served as organist for Saint John's Church, while John, his brother, taught
music in their home. On the side, they and their relatives had a tobacco
shop and a carpenter's workshop. Only a handful of Italians were in trade
in the city, among them the De Lamannos and the Lenos. There were no
Italian saloons and no Italian boarding houses.

The enterprising Ponzillos soon filled both of those voids, opening a
saloon and a boarding house at numbers 10 and 12 Myers Alley. This narrow,
unpaved street was in the heart of downtown Schenectady, just a short walk
from the Mohawk River. It lay between Fonda and Romeyn Streets, about a
block from the Schenectady Locomotive Works, running for a few scant
yards and ending to the east at South Avenue and to the west at another
short transverse, Gleason's Alley. It is a sign of the Ponzillos' determination
and energy that they got both of their businesses listed in the city directory
of 1890, when virtually all the Italians there were day laborers. At that time
the city had a population of nineteen thousand; fewer than twenty Italians
were in trade.

Maddalena Conte arrived in the United States in 1887, thirteen months
after her fiancé, Bernardino Ponzillo; she was seventeen at the time. Chaper-
oned by her mother, Fortunata Esposito Conte, then forty-three, Maddalena
landed in New York City on July 8, 1887, on board the steamship *Alexandria,*
coming from Naples. Because, according to Ponselle family tradition, Bernardino and Maddalena had become engaged in Caiazzo, it is likely that
Fortunata came to see her young daughter's marriage celebrated. She gave
her status as "wife," so she evidently had a husband still in Italy.

Like the earlier arrivals in the family, the mother and daughter knew where their future lay and went directly to Schenectady. There the marriage took place almost at once, and Carmela Maria Ponzillo, the couple's first child, was born in the family boarding house on Myers Alley on June 7, 1888. Her parents called her Carmel. A son, Antonio, called Anthony or Tony, was born on June 4, 1890. Then and for many years to come, only Italian was spoken in their home. With the saloon and the boarding house to operate, the family prospered, perhaps because they had so little competition, although one other family on Myers Alley was also taking in Italian laborers by 1890. Then as now, the cruel winters of the Hudson Valley took their toll on everyone, particularly on immigrants who had come from the mild climate of the Terra di Lavoro, and soon after Tony's birth, Ben and Maddalena Ponzillo began to think of moving to a more hospitable environment.

The question of where to go was easily solved, with Connecticut the first choice, for other Ponzillos were already there and had been having children in America as early as 1883. They lived in East Haven and were a part of one of the state's many large Italian enclaves. Soon they were joined by Federico Ponzillo, who lived in Orange. Alfonso Ponzillo, Bernardino's older brother, had settled in Waterbury in the late 1880s. Born in Caiazzo in March 1857, he had married in Italy and emigrated with his wife, Maria. He and Maria appear in the census as "Ponsalo," with their three daughters and their son, Antonio, born in 1889. Rosa and her sister and brother knew this family well; their uncle lived in Meriden for a time after Carmela and Rosa left home for New York. Other relatives settled in other towns of New Haven County, and eventually they formed a kind of clan nucleus in the region.

In 1892 Ben, Maddalena, Carmela, and the infant Tony left Schenectady and joined Alfonso and his wife in Connecticut. The young cousins grew up together there, with both little Antonios named for their Ponzillo grandfather in Caiazzo. Again Ben went into business, this time as his brother's partner in a small Italian-speaking community. Although the two families remained together for some time, by 1897 they had separated. Alfonso and his family moved to Southington in Hartford County, where in 1900 they were tallied in the census as living on Mill Street.

*M*ERIDEN, CONNECTICUT: A PERMANENT HOME

Ben and Maddalena and their children settled finally in Meriden, just north-west of New Haven in the hill country of central Connecticut. Compared with the industrial slums of Schenectady, Meriden seemed positively rural, with many parks and open lots scattered through it. A modest market town in colonial times, it grew slowly, although a major stagecoach route had connected Hartford, the state capital, and New Haven through Meriden as early as 1784. No heavy transportation passed through there until a railroad cut through the fields and swamps to the west of the original community in 1838. The trains brought commerce and manufacturing and, with them, immigrants. The most aggressive development in Meriden began in the late 1800s and continued into the first years of the present century. Gradually, like dozens of New England manufacturing towns, it became two communi-ties, separated by the tracks of the New York, New Haven, and Hartford line and connected by West Main Street, the east-west route through the state.

The old heart of Meriden was the traditional "city on a hill" of the eastern United States: Protestant and prosperous, with a neatly trimmed town green, classical church spires, and white clapboard houses with a wealth of Palladian and Greek revival details and dark green shutters. Be-yond the tracks and well below historic Meriden was the second enclave, the West Side, far down the hill from the town center. This was the neighbor-hood of hundreds of immigrant families. In the 1900 census of that part of Meriden one finds a single Swede, one family born in France, and then the Italian colony. The Italian immigrants lived mostly on Bartlett and Foster Streets and Lewis and Springdale Avenues. Many of them had arrived in the late 1880s and 1890s, having married in Italy and come to the United States with young sons and daughters, while others, mostly single men, had come in droves to live as lodgers. This meant that few Italian-Americans in the West Side spoke English, for they had not been there long enough to learn.

From their surnames it is plain that these family units are almost with-

out exception from the south of Italy, and this small ethnic group exempli-
fies perfectly the social and political issues raised by their tight unity. All
Sicilians and Neapolitans could understand each other, although local dialects differed greatly, even from one village to another; but many of the
immigrant adults born in Italy just before or after the founding of the nation
between 1859 and 1866 never mastered English at all. Because of this, anyone
who associated with these Italian cultural clusters, even in the 1940s and
1950s, can name many men and women who spoke fractured English even
thirty-five years after coming to this country. Apart from language, their
appearance also set them apart. Both Carmela and Rosa Ponselle recalled
that non-Italian schoolmates made remarks about their olive complexions,
black eyes, and thick black hair. In her memoir Carmela wrote that when
she was young, "school girls called me 'The Gypsy' . . . [and] talked about
my dark skin." The suspicion generated in America by the southern Italians'
closed population cells and clannish behavior made them the object of prej-
udice and open hostility. In northern Italy, after immigration from the south
began, it was said that "the most hated people here are the Terroni." They
were "Bedouins dressed like civilized people." Unfortunately, this same prej-
udice often made itself felt in the United States. Every Italian-American,
even today, can remember a time when "Wop," "Dago," "Cravatton," "Ca-
fone," and "Terron" were hurled at them or at someone they knew.

The early Italian-American households were often large, swollen with
grandparents, parents, children, cousins, and sometimes boarders, almost
all Catholic and, with few exceptions, separated from the English-speaking,
Protestant community. Mistrustful of American customs, the older generation of Italians feared that their children would lose their ancient Mediterranean heritage and traditions, go astray, forget the catechism and their moral
precepts, and worse, be "dishonored," according to the timeless and arcane
meanings invested in that word. As they had on the other side of the Atlantic, many of these immigrant families resisted sending their children to
school, usually because they were said to be needed at home. This was an
explanation truant officers rarely accepted. Frederick Grannis, the police-
man whose duty it was to track children missing from school in Meriden,

said that he had to visit the Ponzillos often. He remembered that "the girls" were kept home became "they had no decent clothes to wear." He was shown their piano, though, which was in a bedroom; Carmela and Rosa sat on the edge of the bed to play it. Later Tony said that his father kept him from school so he could work in the bakery.

The problem of the English language opened huge rifts in many of these households. When American-born children of Italian immigrants spoke English at home, they were often reprimanded or even beaten. One anecdote from a son of immigrants living in New York City shows how wrenching and bizarre these situations could become: when he spoke English at home, his father slapped him and gave him orders in broken English: "Speak the speak your mother speaks!" Although his family was in trade, and no one was a day laborer, none of his elder siblings was allowed to go to school beyond the required years, and he had to put up a long fight to get to high school and college.

Suspicion like this was not uncommon in Italian-American families, where the need for labor was at odds with the children's hopes and plans; it became a source of frustration, rancor, and anguish. Thousands of fathers like Ben Ponzillo urged their sons to take up the family's trade and treated them as apprentices; but the fear that a son would somehow become too educated or surpass or outreach his father was deep-seated. The daughters often found their formal educations cut short, for they had to help out at home, sometimes with piecework from factories, or find work outside, but they were always expected to marry respectably to an Italian Catholic and have children. All of these problems arose to a greater or lesser degree in Italian-American households. In the Ponzillo home they forced decisions that shaped the future of the whole family.

In their house, as elsewhere, two generations were marked by this polarization and the search for identity in a country where so many of their people were shunned or mocked by non-Italians, whether of English, German, or Irish extraction. The Ponzillos differed from others, though, because Maddalena was determined to see Carmela pursue a career in music and, as Rosa later said, to see that her younger daughter would go to college. In spite of the forces pulling them in two different directions, the fierce loyalty of the American-born generation to their Italian past held; the Ponzillo girls never denied their Italian culture.

If Schenectady was the home of the electrical and locomotive industries, Meriden was the silver capital of America, with large factories and dozens of small, home-based shops for the manufacturing, sale, and repair of sterling and plate. The demand for blue-collar labor in these factories brought so many day laborers that by the time Ben and Maddalena Ponzillo got to Meriden, many couples were supplementing the family income by taking in boarders. This the Ponzillos also did.

The Ponzillos' first home in Meriden was near the corner of Lewis Avenue and Bartlett Street, in the Italian quarter. Maddalena became pregnant with their third child and gave birth in the house at 175 Lewis Avenue, assisted by her mother, Fortunata Esposito Conte, who lived with the Ponzillos during several periods after the turn of the century.

Rosa Ponzillo was born on January 22, 1897, and, through an error, was entered in the civil records as "Therese Bonsillo." The birth was registered by a German woman, Frieda Stark, who was perhaps a midwife. The baby was named Rosa and was baptized on March 20, 1898, in the parish church of Our Lady of Mount Carmel, on Goodwill Avenue in Meriden. The page of this register of baptisms tells its own story: the priest wrote (and probably spoke) almost no English; the only two non-Italians are "Tommaso Farland" and "Alberto Kelly." Rosa's godparents were Giovanni Battista Jagness and Teresa Ongiano. Rosa's name on her birth certificate was rectified years later from the baptismal record. In the original civil document, her father is "Bernhardt Borillo, a laborer," and her mother is "Magdalena Count." Surprisingly, Caiazzo, correctly spelled, is given as the birthplace of both. Carmela, who was eight and a half when Rosa was born, remembered that her baby sister had blond hair and blue eyes, both of which soon changed.

Within a few months the family had moved to 168 Foster Street. Ben Ponzillo did as he had in Schenectady and paid for a listing in the city directory of 1897, where he has not one entry but two: *Benjamin* Ponzillo is a "coal and wood dealer," and *Bernardino* Ponzillo, just below, is a "contractor." Home and business are both in the same building on Foster Street. Again he distinguishes himself from dozens of Italians immigrants of the time by being independent, an entrepreneur. With his wife he raised the family to the respectability of the trade and merchant class by broadening the scope of their enterprises.

When the 1900 census was taken, the Ponzillos were living in larger quarters at 164 Foster Street. Carmela, Tony, and Rosa are correctly identified, with their ages and birthdates. By then Ben and Maddalena had taken in three boarders to supplement their income: Joseph Rosoni, age thirty-two, and John Spatone and Francesco Lucci, both thirty-five—day laborers and Italian-born. The house next door had only Italian residents, the Mirabellis, a family whose children were the exact contemporaries of the young Ponzillos, and the Mastroiannis and their boarders. Carmela described the "depressed, old, worn, bare wooden floors" and a "tiny kitchen" in the home of her childhood; there she dreamed of "having carpets and everything" and wanted "to be a great lady." In fact, curtains were a sign of status in these communities, while carpets meant luxury.

Apart from Ben Ponzillo's extraordinary decision to buy listings in city directories, the family also departed radically from Italian-American custom in the matter of Carmela's education. In 1893 or 1894, when she was five, she was sent to live with cousins in New Haven and enrolled in Saint Mary's Convent School there. In Italy, as in the United States, the idea of early childhood education had first been posed about thirty years earlier. Among the founders of the kindergarten movement in Italy were Verdi's mother's family, the Uttinis of Piacenza, who established day care and educational facilities in towns and villages up and down the Po Valley and corresponded with the German educator Friedrich Froebel, among others in Europe. Verdi and his wife often provided urgently needed funds to these nursery school–kindergartens.

Even for a traditional American family the idea of sending a five-year-old girl away to school was daring; for the Ponzillos, who had been in the United States less than seven years, it was one of the most extraordinary steps that a family in their situation could have taken. Carmela remained in

New Haven for about five years and did not return to Meriden until she was ten; Rosa was still an infant. With Tony, Carmela then attended the Columbia Street Grammar School, two blocks from home. Soon Carmela became the head of her class. She recalled being embarrassed because her mother dressed her then in "gaudy colors, a dress of purple Canton crepe, with a red velvet yoke trimmed with blue satin ruffles, and large white ribbons in my black hair." She longed for a "pure white batiste gown" so she could look like other girls her age. Independent as she was, she decided when she was twelve to work at the local five-and-ten, where she could "earn a few dollars." Her four hours a week, on Friday and Saturday evenings from five to seven, brought in pin money and may even have added pennies to the family till at a time when Ben Ponzillo began an ambitious expansion of his holdings in Meriden. Rosa was then about four and Tony was in elementary school.

By this time the Ponzillos had laid the foundation for what eventually became their commercial enterprises in Meriden. Ben and his wife and children all worked in their operations: coal, wood, a bakery, a vineyard–truck farm, and a small grocery store. These they developed over the decades. In 1894, while they were still living on Foster Street, Ben bought a property there; it is probably this expansion that allowed them to own a single-family home and take in three boarders. Six years later, in September 1900, he and Maddalena together bought their lot and bungalow-style home at 159 Springdale Avenue. Under his title of contractor he began to enlarge the house at once, adding a second floor and an exterior wooden staircase at first and later topping it off with a third floor. The house was on the north side of the street on a piece of land that reached back into the block. The Ponzillos added more land there in February 1901, when they also bought lots on Water Street, adjacent to their house and behind it on a dead-end road that runs back to now-abandoned railroad tracks. In 1906 they enlarged this plot. At some point, perhaps even before 1900, they had bought wooded lots on Gracey Street, about a mile north of their house. There Ben cut trees to sell in his wood business. All of these properties were mortgaged, as deeds show; Maddalena held the co-title on all deeds except the one registered in

1894. In the district court and probate registry in Meriden, she is described as having "an undivided half-interest" in everything they owned. This, too, was a departure from Italian tradition.

The house at 159 Springdale Avenue was the family's home from the third year of Rosa's life and was the center of the family's business operations as well. Ben and his laborers operated the wood and coal business; an Italian immigrant ran the bakery that Ben built in the yard behind the house on Springdale. Later Tony worked in the bakery after school and on Saturdays; in time, his father ordered him to leave school and take it over. Maddalena managed the small Italian grocery they opened in what had originally been the living room of the Springdale house. When it began operations, Ben had to build the white wooden stairway on the side of the house so they could reach the second floor. In the little shop she sold pasta, salami and other cured meats, dry biscuits, provolone and other cheeses, fresh bread made in the adjacent family bakery, and a variety of household needs such as soap and scouring powder. A storage area occupied the rest of the first floor. Ben planted grapevines on trellises in the backyard, harvested and sold grapes from them every fall, and made his own wine.

In effect, the Ponzillos recreated the small family businesses found in thousands of towns and villages in Italy, from the Alps to the southernmost cape of Sicily; however, they pursued not one type of commerce but several, and simultaneously. They were fortunate indeed to be able to do so without counting on the free labor that a large family of children offered to many Italian families. But the Ponzillos did succeed and remained among the few who were never forced into digging sewers and subway tunnels or working on the railroad or in factory jobs. The middle-class life in trade that they created for themselves let them eke a decent, honest living out of their city land and the empty plots they added to it. So long as the American economy remained fairly stable, the Ponzillo family prospered.

Tony Ponzillo, in a 1977 interview, remembered that his mother was "an angel," respected throughout the West Side for her goodness and concern for others, while his father was strict with a "hardness" to him. Carmela, he said, inherited Ben's ambition but was kinder and more loving.

Rosa, in many interviews, spoke of fond memories of the family's home, the bakery, her mother's little grocery, and the neighborhood. The property deeds and the census show that on Springdale Avenue they were surrounded on all sides by Italian immigrants. In the house next to theirs was a saloon, operated by their friends. On Lewis Avenue the business district served the diverse West Side population.

It was a place where a good deal of open land remained, where the air was clear and the streets clean. The life of the Italian-speaking community centered on the parish church, Our Lady of Mount Carmel. In this world Rosa Ponzillo was happy and loved as "Babe" by the protective Carmela. To her mother she was Rosina. Rosa's bond to her mother was always strong, although her relationship to her severe father was somewhat strained. This, though, was not unusual in an Italian-American family, where the father ruled—or tried to. With her Conte grandmother living in the house, with Carmela almost nine years older than she, and with a loving older brother, Tony, to protect her from the neighborhood bullies, Rosa was the darling of the Ponzillos, "coccolata," coddled as she could never have been in one of the many nearby families that had eight or ten children. Carmela, who possessed a strong sense of family pride from the start, remembered her own lack of respect for their neighbors' crowded, noisy households. In the Ponzillo home things were orderly, particularly because Maddalena was a quiet, serious woman who, during Rosa's childhood and for decades to come, remained protective toward her "baby daughter." Rosa, her mother's favorite, got more than her share of attention in the house.

After Ben added the upper floors to the building, the grocery and provisions storeroom took up the whole main floor. On the expanded second floor were a living room, kitchen, and bedrooms. On the new third floor, more rooms were added. Even today the house at 159 Springdale has this same general plan, although the grocery is gone and the living quarters have been restored to the ground floor. The outside staircase is still there. Within this little enclave the Ponzillo children grew up as part of a close, self-contained family unit, surprisingly independent from the outside, for they were among the few who could provide their own fuel and most of their own food.

Rosa's parents and grandmother spoke Neapolitan among themselves, she recalled in an interview for the Ithaca College Oral History Project. "Between my father, grandmother, and mother, they spoke it most of the time, and once in a while Daddy would come in and all of a sudden 'go English' on me. He had to speak it with a broken accent, but Mother's was still more broken." She said that "of course the Neapolitan came out faster" and was easier for them. She learned it because she was "quite a good parrot" in picking up language and learning to carry a melody quickly. "I did know the sound of it very well, and I could understand everything in Neapolitan, and if I had to sing a Neapolitan song, I had the right feeling and temperament for it." From some of Rosa's later interviews, particularly those for radio, it is clear that she could speak Neapolitan very well.

In many ways, hers was an ordinary Italian-American, Catholic childhood, with her parents in trade. The Ponzillo house differed from others in the West Side, though, because it contained many musical instruments, accumulated by Tony. Ben Ponzillo played his accordion, the sound of which fascinated the young Carmela, who also learned to play it.

Rosa, who had been baptized at Our Lady of Mount Carmel, attended mass there with her family and had her confirmation with boys and girls of her age group. She often told interviewers that she revered Nellie Melba and tried to convince the parish priest to let her be confirmed as Rosa Melba Ponzillo, something he would not permit. He confirmed her as Rosa Maria. Carmela's influence on that moment can perhaps be discerned, for Rosa wore the "pure, white batiste dress" of her sister's dreams on confirmation day. As a child, Rosa played with the sometimes rowdy neighborhood companions but stayed aloof from disputes and rows. Then, as later, her placid, sweet disposition and sense of humor were her greatest assets. Always respectful and ready to please, she was obedient and cooperative, even as a child. These traits of character helped her throughout her career, particularly in her relations with colleagues and with Giulio Gatti-Casazza, the director of the Metropolitan Opera, who guided her from before her debut to the years after his retirement.

If Rosa had one "sin" as a girl, it was sneaking food from her mother's grocery shelves. In Rosa's own words: "My mother used to say that I would eat up all the profits between meals; and when mealtime came, I would never be ready for dinner because I had already eaten salami, cheese, and homemade hot bread." As a result, she grew into a sturdy teenager with no serious health problems, about five feet eight inches tall, and weighing, she said, around 160 pounds, so long as she kept her weight under control.

Rosa described her childhood and youth in simple terms during a program for Radio Free Europe: "My school and formal training were next to nil. . . . I was just born to sing, and all I wanted to do was sing, and all I could do was sing. My one aim in life was to sing, and I didn't care where or what, so long as I sang. That was my goal."

THE SINGING PONZILLOS: MOTHER AND CHILDREN ~

Rosa said that she was introduced to music in childhood by her mother, Carmela, Tony, and the parish organist. For the Ithaca College Oral History, she spoke of Maddalena's gift:

> My mother had a wonderful ear and a sweet, high voice, but never cultivated. . . . I think my mother would have been meant for the stage, had she been given half a chance, but you know, in Italy the education and all those privileges go to the males, the sons that are born in the family; all the females have to just wait until they are of marriageable age, and then their husbands will take care of them. . . . But my mother wanted to take singing lessons, and all they would let her do was sing in the church; they said, 'No, no, the stage is no place for a woman,' so she became resigned. But she had a phenomenal ear. We could take her to an opera or anything, and she would come out humming it, pitched way up high. I think she would have been another Lily Pons, it was pitched so high.

Music ran in the Conte family, and several Conte cousins became professional or amateur musicians in New Haven.

Rosa often acknowledged her great debt to Carmela, who, in a way, forced her into a career, as we shall see. Carmela had "ambition," Rosa said; she also spoke of Tony's participation in town band concerts and parades. In his third-floor room he stored all kinds of instruments, which Rosa, self-taught, learned to play. Her closest childhood friend, Lena Tamborini, dared her to learn to play the violin, which she did.

Carmela's early training in music outside the family home came in the choir of Our Lady of Mount Carmel, where she became the protégée of an unmarried Irish woman, the organist Anna M. Ryan, who later became the teacher of the other two Ponzillo children as well. If ever a story had an early protagonist-heroine, Anna Ryan is that heroine. She taught music, piano, sight-reading, and basic vocal technique to Carmela, Tony, and Rosa, then saved the money to get Carmela to New York, supported her during her first two years there, found her a good voice teacher, found paid work for her as a church soloist, stood by the sisters when Rosa came to New York, and became their live-in housekeeper and music teacher. She figured in their lives (or they in hers) until her death in February 1943.

This is how Carmela described her own early ventures in Meriden: When she was about thirteen or fourteen she left the five-and-ten and began to work for Hurley's Millinery Shop. Earning fifteen dollars a week, she made, designed, and sometimes modeled hats. Carmela described herself as "dramatically inclined . . . with one thought in mind, that I was going to be a great singing actress." By then, she had been in the children's choir for several years, was teaching Sunday school, and had been named the female soloist in the adult choir. From Rosa's accounts we know that Carmela could cover both the mezzo-soprano and lyric soprano ranges.

In her memoir Carmela described the arrival of Anna Ryan, who, perhaps more than anyone else, shaped the lives of these young Ponzillos. This unassuming young music director was the daughter of Patrick F. Ryan and Katherine Degnan, natives of Ireland who were living at 132 Hobart Street in Meriden. Born in Meriden in May 1874, Anna Ryan was a professional by 1905, listing herself as a music teacher in the city directory. Her mother's death, which occurred sometime before 1900, left Anna as the housekeeper for her father, herself, and her younger brother and sister, Joseph and Kitty. Her first job was as assistant organist at Saint Rose's Church in Meriden; she later became organist and music director for the Ponzillos' parish, Our Lady of Mount Carmel.

It was then that Carmela, still a girl, went to a choir practice. "During a rehearsal for the Mass," Carmela's memoir continues, "[Miss Ryan] turned to see where this mezzo-soprano came from; she stopped suddenly to ask, then the children yelled, 'It's Carmela!' " After other rehearsals, Ryan encouraged Carmela to study music seriously; for the moment, however, she was content to teach her piano herself as she continued to guide her vocal development, within the range of the parish choir and Carmela's solo opportunities. As Carmela recalled, "She said that I should . . . study piano for two years and then she would take me to New York to a great voice teacher. The stage in those days meant disgrace to the Italians; no lady was on the stage."

By the time Carmela was nineteen, the city directory of 1907 listed "Carmela Ponzillo, vocalist." Rosa had followed in her path and had begun to sing around the house. Soon after her fifth birthday, which Rosa remembered because her mother gave her a fine party, she would pretend to play the piano by putting a piece of sheet music against the windowpane and fingering an imaginary keyboard on the sill. Like Carmela, she was blessed with a large, mature voice. Rosa recalled the day when Ryan, walking up Springdale Avenue on the way to buy bread from Maddalena, happened to hear a voice from inside the Ponzillo house singing " 'O Sole Mio." She believed that it was Carmela, but in fact it was Rosa. Soon "the little Ponzillo" was singing at Our Lady of Mount Carmel. In her oral history interview she recalled this period:

We were churchgoers then. We were Catholics, and Mother and Dad used to go to the mass every Sunday. I would go there and was interested in hearing the choir. And it wasn't long after that that I was asked to join the choir . . . I was singing the Ave Marias. The solos were taken away from the [other singer], an adult. . . . Gounod's "Ave Maria," Schubert's "Ave Maria," and whatever solos the mass encompassed; so I was chosen for that. . . . from there on, all my interest was singing. . . . It just was there. I don't know where it came from. . . . In school the children would laugh at [my] voice. It was a mature voice, a developed voice. It was never a child's voice.

Rosa soon was studying piano with Ryan, who had also taught Tony by then. All of this happened in the era before the Victrola became a standard item among the furnishings in most Italian-American homes. Caruso made his first European recordings for the Gramophone and Typewriter Company in the spring of 1902 in the Grand Hotel de Milan, the building where Verdi had died fifteen months before. Fred W. Gaisberg, later a close friend of Rosa Ponselle, was one of two technicians manning the machinery during that and subsequent sessions for that company. The tenor's old Pathé Frères cylinders date from 1903; his first Victor Talking Machine Company recordings, made in Camden, New Jersey, date from 1904. Because it took years for these to reach a mass market, the Ponzillo children had no access to a Victrola and no first exposure to music through the old wax records. In this they were disadvantaged compared with the children of immigrants who arrived in America after the "first wave." Rosa was explicit about this in interviews. But with their two daughters and son all evidently gifted musically, Ben and Maddalena bought an upright piano, which was much more useful for the purposes of these budding musicians. As we shall see, Tony might have had a respectable singing career if World War I and his parents' needs had not drawn him in other directions. Under Anna Ryan's hand Rosa and Carmela became fine pianists and expert sight-readers who could also arrange music as needed in their later careers.

Rosa, in effect, became the star music pupil in her school because of her sight-reading. With some pride she described being called out of her classroom to help the district music teacher during the once-a-week lessons; on some occasions she was asked to teach sight-reading to other students. She said she had little interest in other subjects, though. She hated school generally because she was "not a morning person" who, as a child and as an adult, functioned poorly early in the day. This may explain some of the visits by Grannis, the truant officer, but when the family fell on hard times and could not clothe the girls decently, that also would have kept them from school. In spite of Rosa's dislike of formal schooling, Maddalena was determined that Rosa should go to college. She never did, because her precocious development as a singer soon took her out of the house, out of Meriden, and finally, out of Connecticut.

Carmela said that she contributed money out of her own modest earnings at this time to "give Rosa a better start than I had had." She bought "cute little dresses" and insisted that Rosa get piano lessons. In her memoir Carmela remembered that Rosa had played the piano by ear long before she could read music; "when she was ten, she sang like a girl of eighteen." Rosa also won a citywide prize in a piano competition.

Encouraged by Anna Ryan and driven by her own ambition, Carmela said that by the time she was fifteen she was earning enough to help at home and "couldn't stand the small town of 20,000 inhabitants" any longer. "I asked Miss Ryan please to take me down to New York and [let me] meet the vocal teacher [she had talked about]." She also told her parents of her plans. Quite predictably, her father was opposed to such a move, while her mother stood behind her. Rosa remembered the emotional scenes at home as Carmela's future was being debated. Her sister, not yet an adult, left Meriden when she was eighteen. "Mother and I were great pals," Carmela said. "She gave me $10. That was all I had to come to New York with: $10 and a suitcase." But she also had Ryan's support, then and for years to come. In the city Carmela soon found a job, a respectable place to stay, and a voice teacher.

Rosa, the only daughter left at home, developed rapidly as a person and a musician in the healthiest environment imaginable. In her oral history interview she recalled that she was not spoiled: "My mother was quite a disciplined person, quite a disciplinarian. She would not take any nonsense or back talk. She had a full-time job there, with three businesses going at once. . . . I would play the piano, read music—'My Hero' and 'Rose in the Bud' and all those lovely classic ballads of those days—and just read any kind of music." She was studying piano with Ryan at the time. Rosa also followed Carmela's example when she was about twelve by getting a job at the five-and-ten "to earn a little extra money. Not that I needed it, because my mother and father [were] very good to me; but [I worked] on Fridays and Saturdays . . . to make a dollar and a half for the weekend. . . . In those times, that was quite a bit of change. . . . Friday night from five to nine, or something like that, on Saturdays till ten; and I'd make a couple of extra dollars and I'd think, 'Wasn't that wonderful!' I'd buy what I wanted with it." Her job was playing sheet music, and sometimes singing it, for the customers.

She longed to have lovely things. Carmela recalled a weekend visit to their home: "Rosa admired my beautiful green fall outfit. 'Oh,' she said, 'Carmela, I'd like a dress like that!' So I told her she must work; I told her to sing right there in Meriden in the moving picture house." Rosa, many years later and far away, remembered that same day, a day of immense importance for her career because it marked the first time she sang an audition on a stage in a theater and got a job because of it. She too said that she had admired Carmela on that occasion: "She was a very beautiful woman, and to make extra money on the side, she would model clothes." Carmela was "all dressed up in beautifully fashioned clothes, and I used to look at her and say, 'Oh, I wish I could have pretty clothes like that.' And she said, 'Well, when you grow up and earn your money like I do, you can buy all the pretty clothes you want. . . . And by the way, you are big enough to be able to earn your [own] money. So come on.' " They went to downtown Meriden.

Rosa recalled in her Radio Free Europe program that Carmela took her to the Crystal Theatre first. Carmela said Rosa did "an audition singing popular ballads before the screen. She starts at an income of $15 a week." Rosa's account continues:

I started at the Crystal, and I got twenty-five dollars a week. The competitor to that company, the [manager of] the Star [Theatre], saw how it clicked and what a big success it was—the first time it had happened in Meriden, Connecticut, that Meriden's own little daughter sings in the movie house. So he thought "Well, it is a good idea. I'll see if I can offer her a little more and take her away from the Crystal." Well, the Star proceeded to do that, and I sang there for a raise of, I think, ten dollars a week. And he had a little theater in Southington, where he went every weekend, and so I made another fifteen or twenty dollars a week, so I was able to buy myself pretty clothes and not have to envy my sister, Carmela, who was then making quite good in New York.

Rosa's recollections of these first engagements were vivid: "They had these silent films, and these illustrated songs were sung from a booth way off in the corner, and the scenes were flashed up on the screen, and I was singing the songs appropriate to the scene you saw on the screen in silent days." She later said that she earned as much as fifty or sixty dollars a week by appearing regularly in several towns.

These theater managers were not the only ones who appreciated Rosa's voice. With her solos in church, her demonstrations of sheet music in the five-and-ten, and her appearances in motion picture houses, she soon became known around Meriden and even beyond for the beauty of her voice. Rosa said that an acquaintance, a painter whose brother was a singing teacher in New Haven, learned of her from someone in the city. "Mr. Battelli . . . had heard of me through someone who had heard me in Meriden. He came to my mother and my father and wanted to talk to me about accepting this position in New Haven," a job at the Café Mellone, "a very exclusive dining place" that presented two singers every evening to entertain the customers. Occupying two buildings at 35 and 37 Center Street in downtown New Haven, it belonged to James G. Ceriani, a Milanese. Single when Rosa first met him, he later married a woman of Italian origin and lived in a fine house at 40 Richmond Avenue. In his "family restaurant" Ceriani catered to a mixed clientele of old New Englanders, Germans and Italian-Americans, Yale professors and students, and a large contingent of musicians and music lovers. Highly respected in New Haven, popular and ambitious, Ceriani continued in business there for decades, eventually bringing a relative from Italy to help him.

At first Maddalena Ponzillo would hear nothing of Battelli's suggestion, Rosa said. "Of course, my mother had a fit. 'My daughter! At that age! Leave my home! Oh, no! No!' But the time did come that some arrangement was made that I would live with my mother's . . . second cousin." This was probably Sebastiano Conte, a native of Caiazzo who lived in New Haven for sixty years and died there in 1944. The Conte family boasted many professional musicians who worked in Connecticut, among them music teachers; one pianist who played at the Shubert and Palace theaters in New Haven and in the Governor's Footguard Band; a clarinetist who led the band at Donat's Restaurant in New Haven; and a Juilliard graduate who was younger than Rosa Ponzillo.

Later Rosa moved in with Margaret and Rocco Da Vino, friends of Carmela's. The Da Vinos' modest home at 22 Middletown Avenue became Rosa's second residence in New Haven. In that city she sang first in a motion picture house called the San Carlino, named after the Teatro San Carlo in Naples; there she sang for movie audiences, as she had done in Meriden, Southington, Waterbury, and Ansonia. At Ceriani's Café Mellone she won the audience's affection with her simple ways and glorious voice. In her oral history interview Rosa said that she

> made a big success there. I sang the classic ballads—no opera; I did not know opera then. They had another girl for the popular songs. This Mr. Ceriani used to marvel and stand there and listen to my voice. He said, "This is so beautiful! You belong in opera, you belong in opera!" I didn't know [anything about] opera! Metropolitan Opera! I said, "No, I love to sing, I don't care where I sing." I had no ambition, no aspirations for opera, nothing of the sort. As long as I sang, whether it was at Loew's or in vaudeville or at a party; as long as I sang, that's all that mattered. I didn't dream of one day singing at the Metropolitan.

A soprano like Rosa Ponzillo's would have attracted attention anywhere, but she was particularly fortunate because of New Haven's Italian population and its university-based music-loving culture. One popular teacher with a sterling musical pedigree said that he coached Rosa while she was at the Café Mellone and urged her to go to New York. This was Max Dessauer, who was also a conductor. Ceriani's was the favorite restaurant of his family and especially of his sister Erna, a pianist. She married Isidore Troostwyk, another musician, and became the grandmother of Elaine Troostwyk Toscanini, a New Haven native and the wife of Walfredo Toscanini, the grandson of Arturo Toscanini. In New Haven at that time there were few families that could boast the professional credentials of the Dessauer-Troostwyks, one of whom, Isidore, had studied with the violinist and composer Josef Joachim. While we do not know who first taught opera arias to Rosa Ponzillo, the fact that Ceriani was pushing her toward opera and that he was willing to pay for her lessons may mean that Max Dessauer, a patron of the Café Mellone, coached her, as he said he had, although he, like her other teachers, would have done nothing to change her natural method of voice production, which she was always unwilling to let anyone manipulate.

Rosa, under contract to Ceriani, continued to sing in New Haven until one brief interruption in May 1915, when she was eighteen. One night as she was leaving the restaurant with him, she was attacked on the street by a drunk. When Ceriani dragged the man away from her, the attacker fell, fractured his skull on the curb, and died. Rosa, in shock, was sent back to Meriden the next day, accompanied to the station by Margaret Da Vino; Ceriani was charged with manslaughter. As a result of testimony at a hearing, the charges were dropped.

After this incident Rosa returned to the Café Mellone. According to her Radio Free Europe program, Ceriani proposed that she study abroad.

> He also said, "I'm going to take you down to New York to see your sister, and you should hear your first opera at the Metropolitan." I said, "That'll be a thrill." . . . I stayed with my sister, and he took me to my first opera. And who do you think it was? Caruso with Farrar in *Butterfly!* We sat way up in the balcony then and were the first to arrive and the last to leave [because] I was so [overcome]. He said,

"Rosa, one day you are going to be singing there." I said, "Oh, come on, Jim." But he said, "Oh, yes, you are. Your voice belongs in opera, it doesn't belong in the Café Mellone. . . . You belong there; you don't belong in New Haven."

Ceriani also took her to see Claudia Muzio with Caruso in Italo Montemezzi's *L'amore dei tre re.* "I just cried buckets full of tears." But she swore that she still had no ambition to sing opera. To hear her tell this story, with her rich, dark voice and heightened, dramatic tones, to hear her say "Far*rah*" with the New England accent she never lost, is to hear Ponselle at her most characteristic.

The question of what Rosa actually saw in the Metropolitan Opera House and when she saw it is addressed in another chapter, but three things are certain: she was in her teens at the time, Ceriani did take her there as his guest, and he did continue to encourage her to study further. He urged her to go to New York City for lessons and repeated his offer to underwrite all her studies abroad and "make all the arrangements" if she would go to Europe. She declined: "I said, 'No, no, no, I am satisfied singing here.' I had no ambition. . . . I didn't want to get on a boat and go to Italy; I didn't want opera." She did, however, let Ceriani take her to New York to visit Carmela, who had settled on the Upper West Side with Anna Ryan.

"PROSPEROUS" CARMELA AND TONY IN NEW YORK CITY ⌇

The private house Rosa stayed in, then and later, was a five-story brownstone where Carmela lived, on West Sixty-fourth Street just west of the intersection of Broadway and Columbus Avenue. This was five blocks north of the showcase blocks at Columbus Circle, where Broadway branched off to the northwest and Central Park West began. The rich social and architectural fabric of this neighborhood is described best in Peter Salwen's *Upper West Side Story,* a fascinating guidebook to what became the "bedroom community" of the entire entertainment business. Carmela's second voice teacher in New York, Paul Savage, lived at 8 West Sixty-fourth, east of Broadway, although he had his studios in Carnegie Hall. His wife was an aspiring singer.

Tony Ponzillo, who followed Carmela to the city in 1911, found a job as a salesman at Macy's and rented a room in the Euclid Hall, a beautiful apartment hotel at 2345 Broadway, near Eighty-sixth Street. The violinist Mischa Elman was its most famous tenant. Tony Ponzillo had actually achieved what many young hopefuls only dreamed of, for he had been given an audition at the Metropolitan Opera. After it, he had been told to study further and ask for another audition later. His career was interrupted when he returned to Meriden to help his parents; later, when World War I broke out, he served in the U.S. Army.

As denizens of the Upper West Side, Carmela and Tony had settled in the right neighborhood for ambitious singers. Rents were still cheap, and although many heads of household took in boarders who were laborers or mechanics, scores of lawyers, judges, and men and women from the music business had already settled there. Just opening up, the Upper West Side boasted many elegant apartment houses such as the Ansonia, which became the "White House" of opera, the Majestic, the Prasada, the Dorilton, and the Dakota, some of which later were designated national landmarks. These grand buildings, the gorgeous, new theaters on Broadway, and the fine private homes stood next to empty plots or even manicured private gardens; but many garages and service buildings such as the fabled Liberty Storage Warehouse dotted the neighborhood. Clean streets, sunlight, and open air distinguished the area from crowded, dirty Hell's Kitchen and San Juan Hill, a few blocks to the south and west.

The brownstone where Carmela roomed was at 125 West Sixty-fourth Street. It belonged to the McCabes, "Irish widows and old maids," as Rosa described them. They had been taking in roomers at least as early as 1910, when Margaret McCabe, an Irish-born widow, then fifty-five, was running a rooming house and providing shelter to her six children, one of whom, Mary, was then just seventeen. She also had bedrooms for two artists and a waitress in a restaurant. By 1915 the roominghouse was being operated by

Miss Mary F. McCabe, the "sainted" Irish woman Carmela designated as "Miss M. Mc——" in her 1933 memoir. The two McCabe sons had moved out, leaving Mary, her widowed mother, and the "old maids" Rosa remembered: Sadie, a stenographer at the gas office; Fannie, an operator at a department store; and Alice, who helped out at home. When Rosa Ponzillo came to New York to visit Carmela, the daughters of the house were in their late twenties or early thirties. Fannie was Carmela's age. When Carmela lived there, the McCabes had at least two other lodgers: a woman in vaudeville and her husband, Mario Gambardella, a tenor who was trying to break into opera. He was studying with a well-known teacher, William Thorner, a friend of the biggest stars.

Carmela's wise choice of residence put her in the heavily trafficked neighborhood that has sheltered legions of singers, conductors, instrumentalists, voice teachers, coaches, stage directors, costumers, agents, and managers ever since it was first opened to development. From Lincoln Square, as the intersection was then called, you could reach almost any point in New York City. The Ninth Avenue El crossed Broadway at Sixty-fifth Street. The IRT subway line, which opened in 1904, ran under Broadway, carrying its human cargo from the express stop at Broadway and Seventy-second Street to the theaters of the Great White Way and to the old Metropolitan Opera House, which had been opened in 1883 on Broadway, between Thirty-ninth and Fortieth Streets. The Times Square IRT express stop had entrances and exits under the opera house, a few steps from the stage door. A local stop at Fifty-ninth Street fed the offices of many music managers who had moved their operations to Fifty-seventh Street and the Carnegie Hall area. Like the Galleria Vittorio Emanuele in Milan, the Upper West Side was the very show route of the entertainment parade, where celebrities from classical music, vaudeville, cabaret, legitimate theater, the motion picture industry, and, after 1917, jazz strolled, shopped, and chatted. It was the best place to meet colleagues and possible employers "by accident." Caruso's early lease at the Majestic, on Central Park West between Seventy-second and Seventy-first Streets, put him conveniently near Gatti-Casazza and Toscanini, both of whom lived at the Ansonia, as did Florenz Ziegfeld and his wife, Anna Held.

Later more than twenty of the Ponzillo sisters' closest friends lived there. David Belasco took a house on Seventieth Street before moving to the Hotel Marie Antoinette, on Broadway and Sixty-sixth. The whole strip from Columbus Circle to Ninety-sixth Street blossomed with theaters like giant flowers. The Majestic, the Circle, the Colonial, built before Carmela reached the Upper West Side, and the Riverside, built later, housed vaudeville or films or both. The Ponzillo sisters appeared eventually in two of them.

Carmela felt at home in this lively environment and prospered through her own hard work, after an initial boost from Ryan: "Miss Ryan paid all my railroad expenses and my room and board for two weeks. . . . She came to New York each weekend and taught piano lessons." Once when Ryan arrived, she found Carmela "penniless, hungry, and broke," but the young singer's situation improved when she found work as a cashier and window dresser for a jeweler at Fifth Avenue and Forty-second Street. He hired her because she "did all the bookkeeping at home for Daddy." When Carmela asked Ryan to help her find work singing in church, they both applied through a specialized employment bureau. Carmela was then engaged to sing in the quartet at Saint Patrick's Church in Long Island City, where Ryan became its organist. She then moved in with Carmela.

Carmela's room cost her only $3.00 a week, one fifth of her salary, because "boarding" ranked far down the economic scale from the rate of $2.50 a night at the Hotel Marie Antoinette. Lunch in a cheap restaurant was fifteen to forty cents; dinner in an elegant dining room was $1.25. Carmela's biggest problem was her voice lessons, first with Giovanni Martino, then with Paul Savage. Originally she could afford only one a week on her cashier's salary, but with additional income from Saint Patrick's she could manage two lessons. But even that was not enough. Soon she read an advertisement for a modeling job: thirty-six-inch bust, twenty-five-inch waist, forty-inch hips. Carmela, at five feet six and a half inches and 140 pounds, borrowed Ryan's "tight-fitting, cream lace dress" and a "black picture hat with a red rose." Adding a green parasol and pretending to be a customer rather than a job applicant, she sailed past the line of young hopefuls outside the door and walked grandly into the showroom of a wholesaler, Mr. Nyberg. He thought the whole thing a great joke and hired her as a model and cashier. Between her salary and commissions, Carmela earned fifty dollars a week, staying there about three years.

She continued to take regular voice lessons until Edmund Stanley, an impresario and star of light opera, heard her in Paul Savage's studio and offered her work. "He said he would teach me acting," Carmela recalled. "I nearly died of joy!" She sang in "small Fox and Loew's theaters, four or five shows a day, for one year" before pushing into vaudeville in "the Fox big time" as a single act and filling in the empty days as a dinner concert singer in Wallick's Hotel. Just down the block from there she went into the Longacre Stationery store and bought her first scrapbook. In it she pasted her first notices. In September 1912 she also got cast in a musical, *The Girl from Brighton,* which opened at the old Academy of Music (later a Fox theater), on Fourteenth Street. She eventually broke into the Keith circuit.

In these early years of her professional life, Carmela was married for about six months to Dr. Henry J. Giamarino, a Connecticut surgeon whom she had known for many years. When Carmela was first rooming in New York, he was still at home with his two unmarried sisters and his aged, widowed father in their house on Chapel Street in New Haven. Four years older than she, Giamarino (according to Carmela's account) demanded after their marriage that she stay there and be a "normal housewife." This, of course, was what her father had also demanded, and that she was unwilling to do. Carmela and Giamarino argued about this issue for some time. Because he refused to make even the slightest concession to her career in the theater, they fell back on divorce—something unthinkable in their Italian-American, Catholic world. Another factor contributing to the friction may have been Giamarino's Italian-born father, who was about Ben Ponzillo's age and was strenuously opposed to having "Miss Operetta" as a daughter-in-law. Forced to choose between her career and the conventional role of an Italian-American wife, Carmela remained on the Upper West Side.

Far from alone, Carmela had Anna Ryan with her in the McCabes' rooming house on West Sixty-fourth Street. She also made many friends through her profession. Among them was a young New Yorker whom she met at her teacher's studio. This was Edith Prilik, an aspiring soprano whose Jewish family often invited Carmela to visit them, first in their home on the Boston Post Road in the Bronx. They later moved to upper Madison Avenue. Prilik soon gave up her hopes for a career of her own and worked for decades as Rosa's secretary; but when Carmela first met her, she was an ambitious singer like so many in the young Ponzillos' circle. The moral and financial support of Anna Ryan and the friendship with Prilik helped Carmela through hard times, when she was pursuing her own interests and laying the foundation for the next Ponzillo to come: her sister, "Babe," Rosa.

CHAPTER 3

Those Tailored Italian Girls in Vaudeville

A family financial crisis in 1915 played a large role in determining the future course of the sisters' careers. Carmela learned of it during a weekend visit with her parents, as she wrote in her 1933 memoir and confirmed about a decade later in an interview. This was while Rosa was living and working in New Haven. She found that her parents were about five years behind on their payments to the tax collector and owed large sums to mortgage holders. An attachment had been placed on the house, Carmela said.

> I phoned Rosa to come home, and . . . she saw that our little home-stead was attached. Babe said, "What does that mean?" "It means that [we're] being put out of our home and are losing it." So she said, "What shall we do?" I told her that we must work, and she said, "At what? How much money do we need?" I told her that all we needed was $500.00 in order to get back our homestead; then she began to cry and said, "Where will we get some [money]?"
>
> Then I decided that she must leave her New Haven position and come to New York. She said she could not come right away, that she [would] come in a few weeks, that she would have to live up to her contract [with Ceriani]. So I returned to New York and played a

> singer [*sic*] for three months on the Keith vaudeville circuit, sending
> money to [our parents'] creditors, paying on the installment plan all
> the back taxes, interest and the mortgage [payments] on the house.

This story was confirmed by Tony Ponzillo in a later interview, when he
recalled that her financial help and that sent later by her and Rosa together
saved the family from ruin. From the records in the Registry of Deeds in the
Meriden Court House, it is clear that both Tony and Carmela held the title
to part or all of the Springdale Avenue and Water Steet properties between
1912 and 1918.

Carmela's account goes on to say that three months after her meeting
with Rosa, she told her manager, Gene C. Hughes, that she had decided to
take her "baby sister" into her act. The popularity of sister acts at that time
was surely a factor in her decision, and it may be that she simply was not
successful enough on her own. In *Vaudeville: From the Honky Tonks to the
Palace,* Joe Laurie Jr. describes sister numbers as "classy" acts, of which there
were dozens on the route. According to the vaudeville historian Douglas
Gilbert, after 1910, women performers became more dominant, sometimes
outrivaling the men. Surely, though, the Ponzillo family's situation was a
powerful factor in Carmela's decision to remove the teenage Rosa from the
relatively safe Italian-American environment of New Haven and Rocco and
Margaret Da Vino's comfortable, blue-collar household and thrust her into
the boisterous vaudeville arena.

$\mathscr{L}$AUNCHING THE SISTER ACT ∾

Carmela was fortunate in having an agent who would at least consider her
project. Gene Hughes was a respected manager who, unlike many in his
trade, had incorporated his small business, with himself as president and
treasurer and Lina, his wife, as secretary. Describing himself as a "promoter," he had two offices in the heart of Times Square: one at 220 West
Forty-ninth Street and the other in Room 1002 at 1564 Broadway, the Palace
Theatre Building. The Hughes family lived in one of New York's most re-

spectable neighborhoods, with an apartment at 350 West Eighty-eighth
Street, near Riverside Drive. If, as Rosa said, she and her sister visited
Hughes in his home, this is where they were entertained. A beloved figure
in vaudeville management, Hughes was also the agent for Laurie, who described him as giant of a man, weighing over 250 pounds. With a friend, he
was said to be able to "finish two cases of champagne at one sitting." Hughes
had been the president of the Vaudeville Comedy Club, which counted Al
Jolson and other celebrities in its membership, and was known for his fairness in that rough-and-tumble world.

According to Carmela, Hughes said, "[Bring] her down and I'll look
her over." She wired to Rosa to come down. "I met Rosa at the station. I
was surprised at her appearance [because] she had developed so suddenly. I
gave a start. I thought for a moment that I would faint. My first words were
'Why did you get so fat?' And she began to cry and said, 'Don't you like my
suit?' She wore a tan suit and coat with a pleated flounce. She was then a
girl of 17 weighing 195 pounds. So there were more heartaches and struggles." Carmela then describes Rosa's introduction to her agent:

> I took her up to see Gene Hughes, my manager for the big-time
> Keith [circuit], at the Palace Theatre Building. When I presented
> Babe to Mr. Hughes, I shall never forget the expression on that man's
> face, when he took a good look at Babe. He called me aside and said,
> "Carmela, you'd better continue with your single act. You're a big
> hit; don't bother about a sister act. You'll have to start all over again,
> and [anyway] she's an amateur and knows nothing about the stage."
>
> I told him, "Don't worry about her appearance; . . . I'll take her
> in hand and put her on a diet and buy her a new corset and proper
> clothes, and there'll be a great change." And he said to me, "A mira-
> cle will have to be performed." I told him please to leave that to me.

As one might expect, Rosa's account differs from Carmela's. Rosa later
recalled that Carmela had never heard her sing in the full voice required for
the operatic arias that had become standards in her program. It was during
one of Carmela's frequent visits to Meriden that she went down to the Café

Mellone in New Haven one evening to hear Rosa, who had by then gained a considerable amount of experience as a teenage "cabaret singer," as she was billed. The sisters planned Rosa's expedition to New York after Carmela's visit, with the help of Ceriani, who, protective as always, accompanied her to the city at least once.

Perhaps during this excursion he took his young protégée to the Metropolitan Opera. Later Rosa said that she first attended the Metropolitan with him on Valentine's Day in 1916, months after their official debut on the Keith circuit, but this is surely wrong. They sat in the gallery. What they saw is by no means certain, because Rosa gave several different accounts of her first experience at the Met. Sometimes she said that the first opera she saw there was *Tosca* with Farrar and Caruso; but in her 1952 *Opera News* interview she said that she first went to the Met when she was fifteen, in 1912, and was "thrilled" by *L'amore dei tre re* and "the *Butterfly* of Farrar and Caruso." In a much earlier interview, just after her Met debut in 1918, she said that Carmela "and friends" took her to hear Caruso and Farrar in a matinee of *Carmen* before her meeting with Hughes and before she and her sister began to tour in vaudeville. This is probably the afternoon performance of *Carmen* on February 15, 1915. Of all Rosa's accounts, this is the most believable, simply because she gave it so soon after the event. Whatever her first experience at the Met may have been, it is likely that she did see at least two operas there, first as Carmela's guest, then as Ceriani's.

Several days later, Rosa and Carmela were invited to Gene Hughes's Upper West Side home. Rosa recalled her youthful awkwardness and her weight, which, she said, had reached 180 pounds. With her height at about five feet eight inches, she seemed too heavy and too tall for the vaudeville audience, which favored such slender beauties as Anna Held, Elsie Janis, Eva Tanguay, and the petite Fritzi Scheff. In spite of his dismay, Hughes let Rosa audition for him that day; she accompanied herself as she sang Scheff's arrangement of Victor Herbert's "Kiss Me Again," from his most popular operetta, the 1905 *Mademoiselle Modiste*. Hughes apparently did not ask her to sing anything else. The sisters had at last got his attention but did not yet have a firm commitment from him.

Carmela gave her sister her early stage training for the big vaudeville theaters, showing her how to move onstage and how to dress. Because they were short of funds, they found it difficult to buy what they needed to effect this transformation. It is likely that either their landlady or Anna Ryan gave them money to help them through this crisis.

The enterprising Carmela also persuaded Adolph Lorber, the owner of the elegant Lorber's Restaurant, to give her work, which he did, perhaps because she had been so successful at the much more famous Reisenweber's Hotel Café, the crown jewel of Columbus Circle. Carmela described her effort in her 1933 memoir:

> [In] the meantime, I applied for a position at Lorber's Restaurant, opposite the Metropolitan Opera House. "Pay me $100 a week," [I said.] I thought that would at least pay our [expenses] and get our music material for the audition and send money home. . . . Then I brought Rose down to Lorber's for dinner one evening and asked Lorber to engage her also. He said he could not afford two singers, so I told Rose that when I sang [she should] join the shows with me from her table. We were a sensation. So I told Rose not to worry, that something would break; [then] Lorber said: "If she'll take $25 a week and three meals a day"—and that was the best he could do. I said: "She'll take it for a few weeks," as we were getting ready to go into vaudeville. He didn't like the idea of our leaving him in a few weeks. We weren't booked as yet for vaudeville; but I took it for granted that we would be booked, for God never failed me in my faith.

According to Carmela, Rosa began to work with her at Lorber's the following week. "We sang at dinner time, first [show] 8:30, two songs apiece and duets; then at [after]-theatre time, 11:30 to 12:30. Spent days studying and [preparing] our vaudeville act; [we] engaged a man to teach us the right songs. We bought our own blue satin [drapery for] scenery on the install-ment plan, but we had no money for our gowns as yet." Hughes helped them stage the act. The thrifty sisters carried that blue drapery along to their new apartment at 307 West Ninety-seventh Street, then moved it to 260 Riverside and to 90 Riverside. Finally Rosa took it to Villa Pace, near Baltimore.

With additional concert engagements that came from people who heard them at Lorber's, the sisters managed to get by in the months before Hughes finally agreed to hire them. But more than a make-do measure, this was a clever twist of strategy, for Lorber's, at 1420 Broadway, was the most popular refuge of the opera audience as well as members of the Metropolitan roster and staff. The Ponzillo sisters, in a sense, sang three unofficial "auditions" for the Metropolitan every night. They could not possibly have found a better stage than Lorber's, and although neither Carmela nor Rosa ever mentioned meeting anyone from the opera business there, it is certain that people from the Metropolitan must have heard them.

The sisters faced two obstacles: to polish their act and to transform an overweight Rosa into a potential vaudeville star. Carmela described their struggle:

> Now the real worry was to get after [Rosa's] personal appearance and make her look thin, [for] 195 is a great deal of excess baggage to try to melt down in a short time. But [because she was] tall and had pretty hands and feet, she at least gave me a line to work on. The next day I bought her a new corset, laced her in, and let her long black hair down over her back. She looked more like 17 than 30 [as she had looked] when I met her at the station. So I drew a long sigh of relief. . . . At that moment, I was most grateful for possessing the gift I [had] for dressmaking and millinery, for it came in [handy] at the proper time.

Their next challenge was to get Hughes to give Rosa another chance. It is much to the credit of Mary McCabe, their generous landlady, that she let them use the entire main floor of her house to entertain the agent at dinner. Carmela remembered that she made the kitchen, dining room, and parlor available—no small accomplishment in a rooming house. It was a matter of good faith, for Carmela, often with Anna Ryan, had already lived on West

Sixty-fourth Street for five years. Miss McCabe, "a kind and religious woman," had already taken an interest in Carmela's fight for work and recognition. The woman, Carmela admitted, had let her rent go unpaid for weeks, evidently because Rosa's stay in New York was taking its toll on the Ponzillos' limited resources. On the day set for Hughes's visit, there was no question about the menu; the sisters made a spaghetti dinner. It was a Sunday noon. "We prepared a banquet for him," Carmela wrote. "When he met us at the door, he said, 'Is this big, fat Rose? Well, Carmela, you're a wonder!' And he put his arms around Rose and said, 'Well, now you're beginning to look like something!' And I said, 'Fine feathers make fine birds, if you know how to use the feathers!'" Carmela, writing her memoir, crossed out the words "big" and "fat" but made no other changes in her account.

During her 1952 interview for *Opera News,* Rosa laughed as she remembered that Sunday: "Mr. Hughes was obviously impressed with Sister and with our cooking, but when he took a look at me and heard that I wanted to break into vaudeville, he must have thought we were crazy. I was square then, just like a box; and he told me so right away. '[You're] too fat!'—That was his decision; but he offered to hear me sing. I did 'Kiss Me Again' from *Mademoiselle Modiste* and must have pleased him, for he signed me right away."

Carmela remembered the event somewhat differently. After dinner she told Rosa to go to the piano and sing "Kiss Me Again" as she had never sung it before. Rosa said, "I'm ashamed." Carmela, very much the older sister, reminded her, "Dear, we're going to make good and pay [for] our homestead for the folks; that's what we're here for." Hearing that, Rosa "shyly and slowly" went to the piano and sang "Kiss Me Again." Carmela saw her "rolling those big, beautiful brown eyes and almost acting the song for Gene Hughes." At first he was "speechless," then came over and said, "My God, Carmela, she actually can sing! And what a voice!" As Hughes left, he hurriedly whispered into Carmela's ear to come to his office the following morning. Although he had, as she expected, "gone crazy" after hearing Rosa sing, he had not yet committed himself to putting her in vaudeville.

At Hughes's office the next day, Carmela told him that she and Rosa were ready with a fully rehearsed vaudeville program. Ever cautious, he reminded her again that she would be starting all over if she were to join forces with Rosa. But, as Carmela wrote, "I had decided that she must join me as a sister act." Rosa would not go back to "doing club work in New Haven earning $50.00 a week." Hughes put on additional pressure, noting that "Babe was unknown and inexperienced." Carmela answered that Rosa was "a very brilliant child" and that "it would not be long before she would be famous overnight." Defeated, Hughes agreed to book the sister act. Carmela's memoir describes their first tryout at a dingy and unfashionable moving picture theater at First Avenue and 110th Street. This is beyond doubt the small nickelodeon owned by Mrs. Mary Marino, not at 110th (because that block was occupied by the Consolidated Gas Tanks) but at 111th and First: 2157 First Avenue, a building that is still standing. Hughes booked the Ponzillos with only four days' advance notice, Carmela recalled. Their debut there probably took place in the spring of 1915.

There is some evidence that the Ponzillos may have had either a longer engagement or repeat engagements at Mrs. Marino's theater, for someone they later knew well was then living next door to it. This was Giuseppe Russo, the man with whom Rosa Ponselle had a long romantic attachment in the early 1930s. Russo, whom she called "Pippo," lived with his parents and three sisters and a brother at 2159 First Avenue. Like the Ponzillos, he had parents who both had been born in Italy; his father was a laborer. At the time the young Ponzillo sisters were making their debuts at 111th and First Avenue, Pippo Russo was a teenager. And while it is possibly a coincidence that he lived next door to the tiny theater where Carmela and Rosa first appeared as a sister act, it is more likely that Pippo Russo met the Ponzillos then and renewed his acquaintance with them later.

The sisters' official debut in 1915 was booked into the Star Theatre on Lexington Avenue and 107th Street. Carmela, in an interview in the second Ryan scrapbook, described it as "the old Star Theatre on the Upper East Side." On a main street at the edge of Italian Harlem, the Star proved to be a perfect venue for the Ponzillo sisters' first major engagement in vaudeville.

Like theaters in New York's downtown Little Italy, it served a largely non-English-speaking, recently arrived immigrant population that was over-whelmingly southern Italian and Sicilian. When widespread telephone use became common in that neighborhood, almost all the numbers were listed to Italian names, among them some that figured heavily in the opera busi-ness, such as Joseph Rubabbo, with his Savoy Film Exchange and theatrical lighting shop, just north of Mrs. Marino's theater.

The Star, which had originally been called the Boricua Theatre, had in 1902 presented Franz von Suppé's *Boccaccio,* produced by the Robinson-Temple Opera Company and Charles Jones, an associate of the opera impre-sario Henry W. Savage. By 1912 and 1913 the theater, renamed the Star in 1903, was featuring dramas such as *Uncle Tom's Cabin* and *The Count of Monte Cristo,* which alternated with comedies by the Academy of Music company, where Carmela had sung in 1912 in *The Girl from Brighton.* It also offered general family entertainment in a "continuous performance of vaudeville and the latest photo plays" on Sundays from 1 to 11 P.M. Later, vaudeville took over completely, perhaps because it was suited to the neigh-borhood into which hundreds of families had moved to escape Manhattan's downtown ghetto.

Jerre Mangione and Ben Morreale, in *La Storia,* call Italian Harlem "the largest and perhaps the drabbest of the Italian enclaves" in New York City; it had grown from 1880 to 1900 into the largest Italian community in the nation. Reaching from the East River to Third and Lexington Avenues and from 106th Street to 116th, it provided housing in five-story walk-up build-ings and shopping in dozens of little mom-and-pop stores that fronted on the streets. Because the buildings were slightly newer than those in the Mul-berry Street community, they sometimes had one toilet per floor and bath-tubs in the kitchens. These, however, were rare in the older buildings. Busy street markets offered all the southern Italian foods. Three of the most popu-lar restaurants were Ricciardi's, Vesuvio, and La Porta Pia di Roma.

One of the best-known Italian-American families was headed by Marzi-ale Sisca, who lived first on Pleasant Avenue, east of First, then in a handsome residence on the north side of Ninety-fifth Street. With their publishers, poets, lyricists, journalists, and physicians, the Siscas served many in this Italian-speaking population. Marziale Sisca published the popular Italian-language magazine *La follia,* which he founded in 1893. He was the first Italian critic to review Rosa Ponselle's opera debut in 1918, having attended *La forza del destino* with his son, Michael, then fourteen. It was Michael who later took over the editorial duties, and *La follia* is still published under his direction. The magazine boasted Enrico Caruso as a regular contributor, for the great tenor gave the Siscas his caricatures, more than one hundred of which they published. The Siscas also had a collection of Caruso's letters, sent during their intimate friendship to "Carissimo Marziale." They also have early motion pictures of Caruso with Michael. Marziale's brother wrote the lyrics to the classic Neapolitan song "Core 'ngrato," with its passionate plea to "Catarì, Catarì."

Because he grew up in that world, Michael Sisca still recalls the Star Theatre. In a 1996 interview he described it as "a dump," though he fondly recalled the Italian shows produced there in his childhood and teen years. "The Italian people used to go to all the shows there," Sisca said. "It was a strictly Italian neighborhood, and very poor." Three of the show business personalities who performed on this circuit were the actor William Ricciardi, whom film fans may recall playing a bit part as the bulbous-nosed coachman in *San Francisco,* which starred Jeanette MacDonald and Clark Gable; Eduardo Migliaccio, Caruso's friend, who played under the stage name Farfariello; and the comedian Rotario De Rosalia, a Sicilian who played the immigrant as millionaire or the Italian barber. An impersonator who mocked the rich Italian banker and, later, the Italian bootlegger, Migliaccio also did skits and performed at private parties in the homes of Italian families. The Siscas were among the many who hired him. Michael Sisca recalls going at least once to Italian vaudeville with Caruso.

Rosa Ponselle described the Star Theatre as "a fleabag of a place" where the highest-priced tickets were twenty-five cents. From handbills and other advertisements of the sisters' act we can see that a quarter was generally the lowest ticket price in the more important vaudeville theaters. The price of admission at the Star was adjusted down for the purses of the struggling immigrants of Italian Harlem, who would have been hard put to pay downtown and Broadway prices. A similar low-price structure was set for grand opera given mainly for the Italian community by the impresario Alfredo Salmaggi, who emigrated from the Abruzzi region of Italy to the United States in 1918 and began his career as a producer that same year. At New York's Hippodrome Theatre, Ebbets Field in Chicago, Coney Island, and the Brooklyn Academy of Music, Salmaggi's audience was always promised reasonable prices; tickets ranged from twenty-five to ninety-nine cents, a bargain for fully staged opera. The highest price guaranteed his patrons a box seat near whatever celebrities the colorful impresario managed to attract.

The Italian-American audiences for both vaudeville and opera came to take part in the staged events rather than merely see them. While they were generally respectful to operatic artists, they sometimes sang along with the performers or shouted to them across the footlights. "Hey! This is how it goes!" came the cry from the balcony when an unfortunate tenor forgot the words to a single phrase of *Il trovatore*; dozens of paying patrons began to sing along with him and the orchestra. This noisy audience often demanded encores, sometimes making it impossible for the show to go on until two or three were given. On one occasion even a single phrase—Cavaradossi's "Vittoria, vittoria!"—was belted out four times before the public would let *Tosca* continue. On other evenings, a single aria or a duet would have to be repeated. Sometimes the police had to intervene to stop a near-riot.

If the Italian-American opera audience was that unruly, the people who went to vaudeville were even more disruptive and, at times, wildly disrespectful. A glance at the vaudeville bills featuring the Ponzillo sisters, some of which are described later in this chapter, shows that the acts on the program offered a golden opportunity to anyone wanting to interrupt the show. The Italian-American paying audience, like that in Italy itself, always considered itself an "actor." Even during the showing of Italian motion pictures, people sitting in the auditorium shouted advice to actors on the screen, cursed the villains, or commented on the action. These were participatory events, and for the two young Ponzillos this debut was a real baptism by fire.

As the sisters left Adolph Lorber's restaurant on a Monday night, Carmela cast what she described as a longing look toward the opera house and said, "See, Rose, there's my dream and aspiration. Soon it won't be long that you and I are going to sing there." Like Ceriani, she encouraged her younger sister to believe that there lay her true destiny, "if she was serious and worked real hard." Fairly typical was Rosa's response: "Carmela, you must be crazy!"

Their last appearance at Lorber's came only a few days before their debut at the Star in 1915. When they spent their last cash on the blue drapery that was to serve them so well then and later, the sisters had nothing left for gowns. Carmela went to Gene Hughes's office, hoping for an advance, but for whatever reason, the promoter refused. Carmela suggested that they appear as "students" for three or four days, until they could earn enough to buy proper gowns. Knowing the millinery trade as well as she did, she went downtown and bought Chinese silk ties with colored flowers on a black background, black satin tams or berets, black satin skirts, and black patent leather slippers. Some of the clothing may have come from their relatives, for one of their mother's cousins, Frederic Faraone, was in the leather business on Gold Street in lower Manhattan, while Alfredo Giannelli, their father's cousin, was a dressmaker at 883 Sixth Avenue. When it came to makeup, both sisters had already had enough experience to handle the challenge of the Star. They both had long hair, Carmela's reaching below her waist and Rosa's falling over her shoulders and down her back. They fastened two long braids with white satin bows and presented themselves on the bill as as "Those Tailored Italian Girls."

When they arrived at the stage door of the Star, the manager, knowing that this was their opening, asked where their trunks were and what their wardrobe was like. Carmela replied that their "costumes" were what they were wearing. With that the manager exploded: "Who ever heard of such a crazy stunt?" He then called Hughes, punctuating his end of the conversation with "a lot of swearing." To his credit, Hughes stood by his performers and ordered the stage manager to use the sisters, dressed just as they were, as the first act in the matinee show.

The opening spot at the Star was scheduled for 2:30. With Carmela warning Rosa to sing out and not to be clumsy in making her entrance and exit, the Ponzillos introduced themselves to big-time vaudeville. It is safe to say that there were not many English-speaking people in the audience that day, for in that neighborhood, even decades later, most people understood only the dialects of southern Italy. "Proper Italian" and other languages were not generally used. Before so many southern Italians, the two sisters were truly at home.

On that first afternoon the card on the easel read: "C. and R. Ponzillo," Carmela said. As they often did in later appearances, the sisters alternated their voices, in effect playing a game with the audience, which was challenged to say which of the two women was singing which phrase. Carmela switched "from soprano to alto" and, she added, "so did Babe." They opened their program with the Barcarolle from Jacques Offenbach's *Tales of Hoffmann,* a duet. For their second number, Carmela sang Paolo Tosti's "Goodbye," which was followed by Rosa singing "Kiss Me Again," her signature piece. Together they sang " 'O Sole Mio," "Comin' through the Rye," "Swanee River," "Annie Laurie," and "Old Black Joe." According to Rosa, all of the arrangements were hers. Carmela later described their success that day as "a sensation" and added that they got so many encores that the following acts were dangerously delayed. At the end of their part of the show, Carmela made a little speech. Even the tough-talking manager was won over; Carmela recalled that he came to their dressing room after they finished and said, "Well, Ponzillo, as far as I'm concerned, you girls could sing in your natural birth outfits." Carmela called Hughes to say that they had had an enormous triumph. Soon after, they saw their name go on billboards as "The Ponzillo Sisters, Opera Singers."

At the beginning of the sisters' career as a duo in vaudeville, Carmela, who had been making about $150 a week as a solo act, had to take a substantial cut in salary, for she and "Babe" were initially paid only $125 a week. Out of that they had to give Hughes his 10 percent commission. The drop in income was no doubt due to the promoter's practice of booking them into theaters of the lowest category, at least at the start. But Carmela, who told interviewers at this time that she had been "on her own" for seven years and was a veteran of vaudeville and musical comedy, believed that "with hard work we would make up the difference in a short time." This they did, but they certainly had to struggle for their success.

Their next engagement, one week after their opening at the Star Theatre, was in the summer of 1915, in Newark, New Jersey, at Proctor's Theatre, where they were praised for their "voices of great sweetness and power." One was a mezzo of unusual range, a newspaper critic wrote. "Nature has been very bountiful to these gifted girls," said another. In the same city one writer identified Carmela as "a dramatic soprano" and Rosa as "a mezzo soprano." One of the sisters (the article does not make clear which one) was criticized for having high notes that were "a trifle metallic," but in their duet—probably the Barcarolle—they achieved a "harmony that at times really stirs the soul." They also played Proctor's in Passaic, New Jersey, and at the Majestic in Paterson, which had a huge Italian-speaking population and supported occasional opera performances with well-known singers. Here they were "the hit of the show." The critic added that "both have beautiful voices and use excellent judgment in the selection of their songs."

A notice in *Music Trades* shows how they were broadening their repertory in vaudeville. Seven numbers were eventually added, including "A Little Bit of Heaven," "She's the Daughter of Mother Machree," "The Little Grey Mother," "In the Garden of the Gods," "If It Takes a Thousand Years," "Are You from Dixie?" and "Good-bye, Good Luck, God Bless You." Other newspaper articles mention additional songs, showing how conscientious the Ponzillos were about varying their program. This was particularly important because, as their reviews prove, they were booked in some cities more than once a year, and occasionally they would move from one theater to another in a given city during a one-week or two-week engagement. While some old favorites were always welcome, it was important to give the public something fresh. In an era when many cities had several daily newspapers, there was a small corps of surprisingly sophisticated critics to be won over. And they did win them over; it is the critics who testify, time and again, to the Ponzillo sisters' growing and quite astonishing popularity.

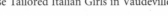

EADLINERS

Their first extensive tour began later. When Hughes booked the act into the Royal Theatre in New York City in September 1915, the *New York American* carried a note about their "good looks and excellent grand opera voices." By the middle of that season they were in Pittsburgh, appearing at the one-thousand-seat Davis Theatre on what was called their "first American tour" in one paper and their "maiden tour" in another. Because Carmela saved the clippings but often did not identify the newspaper by name, we sometimes have the critics' accounts without their credits; but the local press was evidently captivated, for it devoted a surprising amount of coverage to them. The sisters were described by one enthusiast as "the Ponzilla [*sic*] girls, Italy's famous and beautiful grand opera prima donnas." They had clearly discovered what would attract their audience, for now they were "purporting to be from Italy" and claiming to be "native Italians, [who] have sung all the leading soprano and alto roles in Italy and know grand opera." Said another reviewer: "The two Ponzillas [*sic*] brought a real bit of grand opera quality to their act . . . [and were] a delight and a joy to the ear." This critic, who found that their program was "sung at too fast a tempo," remarked on their "alleged Italian ancestry" and their "admirable English accents." But the "two dark-haired young girls . . . took the large audience by storm . . . with such singing as one rarely hears. One is a lyric-dramatic soprano and the other a contralto of almost soprano range." He went on to praise their "dignity of execution and beauty of harmony." In another Pittsburgh paper the critic remarked on their ancestry: "Italian girls, but possessing perfect English accents." Like many others, he could not distinguish between their voices in the duets.

It was in Pittsburgh that Carmela, the "spokeswoman" for the act, began to give interviews. On June 19, 1916, described as "exceedingly beautiful" and "fresh from Italy," she embroidered somewhat on their story, saying that they were "making their maiden tour of the States, their first tour in vaudeville." They had been singing in the grand opera houses of Milan, Florence, and Rome but had a genuine interest in American culture; they

were "interested in ragtime and seriously studying American ragtime melo-
dies." In their "native Italy," Carmela said, they had "heard very little ragtime," but she boasted that she knew a great deal about its history. She also
praised "the real Negro ditty" as "a classic."

An early interview was given after Carmela shared a program with the
notorious Evelyn Nesbit Thaw, the "Girl in the Red Velvet Swing," former
mistress of the architect Stanford White and the wife of his murderer, Harry
K. Thaw. Carmela, called "Pontzilla," was "supposed to be a Spaniard, but
her features are undeniably Jewish; but she can sing and has one of the best
soprano voices ever heard in vaudeville: a commanding presence." This was
not the only reference to a "Spanish" background, although the sisters were
usually billed as Italian and were then passing themselves off as native-born
Neapolitans. In one interview Carmela compared the climate of Naples with
the Atlanta climate. They were "similar."

In another interview during this first tour (again from an unidentified
newspaper), a journalist wrote of "the stream of Spanish blood in their
veins" and described Carmela's claim that both she and Rosa had received
their musical education in Milan, where their mother had known the parents of Lucrezia Bori "when Bori was making her debut as Micaela." They
were "intimate," Carmela said. It would be easy to dismiss this as empty
boasting; but, as we have seen from the American immigration records,
some of the Contes did indeed come to this country from Milan, having
done what so many southern Italians did after the unification of Italy: mi-
grate to the north. This raises at least the possibility that a member of the
family of Maddalena Conte Ponzillo had some acquaintance with Bori and
her family and some contact with the most important center of opera in
Europe. So far as one can discover, this dubious story is the only reference
to the Conte family's interest in grand opera.

Because the Ponzillo sisters' "maiden tour" was such a success, Hughes
lost no time in bringing the sisters back to New York City that summer,
booking them at the Palace Theatre in the heart of Times Square from July
3 to 10, 1916. *Billboard,* which was already the most important entertainment
publication in the country, praised their act exuberantly in its issue of July

10 as "a riot. . . . The girls possess remarkable voices [with] a wonderful range." The *New York Morning Telegraph* carried a headline: CARMELA AND ROSA PONZILLO. It was followed by an article that described them as "two singers . . . that have made a remarkable hit at the Palace." Here, too, they were identified as "these lovely Spanish girls." The *New York Star,* covering the news of "the week ending July 16," reported that the show began with a dog act and included an interlude with "Anna Held, comedienne," one of the most famous entertainers of that period. As the headliners, "the Ponzello [*sic*] sisters were a hit with their piano and songs. . . . They are second to none" and "stand in a class all alone." The writer also complimented them on their "new dresses, which made them look great." In some other season of the year this would have been the perfect opportunity for Carmela and Rosa to be heard by someone associated with the opera business, or even with the Metropolitan. But not many important figures from the Metropolitan were likely to have been sitting through vaudeville shows in New York that summer. Nevertheless, this was a significant advancement for Carmela and Rosa. Times Square and the Palace, after all, had a mystique all their own.

Still under Hughes's management, the "Two Italian Girls" appeared at the end of August at Morrison's Theatre on Long Island during the all-important week before Labor Day. In the *Rockaway News* of August 30 they received a highly personalized review, where "Miss Carmela" was praised for her rendition of "She's the Sunshine of Virginia" and "Miss Rose" for her incomparable "Kiss Me Again." At the end of the act, they sang their popular duet " 'O Sole Mio." "Excellent!" the reviewer wrote. Their return engagement was guaranteed, and the following summer found them back on New York City's beach circuit again.

By September they were at the B. F. Keith Theatre in Philadelphia. Like their arrival at the Palace in Times Square, this was a step upward from their 1915 engagement at the William Penn Theatre in the "City of Brotherly Love." At the Penn they had been billed as "an act of the better sort" on a program that included Joe Laurie Jr., who remembered them with genuine affection in his history of vaudeville, along with Aleen Bronson, several dancers, a gymnastic act called the Seven Bracks, and "The Clown Seal, an Animal of Rare Ingenuity." Of course, the Ponzillos stood out, with their "beauty of voice and excellent musical training." Among other popular songs, they had sung Carmela's favorite, Tosti's "Goodbye" and Ethelbert Nevin's "Mighty Lak' a Rose." That autumn they were praised for their artistry in the *Philadelphia Record* of September 26. "With their jet black hair, charming stage presence and the most beautiful voices that have come to vaudeville in a very long while," they were a sensation, surpassing the dancers Adelaide and Hughes, who performed "an allegory of the world at war and the unsuccessful attempt to bring the United States and Mexico into the open conflict." Here the sisters played second in billing to Hugh Herbert, one of the most beloved comedians of vaudeville and, later, motion pictures. In October 1916 Carmela and Rosa arrived at the Keith Theatre in Washington, where they were reviewed as "dramatic soprano voices of exceptional quality in tone and volume." This house, smaller than the eighteen-hundred-seat New York Palace, had one thousand seats and presented no real challenge to the sisters. At this engagement, Rosa was singled out for her gifts: "a range of three octaves" and artistry as "an accomplished pianist."

They swung up to Buffalo and Toronto next, appearing in Shea's theaters in both cities. Joe Laurie Jr. wrote of the chain's owner that "there never was a sweeter or nicer Irishman than Mike Shea." He defied "Keith's orders" and paid Carmela and Rosa $400 a week, instead of the $350 they had been contracted for, and clearly was fond of them. The *Buffalo Enquirer* of November 7 greeted "the daughters of Sunny Italy," who "captivated" the audience. In Shea's Theatre in Toronto they were the "hit of the bill, with their magnetic, joyous personalities." Here they appeared with the Singing Bicyclists. This tour probably also included the Palace Theatre in Springfield, Massachusetts.

At the end of the month Hughes called them back to New York City, where they got a fine review in the *Brooklyn Citizen* of November 28 for their performances at the important Bushwick Theatre. They "made a tremendous hit with their excellent singing . . . [and] splendid voices." A return engagement to the Davis Theatre in Pittsburgh was scheduled for mid-December. There the reviewer for the *Gazette* welcomed them as "a singing act of superlative merit." Praising them for having gained so much in "dramatic expression" in the six months since their previous appearance in the city, he singled out two songs that were particularly appealing: "Goodbye, Summer" and "Mother Machree." When they returned to Proctor's in Newark their notice read: "Nothing better in vocal music has been heard . . . this winter." Another New Jersey newspaper wrote that they were "finished artists; and the volume and sweetness of their voices have been remarked upon by many music critics." Carmela and Rosa spent Christmas of 1916 away from New York, playing in a Keith's theater in an unidentified city. On this occasion the critic complimented them for their staging, something that other journalists rarely mentioned. It included "a piano and a rose-shaded lamp [as] the setting for the sumptuous beauty of the 'Two Italian Girls.'"

In 1917 the Ponzillos undertook several long tours that swept through the South, the Midwest, and New England. They returned to Washington, played at the Maryland Theatre in Baltimore, and went on to Atlanta, where they conquered the audience and the very knowledgeable critics. "[They have] the most melodious voices that blend in delightful harmony, and they are dramatic singers of most pleasing appearance," wrote one reviewer. He added that Tosti's "Goodbye" and "Swanee River" brought "storms of applause." When Carmela was interviewed in the *Atlanta Constitution* she remarked, as she had done in other cities, that the weather there was "something like our winters in Naples" and added that "Rose wants to come when she can go swimming in Piedmont Park." At the Temple Theatre in a city that Carmela did not identify, the program included trained dogs, cats, and pigeons as well as the Imperial Cyclists, who played basketball as they did stunts onstage. "The Italian nightingales," though, "brought tears to the eyes of many in the house." Rosa later recalled their engagements in New Orleans and other southern cities.

The two sisters had moved beyond the split-week engagements that were the bane of performers and been promoted to long runs in major cities, a mark of accomplishment. When a two-week summer run in 1917 at the

Empress and Ramona theaters in Grand Rapids, Michigan, allowed Carmela and Rosa to rent a cottage in a nearby resort area, they were able to entertain friends "with an Italian supper." The reporter noted their love of beauty: "The rooms were fragrant with wild flowers, and a large bowl of American Beauty roses" provided the centerpiece of their table. Others had already written about the way they decorated their dressing rooms with flowered cretonnes and pillows and other small touches that brightened up the otherwise dingy cubicles.

The Ponzillos toured extensively in the Midwest. During this trek Carmela described the long, often difficult road she had traveled to reach what was then a peak of fame. It had taken her seven years, she said, as she "fought against great odds for her success." One writer said that after a six-month stint in a jewelry store at Fifth Avenue and Forty-second Street, she had been lucky to have studied with Paul Savage. Living in a furnished room, she later became a saleswoman in a wholesale dress house and a soloist in "churches in Greater New York." Her early career in vaudeville and musical comedy, she said, had prepared her for four years as a "parlor entertainer" for New York's richest families; she had also sung cabaret at Wallick's Hotel in the city. Carmela had nothing but praise for "Rose Ponzillo, who is a lyric soprano of exceptional ability and possesses a truly wonderful voice." She also recalled Rosa's work as "a former cabaret singer in New Haven" before they got into vaudeville.

The sisters had also appeared in Massachusetts, singing at the Colonial in Boston and in Fall River's Savoy Theatre. "They will never be forgotten for the surprise of the vocal treat that they have sprung on an unsuspecting audience." In a City Theatre on this same tour, they sang with "beautiful and full-throated voices" on a program with the Five Mowatts, a juggling act. Far from home and "east of Boston," the Ponzillos arrived in Portland, Maine, where they played in Keith's Theatre and were received as visiting divas. The Portland paper gave a nod to Marlo and Duffy, two gymnasts, but devoted serious column space to " 'These Italian Girls,' the most delightful songbirds who have ever been seen and heard this season. Their voices are superb." Another Portland journalist wrote: "Seldom have two artists been accorded heartier and more spontaneous applause." And from another clipping: " 'Those Italian Girls' simply captivated Monday's matinee audience. [It was] a triumph."

Closer to their family's base, Carmela and Rosa played in Pawtucket, Rhode Island, appearing at the Scenic Theatre with Lou Granato, "The Human Parrot," a troupe of acrobats, and a minstrel act. There the "Two Italian Girls" were praised for their "high class singing, . . . classical numbers and the better grade of old-time ballads." They returned to theaters of the Poli chain, where Rosa had sung in her early teen years, playing in Waterbury, where their uncle, Alfonso Ponzillo, and their aunt and cousins still lived. This chain was owned by Sylvester Poli, born in Lucca, who had become a revered figure in Italian-American communities of the Northeast. Having landed in the United States in 1881 as a penniless sculptor, he had developed his theaters from a sideshow he had managed in Rochester, survived through craft and thrift, and created one of New England's important small chains. It was "Old Home Week" at Poli's in New Haven, commented the reviewer, when "the Ponzillo girls were welcomed back for the first time in several years." When they played Poli's in Meriden, the scene of one of Rosa's first professional theater engagements, the pride of their parents was matched by that of their home city, which praised their "wonderfully sweet voices." At Poli's Palace in Hartford the reviewer pronounced their act "well arranged" and congratulated them on their "exceptionally fine voices," which held up as they delivered "encore after encore." The *Hartford Courant,* Connecticut's most important newspaper, declared that theirs was "the classiest singing act that has ever appeared at the Palace Theatre."

With reviews that matched or bettered those of many of the grand celebrities of vaudeville, Carmela returned to New York while Rosa stayed at home briefly. Said Carmela: "This was during the summer [of 1917], and we liked working in the summer. [Then] we were booked at Brighton Beach at Coney Island. We were booked like circus horses." But when her doctor ordered her to take a week's rest near the sea, Carmela chose a hotel in Far Rockaway and went to see the new theater. She found it "a beautiful place, right in the center of the park, with a beautiful hotel opposite. I immediately sent for Rose; and we spent a quiet week in Brighton."

Their affairs, though, were in disorder and their future in vaudeville threatened by a contract dispute that involved Carmela and the neat, mustached Edward F. Albee, B. F. Keith's partner. When their contract expired, Albee had offered the sisters another twenty-week contract at their old fee of four or five hundred dollars per week. As she learned, Hughes had signed without telling Carmela. "I went wild," she recalled. "I refused the contract. We were [even] billed for a return engagement at the Palace [on Broadway] without my knowledge." At that point Albee, acting for the Keith circuit, sued for breach of contract and had Carmela served with a summons, for she was demanding one thousand dollars a week, which Albee swore he would not pay, perhaps because of the earlier dispute with Shea over the Buffalo and Toronto fees. Eventually he sent for her; they argued; finally the case was settled out of court and in Carmela's favor. "The new contract [was] signed by me at $1,000 a week for twenty weeks." Defending her stand, she had argued that while Eva Tanguay and other stars were getting two thousand dollars a week, she was not about to sell the two Ponzillo sisters short at five hundred dollars. An interesting observation about the sisters' fees was made by Laurie, who said they "should have had $2,000" because they were so good.

With that battle won, the management of the New Brighton Theatre in Brooklyn ran a bill in August that featured the sisters and Elsie Janis, who sang patriotic songs, for the United States had been fighting World War I for several months by that time. Repeating their triumph at the Rockaway the previous year, the sisters were "a pronounced hit" and the best act on the bill.

On October 29, 1917, Gene Hughes again billed them at the Palace in Times Square. A glance at the full program, which is in the collection of the Ponselle biographer Enrico Aloi, shows eight acts. Two dancers performed "a reminiscence of the battle and entertainments they gave the wounded in Red Cross hospitals." The "Stepping Stars" were on "furlough from the French front," the bill said, hailing their "Waltz der Front," their Fox Trot, and the "new Paris Gowns of Miss Walton," who had bought them from Paquin and Callot Soeurs. Second on the bill were an "Xtra [*sic*] Feature,

Two Fascinating Italian Girls with Grand Opera Voices, Carmela and Rosa Ponzillo, in a New Programme of Superb Selections." They were followed by a song, dance, and comedy act; a skit featuring William Cressy and Blanche Dayne; Swor and Avery, "impersonators of Southern Negroes"; a patriotic skit; two comedians; Meehan's Dogs; and at the end, the headliner: Blossom Seeley and her "Syncopated Singers," who offered a program of "Jazz Melodical Delirium Tremens of Ragtime Running Wild." Her troupe was based in "Seeley's Syncopated Studio, where the art of Jazzing Things Up Reaches the Entertainment Limit." And the last line: "Oh! Hearken to that Jazz Cornet!"

Carmela, with her eye for detail, compared the sisters' 1916 appearance at the Palace to "a debut at the Metropolitan Opera." For their first engagement there, both wore black gowns: Rosa in fitted velvet trimmed with spangles; Carmela in a similar gown with a net train. Both wore black silk ribbon bandeaus covered with spangles. "Our hair reached almost to our knees, and [I] had a red rose in my hair." Their setting at the Palace, a "drawing room with beautiful lights," was "most flattering." Their costumes for their return were not well received by the critics.

Although we do not know the music of their program in 1917, Carmela did leave a record of their earlier successful appearance there: Offenbach's Barcarolle, to open the show; then Tosti's "Goodbye," which she sang; Rosa's "Kiss Me Again"; and " 'O Sole Mio," their favorite duet. Their encores at the Palace were "Old Black Joe," "Comin' through the Rye," and "Swanee River." In a sense, their October 1917 engagement at the Palace represented the peak of their success in vaudeville, where they had come from the most inauspicious beginning imaginable—$125 a week at the Star in Italian Harlem—to an undisputed triumph in the tour, with renegotiated contracts, bringing them first to $250 a week and later to $500. With their new contract and its $1,000 fee settled in the summer of 1917, they enjoyed popularity as "the class act" on the best circuits in the trade, although it is true that the twenty weeks that Carmela negotiated was a step down from the forty weeks that all vaudevillians saw as the passage to eighty, the most prestigious contract of all. With eighty weeks, Douglas Gilbert said, "your career was made." The sisters were rivals of women with international careers and years of experience in music halls and the legitimate theater, yet they maintained their refined image, never vulgarized their program, and never violated the tenets of good taste that marked their act. Laurie, for example, described the "blueys," or salacious jokes delivered by some of the women on the circuit; Carmela and Rosa never resorted to those. From beginning to end they put themselves on a pedestal and never left it.

After the prestigious autumn stint at the Palace, the sisters again toured New England, "all return engagements, and of course, that meant new songs and new gowns," Carmela said. They also returned to Pittsburgh, where they had won over a core of followers. For this two-week stay they were billed as headliners with Eva Tanguay. Once during their act Carmela fainted onstage. Carried into the wings, she was revived by the stage manager, who gave her sips of water. Later they got a big ovation, which set Tanguay off in a fit of jealousy. Carmela wrote in her memoir: "You should have heard the slamming of doors when we'd pass each other's dressing rooms!" Later, though, all bitterness was forgotten, for Tanguay was in the audience when Rosa Ponselle made her Metropolitan Opera debut and was one of the first to congratulate her in her dressing room.

Several unexpected events changed the course of their careers soon after their 1917 tour. Both sisters were suffering from a nagging fatigue that short vacations of one or two weeks did not dispel. Carmela, particularly, seemed exhausted and frustrated at not having time for uninterrupted vocal study. She, much more than Rosa, was determined to break into opera somehow. Almost thirty, she had to make an important decision: either remain in vaudeville for the rest of her career or prepare for auditions for American opera houses. It seems that neither of the sisters considered taking the standard route for American singers: going to Europe to study, making a debut abroad, and then returning to the States. If, as their future mentor, William Thorner, said, an investment of five thousand dollars was needed to launch an opera career, then their choice is easily explained.

A serious setback came when Gene Hughes died, leaving them without a manager. At that point Edward Valentine Darling, the "Grand Master" of the Palace and the head booker of the Keith circuit, telephoned to Carmela with an offer to rebook their act at the Palace in New York on very short notice. She refused at first, then (according to her memoir) asked for two thousand a week and enough time to put a new act together. Darling said, "Carmela, you've gone crazy!" and hung up on her.

Carmela, by that time, had acquired a reputation for hard bargaining. Just on the face of it, her salary demand seemed outrageous, simply because it represented such a huge increase from their original 1915 fee and was double the fee she had accepted after her latest dispute with Edward Albee. Judging from their popularity, though, the Ponzillo sisters deserved it. Having played the lowest houses, they had risen through the ranks of modest performers to a place near the top of their profession. In some theaters they were headliners, and even when they did not get that billing, at the Palace on Broadway, for example, they won the critical acclaim that had kept Hughes happy. He obviously had liked them and had invested a great deal in their careers, from the days of their appearances at Lorber's to their triumph at the Palace. But Hughes's death brought that phase of their lives to an end. Another agent—Darling, for example—might take a tougher stand in negotiations over their fees, for they were not as famous as Seeley, Janis, Tanguay, or Thaw, although they were certain of frequent billings with stars.

From recordings of their vaudeville repertory that the Ponzillo sisters made in 1918 and the 1920s, all the qualities that impressed the critics come rolling out on the wave of their pure sound. The standards, such as "Comin' through the Rye," " 'O Sole Mio," and the *Hoffmann* Barcarolle, recorded for Columbia, show the generous warmth and power of their voices, while the unmatched beauty of Löhr's "Where My Caravan Has Rested" reveals an earthiness, an honesty, and an utter lack of condescension. The innocence paired with the compelling and often sensual quality of Rosa's "Kiss Me Again" are perhaps unmatched by any of her other program choices. "Un bel dì" from *Madama Butterfly,* recorded in 1919, shows the confidence that came from several years of performing in motion picture houses and restaurants. Carmela's mastery of her voice is also beyond dispute.

In spite of the sisters' popularity, though, it seems that after Hughes's death no other vaudeville manager was interested in them. Thus their decision to leave vaudeville was to a certain extent forced upon them when they finished their last tour. But this was a moment when their lives were changing in other important ways as well. The sisters had lived frugally; they were sending money home and had been able to pay off almost all of their parents' debts. Old wounds had healed; Carmela said, "Father and I became pals again, [even though] he had disowned me as his daughter when I left home to go on the stage." As we know from later correspondence, Carmela and her father remained close until his death, keeping in touch by mail and by telephone.

By that time, Carmela had had at least two voice teachers in New York City. The first, Giovanni Martino, had been recommended to her by Anna Ryan. Although he was in early middle age and had been teaching in the city for several years, he became a member of the Metropolitan Opera roster in 1919, remaining there until 1927. Martino clearly remained a part of the sisters' circle of friends: a Keystone View photograph of 1922 shows Martino standing next to Rosa at her birthday party, and he was an honored guest at the Hotel des Artistes when the president of the National Concerts management bureau fêted her and William Thorner in 1919. Carmela's later studies with the much more famous Paul Savage had been interrupted by the vaudeville tours, which had made it difficult for her to maintain her voice at peak operatic condition. She also had to find someone to prepare the repertory needed for auditions. Rosa, in her 1952 *Opera News* interview, said, "Carmela had the idea [of going into opera] first. She decided vaudeville and a lifetime of 'Tailored Sisters' acts was not for her."

THE WILLIAM THORNER VOCAL STUDIO ～

Both Rosa and Carmela agree that these considerations influenced Carmela's decision to take lessons from "the famous teacher" William Thorner, in Rosa's words. When Carmela was interviewed by Terese Rose Nagel for the *New York Sun* just after Rosa's debut, she recalled her early years in the city, then discussed her engagement at "Wallick's, at 43rd Street and Broadway," and the chance encounter with Hughes, who launched her in vaudeville. An acquaintance who had heard the sisters in vaudeville, Mario Gambardella, convinced her that "their place was in the opera, not in a variety house," and offered to introduce Carmela to William Thorner, which he did in the autumn of 1917. Carmela's professional relationship with Thorner eventually provided both sisters with their first real chance to join the roster of an opera company.

Thorner's residence and studio were in an elegant apartment at 2128 Broadway, in a building that was demolished in 1929 to make room for Samuel "Roxy" Rothafel's Beacon Theatre. At the very heart of the "residential quarter" of the music business, it stood diagonally across from the fabled Hotel Ansonia. Thorner and his wife had decorated their high-ceilinged suite with European taste. It had elaborate carved moldings; imposing fireplaces with fluted columns and graceful wreaths were topped by mantels where porcelain figurines and antique lamps were displayed. Double wall sconces with glass shades helped to light the rooms. Thorner had, as a fire screen, a bronze shield nearly three feet across. Healthy potted plants stood in fine cachepots, and tall porcelain vases held bouquets of fresh flowers. The floors were covered with expensive Oriental rugs. As proof of his contacts with opera stars, signed photographs of his celebrated friends covered the walls of Thorner's living room, where places of honor were reserved for Jean and Edouard De Reszke and Amelita Galli-Curci, his protégée. Portraits of Enrico Caruso and Antonio Scotti hung over the grand piano in his studio. Period photographs of him in this sumptuous setting show a "grand master" of his art: Thorner appeared robust but not fat, and the classic lines of his face reinforced this impression of dignity and strength. His publicity photographs were made by Count Jean de Strelecki, not by any of the everyday photographers on the scene.

In 1916 Thorner was teaching a large coterie of sopranos, a single tenor, and a bass. Among his pupils were Eva Didur, the daughter of the celebrated bass Adamo Didur, and the soprano Ganna Walska, who was already billing herself as "Madame" as a sign of her rank. Walska had studied in Paris with Jean De Reszke before coming to the United States in 1915 and, with the help of Otto Kahn, had studied with Wilfrid Pelletier and sung at the Century Theatre. Later Thorner succeeded in getting her a contract at the Chicago Opera Association. Although her planned debut there was a fiasco, she remained the companion and, later, the wife of the financier Harold McCormick, her third or fourth husband, who divorced Edith Rockefeller so he could marry her. Walska was said to be an inspiration for the diva Susan Alexander in Orson Welles's *Citizen Kane,* just as McCormick, according to sources close to Welles, was one of the real models for Charles Foster Kane.

When Carmela Ponzillo was introduced to Thorner, he was riding high on the nationwide sensation created by Amelita Galli-Curci, who was hailed as the "Second Adelina Patti" and the worthy heir to the crowns of Nellie Melba and Luisa Tetrazzini. Scouting Italian theaters, the teacher-manager had met the coloratura in Catania in 1914. A journalist for *Town Topics* wrote on October 24, 1918, that when she "completed a tour in South America, she chanced to meet an old acquaintance from Italy, who requested permission to speak to Cleofonte Campanini, General Director of the Chicago Opera Company, with a view to his engaging Mme. Galli-Curci." This old acquaintance was William Thorner. In a feature story and interview in the *Fort Wayne* (Indiana) *Journal Gazette* of March 30, 1919, Thorner described his battle to get her an American contract: neither the Metropolitan nor Chicago would hire her. But with Thorner's training, Galli-Curci got her voice under control. "The faults that made Gatti-Casazza, manager of the Metropolitan Opera, and Campanini reluctant to regard her seriously have been largely wiped out," Thorner said. "I personally am proud to have given her some advice, for which to me she has expressed the highest esteem, as having contributed to her great triumphs." He continued with a detailed analysis of the particular qualities of Galli-Curci's voice. Thorner was said to have laid siege to Campanini to get the soprano her first contract with Chicago at three hundred dollars a performance. After her debut in the early winter of 1916 this was raised to one thousand dollars, solid proof of her mercurial rise to fame. Her first recording contract was also secured by Thorner.

Although he had not been able to get a contract for Walska at the same time, Thorner had got her an audition with Campanini, who told her to let him know when she was ready. Later Thorner coached Rosa Raisa and the Metropolitan tenor Sydney Rayner; and in 1920 Mario Chamlee, another of his students, made his Metropolitan debut as Cavaradossi in *Tosca* with Geraldine Farrar in the title role. He also placed Anna Roselle, Yvonne D'Arle, and a number of minor figures in opera. His most famous pupil by far was Al Jolson, whose lessons with Thorner are described in a clipping in Ponselle's scrapbook for 1922–24. While Jolson was learning Mozart arias, crowds of fans used to gather outside Thorner's studio windows for a "free concert." In addition to his contacts with managers and celebrities such as Jolson, Thorner was a close friend of Caruso and of Victor Maurel, one of the greatest actor-singers of the previous century. Maurel, after his retirement from the European stage, had settled in New York, where he lived in an imposing residence at 14 West Sixty-eighth Street. Regularly Thorner asked such famous artists as Adamo Didur, Giuseppe De Luca, Raisa, and Maurel to sit in on lessons with promising young singers. As we shall see, both Maurel and Raisa's friend Romano Romani played major roles in shaping Rosa's career.

When Carmela began to study with Thorner, it is fair to say that she did not have at her disposal the fifteen hundred dollars a year that he said was necessary for serious study in America; but the Ponzillo sisters' last vaudeville contract, at one thousand dollars a week, may have left her with some small reserve. Rosa, who had no voice teacher in New York in this period, seemingly had no work at all and was waiting to return to the vaudeville stage. Oddly, Carmela had not told her that she had turned down the last offer made to them by Edward Darling. "I did all the business," Carmela said, by way of explanation, referring to her curt exchange with Darling; but that does not account for her failure to tell her sister of this wrenching change in their lives. Carmela recalled that she was worried about "Babe, this child with that great talent," but had no plans for her immediate future.

Carmela's recollection of her momentous decision to return to serious study began with her observation that "Galli-Curci made her sensational debut [in 1916]. . . . I then had heard of William Thorner, who taught [her]." Carmela's lessons had hardly begun when she was diagnosed with acute appendicitis and had to be operated on at Flower Fifth Avenue Hospital. Recovered, she went back to her studies:

> [I] started out one morning for my lesson with Mr. Thorner. I thought that if Babe would hear the improvement in my voice, she would be inspired to study. . . . So one morning she asked me if I was studying voice, and I said that I was. She said, "What's his name?" I replied, "William Thorner." I just watched her eyes sparkle; that was all I needed to know: [that she had] the interest and that the thought registered. . . . Mr. Thorner had become interested in my talent; . . . I wanted him to hear Rose and get him interested in her.

Rosa followed Carmela that morning

> up in the elevator to Thorner's studio. I shall never forget her big eyes shining when she saw his studio! I introduced Rose to Thorner, then I asked him please to hear Rose; but he said he was not interested in two voices [from the same family] and that he should only [train] me. I insisted on his hearing her. He said, "If she studies hard, she may some day sing well." Then I asked her to sing a song that she knew well, "Kiss Me Again," and play her own accompaniment. He was rather taken by surprise, for he had only given her vocal exercises before. Still, he said that he could not possibly train us both.

Knowing of the Ponzillos' situation, Thorner may not have wished to sacrifice two of his precious hours for what was probably a reduced fee. Finally, though, he agreed to add Rosa to his roster of students: "Well, I'll take her and see what she can do. If she's studious, I will teach her." This was a great triumph for the sisters.

Rosa Ponselle's 1952 interview for *Opera News* fixes these events in the spring of 1918; but, as we know from Thorner's sworn testimony in a later litigation, he first began to teach both of the Ponzillos in November 1917. Rosa, in *Opera News,* said, "Up to that time, I had never studied voice." She went on: "Celebrities dropped into the studio to hear Thorner's pupils sing, and Carmela was so thrilled at the unofficial 'audience' that she persuaded me to go to Thorner too. I auditioned for him; he accepted me and became my first vocal teacher. I was already twenty and until that time had learned music mostly by ear. Word got around of the two vaudeville singers from New Haven."

One day when he had both Ponzillos singing in his studio, Thorner, as was his custom, invited a friend to hear them. This was Victor Maurel, who was then sixty-nine years old and a living legend in opera. He had sung the world premiere of Antonio Carlos Gomez's *Il guarany* for his La Scala debut and gone on to create Simon in Verdi's revised *Simon Boccanegra* in 1881. It was widely believed that Verdi's decision to undertake this revision depended in part on the likelihood that Maurel would sing it. When Verdi was composing *Otello* he made a special trip to Paris in 1886 to persuade Maurel to sing Iago, and at one time he even considered naming the opera after its villain. Maurel's absolute triumph in this role in 1887 at La Scala was followed by another when he was the protagonist in *Falstaff* in the same theater in 1893.

It was Maurel who first suggested to Verdi that he write an opera from Shakespeare's *Merry Wives of Windsor*, a text of which he sent to the composer from Paris. At first, Verdi refused to consider it, insisting that his career was over; but later he wrote to Maurel to inquire about a French production of the play that was then on the boards. While there is no doubt that Verdi's and Arrigo Boito's shared love for Shakespeare was the main factor in their collaboration on *Falstaff*, as it had been on *Otello*, it is also certain that Maurel corresponded with Verdi about the play. We can still hear his interpretations of arias on recordings, where the dramatic insistence and the "extraordinarily fine pronunciation" (Verdi's words) clearly show why Maurel had one of the greatest careers of the last century.

The Maurel we see in photographs of this period, six feet tall and perfectly groomed, remained as elegant as he had been decades before; two New York writers described him as "the handsomest man I ever saw." Still active in theater, he had given a number of New York recitals and had returned to the stage briefly in 1913. He attended the Metropolitan Opera regularly and,

shortly after he met the Ponzillo sisters, designed the sets for the 1919 production of Gounod's *Mireille*. This was a relatively easy task for an artist
who was the son of a famous architect; Maurel had been an amateur painter
and sculptor all his life and had continued to paint in his home on Sixty-
eighth Street. Lillian Gish, then an aspiring actress, bartered one-half hour
of time as his model for one-half hour of his voice lessons. He also invited
famous singers to give private recitals in his salon. After the death of his wife
he moved to a suite in the Riverside Studios Hotel at the corner of Seventy-
first Street and Riverside Drive. He died there in 1923.

At the moment when Maurel first heard the Ponzillo sisters he was still
teaching voice in his home, as he had been since 1909. As a courtesy,
Thorner asked him what he thought of his students and expressed particular
interest in Carmela. After hearing them, according to Rosa, Maurel delivered
his verdict: the younger sister had the better voice and more promise. His
opinion may have influenced Thorner to give Rosa more attention, for Carmela, in her memoir, said that after a "few months of study" he was aston-
ished at Rosa's "rapid progress. He immediately offered [Rosa] a contract to
study with him." As in most of these "study contracts," the teacher offered
his pupil lessons that were free or almost free in exchange for a percentage
of future earnings. This alone shows that Thorner felt that Rosa would have
a career, for a teacher as famous as he was could pick and choose among
the thousands of young hopefuls that pounded the streets of New York seeking work. This was in December 1917, and the agreement was oral, not written, according to Thorner's later testimony. Rosa, who said that Carmela's
lessons with him had begun early in 1918, remembered that she and "Sister
saved money [so] Sister could become one of his pupils." They made the
sacrifice to cover this extraordinary expense because "everyone told Carmela
that Thorner knew Caruso, Thorner knew Gatti," and that lessons with him
were a "good investment." As later events prove, the sisters were not wrong.

Rosa's 1952 interview for *Opera News* described the day that Caruso first
heard her sing. "One day late in the spring, after the Metropolitan had
closed, Enrico Caruso walked into the studio. You can imagine the thoughts
that went through my mind. Five years before, I had listened to him, a god

on that big stage. Now he was in the same room [with me], and I was going to sing for *him*. It seemed like some crazy joke; and I thought for a minute that I was going to laugh." Rosa remembered Caruso as entering the studio "jauntily, looking every bit as dapper as he did in all his photographs. He was wearing a light-colored fedora, tipped to one side and creased in the middle. He had one of those high, stiff collars, gloves and a long cigarette holder; he carried a cane, always a cane. He was such a lovely, beautifully groomed man. He was of good, medium height with a broad chest, very wide shoulders, and was narrow in his hips. His bone structure was very square: square jaw; wide, strong chin; and a prominent, noble nose." Quite naturally, she never forgot that first encounter. "Looking at my face, Caruso made a good guess [about my origins] and spoke to me in Neapolitan dialect. '*Scugnizza*,' he called me—a little street urchin! 'Do you know that you look just like me?' "

In later recorded interviews Rosa rendered his easy greeting in her own Neapolitan dialect: "Oè, Scugnizz', sa che si sommiglia a mme?"—all gloriously elided, with the falling accent on the last syllable of *Scugnizz'* and the rising tone and luscious doubled *m* on *sommiglia* and *mme*. As she pronounces them, *sommiglia* and *a mme* speak volumes for her command of the language of the Terra di Lavoro. It is liquid gold, with melted vowels and gentle consonants.

In this way the son of the Carusos of Piedimonte d'Alife greeted the daughter of the Ponzillos of nearby Caiazzo. And Caruso was not wrong: he did resemble Rosa Ponselle, just as he also resembled her mother. In some of his caricatures the resemblance seems almost uncanny. It is no wonder that, as Michael Sisca says, Caruso considered Rosa his protégée, his "find."

Responding to his gambit, Rosa, bold and fresh and young, answered him: "I wouldn't mind looking like you, if I could only sing like you!" She recalled being "more excited than nervous at the time. Perhaps I thought I was pretty smart."

Surprised and amused, he laughed. "His eyes narrowed, and he nodded a few times. All he said was: 'We'll see; we'll see.' But I'm sure he was thinking, 'What nerve! What ambition! She must have what it takes!' "

With the audition in Thorner's studio recast as a friendly exchange between two émigrés with the blood of the Terra di Lavoro running in their veins, things took a decidedly positive turn. Rosa added that Adamo Didur attended this audition, as did Raisa and her husband, Giacomo Rimini. From this it seems likely that Thorner hoped to place Rosa or Carmela with the Chicago Opera. In her 1952 *Opera News* interview, Ponselle said, "I had sung only a few passages when Caruso began to sing with me. Of course, I could scarcely believe my own ears and almost collapsed with fright and excitement." She also said in another interview that she and Carmela "ran through" their repertoire, mostly Verdi, singing all the big, technically difficult arias from *Trovatore, Gioconda, Aida,* and others. "It was a very ambitious program, considering that I never had any voice training, and my sister very little. I remember that as I sang he studied me carefully, his eyes squinting shrewdly as he sized me up."

At the end of the audition Didur, Raisa, Rimini, and Caruso applauded,

and we got all sorts of words of encouragement from these great artists. As we were getting ready to leave, Caruso walked over to me and said, "You're going to sing with me yet. I don't know when, maybe a year, maybe two, but you will." Of course, I was absolutely paralyzed when I heard that. I had never had any serious aspirations as an opera singer, and here was Caruso telling me that I would soon be singing with him! Then he put his hand on his throat and said, "You've got it here," meaning the voice. He moved his hand to his heart and said, "You've got it here," meaning the emotions. Then he pointed to his head and said, "The rest depends on what you've got up here,"—the brains, the ability to memorize—"but I think you've got it."

When Rosa asked when she might hope to sing at the Metropolitan with him, he answered, "That is in the lap of the gods." Carmela said later that Caruso was truly "carried away by her voice." This is surely no exaggeration, for the facts speak for themselves. With *La forza del destino* in mind, and with Claudia Muzio, the original choice for the role of Leonora, not available, Caruso had conducted an audition in ideal circumstances with a young woman who gave him ample proof that here was the soprano he had been searching for: the right voice, if not an experienced artist.

The importance of Rosa's lessons in Thorner's studio can hardly be overstated, for he, with his wide range of contacts, had arranged for her to be heard by several of the most famous singers of the era, one retired and the others active, at a time when they all were trusted friends of Giulio Gatti-Casazza. These links to the Metropolitan Opera were a windfall for both Rosa and Thorner, for his contract with her stipulated that he would try to place her "either with the Metropolitan Opera or the Chicago Opera"; of the two, however, the Metropolitan was by far the better opportunity. Thorner also invited Rosa and Carmela to his home to watch his Friday night card games, where other opera stars sat around his table. They were among his guests at his New Year's Eve party in 1917. What Thorner did for Ponselle had much more long-term and inherent value than what he did for Galli-Curci, for when Ponselle auditioned for Caruso, the Chicago company had unfortunately begun to feel the pressures that eventually led to its closing. Campanini, Thorner's close friend, was already ill; he died in 1919, leaving the teacher without the strong support he needed in that venue. Furthermore, from the memoirs of Thorner's protégée Ganna Walska and of Mary Garden, who became the Chicago Opera's general director after Campanini died, it is clear that the lack of order and even of common sense was about to lead to reorganization. McCormick, Walska's future husband, intended to help bring the curtain down on a failing enterprise. Had Ponselle been engaged for Chicago, her career might have been interrupted at the start and never have run its course as it did in New York.

In her 1952 *Opera News* interview Ponselle remembered how excited she and Carmela were after their audition for Caruso. "No one can know the happiness Sister and I felt that night. How we re-lived every second of the day! We waited to hear the results of 'The Caruso Afternoon,' as we called it; and soon learned that Caruso had told Gatti-Casazza that I, Rosa Ponselle from New Haven, was what the Metropolitan needed for *La forza del destino,* which Caruso was crazy to sing. In a day or so, both Sister and I were called in for an audition."

CHAPTER 4

The Metropolitan Opera

1908–1918

Evidently convinced that he had found the right soprano for *La forza del destino*, Caruso went directly to Gatti-Casazza to arrange an audition, not for Rosa alone but for Carmela as well. Their status as Thorner's pupils and young members of his social circle added a certain cachet to Caruso's recommendation; and even if Gatti had not known Thorner well, his reputation as a teacher, his former business association with Jean and Edouard De Reszke, and his personal friendships with such luminaries as Maurel, Caruso, Galli-Curci, Raisa, and Didur would surely have gained the Ponzillos a hearing at the Metropolitan. In 1915 *Theatre* magazine described Thorner as "the Christopher Columbus of vocal landmarks," someone who could be counted on to bring real talent to the management. As we shall see later, Gatti wrote in his autobiography that it was Thorner, not Caruso, who first brought the Ponzillos to his attention.

THE PONZILLO SISTERS' FIRST AUDITION FOR GATTI-CASAZZA

With Caruso's guarantees added to Thorner's, the Ponzillo sisters were in an enviable position, having finally got the break they had literally been praying for. They had passed what was probably the most important test of their professional lives at a crucial moment when they had not been singing regularly in public, and had so little money and so few engagements that they often went back to their parents' home in Meriden on weekends. Rosa said that after Edward Valentine Darling and Edward Albee refused them new Keith vaudeville contracts, they went back to singing occasionally at Lorber's and in other café concerts. After the United States entered the combat in World War I, they also sang in war bond rallies. Their help at home was welcome, for Tony Ponzillo, their brother, had been sent to train in Texas after joining the army. It was a time of great instability in their lives, when their regular, daily, onstage use of their voices had come to a dead stop. For all these reasons, their "recital" for Caruso, Raisa, Rimini, and Didur had something of the miraculous about it.

When we ask ourselves "What did Caruso hear?" we can find the answer, in part at least, in Rosa's and Carmela's earliest Columbia acoustic recordings, where some of their vaudeville program is also preserved. What Rosa called their "audition repertoire" in classical music included several arias sung by her, including two from *Il trovatore*, "Tacea la notte placida," with its florid cabaletta, "Di tale amor," and "D'amor sull'ali rosee"; "Suicidio" from *La Gioconda*; "O patria mia" and "Ritorna vincitor" from *Aida*; "Voi lo sapete" from *Cavalleria rusticana*; and "Un bel dì" from *Madama Butterfly*. Carmela sang "Stride la vampa" from *Trovatore*, "Che farò senza Euridice" from *Orfeo*, and "Voce di donna" from *La Gioconda*. They also sang at least two duets, perhaps from *Aida* and *Gioconda*. Although these are not among their first recordings, an example of how they sounded together is found in the 1919 Barcarolle from *Les contes d'Hoffmann*. The CD anthology *Rosa Ponselle: The Columbia Acoustic Recordings* includes many of what Rosa called her "audition" pieces, as well as arias from *Norma*, *Ernani* and *I vespri siciliani*, all of which show clearly why Gatti became convinced that she could manage the great dramatic coloratura roles. The sisters' duets from vaudeville, " 'O Sole Mio," "Comin' through the Rye," and "Where My Caravan Has Rested" also tell us how they sounded when their extraordinarily rich and perfectly matched voices were paired in less demanding music. Because many of these recordings were made within weeks or, at the most, months of Rosa's Metropolitan debut, and some within seven or eight months of the Caruso audition in Thorner's studio, there can be no doubt that they accurately reflect what Caruso heard.

One day after judging Rosa and Carmela in the informal audition, Caruso visited Gatti in his office. As their conversation was later reported to Rosa, Caruso said, "I found the perfect voice for *Forza del destino*, for Leonora."

"Where? Where? What experience has she had?" Gatti asked.

Caruso drew a long breath and calmly replied, "Well, she's sung in vaudeville with her sister."

"What? Vaudeville! Vaudeville! What do you expect me to do? Cut my throat? From vaudeville to opera!" was Gatti's response.

"You just listen. Then you tell me," Caruso insisted.

In spite of his reservations, Gatti telephoned to Thorner and said, "I understand you have two young operatic voices there. I would like to hear them." Thorner thanked Gatti for agreeing to hear them. The actual time of the appointment was fixed by Giuseppe Bamboschek, Gatti's musical secretary, who later became a conductor and remained one of Carmela's closest friends for decades to come. Thorner then told the two sisters his good news. Rosa recalled that "it was just a matter of two or three days" before she, Carmela, and Thorner went to the opera house, where Gatti and Caruso were waiting for them.

If they had an enthusiastic advocate in Caruso, they faced a diffident, skeptical Gatti, who was exhausted by the disruptions World War I had brought to his two previous seasons. At the moment of the Ponzillo sisters' audition, in May 1918, the fighting raged on in Europe with no end in sight. Singers Gatti wished to engage were stranded abroad, and if they were German, they would not have been welcome in any case. Systematic repertory planning had been abandoned; the uncertainty aggravated every other problem faced by the meticulous, orderly general manager. Even under the best circumstances, Gatti said, his natural reserve held in check any praise of an auditioner; but in the spring of 1918 he was in a foul humor.

In his memoir Gatti's own account of the auditions he held proves how cautious and measured he always was: "I have often been asked what happened at the auditions of newcomers like Ponselle, Tibbett and Pons. My answer is: Nothing. We engaged the artist without any to-do. Personally, I am not, in general, enthusiastic. I merely say, 'All right, if you wish to join the company, we will discuss terms.' I do not distribute compliments, as some people [do] who immediately cry out, 'Marvelous! Heavenly!' It is a question of policy. For my part, I say nothing."

So far as we know, Gatti, Caruso, Otto Kahn, and "all the other directors at the Met" heard the audition. Rosa said that word "had gotten around like wildfire; they all wanted to hear Caruso's 'find.' " In several printed and taped interviews she said that she sang "O patria mia" from *Aida*, "D'amor sull'ali rosee" and "the andante and allegro from 'Tacea la notte' " from *Il trovatore*. Carmela sang Laura's aria from *La Gioconda*. Then the sisters sang two duets, one from *Aida* and one from *Gioconda*. Because they had sung these pieces for Caruso in Thorner's studio just a few days before and because they had been singing together for years, the Ponzillo sisters were more confident and experienced than most newcomers called to audition at the Metropolitan. On that day, the years of study and hacking on the vaudeville road stood them in good stead as they faced one of the most critical audiences in the world. On one occasion Rosa said that Margarete Matzenauer, Giovanni Martinelli, and other Metropolitan stars were also in the room. While the Ponzillo sisters were surely nervous (Rosa, especially, said that she always suffered stage fright, at least before the curtain opened), their professionalism and high level of musicianship won them the respect of everyone there.

When the audition ended, Gatti thanked Caruso for bringing the sisters to his attention. As Rosa recalled in her 1952 *Opera News* interview, "Gatti gave me an assignment and told me to come back within a week. He might as well have given me the Koran to learn from memory, for my assignment was to learn 'Pace, pace' from *Forza* and 'Casta diva' from *Norma*. If I had known then what I know now, I would have fainted, but I didn't; and I simply said, 'All right, Mr. Gatti,' and left the house, thanking him profusely." In another interview she said that, "having heard the agility from the 'Di tale amor,' he said, 'Who knows? Maybe we'll have another Norma.' The last one to sing Norma was Lilli Lehmann, thirty-eight years prior to my debut in the role." She also remarked on Gatti's "foresight" in typing her voice and perceiving her potential for singing such a difficult role.

𝒯HE SECOND METROPOLITAN AUDITION ⁓

No matter what joy the sisters may have felt at Rosa's success, the fact that Carmela was not asked "to prepare anything new" was disappointing, for it was she who had worked so hard to get into opera and had cherished for so long the hope of joining the Metropolitan. Ever loyal, she continued her tireless promotion of "Babe" through those exciting weeks and the many decades to come. Carmela, in her memoir, wrote nothing about her dismay: "I was so interested in Rosa's career that I had entirely forgotten mine." She had to face reality: with Julia Claussen, Louise Homer, and Matzenauer on the roster, all backed by competent second-level mezzos, Gatti simply had no place for her then. Rather than go back to her old life, she remained at Rosa's side, returning to concerts and vaudeville only later. The sisters also began to insist that their mother leave Meriden and join them in New York, and while that did not happen at once, Maddalena Conte Ponzillo did spend a great deal of time with them in the summer after 1918. She was also a frequent visitor to their new two-bedroom apartment, at 307 West Ninety-seventh Street, near West End Avenue. It was their second move since leaving Mary McCabe's boarding house, for they had lived briefly near the intersection of Broadway, Columbus Avenue, and Sixty-fifth Street.

"How I worked in that week to learn those two awful arias from scratch!" Ponselle recalled in *Opera News*. "*Norma* and *Forza* were strange wildernesses to me. I was a novice who knew nothing about opera; I worked day and night. Meals were forgotten and so was sleep, as I tried to master them. But in a week I was back at the Metropolitan, shaking in my boots, to make my second audition for Gatti."

One source of unflagging support was the conductor and composer

Romano Romani, who had begun to coach Rosa in the spring of 1918 at Thorner's request and had prepared her for the first Metropolitan Opera audition. A cultivated northern Italian musician, Romani brought a whole repertory of sophistication into the Ponzillo sisters' realm, a taste far more elevated than that of the Illinois-born Savage or even of the blasé American Thorner. Born February 6, 1882, in Leghorn, Tuscany, he attracted attention as a gifted child pianist who was growing up just as Verdi's long career was coming to an end. Verdi died in 1901, leaving Puccini as his artistic heir and "crown prince," as many in Milan called him; young Romani was fortunate in becoming Puccini's protégé. They were from the same soil; they understood each other. The older composer, a native of Lucca, established his permanent residence at Torre del Lago, near Viareggio, but also kept an apartment in Milan, where young Romani studied after a stint at the Royal Conservatory in Naples. At the Milan Conservatory he remained close to Puccini and got to know Pietro Mascagni as well. As the charming young representative of the Columbia Graphophone Recording Company in Milan, the nineteen-year-old Romani began to cultivate many of the famous artists who remained his friends. He also conducted for many of their recordings, as he later did for Rosa. Even as he pursued his career as a coach and teacher, he composed three operas. *Zulma*, his first, was given in Rome with the celebrated soprano Eugenia Burzio in the title role. Of *Rosana*, another of his operas, little is known, but his *Fedra* won the famed Casa Sonzogno Prize. Romani succeeded in getting it produced in Rome with Raisa in the title role and the tenor Hipólito Lázaro as the male lead. Later, as we shall see, Ponselle sang *Fedra* at Covent Garden in London. Romani began his long association with Raisa as a serious composer and trusted friend just as the young Polish woman was emerging as a major dramatic soprano. He first met Carmela and Rosa Ponzillo after a Raisa concert in New York in the early spring of 1918, although he later said that he had also heard them in vaudeville at the Palace and at the Riverside Theatre on Broadway at Ninety-sixth Street.

Because of his connections, particularly with Raisa, Romani also knew

Thorner and may have served as accompanist for Rosa's and Carmela's audition for Caruso in Thorner's apartment. Although Thorner's regular accompanist for years was Ina Grange, a woman in late middle age, Rosa recalled that a man accompanied her and her sister during their Caruso audition. Everything leads one to think that it was Romani at the piano. For decades to come he would be a steadying influence in Rosa's life. Fifteen years older than she, and a serious professional, he called her "Rosina"; as she was preparing the second audition for Gatti, he gave her the moral support and expert coaching that were essential if she were to make another favorable impression at the Metropolitan.

Rosa said that she was not familiar with either of the arias Gatti had asked to hear. Indeed, in one interview she said she had never even heard of them, nor is there any reason to think that she should have, because neither *La forza del destino* nor *Norma* belonged to the repertory then. *Norma* had last been heard at the Metropolitan in 1892 with Lilli Lehmann in the title role, while Gatti's planned production of *Forza* was a first at the Metropolitan, though not the first in America. The Academy of Music in New York had offered *Forza* in 1880 with Italo Campanini as Don Alvaro, under Luigi Arditi's baton.

As Rosa was preparing the two arias, she had just over a week in which to master extremely difficult music and two styles that differed radically from each other. This was a tremendous challenge for a young woman of her background who had just turned twenty-one three months earlier, had never been on the opera stage, had seen only two operas in her life, had had only "secondhand" study through Carmela for years, and had been taking lessons with Thorner for less than six months. But Rosa's sight-reading, memory skills, and musicianship, about which there was never any serious dispute, made this feat possible.

Ten days after the critical first hearing, Rosa said, the two sisters returned to the opera house. This time Rosa was to sing on a stage in one of the large rehearsal halls, while Carmela stood near her with a bottle of smelling salts—a sure sign that she knew how vulnerable Rosa was.

Rosa, in her *Opera News* interview, remembered her fear:

Can I ever forget that day? I got through "Pace" all right; but in the middle of that terrible second half of "Casta diva" my breath simply stopped, and I fainted dead away, right in the middle of that stage. Sister rushed out from the wings and, working with about ten other people, revived me. I was thinking of "suicidio" all right; I was sure that my chance was killed, that I would be thrown right out the Opera House door. I cursed myself for every missed meal and hour of sleep. As I got to my feet, dying of shame, Gatti came over and, like a father, asked me if I would come into his office. Naturally, I expected to be thrown out.

She later attributed her fainting to "nerves, fright, and a slight indisposition and an accumulation of things. . . . Dear, dear Caruso was more upset than I."

Wilfrid Pelletier, the French Canadian conductor who joined Gatti-Casazza's musical staff at the Metropolitan Opera before Rosa Ponzillo's first auditions, said that Thorner had indeed arranged for her to sing for Gatti. In his autobiography, *Une symphonie inachevée*, Pelletier wrote that "this girl, intimidated, did not give her best [in the first audition], but her voice seemed sufficiently interesting for him to offer her another chance. This time, Rosa was in full command of her means: she sang with a surprising style for a young artist. Proud of his discovery, Gatti offered her a contract with the Metropolitan." Later Pelletier wrote:

Ponselle was a true vocal phenomenon. . . . She sang with a perfect voice, with faultless musicality. This was so extraordinary that the critics, rather reserved about a debut such as Ponselle's, spoke of her voice as a gold mine, with her delicious middle and low notes, and with her flexible and brilliant high notes. What Caruso represented in the world of tenors, Ponselle was to the world of sopranos. . . . To so many natural gifts, Ponselle added her conscientious work, which could sometimes go beyond the point of scrupulousness.

In another account, on the occasion of the hundredth anniversary of Caruso's birth, Ponselle said that she "*almost* fainted with excitement" and that "my sister was in the wings with smelling salts and caught me as I fell." In taped interviews, Rosa said that she simply ran out of breath and was overcome by emotion.

To his credit, Gatti came forward to console her. He said, "It was nerves. You're young; you've the stamina; and, besides, we're not doing *Norma* tomorrow."

Gatti then asked her to come into his office. Rosa thought, of course, that she was going to be dismissed; but he offered her a contract instead.

"Here, sign this," Gatti ordered.

"Sign what?" Rosa asked.

"Your contract to make your debut with Caruso in *La forza del destino*. Do you think you could be ready by November?" Gatti asked her. She nodded. Thorner read the agreement and Rosa signed it.

Gatti's account of Rosa's entry into the Metropolitan is also worth including here because it differs somewhat from hers:

> The story of Rosa Ponselle is an interesting one. One fine day, William Thorner met me and said, "Mr. Gatti, I have a young woman, a pupil of mine, an Italian-American who really has an admirable voice. She and her sister have been appearing in vaudeville. But you must remember that this is not the ordinary singer. This is a special case."
>
> We gave this girl, as well as her sister, an audition. She was nervous, upset and somewhat ill. Nevertheless, I could see that this girl had a magnificent voice. We allowed her to come back a few days later and gave her another audition. This time she sang perfectly, with a beauty of voice and style that was truly amazing in a young and inexperienced singer.
>
> I had already turned over in my mind the possibility of [presenting] *La forza del destino*. When I heard her the second time, I decided at once to go through with this. . . . Caruso graciously agreed to sing

the role of Don Alvaro; and we went ahead with preparations for the event.

I have been asked how I dared to give this inexperienced young artist so difficult a role to begin with. I will admit that it was a somewhat difficult problem, since the girl's only experience had been in vaudeville. But I took the chance. I decided to run the risk, although I felt a certain amount of assurance, since the young singer was extremely musical and very sure of herself. . . . On the stage, she is absolutely sure.

Looking at the first contract Gatti offered "this girl," one sees that he risked a great deal in terms of the *Forza* and his demand that she master several other operas and Verdi's Requiem in just over four months. She was engaged for a period of twenty-three weeks that included fourteen days of rehearsals and a season that ran from November 11, 1918, through April 20, 1919, with the company reserving the right to extend her employment for an additional week, if necessary. Her salary was $150 a week; she could be asked to sing three times a week or (for a limited period of two weeks) four times a week. The operas she was required to prepare were *Aida, Il trovatore, Cavalleria rusticana, La forza del destino, La Gioconda, Tosca,* and *Un ballo in maschera*; the Verdi Requiem was the only sacred work. Of these, the first four operas and the Requiem had to be ready for production by November 11.

The Metropolitan held the right of renewal for 1919–20 at $300 per week, plus $100 for extra performances, and for 1920–21 at $650 per week, plus $250 for extra performances. Each year she would be notified "on or before the first of May" whether she would be reengaged for the next season. One strange clause stipulated that the Metropolitan could limit her season in 1920–21 to three months "or prolong such season from fortnight to fortnight up to five months." She was also prohibited from singing in opera for any other company from June 4, 1918, until April 1921; she was allowed to sing in concerts outside her contracted period but not before her debut. She could accept concert engagements within the Metropolitan's season only on the company's approval.

Other clauses concerned the Metropolitan's guarantee that Rosa would never be required to sing more than twice "in succession" and "never twice on the same day." The penalty for illness was fifty dollars, deducted from her paycheck for each appearance missed because of illness. If she were ill for more than seven days, the company could deduct one seventh of her paycheck for "each day of such disability." One clause stated that the artist should provide her own "gloves, feathers, wigs, tights, boots, shoes and other similar articles." The company provided the costumes; but if the singer had her own, she could use them if they "conform[ed] to the artistic style of the ensemble for the respective performances."

She signed the contract "Rosa Ponzillo," with "Rosa Ponsell" under the first name. There is an added, smudged "e" or "o" at the end of "Ponsell." Her address was given as "159 Springdale Ave., Meriden, Conn." It was Thorner who negotiated the terms, doing the best he could for a singer without experience in opera in a situation without precedent.

To the Siscas, Caruso confided that Gatti had originally planned to have Claudia Muzio sing Leonora but, after hearing Rosa, assigned Muzio the *Aida* scheduled for the second night of the 1918–19 season, while Rosa, officially a member of the Metropolitan Opera roster, was given the new production of *Forza* and, with it, the chance to become Caruso's "little urchin" and partner. His decisions about her were crucial to the launching of her career, for although he always deferred to Gatti, calling him "Direttore" and "Padrone" ("Master"), in fact Gatti let Caruso dictate most matters relating to the operas he chose to sing. Caruso told Marziale Sisca that he felt directly responsible for Rosa and intended to see that she was treated well. He also told his friends that he remained in Gatti's office after Rosa's contract was signed and told Gatti that he was confident she would succeed. Gatti, ever laconic, said that if she did not, he would take the first ship back to Italy and never let his face be seen again in the States.

 ## GATTI-CASAZZA'S FIRST DECADE ～

In the weeks when Gatti gave Rosa her two auditions and a contract, he was as confused and discouraged as he had ever been in the twenty-five years of his career. Little remained of the great optimism that had fed his first years at the Metropolitan. At the beginning of his tenure, Gatti, in collaboration with Arturo Toscanini, brought the opera to a level of excellence few could fault. When the Gatti-Casazza era began, with the 1908–9 season, the gentleman impresario from Ferrara had already won the highest respect as the man who created a new Teatro alla Scala in Milan out of the ruin into which it had fallen during the last years of Verdi's life. As the nineteenth century was winding down and one bankrupt impresario succeeded another, Verdi himself had often urged the closing of the great Italian theater, but Gatti and Toscanini had come to save it. Toscanini, even more than Gatti, guaranteed the artistic integrity of the venerable institution and succeeded in carrying its music into the twentieth century while preserving the best of its past. On their triumphs in Milan their international reputations were built.

In New York the support of Otto H. Kahn, "the godfather of the Metropolitan" and chairman of its board of directors, bolstered Gatti's position from the start. With another enthusiastic board member, Rawlins L. Cottenet, Kahn had successfully conducted the secret negotiations in Europe that brought Gatti and Toscanini to New York. With other important American bankers and businessmen, Kahn made possible the "new" company that gradually took over its stage after 1908.

When Gatti and Toscanini arrived for the 1908–9 season, Caruso's immense popularity and Antonio Scotti's hardy professionalism bolstered the men's roster, while the women's side depended on such stars as Frances Alda, Emmy Destinn, Emma Eames, Geraldine Farrar, Olive Fremstad, and that living legend Marcella Sembrich. Although it lost some of these vocal assets, the Metropolitan thrived. As Gatti and Toscanini soon discovered, Kahn was willing to spend enormous amounts from his personal fortune to make this company the greatest in the world. Puccini, whom the former impresario Heinrich Conried had invited to oversee *Manon Lescaut* and *Madama Butterfly* early in 1907, was asked to return to produce the world premiere of his new work, *La fanciulla del West* in 1910.

Kahn, who always valued public relations, made sure that the Metropolitan was widely covered in all the papers. He cultivated journalists and did everything possible to guarantee favorable reviews. Stars drew overflow audiences in the opera house in New York and in the Metropolitan's "tour cities," Philadelphia and Baltimore. With Kahn's backing, the company even got as far as Paris, where it played in the Châtelet. Despite the continuing disappointment of Kahn's cherished New Theatre, where nineteen operas were produced in 1909–10, Gatti flourished. Gatti's rivalry with Oscar Hammerstein effectively ended in 1910, when Kahn arranged for the Metropolitan to buy out Hammerstein's interests. Hammerstein was enjoined not to produce opera in Boston, Chicago, Philadelphia, or New York for ten years. In her book *The Miracle of the Met* Quaintance Eaton wrote that Kahn's grandiose schemes kept the company going until the outbreak of World War I. Gatti had lost Eames, Sembrich, Fremstad, Gustav Mahler, and even Toscanini, who left the company in 1915. Even this weaker Metropolitan still counted some of the world's most famous singers in its ranks, and Gatti went abroad each year, seeking new artists.

Not even the outbreak of World War I had put a stop to his searches, which were often covered by the press. News organizations in America and Italy published photographs of the courageous Gatti boarding a New York–bound liner in Naples in the autumn of 1914 with his flock of Metropolitan artists: Toscanini, Caruso, Farrar, and Destinn, accompanied by Giulio Setti, the chorus master. Like a shepherd, Gatti gathered them in and brought them safely home. With this gesture he lifted the company's spirits and reassured the Metropolitan's patrons about the quality of his productions; yet he felt threatened at every turn, trapped in a situation that was beyond his control, for he counted on the expertise and experience of European-trained singers. His recruiting abroad did not mean that he was prejudiced against American artists, for he was not. Pennsylvania's Paul Althouse (the first American who starred at the Met without European training or experience) and Louise Homer, Maine's Lillian Nordica, and Massachusetts's Farrar, among many others, had long since "made the Met safe for Americans." Gatti simply wanted the best of all worlds, but during the war this was beyond him. The 1915–16 season saw the departure of Destinn, the imposing lyric-dramatic soprano who had been a mainstay of the company since 1908.

Again that summer Gatti went abroad, but his return on the liner *Lafayette* in 1916 had a feeling of finality about it, for that autumn no one knew when ships would safely sail from America to Europe again.

At home Gatti was facing the worst crisis of his administration. As he recalled in his *Memories of the Opera*, the 1916–17 season ended with the United States officially entering the conflict. The announcement that Congress had voted to declare war came in April, on Good Friday during a performance of *Parsifal*. The season ended without interruption, but for the first time in his professional life the general manager had almost nothing ready for the year to come. Gatti later recalled his woes: "Our repertoire for each succeeding season was usually prepared by the previous February. This year, the season ended and the repertoire had not yet been selected. We were naturally much concerned as to the public attitude toward the production of German opera." Some members of the press had encouraged him to present German works because, as they said, "this country, in a question of art, is broadminded." He was given unofficial authorization to continue offering German operas with German artists. Having also conducted an informal survey among "the leading critics," he always got "yes, yes, of course" for an answer.

Thus reassured, Gatti had planned a repertoire of German, French, and Italian operas for the years to come. After American soldiers began to die on the battlefields of Europe, however, public opinion turned. Clamor over the German citizenship or pro-German sentiments of certain artists aggravated the situation. Margarete Ober fainted in the wings of the Metropolitan on the night that the announcement was made that Congress had declared war. The soprano Johanna Gadski resigned from the company, even though her husband, Captain Hans Tauscher, had been acquitted by a jury of dynamiting the Welland Canal. Confronted with rabid and propaganda-fueled anti-German sentiment, Gatti began to consider putting into effect a plan to ban German opera altogether. The 1916–17 season found Gatti, as he said, fighting what he thought might be the last of many battles "for the very existence of the Metropolitan."

By the beginning of the 1917–18 season he was feeling particularly frustrated at having been confined to American soil. Gatti called this year "the hardest I had ever had up to that time, taking into account even the days of the co-management [with Andreas Dippel from 1908 to the spring of 1910] and the competition with [Oscar] Hammerstein. That takes in the five [years] at Ferrara, the ten at La Scala and the ten here."

In spite of his discouragement, the audiences and critics found much to like, for the season brought the successful debut of the English soprano Florence Easton, who first appeared in December as Santuzza in a *Cavalleria rusticana* that the critic Richard Aldrich of the *New York Times* described as "the picture of Italian life among the lowly."

In February 1918 Caruso's Jean of Leyden in the revival of *Le prophète* was hailed as "superb," with "an earnestness and dignity, a beauty of voice and restraint of action" that characterized the great artist he had become. The tenor celebrated his forty-fifth birthday later that same month.

From reviews like these one can see that in spite of Gatti's despair, the 1917–18 season, like every other one, had its successes. Even the unusual "ballet opera" or "operatic pantomine" *Le coq d'or* found favor with William J. Henderson of the *New York Sun*, who mentioned both the impresario and Kahn in his review of the first American performance of the Rimsky-Korsakov work. "Mr. Gatti-Casazza is a person of exceedingly solemn mien and a grave cast of thought," Henderson wrote. "It is too much to believe that he alone is responsible for the challenge flung into the face of weary society from the stage of the Metropolitan Opera last night. Nor is it a solution of the problem to conjecture that Otto Kahn commanded the production." Nevertheless, the Metropolitan successfully produced the "fantastical, whimsical, delicious bit of foolery" and "credit is due to everyone concerned in it." To win praise like this from the serious Henderson was sheer triumph.

Still Gatti's depression did not abate, particularly because the "German question" raged on. Even a serious publication like *Etude* was conducting a reader survey and contest entitled "The Trial of Richard Wagner," announced in its February 1918 issue and about to be published in July. When the 1917–18 season ended, no one knew exactly which of the reader-essayists would win the prizes; given the frenzy of war propaganda, the verdict in the "case" might have been expected to be totally negative. As it happened, *Etude* presented both sides, the positive contributors praising Wagner's music as art and therefore universal, while the negative side of the "debate" called him "a megalomaniac." Others saw in Wagner a German monster. This *Etude* contest also offered an opportunity for patriots to come forward. "Give American music a chance," one winner demanded. "German opera has been given preference for too long to the exclusion of much good music of our Allies, French and Italian in particular. . . . Why not banish everything that even suggests Germany and put 'America First.'—English-speaking North America! Give the public what they want and give American music a great opportunity." The subtext here was "give American singers a chance," for the foreign singers' struggles with sung English had given rise to criticism in print and in the corridors of the theater.

Such anti-German sentiment prevented Gatti from returning German opera in general and Wagner's works in particular to the repertory as he believed should be done. This meant presenting more Italian and French operas. Farrar remained immensely popular, reigning supreme as Tosca, Butterfly, and Carmen (although she got a scandalously bad review for her Thaïs). Claudia Muzio, who made her debut in December 1916, had been assigned *Aida* and *Trovatore*, to which she later added *La bohème* and *L'amore dei tre re*, among other operas; but she had not yet won the heart of the audience as others had. She remained largely a young woman with much promise but as yet no star. Roles such as Santuzza in *Cavalleria rusticana* had been given to Melanie Kurt, known for her Kundry and Leonora in *Fidelio*, and to Matzenauer and Easton. Marie Rappold, an aging holdover from the Conried days, was assigned *Aida* and the *Trovatore* Leonora; she was not likely to arouse enthusiasm in the audience, however, for she had been a familiar figure on the Metropolitan stage since 1905 and now faced the inevitable end of her career. In fact, Rappold left the company at the end of the 1919–20 season. In this situation Gatti needed new sopranos who were strong yet flexible, lyric-dramatics who could at least cover the ground from Santuzza to Aida. But with European singers not available to him and American conservatories not turning out crops of young American singers for the heavier repertory, he was bound to be frustrated in his search.

Beyond the daily exasperations of running the opera company, there was also the matter of Gatti's age and temperament. After a quarter century of professional life, his patience had begun to fray. Orderly and conservative as he was, he had come to depend on his annual routine: the New York season, then his visits to a villa on Lake Orta and to his brother's house on the Grand Canal in Venice, calls to the great theaters, and brief vacations with friends and colleagues. But when he first heard about Carmela and Rosa Ponzillo, in the spring of 1918, he had been "confined," as he said, to American soil for nearly two years and was worn down with his burdens.

Beyond his fatigue, Gatti had every right to be skeptical about the two Italian-American sisters from the vaudeville stage simply because they were so far removed from his ideal, polished professionals, the singers he needed. Not even the recommendations of Thorner and Caruso could outweigh the liability of their lack of experience, Gatti reasoned. The Metropolitan did not take such risks; it was not a training institution. Among the American woman artists Gatti said he most respected were the glacial Emma Eames, Shanghai-born and Boston-trained, who had gone to Europe to study with Mathilde Marchesi in the studio that produced Emma Calvé, Melba, and Garden; Lillian Nordica, whom Gatti knew only briefly; the cultivated and genteel Louise Homer, a native of Pittsburgh who studied in Paris and sang there and in London before returning to the States; and Farrar, who, following Nordica's advice, studied in Berlin and sang there and in Monte Carlo before coming to the Metropolitan in 1906.

All these women had had careful training and broad experience in Europe before reaching the Metropolitan. They had been honored by heads of state and high society as few singers in the past had been; famous teachers, critics, and the leading impresarios of the world had recommended them; and some of them had even been received at court by the crowned heads of Europe. They knew how to walk and dress properly and had "front parlor manners": they knew how to curtsey to royalty and aristocrats, pick up the correct fork at dinner, and step out of a carriage or automobile gracefully.

As far as anyone knew, the Ponzillo sisters had nothing of this background for the Met to count upon. In the eyes of the powers-that-were at the Metropolitan, they were nothing more than the daughters of simple immigrants, Italian-American tradespeople from central Connecticut. Products of the public school system, the Ponzillos had never attended conservatory and, apart from Thorner, had no mentor to oversee them. But more than anything else, it was their years in vaudeville that weighed against them. Though it was entertaining, "vaude" was still considered low-class entertainment, where comedians, dog acts, trained bears, and acrobats shared the program with "singing artists," no matter how good they were. With the Metropolitan's boxes filled with the cream of New York society, the Ponzillos had grave shortcomings, in the opinion of the staid, conservative gentlemen who ruled the opera house. Among the board members, Otto Kahn was the most modern, for he often went to popular theater and music halls and, later, to Minsky's burlesque theater, where he took members of the Met press corps as his guests. Rosa and Carmela could never have got a hearing at the Metropolitan without open-minded men like Kahn behind Gatti, for Kahn himself had brought a new outlook to the company.

It says a great deal for Gatti, though, that he was willing to risk a season's most important new production on a soprano who had so little experience in singing with an orchestra—the critical test for opera singers. Once, Rosa had sung "Voi lo sapete" from *Cavalleria rusticana* in the San Carlino Theatre in New Haven with a twenty-piece orchestra behind her, but so far as we know, she had no other experience with orchestral accompaniments for operatic music. When she and Carmela sang the Barcarolle from *Les contes d'Hoffmann* in vaudeville, Rosa played the piano accompaniment. And although it is true that they sang all the time with vaudeville orchestras, some as small as six instruments, not even Rosa's and Carmela's important concerts in Newport and at Narragansett Pier in Rhode Island had had full orchestral accompaniments. Their programs there had been chiefly made up of popular songs and ballads, not opera. The greatest risk to the Metropolitan was not whether Rosa could learn the score but whether her voice could stand up against an entire evening of being projected over a full orchestra playing a heavily scored opera in a huge auditorium.

Although this was one of the significant arguments raised against engaging Rosa, Gatti was convinced after just two hearings that she could pass that test. As he said, he took full responsibility for the young soprano before the patrons, the critics, and the board. He even created a new stage name for her. Gatti at first favored "Rosa Gloria" but eventually settled on "Rosa Ponselle." Carmela, a veteran of many battles with managers, argued with Gatti over the change, which he defended on the ground that people would find "Ponzillo" hard to pronounce. He prevailed, leaving Carmela angry and troubled at the idea that she and her sister would no longer share the same surname. At least for a while she remained "Ponzillo" on concert and vaudeville bills, while Rosa became "Ponselle."

Rosa Ponselle's contract was signed on June 4, 1918, and on that date she also fulfilled her obligation to Thorner. Her first student contract with him had provided for the payment to him of a percentage of her fees should she ever get a professional contract with an opera company. At that time, as we have seen, he believed that he might eventually be able to place her with either the Chicago Opera or the Metropolitan. He later claimed that she also made a subsequent oral agreement with him in December 1917, stipulating that she would pay him 10 percent of her salary so long as she was engaged and that she would create a security account against possible default on this agreement. All this leads one to believe that Thorner had taught her without being paid. Holding to her agreement with him, Ponselle signed a letter to the Metropolitan Opera, dated June 11, 1918, authorizing its management to retain 10 percent of her salary during the 1919–20 season and during the seasons to follow, if she was reengaged by the Metropolitan, "in favor and at the disposal of William Thorner, my authorized representative and teacher." Her letter contained words that led to lawsuits and countersuits later: "during the season of 1919–1920 *and eventual subsequent years of my engagement with the Metropolitan Opera Company*" (emphasis added). He deserved this compensation, he said, because he had taught Ponselle, acted to represent her, procured her auditions with Caruso and the general manager, and negotiated her contract. He might also have added that he introduced her socially into the circle of powerful music business figures. With the two agreements signed, Ponselle became a full-fledged Metropolitan Opera artist.

THE REHEARSALS AND PERFORMANCES OF *LA FORZA DEL DESTINO* ∽

With Ponselle's engagement, a new era began at the Metropolitan, for Gatti himself told her that if she made good, he would bring other American-trained artists to the Metropolitan. Both her life and his were changed by the affectionate friendship and sense of trust that grew between her and the Italian-born manager. Gatti, nearing fifty, was one year older than Ponselle's mother, while Ponselle had just turned twenty-one. A warm father-daughter bond was established between them, and as Gatti watched Ponselle develop he came to depend on her as an excellent musician, always the perfectionist, who accepted counsel, followed directions, and caused no friction in the company. Later he discovered the genius, a singing actress who could bring life to Donna Anna in *Don Giovanni*, Gioconda, and Norma, the legitimate heir to and descendant of the legendary sopranos of the previous century. Just as Ponselle's artistry enhanced Gatti's opera company, her personal warmth thawed even the stern general manager, who counted her among his friends from 1918 until long after his retirement. In short, he found in her the obedient and conscientious daughter he never had. After he retired, Gatti wrote to Ponselle, thanking her for having given him less trouble than any other singer in his entire career. It was more than an empty gesture. Ponselle later said in interviews that he was a concerned father to her.

For her part, Ponselle brought a breath of fresh air into the opera house, for she was the first truly modern American singer at the Metropolitan, courageous and, as she said, "brazen." In spite of the restrictions Ben Ponzillo had attempted to put on his daughters, they had both got around them, left home, and become independent professional women. Reversing the traditional situation, it was Rosa and Carmela who sent money home, rather than being young women who waited for a check from their parents. Earlier American singers had grown up with *McGuffey's Readers* and homilies. Ponselle grew up with the popular culture of silent films and vaudeville rather than that of padded, velvet-scrolled family albums, stereopticons, Carnegie Hall, and the Academy of Music. Ponselle's dearest childhood friend, Lena Tamborini, was the neighborhood tomboy. The teenager's bible when Ponselle and Tamborini were growing up was Edith Van Dyne's *The Flying Girl*, published in 1911, when Rosa was fourteen. Van Dyne's heroine, Orissa Kane, pilots a single-engine plane at an aviation meet in California, making an ascent of perfect grace and beauty; she makes half-mile-long stunt dives, escapes death at the hands of a male villain-rival, and, in a gloriously heroic gesture before fifteen thousand spectators, saves her nemesis from dying in the crash of his own plane. Down toward the field Orissa glides, with the rescued villain hanging from the foot rail of her aircraft. To the shouts of thousands of admirers, the "young aviator" is "plucked from her seat" and "held aloft for all to see," the heroine of the "terrible adventure," adored by all.

In Ponselle's youth women were indeed learning to fly, driving cars and discovering how to take the motors apart, patching together motor-powered ice sleds in the family basement, ice skating, demonstrating Harley-Davidsons at the county fair, and playing team basketball in school. And while it is true that certain limitations were placed upon young women in the Italian-American communities, it is also true that the Ponzillo girls defied them, largely with their mother's support. Whatever else they were, they were women who had broken the stereotype.

Ponselle also differed from almost every opera singer of her day in her extraordinary athleticism, which, she said, helped her develop breath control to support the long phrases and fine shading that marked her style. Tall and bursting with good health, Ponselle loved the outdoors and could turn any weekend in the country into some kind of sports competition. The photographs from her earliest album reveal a sturdy, dedicated athlete. At Narragansett Pier in 1915 Rosa is shown swimming between concerts; snapshots from 1916 show a setting in rural Michigan with groves of trees and wicker chairs, the scene of a brief summer vacation during a vaudeville engagement; in 1918 Rosa is lounging on the grass in Riverside Park in New York. Over the years we see her in bathing suits, tennis dresses, and later, tennis shorts; golfing skirts, slit to the thigh, and spiked oxfords for trekking the course; and Alpine gear, with cap, scarf, tailored jacket, and trousers tucked into her boots, pick in hand as she struggles across a glacier. On shipboard she challenged everyone to volleyball, deck tennis, Ping-Pong, and shuffleboard. At home she lobbed snowballs at friends and sledded in Riverside Park in the winter, walked miles every day, biked, and soon after her debut took her first airplane ride. An early snapshot in the first scrapbook shows her in pants and a flight jacket, with a pilot's leather cap, scarf flying as she is climbing into a rickety-looking single-motor plane. This was taken in 1922 during one of her first big concert tours; she is in Memphis, and "Rosa's First Flight" is the caption. In March 1918, even while she and Carmela were studying opera with Thorner and joining his Friday-night card games, Rosa was following the swimming championship meets at the New York Athletic Club, where she attended the finals. During her summers in Italy she swam at the Lido and in Lake Como; her mountain-climbing gear was for use at Saint-Moritz. Later scrapbooks show her on the tennis courts and golf courses in Hollywood and in the pool at Villa Pace. From her teen years through the 1950s Ponselle was a tireless and even aggressive sportswoman. About the only women's sport she did not practice was hunting, off-limits because of her passionate love for animals. It would have been unthinkable for her to kill one.

Utterly lacking prima donna mannerisms at the start of her career, Ponselle was generous, likable, and funny. Fred Gaisberg described her solicitude for others in his two books on the early recording industry, calling her a good scout and adding, "Indeed, I don't suppose she has an enemy in the world."

Ponselle loved banter, as many journalists discovered when she played word games with them and let them know that they had met their match in her. Reading early interviews, no one could be surprised to learn that even in the presence of the great Caruso young Ponselle could muster a quick response to his remark about her Neapolitan features. She loved to tell jokes and play harmless tricks on people. Naturally, she had a seemingly inexhaustible fund of stories about vaudeville. On New Year's Eve 1917, as we have seen, she and Carmela entertained Thorner's guests by running through the songs of their vaudeville repertory with Rosa at the piano. She also amused people by jazzing up passages from *Aida* or playing them in ragtime. With Carmela she sang her wicked parodies of opera arias and duets; on one recording made in her home she even sang the bass aria "Vecchia zimarra" from *La bohème*.

A good-natured sister, daughter, and colleague, Ponselle wanted friends and relatives around her. One associate said, "She wasn't Ponselle; she was an entourage, with people and pets everywhere." Tony Ponzillo, her brother, who served in the army in World War I and made a reputation for himself singing as "Caruso in khaki," was often photographed with his sister in New York after the war, although his military service prevented him from sharing the glory of her debut at the Metropolitan Opera. Wilfred Pelletier remembered that Tony lived with Rosa and Carmela for a while. After he married and had a child, he and his family were often captured in snapshots with Ponselle.

Anyone who has ever interviewed singers knows that they often are at the center of strange entourages. While the Ponselle sisters' household was perhaps no stranger than those of most singers, by middle America's standards it was odd. Carmela and Rosa lived together for more than twenty years, calling each other "Sister," "Babe," and "Toodles." They presided over a Neapolitan kitchen where Rosa fed invading mice and Carmela threatened to kill them. The family pet was Bush, the bull terrier, brought from Meriden and often photographed with one sister or the other. With them was Edith Prilik, Ponselle's secretary, who, according to several interviews, slept on a folding bed beside the piano in the living room.

Anna Ryan, in advancing years, had her own room. She functioned as "housekeeper, confidant, and friend," according to an interview in the first of the James E. Ryan scrapbooks. The phrase is underlined in red, perhaps by Anna Ryan herself. In her piety, she insisted on kneeling on the bare dining room floor to pray. It remained for the others to help her up, as arthritis made it ever more difficult for her to rise. Rosa begged her to use a pillow, which she would not do. "God doesn't want you to do that," Rosa would say. Eventually Rosa bought an ornate Italian prie-dieu so their old teacher could pray in greater comfort. The sisters' mother, Maddalena, often accompanied Rosa on vacations and tours. Like Carmela and Ryan, she came with a purse full of rosaries, religious medals, and prayer cards. Unlike them, she did not carry a missal because she could not read. Carmela was the official head of this household.

The Ponzillos' friends, personal and professional, were welcomed at their table at least once a week. These rituals became as firmly established as did Rosa's biking and sixty-block walks around New York, as established as her study routines, which she kept to because, as she said, she was "a perfectionist" and her strict study patterns were inviolable. When friends came, it was different matter. She put on the only good dress she had at the time, a black lace gown, and joined Carmela in the kitchen, for they loved to cook. Rosa always kept a collection of family recipes with her. Visitors to their apartment remember the sisters lingering over the stove and rolling their eyes as they muttered "incantations" over their spaghetti sauces, the recipes for which they refused to give out. Carmela said God gave her the recipes, but more likely they came from her mother.

On June 4, 1918, with her Metropolitan Opera contract signed, Ponselle faced the challenge of learning three difficult opera scores in just five months. The main sources of her strength in those days were her voice, her natural musicianship, and her steady nature. She did not falter, although the learning process proved to be a lonely job, as she said; never before had she undertaken such rigorous work. But with her family members and most trusted friends nearby, Ponselle had the enormous advantage of a support group within her home while Romani, in his studio, taught her the survival tactics he had learned while acquiring his own polish and expertise as a composer, conductor, and coach.

The first busy weeks after Ponselle signed with the Metropolitan were taken up with the move to 307 West Ninety-seventh Street, where she, Carmela, Ryan, and Prilik shared the four-room apartment. Here the two sisters were interviewed by Terese Rose Nagel of the *New York Sun*, a reporter they came to like and trust. For the first time in their lives, Rosa and Carmela could depend on Ryan to do housekeeping; for both sisters, this was an unimaginable luxury. They brought a grand piano, which dominated their other simple furnishings. So proud of the piano that she let someone take many snapshots of her sitting at it, Ponselle can be seen in these surviving photographs as Gatti, Caruso, and others saw her during her auditions at the Metropolitan: well dressed in a handsome satin gown and jacket, with her parents' Terra di Lavoro features—a riveting gaze, the dark eyes, the mass of black hair, and the broad cheekbones and jaw that led Gatti to tease her about her *faccia tosta*, her "bold, cheeky face." As the snapshots show, she was considerably overweight, a condition she determined to remedy during the summer, hoping to lose about thirty-five pounds.

Just after they moved, one unanticipated worry was Carmela's illness. Although she recovered "very quickly," as she told interviewers, her health may have been one factor that later led Ponselle to think about finding a summer house outside the city. At first, though, in her new and already crowded Upper West Side home, Ponselle began to study *La forza del destino* and Carl Maria von Weber's *Oberon*, two of the scores assigned to her by Gatti. He also promised to let her sing Santuzza in *Cavalleria rusticana* on tour if all went well in the first months of her engagement. Of the three works, *Cavalleria* was the only one with which she had even minimal familiarity. As with *Norma* and *Forza*, *Oberon* was an opera she had never even heard of. It was to be sung in its original English, a language that posed no problem whatsoever, for Ponselle's diction had won her praise from many reviewers who had heard her in vaudeville.

After her first sessions with Romani in New York, the pressure on Ponselle became so great that she felt she had to get away. Seeking a more tranquil environment, she chose a modest resort, Pine Orchard, Connecticut, ten miles north of New Haven. It is now a district of Branford. In a typical gesture, Ponselle moved her entire household there. Romani also joined her, leaving his studio so he could spend the summer coaching her. Reveling in the beachfront house (memorialized in snapshots from 1918 and 1922) were Romani, Rosa, Carmela, Prilik, and a cook. Ponselle golfed, swam, and played tennis; by 1922, when she returned to Pine Orchard, her household had grown even larger, with her mother and a pet dog. One of these photographs is vintage Ponselle: she has a score in one hand and the dog on her lap.

In later interviews Ponselle said of this summer that Romani taught her not just the scores she had to learn but his own technique of singing "Maw-may-me-mo-moo" on Italian vowels to bring her voice into the mask. She preached this correct placement of the instrument to students and acquaintances for years and expounded on it in interviews as well. Rosa said, and Carmela also testified, that from the age of fourteen she had a woman's voice, covering a range of nearly three octaves. Singing came easily to her, in opera as it had in popular music, but these tricks of technique bolstered her mastery of the voice. In a conversation with Hope E. Stoddard in the early 1960s, Ponselle declared that she could never have got through *Forza* without having mastered those vocalises and the practice of "talking to herself in her head" to convince herself that she could in fact reach the highest notes in her range: "I said to myself, 'Top, top, top. Up. Up.'" She also often reiterated her claim that she was really self-taught in all that related to her singing, for Romani, like Thorner, served strictly as her coach and never as her voice teacher.

Of that summer, Ponselle recalled that it was "the most intensive work I have ever undertaken, coaching from morning to night. . . . Unlike many singers who learn the arias first and the connecting recitatives, duets and ensembles later, I learned the whole score of *Forza* from the first page to the last. This method stayed with me through all the rest of my career; and I still believe that it is the best, for it gives the singer the proper perspective and permits him to understand the opera as drama, not just a series of 'show-piece' arias hooked together with incidental, functional lines." This was Romani's gospel, drilled into her during these first months of their long association. His lesson was never forgotten.

"All went well during those months, my vocal confidence increasing with every new line of the score that I mastered. I memorized, line after line, page after page, until the whole of *Forza* was fixed in my mind. Then came problems of interpretation, phrasing, adjusting the voice to the tessiture of the various scenes.—All difficult, but thrilling to learn."

As she remarked later in this *Opera News* interview, Ponselle was making astounding progress. Her study went far beyond music, for Romani was also teaching her Tuscan Italian, then as now considered the benchmark for all who wish to speak the language correctly. This he was thoroughly qualified to do, being Tuscan-born. Although this meant that Ponselle had to learn a third language, adding to her own English and the family dialect of the Terra di Lavoro, she proved to be an apt pupil. Fortunately, though, she never completely lost the caressing, long vowels, especially the indistinct soft *ë*, which are typical of the northern territories of Campania and particularly of the Caserta-Capua region. This is the district where people say *vinne* and *venne* for the Italian *vendi* (you sell); where the Italian *bocca* (mouth) becomes *vucca*, with the explosive *b* lost. *Piove* (it is raining) becomes a slurred *chiove*. *Amore* is *amurre*. *Che vuoi?* (What do you want?) becomes *che bbuoie?*, the speaker leaning into the phrase and binding the two words into one. The aggressive *quello* (that) of correct Italian slides into a gentler *chillo*. *Questo* (this) becomes *chist*, as in the well-known first line of " 'O paise d' 'o sole": "Chist'è 'o paese d' 'o sole," "This is the land of the sun." The last word of the chorus is *ammore*, which often falls into *ammure*. If it were sung as "Il paese del sole," all flavor would be lost. The best-known example of a hard consonant disappearing is in the title of the most famous Neapolitan song: " 'O Sole Mio," the formal version of which would be "*Lo* Sole Mio," now almost everywhere corrupted into " '*O* Sole Mio." The Northern Italian "*Il* sole" is gone.

On Ponselle's recordings of Neapolitan songs such as "Maria, Marì" and on her duet with Carmela of " 'O Sole Mio," one can hear their repertory of Terra di Lavoro vowels and luscious, rolling, doubled (and even tripled) consonants: *mm, nn, bb, dd,* and *ll.* Just a few lines from the early Columbia acoustic recording clearly illustrate how this affected Ponselle's singing:

> Oì, Marì! Oì, Marì!
> Quanto suonno che perdo pe' te.
> Famm'addurmì
> Una notte abbracciati cu te!

Many of these are heard, together with the smooth phrasing of Campania, on Rosa's and Carmela's classical works as well. Like Caruso and Scotti, they used these doubled consonants to produce a rich, golden sound, a sound that differs radically from the tight, closed pronunciation of such northerners as the tenors Giovanni Martinelli and Aureliano Pertile or the soprano Toti Dal Monte. These three present a fascinating case history when compared with Caruso, Scotti, and Ponselle because Martinelli and Pertile came from the same parish near Padua, and Toti Dal Monte was born nearby, as Antonietta Meneghel, in Mogliano Veneto, just north of Venice. In all three, the narrow vowels and incisive single consonants of their native region produce a sound that is at farthest remove from the melting, seductive southern singing that we hear in the Neapolitans—not just Ponselle and her compatriots in opera, but in dozens of singers from the folk and popular repertory who had the good fortune to be born near the Bay of Naples. That southern quality converted millions of Americans to what they believed was "Italian music" when it was in fact a regional genre.

Beyond Ponselle's lessons in proper Italian, she said that she also followed her weight loss program that summer, spending all her free time in the water, on the golf course, or walking. A diet regime also helped her to lose just the amount she had decided upon: thirty-five pounds. By the end of August she was slimmer, her new figure accentuated by her height. With two-inch heels on her new shoes, Ponselle reached five feet ten inches and was a match for most of the men at the Metropolitan.

"Summer ended," she said, "and Romani announced that I was ready to go. Rehearsals began, and I heard myself on the Metropolitan stage for the first time with an orchestra. I felt like a bird trying to fly for the first time; but everyone agreed that I had made astounding progress." Gatti, in an unusually generous expression of feelings, complimented her on her recently acquired northern Italian diction and on her weight loss. She would fight a weight problem that winter and for years to come by walking from her apartment to the opera house, nearly sixty blocks down Broadway, three miles a day, in addition to other walks and exercise. Occasionally she would bike, but Gatti, fearing that she would be hit, tried to persuade her to keep her bicycle to Central Park and the "upper road" of Riverside Drive.

Even before she got to hear herself onstage, Ponselle went through the regular routine of individual room rehearsals followed by ensembles on the rehearsal stage. She described these in many interviews with Francis Robinson, Robert Lawrence, Boris Goldovsky, and Tom Villella, among others. She said that Caruso was "very nervous" because he was "a perfectionist, with that Latin, Neapolitan sensitive nature of his. He was always thinking to perfect [himself]. The world was expecting greater and greater things from him, and each performance weighed heavily on him, especially a premiere."

For once, Gatti put aside his resolution not to lavish praise on singers. Ponselle described the early *Forza* rehearsals: "Gatti was walking around beaming, he was so proud and happy with his cast. Caruso would sit there and listen to my singing, always assuring me and reassuring me and suggesting ways of improving my performance. He was always like this at rehearsals, not at all temperamental. I never saw him have a tantrum or become angry with anyone. He was just as humble and helpful to a singer as he could be. He would say to a singer, 'Try it this way, or that way.' He was very solicitous; all I could see was kindness in that face." Caruso was generous "to a fault" and could never say no to anyone who needed money. "He would indulge them in everything. Once he said to me, 'I never knew I had so many relatives until I became a celebrity!'"

The whole company was satisfied when the dress rehearsal went almost flawlessly, although "as the premiere approached, that was the time that I began to feel uneasy," Ponselle recalled. She conquered her nerves, though, as she declared in her *Opera News* interview:

> The day of the dress rehearsal found me feeling wonderful. I listened carefully for the overture; when it began, I felt as if I were shaking hands with an old friend, so carefully had Maestro Romani prepared me. The curtain went up. Caruso seemed at ease, although it was his first Alvaro. (I learned two days later how he behaved on the night of the performance.) Giuseppe De Luca sang marvelously, as always.
>
> At the end of the rehearsal, Gatti came up to me, playfully slapped my face and exclaimed, for all to hear, "Che faccia tosta!"

That meant "You brazen thing, with your [cheeky] face!" During the whole rehearsal I had felt not one moment of nervousness.

Although she did not know it at the time, Ponselle was extremely fortunate in having the most important members of the press corps in Gatti's invited audience at the Metropolitan that day. None of the reviewers had received much advance notice about the new soprano because Gatti's staff had been ordered not to give anyone a hint of the management's hopes for her. If they were pleasantly surprised, Gatti reasoned, so much the better for her and for the company. For many journalists, she was just one of a long list of aspiring Americans they would hear that season. A one-page article by May Stanley, dated October 5, 1918, listed Charles Hackett, Reinald Werrenrath, Alice Gentle, Mary Mellish, Rosa Eaton, Helene Marsh, Mary Ellis, Margaret Romaine, and Rose Poncille [*sic*] as the ones to watch. Stanley wrote of Ponselle: "Vaudeville tried to get Rose Poncille for its own, but her teacher, William Thorner, saw other and more brilliant fields for her talents and persuaded her to continue her studies until she was ready to launch her operatic career."

Many of these early interviews, some conducted in the living room of the apartment on Ninety-seventh Street, prove to be a mine of information on Ponselle's frame of mind at this time because they offer a transcription of her exact words as she, unguarded and natural, spoke to the press. In the critical years between 1918 and 1922 many women journalists with shorthand skills were sent to interview women like Ponselle for feature articles that are invaluable today. We read of her self-doubt, her worries about looking ungainly on the stage and cracking or losing her voice in the middle of a performance. The stories published before her debut also tell us how little everyone knew about her then. Most writers saw Ponselle as an inexperienced singer on a wildly raked playing field where others were trained for the task before them and she was not. Every story mentioned her career in vaudeville. There was some debate among women interviewers about which of the newly engaged sopranos and mezzos might have the best chance of becoming "Miss Columbia"—the title invented in advance for the star-to-come, the "second Farrar" they longed to discover. Who would it be? Mary Mellish? Rosa Eaton? Helene Marsh? Clearly Ponselle burst on the scene as a surprise to most newspaper people and the audience as well. Given the power of gossip in the music business, it is quite remarkable that Gatti's strategy worked.

Ponselle's account of the day of dress rehearsal goes on: "We all left the Opera House together and went [across the street] to a late afternoon luncheon given by the Knabe Piano Company [which provided the official pianos for the Metropolitan]." The restaurant was Lorber's, the scene of Rosa's first appearances in New York, when she and Carmela had staged their duets there, with Carmela on stage and Rosa in a sort of balcony. Here they had experimented with and perfected " 'O Sole Mio" and "Comin' through the Rye," among many other pieces. Now here she was: "I was the guest of honor—a position I had never expected to hold [in the days] when I sang at that same restaurant with Carmela. That [first] night we won a contract for the [1915 concert at] Narrangansett Pier. That led to vaudeville; vaudeville to the Met; and the Met brought me back to that same restaurant! That's how the *Forza del destino* worked in *my* life!"

This was Wednesday, November 13, when America was still celebrating the Armistice. It had been signed two days before, on November 11, when the joy at this nation's victory coincided with the opening night of the Metropolitan's 1918–19 season: Caruso and Homer in Camille Saint-Saëns's *Samson et Dalila*. It says a lot for the tenor's loyalty to the company that he attended the luncheon after having rehearsed *Samson* on the ninth, sung it for the opening two days later, finished the *Forza* dress rehearsal earlier that afternoon, and still had its premiere ahead of him on November 15. But he did attend and paid solicitous attention to Ponselle; he even stayed until the ceremonial remarks were delivered and guests were beginning to leave.

At Lorber's Gatti and the senior management figures sat at the head table with Caruso, Otto Kahn, and other board members. Although Ponselle was the guest of honor, Giuseppe De Luca and the other newcomers to the roster were not neglected. Romani, also on the guest list, took Ponselle home in a taxi as evening fell. "After the luncheon, I went home to rest," she told

Opera News, adding that she was "completely relaxed until the next morning" and was congratulating herself on remaining calm.

The attack of nerves that paralyzed her was brought on by reading a bad review of the Radamès of the Italian tenor Giulio Crimi, who had made his Metropolitan debut in *Aida* with Muzio, Homer, and Didur on November 13, the evening after the Knabe luncheon. The Sicilian tenor, who was a bit older than Carmela, had made his Italian debut six years earlier and had sung the leading tenor role in Alfredo Catalani's *La Wally* and the first London Avito in Italo Montemezzi's *L'amore dei tre re* at Covent Garden. He had also been the first Paolo in Riccardo Zandonai's *Francesca da Rimini* in Turin. Because Crimi had such a distinguished career behind him, Ponselle had assumed that the New York critics would treat him with respect. They did not.

Seeing their "unfavorable and unflattering" attack on Crimi, she imagined that they would also destroy her because she was "a nobody." To her sister she said, "Dear Lord, what are they going to do to me, if they do this to a celebrated tenor?" With that, all her self-doubt and the repressed fears took over, throwing her into a panic. In one interview she said that it got "steadily worse" and "stayed with me constantly" until curtain time. Neither Carmela nor Romani nor their physician could calm her down. Their mother, who had come down earlier in the month from Meriden, was muttering litanies, armed with a rosary and prayer cards to the saints. Apparently unaware that the critics who attended the dress rehearsal had already judged Ponselle favorably, everyone in her household spent more than twenty-four hours standing by and trying to reassure her. Everyone slept badly that night, and with good reason, for she and Carmela had both had influenza that fall and had been very ill. "Rosa was so sick that we thought she would have to postpone her debut," Carmela wrote. On the day before Ponselle's debut their doctor calmed her with sedatives.

Carmela recalled that the next morning dawned "a cold but beautiful November day." Rosa was so edgy that she had to ask Carmela to help her get into her street clothes. Finally they were ready to start for the theater. Carmela said, "We were all so excited and nervous: my saintly mother, Miss

Prilik, Rose and I arrived at the Metropolitan at six P.M." They allowed "plenty of time" in the hope that the overwrought Ponselle could get better control of herself in a structured situation; at home she had sworn that she had completely forgotten the music of *Forza* and that it had gone out of her mind and her voice.

By the time the four women "looked around her [dressing] room, got her makeup out, and had [the opera house maid], Ethel, straighten her gown" it was about six-thirty. "Suddenly Rose got panicky [and said that] she was so nervous that she could not and would not go on." As she had done so often in the past, Carmela gently reproached her, saying, "Why, Rose, that's not you talking. We were never failures." The two sisters knelt in the dressing room and prayed together. Ponselle, in a later interview, also remembered her mother, off in a corner saying the rosary, and Carmela at her side. Gatti, perhaps remembering that Rosa had fainted during her Metropolitan audition, gave Carmela permission to stand in the wings, just in case.

Ponselle recalled that she could not even lift her arms to put on her makeup. "I was numb," she said. "I thought, 'This is it; I'm going to die on the stage. Oh, my poor mother!'" She was particularly upset because Caruso did not come to her dressing room to reassure her, "his protégée," as she called herself. Later, of course, she learned that he was in an anguished state over his own stage fright. She had just finished dressing when Thorner came to wish her good luck. She thanked him, but when he also asked her to run through some vocalises for him, she refused at first. When he persisted, she tried her voice but could hear nothing.

In her *Opera News* interview she says:

> The fatal moment came when I decided to try my voice. Never realizing the effect a carpeted room with heavily draped windows can have on a voice, I began to vocalize. To my complete horror, not a sound could be heard! I thought my voice was gone! All I could think of was "I'm going to die tonight, right here!" Only the reassurance of Romani got me to go onto the stage.

There we were—a cheerful parade! Romani, obviously nervous; Mother, with her rosary beads; Sister, with the smelling salts. And me, led like a lamb to the slaughter.

When she got onto the stage she found the overwrought Caruso "behind the flats, gargling and spitting his famous salt-and-water drink. Far from taking my 'gelida manina,' he ignored me completely, looked right through me, while he struck his forehead and shouted in Italian, 'Never again! It's too much to ask of any man! I'll never sing again!' And I?—Do you think I was thinking of *Forza*? I was not!" To another journalist she said that she was so unsteady on her feet that she could hear the sound of her heels hitting the stage as the overture began.

As the first act opened she sang "a duet with my stage father, and the big aria, this very difficult aria, 'Me pellegrina ed orfana,' and I got through that, but I don't know how. My tongue stuck in my throat. No secretion. No saliva." It was at the beginning of this scene, after Leonora's father leaves the stage, that Carmela, standing in the wings, saw Rosa sway and thought she was about to faint. A stagehand stopped her from rushing out onto the open stage.

Ponselle's account goes on:

After a few recitatives with the maid comes Don Alvaro—Caruso— through the casement window: and he catches me in his arms, singing "Ah, my love, my darling! How I have lived for this moment!" And between phrases I said to him, under my breath, "I'm dying!" "Sto morendo! Sto morendo!" And he said, "Courage! Courage! I'll sustain you!" between phrases: "Coraggio! Coraggio! Io ti sustengo," in his Neapolitan dialect. And he did. He gave me the encouragement I so badly needed. Through some miracle, we got through that duet; he lived through it and so did I.

During the intermission Ponselle prayed in her dressing room: "O Lord, please help me to get through this second act," knowing that it was almost one hour long, "55 minutes of constant singing, and an almost impossible tessitura for a young girl, or even for a veteran artist, for that matter, including the tavern scene, no cuts."

To the *Opera News* interviewer she said:

> Musically the second act of *Forza* was always more difficult for me than any single part of any opera I sang; and I always felt that the duet with the basso was the most difficult part of that opera. By the time I got to "La Vergine degli angeli" at the end of the act, I was in seventh heaven, for I knew that the worst was behind me. In that scene with Padre Guardiano, Leonora has to be a lyric, dramatic and near-mezzo soprano. She must express fear, fatigue, piety, desperation, remorse, relief and a dozen other assorted emotions—all in phrases placed all over the scale and above and below it as well!
>
> The big aria, "Madre, pietosa Vergine," [and] the long duet with [the bass José Mardones], seemed endless to me. I thought that at every note I was going to crack or drop dead.

She got through it mostly because she kept repeating her formula:

> Top, top, top. Up. Up, to keep my voice light and sustain that extremely high pitch Verdi established for the tone of the opera. The combination of the heavy drama, to which the voice must be keyed in color, and the light, soaring singing assigned to Leonora is the barrier that stands between this opera and most singers—except for such brilliant sopranos as Zinka Milanov. It was not until I learned other operas—*Forza* was my first, remember—that I realized how hard the opera was.

Certainly it was not easy for the others, despite their years of experience, but Gatti was fortunate in having a team of dependable artists at hand. Caruso as Don Alvaro, De Luca as Don Carlo, and José Mardones as the Padre Guardiano guaranteed a given level of success, while the debutantes Ponselle and Alice Gentle, the Preziosilla, brought their youthful voices to the production, as did the Marquis, Louis d'Angelo, who had joined the company in 1917.

Ponselle's recollection of *Forza* goes on:

Of all the operas in the repertory, *Forza* is certainly one of the most difficult to cast. . . . Also it is one of the most difficult operas. . . . It is one of the most appealing; and I will never understand why it is not more popular. Perhaps because it is not well enough known. *Forza* is an intensely human story, encompassing an ill-starred love affair and the solace of religion, two universally known and understood problems. Leonora is no Wagnerian goddess. She is a conscientious daughter, torn between her love for her father and love for Alvaro, a man of another race. In her despair, she turns to God for help and guidance, offering Verdi one of his rare opportunities to write long scenes of deeply religious music. But Leonora is a human being. Her confusion in the first act, her desire to see her father again and postpone her elopement, then her desperate search for the peace of a religious life all unfold for us the innermost heart of a forlorn girl, a real "orfana e pellegrina."

Ponselle relaxed somewhat after a storm of applause greeted her at the end of the monastery scene. Feeling more confident, she stood in the wings during several scenes that followed, fascinated at hearing Caruso and De Luca in their exchanges. Asked about her great last-act aria, she said in 1952, "Of all the arias in the opera, 'Pace, pace' is naturally my favorite. My house is named after it, and it has followed me like a true *forza del destino* all my life. It is the supreme expression of the tormented soul; and when I came to it in the opera, I was always carried away." It became one of her signature pieces in concerts and on recordings.

About the opera itself, she remarked on the weight of emotions in it, saying that they are just as important as fate or destiny. "The text is supreme. It is bosh to talk about poor librettos. *Forza*'s libretto is no more incredible—in fact, less so—than *Trovatore*, with its exchanged children, or *Ballo*, with its unbelievable mistaken-identity plot, or a dozen others. *Forza* tells a credible story, one which could almost be translated into modern dress and be believed. It is full of intense religious feeling, which is inherent in the text. Its story and emotions must be translated to the audience by the singers."

Asked about stage directions and oversight provided by the Metropolitan staff during the rehearsals, she said:

Since there was no precedent for *Forza* when I sang it, I had to work out all my own *scena* for it, without any real dramatic coaching. Leaning heavily on the text, I evolved my Leonora, a warm, passionate girl who was torn first one way then another by her own personality and by circumstance. I found that restrained hand gestures [learned from Carmela and mastered in vaudeville days] contributed more to my portrayal than any other dramatic device. Leonora can't throw herself around the stage. She just is not that kind of person; but she can use her hands, a fact which guided me toward a convincing expression of her character. And since all the nuances and tones of her being are written into the lines she has to sing, I simply studied those lines, word by word, until I knew her better than I knew the members of my own family.

Unfortunately, these remarks reveal how far the company had slid since the days when Gatti, Toscanini, Puccini, and David Belasco were overseeing *Madama Butterfly* and *La fanciulla del West* at the Met. They had served as co-directors, even having a say in the design and building of the sets. But with *Forza*, never before given in the opera house, the company and its artists were entering unknown territory. It was a risky venture, especially because Gatti's 1913 production of *Un ballo in maschera*, to honor the centenary of Verdi's birth, had not been well received. "Unfamiliar Verdi works" (as the critics called them) seemed by definition suspect. The "absurdities" of the *Ballo* libretto were mentioned in the 1913 reviews, while the singers were almost all faulted. Today we can scarcely believe that out of a *Ballo* cast that included Destinn, Caruso, Pasquale Amato, Matzenauer, Frieda Hempel, Andres De Segurola, and Léon Rothier, only Caruso won praise from W. J. Henderson of the *New York Sun*. "It would be unkind to make detailed comment on the singing of yesterday's cast. Mr. Caruso alone stood forth as the artist commanding the respect of the connoisseur. Even his delivery of the music of Riccardo was by no means impeccable, but at its best moments it was admirable."

If *Ballo* called forth this mixed criticism, one can imagine that the much more complex *Forza* would prove to be a larger challenge for the Metropolitan. With this extremely difficult work, we might expect to hear that the management provided extensive dramatic coaching, but evidently the confounding score took up all the available rehearsal time and funds. Ponselle and the company were lucky that she had sufficient training, such as it was, performing in vaudeville and watching motion pictures—her schooling.

Ponselle also said that she found "the most important single fact" about *Forza* to be "that the singer *must* learn to project it without giving too much or too little. If [the projection] is too dramatic, the voice will be torn to pieces in one or two acts. If [it is] too little, no one will understand the opera. That's the secret of a successful *Forza*; and if you can sing *Forza*, you can sing anything."

The young soprano's enormous triumph on this night has rarely been replicated anywhere; Ponselle's Leonora represents one of the greatest debuts in the history of opera. Many reviews and subsequent articles refer to the waves of applause, the dozen or more curtain calls after each act and at the end of the opera. After the performance Otto Kahn came to her dressing room and handed her a small envelope with a thousand-dollar bill in it; this was a gift he often brought as a gesture of appreciation to young performers. Caruso, Gatti, and the cast members and staffers congratulated Ponselle, as did Romani and James Ceriani, who had come to hear his protégée on the Met stage, where he had always sworn she should sing. Vaudeville was represented by Eddie Dowling, Ray Dooley, and one of its authentic celebrities, Eva Tanguay.

At the end of the evening Ponselle went home with her mother, Carmela, and their closest friends. Caruso left with what she dubbed "his entourage—I called them 'hangers-on' [and] he never made a move without them, for they would follow him anyway. It was a ritual with them to plan a big meal in some restaurant [after the performance]; Caruso loved Italian food."

Not even marriage, apparently, had changed the tenor's habits. In August 1918 Caruso had married Dorothy Benjamin, the young daughter of a prominent father who vigorously opposed their romance.

In the days that followed the premiere Ponselle and those around her collected the reviews of *Forza.* The critics' general feelings about the revival can be deduced from one review that described the opera as "ashes" recovered from "oblivion" and "dragged from its tomb," even though the writer, James J. Huneker of the *New York Times,* admitted that "you can't kill Verdi." Yet the score was "crammed musically speaking" with "a surfeit" of "jostling elbows, the melodramatic, the violent and the vulgar; even the barrel-organ flavor is not absent." Huneker went on to a detailed analysis of the history of *Forza* but blasted its "saccharine nonsense" and wrote off the second-act scene in the kitchen of a village inn as being indebted to *Carmen,* although Verdi put in "little trace" of "Spanish local color." He praised other scenes, though, for "impressive music" and, in the last scene, the "powerful dramatic climax." He did admit that though "the old machinery unmistakably creaked," the public was enthusiastic.

The highlights of the evening for Huneker were Caruso's Don Alvaro and "the brilliant debut made by Rosa Ponselle." His observations follow:

> She is comely, and she is tall and solidly built. A fine figure of a woman, was the opinion of the experts; and in a cavalier costume was handsome and—embarrassed. Those long boots made her gait awkward; she was too conscious of her legs, and her gestures were angular. But what a promising debut! Added to her personal attractiveness, she possesses a voice of natural beauty that may prove a gold mine; it is vocal gold, anyhow, with its luscious lower and middle tones, dark, rich and ductile [and] brilliant in the upper register. . . . She is given to forcing the column of breath, with the result that the tone becomes hard [to the point of] steeliness, yet [she has] a sweet, appealing, sympathetic voice, well placed, well trained. The note of monotony in the tone color that occasionally intruded may be avoided. Nuance, nuance, nuance! That must be mastered. Her

nervousness was evident, but after she sang 'Addio' in Act I, she had her audience captured. Her scene and cavatina before the church was astonishingly mature for such a youthful debutante. She sagged below pitch on her last note. Unless we are greatly mistaken, our opera has in Rosa Ponselle a dramatic soprano of splendid potentialities; but she has an arduous road to traverse before she can call herself a finished artist.

The critic also mentioned that Ponselle was "an American, born of Italian parentage."

W. J. Henderson, in the *New York Sun*, wrote that she had one of the most voluptuous dramatic soprano voices he had ever heard. He was, however, an unrelenting critic of her technique and development for years to come. When Ponselle won Henderson's praise, she knew she had earned it.

A long article in the *Musical Courier* entitled "Verdi's *Forza* Resuscitated" belittled "one of Verdi's weakest musical scores" and excoriated its "inane libretto." The writer, though, did not stint on praise of the singers: Caruso offered "the best lyrical and dramatic singing he has given us in a long while" and was "a rare presence" onstage. Of Ponselle, the reviewer noted that she was "one year ago a vaudeville performer" and that she "upset all traditions by assuming a leading role at the Metropolitan and without any previous experience, carrying it to triumphant success. It is no exaggeration to say that she made a sensational impression and was sensationally received. . . . [She has] a voice of rich, sensuous quality, generous in volume and range and capable of all the lights and shades of operatic expression. . . . smooth in texture and perfect in placement."

Predictably, Marziale Sisca praised both Caruso and Ponselle in *La follia* of December 1918, which gave her an early, important review intended for the Italian-speaking population. With the elder Sisca at the debut was his son, Michael, who was fifteen at the time. Michael Sisca's memories of that evening include "Mardones, the greatest bass I ever heard," and Caruso, who was "very excited about [Ponselle's] debut and about *Forza*." Of Ponselle, Sisca recalled in 1996: "She was afraid. She was a smart girl, she learned the opera, but she was very, very afraid." He also remembers visiting Romano Romani's studio at 250 Riverside Drive, where Ponselle was just finishing a coaching session. "Romani said, 'Rosa, please make us some coffee,' and she went out to the kitchen and made it. A lovely Italian girl."

Pierre V. R. Key, a writer and critic, was already collecting material for the biography of Caruso that he and the tenor's secretary, Bruno Zirato, would publish in 1922. Key described "the tonal beauty" of Ponselle's voice, adding that no other soprano had surpassed her "within memory." It was "big, luscious, with a texture like a piece of velvet." He also praised her "technique, her art and her buoyant youth." *Musical America* wrote of her "incomparable charm [and] dramatic ability [and] her voice, of considerable power and a finely musical quality." The reviewer said that she "absolutely captured the audience."

Among the reviews in Ponselle's scrapbooks, which are in the New York Public Library for the Performing Arts, one stands out because its writer, Olin Downes, later became the leading *New York Times* critic and one of the most respected music reviewers in the world. As we learn from his article about *La forza del destino*, he had never heard of Ponselle, knew nothing about her vaudeville career, and had not attended the dress rehearsal, as many of the important New York writers had. Downes, who was then writing for the *Boston Sunday Post*, saw the first performance of *Forza* by accident because, as he said, "I missed the five o'clock train to Boston." With nothing to do that evening, he decided to walk over to the Metropolitan and join the standees in the rear of the auditorium. He was stunned by what he heard. Describing his experience in the *Post* a few days later, he wrote: "Some tall woman with a superb voice [was on the stage]. All through that [first] act, I tried to figure out who that woman could be—a voice with that extra range, as required by the music; with the power, the quality, the color of a dramatic soprano of the very first order." At the end of act 1 Downes spoke to "one of the attachés of the Metropolitan," who said, "That's the girl Gatti-Casazza has taken out of vaudeville." Surely this is the freshest and most spontaneous view of Ponselle's epic debut.

CHAPTER 5

Founding a Career

1918–1921

From the moment the first reviews appeared, Gatti and Caruso could be certain they had made no mistake in risking so much on Ponselle, at least for *La forza del destino*, which she was scheduled to sing nine times that season. Six performances were to be in the opera house and one each in Brooklyn, Philadelphia, and Atlanta. Because they were evenly spaced, the management could reasonably expect Ponselle to sing them all, so long as she did not become ill. Beyond those Gatti and Caruso had few expectations, being far too wise in the ways of opera to plan a future for such a neophyte, no matter how intelligent or gifted she seemed, no matter how much publicity her debut generated.

"THE NEWEST STAR IN THE SKY"

Ponselle became the new darling of the American press almost overnight as the news services telegraphed her story out over the wires. American readers learned all about her past: her origins, the grocery and family bakery, and even the names of Bush and Bessie, the Ponzillos' pet dogs in Meriden; Carmela's struggle, Rosa's history as a largely self-taught creature of genius, and the sisters' vaudeville years. Within ten days dramatic photographs of Ponselle were appearing in local papers as far afield as Wisconsin, Georgia, and California, where editors used old photographs of her wearing long, silk vaudeville gowns and a mantilla. *Town and Country* magazine rushed into print with a Maurice Goldberg shot that showed her in an alluring "vamp" pose, full length and full page, in its December 10 issue. With the exception of the Metropolitan's house photographs of her, Caruso, and Mardones in *La forza del destino,* many of these date from the Ponzillo sisters' earlier appearances. Often Carmela's picture appeared next to Rosa's in interviews where both women were covered, because both were considered newsworthy.

So great was the stress of Ponselle's debut that, she said, on November 16 one of her doctors put her in Saint Raphael's Hospital in New Haven, where her personal physician, Dr. William F. Verdi, served for decades. Knowing her better than anyone outside her family, he was also one of the Ponzillos' closest friends. A contemporary of Rosa Ponselle's mother, Dr. Verdi was, like her, a native of Campania, born in Sorrento in 1872. A veteran of World War I who served with the U.S. Army medical corps, he returned to his practice in New Haven, where he remained the immigrant families' favorite surgeon. He was devoted to Rosa Ponselle, who once sang a private concert in his house. He also had a handsome portrait done of her. Dr. Verdi, after whom a wing of Saint Raphael's Hospital is named, lived across the street from the family of Helen Greco, who has long been active in the New York cultural scene. New Haven was Ponselle's second home, where she had sung for years, where her mother, her cousins, Carmela, Anna Ryan, and Ceriani could stand by, where the Italian-American culture of her childhood and youth flourished in the half dozen music lovers' clubs that sent her flowers and good wishes because she was one of their own.

Even during the week in the hospital journalists were after Ponselle in full cry. When her physician announced that she was sufficiently recovered, she went back to New York, where the next performance of *Forza* was scheduled for November 28. We do not know whether Gennaro Papi, the conductor, scheduled any brush-up rehearsals, but small cast changes make it likely.

Ponselle was kept busy at the theater every day in any case, called for rehearsals for her next opera, *Cavalleria rusticana.* Santuzza was the role that Gatti had promised she could sing, provided her debut in *Forza* went well. He had a habit of not notifying his singers of their roles or announcing his casts to the press until shortly before a given performance, except when he planned a big premiere such as *Forza*. Over the years he had found this a useful way of keeping his artists on a short leash and preventing them from running off to lucrative concerts and recital engagements out of New York; it was only one of many tricks he used to keep his theatrical family at home.

Because of this practice, Gatti could wait until after Ponselle's debut of November 15 to tell her to prepare to sing Santuzza in *Cavalleria* in Philadelphia in less than a month. The date was on her calendar for December 10. The American tenor Paul Althouse was her Turiddu; Sophie Braslau, Lola; Marie Mattfeld, Mamma Lucia; and Mario Laurenti, Alfio. The cast of *Pagliacci* that same evening included Caruso, Florence Easton, Luigi Montesanto, and Albert Reiss. Papi conducted both works. This, Ponselle's first appearance in *Cavalleria*, began her nineteen-year run in the opera, which she sang more than any other at the Metropolitan. Her last was in 1937, as her career was drawing to its end.

The photographs of her in this part, like Caruso's caricatures of her, and particularly of her as Santuzza, show how well she captured the soul of her own people and of an abandoned, betrayed, ruined, and frightened southern Italian girl. So also does Ponselle's early Columbia acoustic recording of "Voi lo sapete," made during the first week of January 1919. Because the aria is short she was able to pace it as slowly and dramatically as she wished, with Romani conducting the studio orchestra, and was thus not threatened by the time limitations that she abhorred—about four and a half minutes was the maximum length on the wax platters. Her young, bright voice, shaded where necessary with a darker, golden coloration, delivers Mascagni's music passionately yet without excess. The critic David Hamilton described her early recordings as "dutiful" and, in an interview, remarked that as a young singer she had no experience with opera itself and no preconception of how it should be done.

Dutiful she surely was, the daughter of a demanding father and a strong-minded mother, obedient to Carmela, Caruso, Gatti-Casazza, and Romani; this is Ponselle at the earliest stage of her development. Her 1919 Columbia recording of "Voi lo sapete" also shows her recently acquired standard Italian diction. The tight, northern pronunciation learned from Romani is clearly heard in lines such as "Tornò; la seppe sposa" and "Quell' invida d'ogni delizia mia." In other phrases, however, she falls back into the language of her parents and grandmother, with its multiple consonants and the corrupted Terra di Lavoro vowels. A raw yet controlled fervor pours out in "Priva dell'onor mio rimango" and "Io piango!" As always, then and for decades to come, Ponselle's musical taste prevails over melodrama. She seems more at ease with it than with some of the other arias recorded for Columbia, for the good reason that "Voi lo sapete" is one of the few arias she had had on her program in 1914 and 1915 when she was the teenage soloist at the San Carlino Theatre and in Ceriani's dinner concerts in New Haven. Unlike the music of *Forza* and *Oberon*, which were utterly new to her, this was something familiar and heartfelt, delivered at a time when she obviously knew the aria but was still learning.

Ponselle's successful debut in *Cavalleria rusticana* in Philadelphia on December 10, 1918, fell within the Metropolitan's long-tested touring schedule, which reached back across the company's first years and eventually became a tradition with the regular Tuesday nights there. Two days later in New York she was rehearsing *Oberon*, which would be her second Metropolitan premiere in less than two months. Because the public still considered German opera unacceptable, Gatti presented Weber's English-language opera as a Metropolitan premiere, reviving a score that had not been heard in New York since 1870.

While the *Cavalleria* and *Oberon* rehearsals were under way Ponselle was also preparing her first Columbia recording sessions with Romani. As an agent and conductor for that company, he was undoubtedly influential in getting her under a contract that gave us the recordings that the discographer Bill Park found catalogued by that label between November 1918 and January 1924. At her first session, just two weeks after her Metropolitan Opera debut, she was taught the techniques of stepping up to and away from the horn (or, later, microphone) to control the volume of her voice as it would be heard on records. These sessions gave us "O patria mia" from *Aida* and an "Ave Maria" that Romani arranged from the intermezzo of

Cavalleria. On November 29 and December 2 and 10 she returned to the studio to record "La Vergine degli angeli" from *Forza*, Tosti's "Goodbye," and "D'amor sull'ali rosee" from *Trovatore*. Other sessions followed in the early months of 1919; in them she sang "Voi lo sapete," "Pace, pace, mio Dio" from *Forza*, "Keep the Home Fires Burning," "Un bel dì" from *Madama Butterfly*, "Vissi d'arte" from *Tosca*, and "Whispering Hope." Not until later in 1919 did she and Carmela record their unforgettable "Comin' through the Rye" and Offenbach's Barcarolle. That year Ponselle also recorded the Sicilienne from *Vespri siciliani* and "Casta diva" from *Norma*, which give us some idea of what Gatti, Caruso, and others had heard in her convincing Metropolitan auditions in the spring of 1918. With these the soprano began a recording career that lasted, with a long hiatus after her retirement, until the 1950s, when she recorded for RCA Victor and made her private recordings at home in Maryland, some with students or Carmela, and some alone.

Oberon, Ponselle's second opera in New York, had its first performance in Metropolitan Opera history at the matinee on December 28, 1918. Ponselle sang Rezia, the leading soprano role, with Giovanni Martinelli as Huon, Althouse in the title role, Alice Gentle as Fatima (quickly replaced by Kathleen Howard), Reiss as Scherasmin, Raymonde Delaunois as Puck, Rothier as Charlemagne, and Marie Sundelius as the Mermaid. All were under Artur Bodanzky's baton. Weber, the composer of *Der Freischütz*, was not new to the Metropolitan, but as one reviewer had declared, the company served listeners who loved "highly spiced" (read: "Italian") music. *Oberon* would not necessarily be appreciated.

By the time the new production opened, Ponselle had sung three performances of *Forza* and the Philadelphia *Cavalleria* and was beginning to gain confidence about maneuvering around the Met's huge stage. Her recently polished stage skills were noted in James Huneker's *Oberon* review for the *New York Times*. "To say that she [has] grown in artistic stature would only be the truth," he said, congratulating her on having mastered a style so different from the Ponselle they had all seen "singing Verdi, with Italian blood in her veins." His few reservations centered on her being "too young," with "too little experience" to be convincing in "Ocean, thou mighty monster," which he found "grandiloquent" and "stilted." That said, he complimented her on her "dramatic temperament, musical intelligence [and] beautiful, natural voice and its remarkable range, from a rich, velvety contralto to a vibrating, silvery soprano." He had high hopes for her and for her "brilliant future." The young Ponselle he described was physically "a buxom, well-proportioned figure," fascinating in Turkish trousers, who captivated the audience and got a great deal of applause. She had "arrived with both lungs."

The striking features of her face are seen paired with a photograph of Carmela in the *New York Sun* illustrating an early interview with both sisters. Two pairs of extraordinarily large and suggestive dark eyes—Carmela's rolled upward toward heaven, Rosa's in a half profile, looking warily out at the reader—bring to life a Mediterranean culture. W. J. Henderson, also writing in the *Sun* and reviewing *Oberon*, criticized Ponselle's imperfect technique but said that she possessed sufficient "voice" and "feeling" and "dramatic instinct" to become one of the great singers of her era.

The intimacy of the interview in the *Sun* is refreshing simply because it shows how free these two sisters were of overblown new-star traits. They were outspoken about their background: both had grown tired of Meriden and of their father's "dull and dreary" coal business; they had struggled to get where they were. Without guile or embarrassment they talked to the writer about their Catholic faith and reassured her that a priest came to their home every year without fail to bestow the traditional blessing of the church on the place where they lived. "Mamma Ponzillo" was also present during the interview. Her daughters said that she left "Papa Ponzillo" in Meriden for "a few days" every week to come to New York to take care of "her girls." All this is delivered straight and square. To many sophisticated New Yorkers this must have sounded like an account of family life tinged with childlike belief and a touch of superstition, things that had already been lost by many, but not by people of Italian origin such as the Ponzillos. Rosa, fresh from her triumph in *Forza*, sounded like a proud schoolgirl when she told of her joy at having learned anything so difficult. Both sisters were "just as unaffected" as they were when they were "living in obscurity" and showed the "simplicity of the truly great."

Rosa showed another side of her character to some writers, for her sharp wit and love of verbal fencing shine out from several of the earliest interviews. For a piece in the *Musical Courier*, undated but clearly identifiable as having been conducted shortly after *Oberon*, she made the writer jump through hoops to get anything out of her. When asked to write a piece for the *Courier*, she answered, "I'm a singer. It would be mere scribbling." Then she invited the interviewer to her apartment, where she played cat to the reporter's mouse.

Asked to tell the *Courier* readers about "the vital moment in her singing career," Ponselle said, "Really, I hesitate to say. My career is only beginning. In opera, I'm in the novitiate."

"Were you nervous, making a debut with the one-and-only Caruso and setting the musical world on its heels?"

"When?" Ponselle responded.

"At your debut."

"Naturally," she answered, sighing. But then "like a shot out of a gun," she turned the tables on the writer. "Wouldn't you be nervous?"

"But I don't sing," the writer protested.

"Suppose you *did* sing?" Ponselle insisted.

By this time the interviewer was in full retreat.

"I'd die of fright!"

"But if you didn't die, and you actually found yourself before the Metropolitan's footlights, looking into 3,000 faces that [looked like] three times that number, how do you imagine you might feel?"

"Scared stiff."

The interviewer said that Ponselle, who laughed "heartily" at her answer, was smarter than "a trial lawyer" and presented her case in a "creamy, dramatic soprano voice."

"So was I, for a minute," Ponselle admitted. "But my nervousness wore off. Then I grew calm—as calm as anything you can think of that is known for calmness." She recalled that she had begun to let herself go after Leonora's big scene in the second act. "Some inner voice kept up a constant whispering that I must not fail." There can be little doubt that this "inner voice" was Carmela's; in her memoir Carmela noted the many times she repeated to Rosa, "We're not failures, my dear," and "We must not fail."

Ponselle went on to say that she had felt the audience's sympathy, had found in Caruso a "foundation of rock beside me," and had kept hearing the "inner voice [that] kept up a constant whispering . . . and steadied me when I became tempted to indulge in some *tour de force*, which my vocal apparatus ached to do."

"So you felt an almost uncontrollable desire to give all you had?" the interviewer asked.

Ponselle nodded and went on.

"It's a strange feeling; yet I successfully resisted it. Had I succumbed, the temptation would have returned at my next appearance in the role. So I am glad. As the opera wore on I cultivated restraint until I felt that I was using no more voice or dramatic action than was suited to each situation. When the end of the opera came, I was physically fresh, despite my mental and nervous fatigue.

"The subsequent *Forza del destino* appearances were further lessons to me in self-restraint. They helped my Rezia in *Oberon*, as they will help my appearances in other roles. Philadelphia would not have had from me such a Santuzza as I was able to offer in *Cavalleria rusticana* if I had not fought against the desire to be ultradramatic. That is not only the young singer's danger; it also hovers over seasoned artists—or so they all tell me."

At that point Ponselle looked across her living room to a signed photograph of Giulio Gatti-Casazza and said, "I owe so much to him. He had confidence in me; I just *had* to do well. From now on I have to give myself unceasingly to my work. The few successes I have had are wonderfully stimulating; but I realize what they mean. The work I did get my opportunity [to do] was much, but it is nothing compared to the work that lies before me, if I am to attain what is expected I should do."

On the day Ponselle gave this insightful interview she had just celebrated her twenty-second birthday and had not yet finished her first season at the Met. In spite of her youth she revealed through her words what a serious, bright and measured woman she had become while still keeping her teenager's love of teasing and her sense of humor. Anyone who regularly interviews singers knows that gushing, smugness, pomposity, or self-congratulation usually comes out in these encounters; Ponselle, however, was clearly different from the others, in this as in her voice and rare musicality. One also can sense her loyalty and sense of obligation to those who had helped her. There is something quite touching in the words "if I am to attain *what it is expected I should do.*" A course had been laid out for her, and she was duty-bound to follow it, to live up to the expectations of her elders, whether they be her parents, her sister, her coaches, or those who were guiding her at the Metropolitan. Remarkably, she never mentioned the words "art" and "artist"—just "work" and "work" again.

The traits reflected in this conversation are some that marked Ponselle's early years. She remained loyal to her sister and brother, helping both and building a house in Meriden for her mother. After it was finished it was occupied by Tony, his wife, and their child. As we see from Ponselle's account books, she helped Anna Ryan until 1943. Ponselle's gifts to charity are recorded from 1921 on, along with bad debts and large loans to Tony and others, including important colleagues. Some of her earliest friends lived to celebrate her seventy-fifth birthday with her in her home near Baltimore. Only a few serious disputes marked the course of her long career.

As 1919 began, other publications besides the trade magazine *Musical Courier* were rejoicing in what seemed to be the most promising debut in many years. *Town Topics*, which was regularly read by everyone in New York interested in high society and the performing arts, reviewed Ponselle's Rezia in *Oberon* and noted in January, one day after her birthday, that she was

> traveling onward and upward artistically, apparently undisturbed by the paeans of praise that have followed in the wake of her every performance of *La forza del destino.* Her success was no flash in the pan. This young American girl is one of the vocal discoveries of our time and is sure to take her place soon with the world's great queens

of song. The way she sings "Ocean, Thou Mighty Monster" . . . is in itself enough to stamp her as a phenomenon in voice and stylistic adaptability. She is in possession of what experts term a "perfectly placed scale," and she has the insight and artistic discretion not to force her smooth, velvety tones beyond their natural dynamic limits.

In an April article the same writer described her "surpassingly lovely voice" and declared that she had been the "one, new sensational vocal hit of 1918–19. She is on the road to big achievements, for she has all the range and warm *timbre* of Raisa, plus refinement and restraint. Also she is a better actress."

One reviewer in an unidentified clipping in Ponselle's scrapbook wrote: "Rosa Ponselle as Leonora was a surprise and a delight. Her voice is fresh, clear and of lovely quality. She used it with a fine grace and effectiveness. In her Mr. Gatti has found something worth while, and, to her credit, she was unheralded [before her debut]."

Another writer, toward the end of the season, described her "velvety and well-controlled voice" as a relief to an audience accustomed to the "shouting" usually heard at the Metropolitan. "The American soprano sang with an intelligence and an artistry that confirm all previous estimates of her."

Even the normally reserved Gatti, who rarely give interviews and disliked journalists as a lot, came forward shortly after her birthday to say, "Signorina Ponselle has a voice like velvet. It is without holes. Most voices are like a garment, thick in one place, thin in others. Hers is strong and even."

One lively description of her, also from her scrapbook, reads: "Were you to encounter Miss Ponselle on the street, in a drawing room, or at a matinee, you would say, 'A good looking girl in an ample way! How brilliant her coloring! How magnificent her vitality!' And when she spoke, you would think, 'How softly girlish is her voice!' From her exudes abundant strength. She is such a girl as one instinctively thinks as 'country bred.'—The nearer to the soil, the greater the singing voice quality."

From all this, one can see that everyone was convinced that opera had found an authentic treasure. Ponselle's success at the Metropolitan in that 1918–19 season made necessary another change of residence to a new, larger apartment at 260 Riverside Drive, at the corner of Ninety-eighth Street, one block from the first place she and Carmela had rented. Giuseppe Bamboschek and Ponselle's accompanist, William Tyroler, lived in the next apartment. Both worked at the Metropolitan. During an interview published soon after the move, Ponselle told about her years in vaudeville, remembering the skimping and saving, then gave Carmela full credit for getting her to a teacher. One day, without preliminaries, Carmela had said to her, "Now it's time to study." Ever obedient, the younger sister trailed along to Thorner's studio. To a writer from *Theatre* magazine who interviewed her one month after her debut and about six months after she began coaching with Romani, Ponselle admitted that originally Thorner had been "impressed with Carmela's voice but heard nothing remarkable" in hers, and that he took little notice of her until after the first Metropolitan audition. She said that it took her about two weeks of study after she started with Thorner to convince him that she had something to offer. Her voice in those student days was "magnificent" and "rambling"; about five months passed before he could "settle" it, she said.

The critic from *Theatre* praised Ponselle's poise and confidence on the operatic stage, noting that both were "born of vaudeville." Her "glorious voice" was "too firm and too strong" to be shaken by nervousness. Best of all, she was "not acting but living her part, as natural an actress as [she was] a singer." She was described as "the girl of the hour, with no prima donna airs. She is extremely tall and dark, not exactly beautiful, but with a happy, natural personality that draws people to her; and she takes her success as if it were a super-Christmas present about which she can be delighted, but not proud."

At the Metropolitan one coach declared that Ponselle learned "like a streak," and that "the stage director need only go through the 'business' once. Ponselle follows him to the last detail, then tries again [after making] her own suggestions." Her story was contrasted to that of Muzio, who was born in the world of singers and singing; Muzio had shared the prompter's box with her father at rehearsals, had been taught arias as a child, and had studied in Europe before stepping onstage. Ponselle had had no such advantages, the *Theatre* critic observed, while sounding a note of warning. "Ponselle's career is almost beyond her control. She has a miracle-voice. And it is said that she can sing florid coloratura as well as dramatic roles. If so, she will be the ideal soprano we have been deprived of for so long, for she will be able to run the whole gamut of operatic heroines." Yet she faced a dreadful summer because she knew so few roles that she could not take advantage of her success. Unlike Muzio, with her lifelong exposure to opera, Ponselle faced "one of the busiest times of her life," with concert offers "crowding in on her." She would have to learn the song repertory if she expected to get through the next season, because her appearances in two Sunday night concerts at the Metropolitan showed her chiefly in "a few Verdi arias. So just as she has learned to be spontaneous on the opera stage, she must learn to be reserved on the concert platform." The writer also acknowledged (as Ponselle had) the enormous contribution Caruso made to her career. "Generous and friendly," he had helped her through her debut because he was "supreme [and] beyond jealousy." Finally, the article ended with a hint of rivalry with Muzio: "Metropolitanites will want to see whether a lifetime of preparedness counts after all [as it does in Muzio's case], or whether a heaven-sent voice makes up for any handicaps."

Rarely has any journalist summed up a sensational debut and set forth so clearly the perils that threatened the future of the twenty-two-year-old soprano while at the same time underscoring her immediate situation. "There is no rest on Ponselle's horizon for a long time to come," simply because she was so handicapped by her limited knowledge and "unable to fill" all the requests made of her. "While Muzio is resting on her laurels during the summer, Ponselle will be out gathering 'laurel-leaves' from opera scores."

After just seven performances at the Metropolitan, the young soprano spoke like a girl to a reporter from one of the New York papers, saying that her debut with Caruso was "very wonderful. I was nervous. I said to myself,

'I will never sing again.' [But] of course, I will sing as often as my contract requires. Really, the most painful part of it all was reducing my flesh. I was very stout, for I had eaten a lot of spaghetti and was very fat. I had to rid myself of 42 pounds. I did it by forgoing pastry and chocolates. And it was hard to learn Italian to sing the roles." The interviewer then asked how Ponselle got into opera so quickly. At that point Romani walked into the room and overheard the question. He cupped his hand to his ear and answered in broken English, "Because she has a marvelous intuition *and this*," pointing to his ear. He then compared her musicality to that of the great Italian soprano Eugenia Burzio.

Answering questions about her family, Ponselle said that ten thousand dollars earned from her Columbia recordings would go a long way toward convincing "Father Ponzillo" that music paid better than operating the grocery in Meriden. And spontaneously, without being asked, she offered this: "I am sorry about my success because I shall never have a husband and a home and children. Prima donnas should not marry."

From these interviews, conducted before the "Ponselle legend" made it so hard to get at the truth, one sees the honesty and openness that affected many of Ponselle's relationships then and later. Because of her youth and inexperience, one perceives how vulnerable she was and how many dangers lay ahead, dangers that she largely managed to avoid. As we read, we can more accurately appraise her conduct of a career and her intelligent care of a voice that lost little or nothing over the decades and can be heard in her 1954 recordings, made in her home near Baltimore about thirty-six years after her first Columbia sessions.

If Ponselle was fêted in New York in November and December after her debut, she was positively deified in Meriden in January 1919. On the morning after her debut in *Forza* a telegram had come from H. T. King, the mayor of her hometown, with his congratulations; he was also planning a huge official reception for her. One week after her twenty-second birthday, Ponselle boarded a train in Grand Central and went back to the place where she was born. When she stepped off in Meriden she found a large, noisy crowd, music, and a welcoming committee that accompanied her to the council chamber in City Hall. Amid the pandemonium described by the Connecticut press, the dignitaries greeted her as the first person from Meriden to attain artistic success. Praised for her remarkable voice, she was also congratulated for her tireless efforts to cultivate it and to learn her profession.

Quite overcome at seeing her whole family and the town council before her, the young woman found it difficult to speak. Only a few simple words came out, convincing everyone that this was the "Rosina" they had always known. Everyone there realized how unaffected she was, still the daughter of the Ponzillos of Springdale Avenue, bringing honor to her people. "You can understand what I feel," she said. "What you have done and what you are doing for me is so unexpected that I can only say that this is the happiest day of my life. I thank you—with all my heart." Not surprisingly, tears welled up, and she could not go on.

Later in the evening, after a visit at home with her family, the city offered a banquet in her honor at the Winthrop Hotel, where more than one hundred guests gathered. For the first time in years Ponselle saw dozens of her schoolmates and the local tradesmen who had known her from childhood. After the speeches the mayor presented her with a large chest full of sterling silver, the product that had made Meriden "the Silver City of New England." All in all, the evening represented the grand triumph of the Italian-American community on the West Side over "The Hill."

The next day Ponselle returned to New York to prepare the first of her Metropolitan Opera concerts. Surprisingly, her first aria in the first of these was "O patria mia," which she often said caused her more anxiety than any other piece. With Mardones she sang the finale from act 2, scene 2 of *Forza*; with Morgan Kingston, another American artist, she sang the Miserere from *Trovatore*. The finale of act 2, scene 2, from *Aida* closed the evening. Papi conducted. Two weeks later she repeated "O patria mia" and added "Un bel dì" from *Butterfly* to her program.

At this time Ponselle was the object of much scrutiny on the part of those who doubted whether she could carry the heavy burden of study and work that Gatti had assigned to her. In January 1919, just before she left for

Meriden, W. J. Henderson had published an article in the *New York Sun* under a headline: PRAISE AND PUBLICITY ENDANGER ROSA PONSELLE'S CA-REER. In full attack Henderson declared that it was "time for first impressions to give way to careful estimates" of what she might accomplish. "The young woman is in grave danger of the ruin of her career through the pernicious operations [of the Metropolitan and] inconsiderate praise [from] her friends."

One headline like that would have been enough to shake the confidence of so inexperienced a singer; but a similar long article appeared in the *Sun* in May—almost certainly by Henderson, although the clipping in Ponselle's scrapbook does not include the author's name. Reviewing the accomplishments of others who had made their debuts that season and examining the American careers in particular, the writer said:

> There was much ado about Rosa Ponselle. There was altogether too much ado, greatly to the young woman's injury. She was already showing the results of [all that] acclaim when the season ended. She was far from being a mistress of vocal technique when she made her excellent debut in *La forza del destino*. When she accomplished her final appearance of the season, she was singing much worse than when she began. Miss Ponselle's friends are not alone [responsible] in this. Much harm was done by that portion of the press that regards it as a solemn duty to "whoop it up" for anyone and everyone on the stage. Miss Ponselle is the most gifted young soprano who has appeared in years. Result: a lot of excitable young men, whose memories of local musical doings extend back perhaps eight seasons, and some [editors] who have no musical memories at all but have misguided opinions as to the duties and functions of journalism, proceeded to fill pages of ecstatic accounts of this singer, even comparing her with such incomparable artists as Patti and Lehmann!
>
> This sort of thing is, of course, ridiculous; but it works incalculable harm. . . . No person whose ear was not deadened by prejudice could have failed to perceive that the quality of Miss Ponselle's tones depreciated as the season advanced.

The writer went on to analyze the voices of Caruso and Scotti, among others. Even allowing for the solemn Henderson's conservatism and granting a certain bias, this was a devastating assessment by the dean of New York critics. Recognized as a venerable curmudgeon, Henderson had first made his mark as critic for the *New York Times*, reviewing the Metropolitan's second season in 1884–85, and had covered almost every important production in the decades that followed. He had heard Francesco Tamagno as Otello, Maurel as Iago, and Caruso's controversial 1903 debut in *Rigoletto*. Henderson had also coined the term "Gerryflappers" for Farrar's young admirers. In February 1919 he wrote an unsparing assessment of another of Thorner's artists that ran under the headline GALLI-CURCI MAY SING FLAT BECAUSE OF POOR BREATHING. A friend of the De Reszkes and Eames, Henderson commanded a knowledge of opera that was perhaps unique for his era; not even Henry Krehbiel, who had reviewed the Metropolitan's opening night in 1883 for the *New York Tribune*, could surpass him. Beyond all else, he knew vocal technique. What he wrote, everyone in the music business read.

By the time his full-page article on Ponselle came out, the audience and New York critics had had a chance to hear her more than twenty times in the opera house. In March she sang the unfortunate world premiere of Joseph Breil's *The Legend*, a short work staged on a triple bill with Charles Wakefield Cadman's slightly more successful *Shanewis, or The Robin Woman*, which had had its premiere the previous season. The third work on the program was John Hugo's *The Temple Dancer*. *The Legend*, conducted by the expert but neurotic Roberto Moranzoni, cast Ponselle with Althouse and Kathleen Howard; it survived for only three evenings. Like several other American operas that Gatti had produced at Otto Kahn's urging, it vanished without a trace. Although Ponselle had little but contempt for it, James Huneker reviewed her favorably, saying that she had to "perform a lot of vocal stunts, and only her extraordinary voice enabled her to encompass some of the long-breathed phrases. She possesses a magnificent bellows."

Although few doubts existed about her ability, all were dispelled when, on March 17, 1919, Gatti-Casazza sent her a letter to confirm that he was renewing her contract for the season of 1919–20. She was to place herself at the disposal of the theater from November 3, when rehearsals would begin, until April 15; she would also be considered for the spring tour. Her fee would be three hundred dollars per week, with an additional sum if she was taken on tour. The signatures at the bottom of the letter, accepting its terms, were "Rosa Ponselle" and "William Thorner, Manager."

Critics had a far better chance to weigh Ponselle's gifts when she sang Verdi's formidable *Messa da Requiem*, which Gatti offered on April 6 with Matzenauer, Charles Hackett, and Mardones under the baton of Giulio Setti, the chorus master. With this assignment Gatti risked showing the company's least mature singer in some of the most exposed music ever written for a soprano. Verdi had composed it for a mature Teresa Stolz, one of the greatest sopranos of the last century and, by some accounts, of all time. Matzenauer, who had made her opera debut when Rosa Ponzillo was just four, could easily dispatch the mezzo-soprano part, originally written for Maria Waldmann. Mardones, acknowledged by many singers (Ponselle among them) as the greatest bass of his generation, sang music that lay perfectly for his *profondo* range. But Ponselle faced a daunting challenge with the Requiem, and it is to her credit that she mastered it. As the 1918–19 New York season was drawing to a close, Ponselle sang one *Forza* in Philadelphia in March. Her April *Oberon* in New York was Ponselle's last performance at the Metropolitan Opera House.

Another career door opened for her in April, when Columbia released her "Un bel dì" from *Butterfly*. The *New York Telegraph*, excited over her "instant fame," hailed her for having achieved a "triumph of dramatic singing" and "conveying heartsick longing for her American lover's return." This is the first review of her recordings preserved in Ponselle's scrapbooks. At the same time the company released Maria Barrientos's aria from *Puritani*. Romani conducted both women in these sessions, giving his sopranos full rein and letting them dominate the orchestra, the critic observed.

After the Metropolitan closed in New York, Ponselle joined her colleagues on the tour to Atlanta, where she opened the 1919 performances with Caruso in *Forza* and also sang her second Metropolitan *Cavalleria*. As before, her Santuzza was partnered by Althouse. The double bill for the Mascagni work in both Philadelphia and Atlanta featured Caruso and Easton in *Pagliacci*. Although travel on the tour train proved somewhat uncomfortable then and later, an easy atmosphere prevailed, a feeling of hearty camaraderie that was rarely felt in New York. When the leading singers stayed together in a luxury hotel and met as guests at social events, they got to know each other after months of wary meetings on rehearsal stages. On tour Gatti's "children" became a family, where Billy Guard and Earle Lewis and Edward Ziegler and their wives became the surrogate uncles and aunts. Mrs. Lewis told Quaintance Eaton that even in New York she had a special mission with the company: being sure the ever-nervous Ponselle came to the theater. On the day of a performance Gatti would ask Earle Lewis to have Mrs. Lewis call the soprano at home to reassure her and allay her attacks of stage fright. She also remembered Ponselle's habit of walking around the opera house block, between Broadway and Seventh Avenue, four or five times before going through the stage door. This always calmed her.

In Atlanta Ponselle, like the other artists, could relax at the end of an unrelenting winter schedule. The weather was good; the singers spent a great deal of time outdoors at private estates and clubs. Ponselle, who had played Atlanta in vaudeville, had a contingent of fans among the city's journalists, who filled hundreds of column inches with her story, year after year, beginning immediately after her debut. When there, the exuberant sportswoman was on display at golf matches and in the pool. Because she was so much younger than colleagues such as Alda, Bori, and Farrar, her interests were not theirs: this was the Ponselle who was already known for biking down Riverside Drive and Broadway to the opera house, who found a way to golf in many cities where operas and concerts were on her schedule and collected snapshots showing her and Carmela in the water.

She later recalled that only on the tour did she have a chance to get to become personally acquainted with Caruso, and then in a limited way. Her friendships with Muzio and Bori also began at that time. At the end of the tour Ponselle sang a clutch of concerts under an arrangement with the Metropolitan and Thorner. It may have been then that she first met Samuel

Geneen of National Concerts, Inc., who later honored her, her brother, and Tony's bride with a dinner at the Hotel des Artistes, one of New York's finest restaurants. Among the guests were Giovanni Martino, Carmela's former teacher, Thorner and his wife, Romani, an associate editor of the *Musical Courier*, and Barbara Maurel, Victor Maurel's mezzo-soprano protégée, with whom Ponselle made recordings in 1919 for Columbia. Although Ponselle's formal association with National Concerts came in 1921, this major management firm, acting with Thorner, booked some of her earliest concerts. The Metropolitan booked Boston and Waterbury.

Like every other singer engaged by the Metropolitan, Ponselle paid a percentage of her fees back to the company, for the management always claimed that without the cachet of its name, the artist's ability to find concert work would be severely limited. This first tour took her to Virginia, North Carolina, Michigan, Massachusetts, Connecticut, Louisiana, and Illinois. Occasionally on the road she would meet colleagues from vaudeville days. In Charlotte she sang with Riccardo Stracciari, a Columbia recording artist and one of Romani's oldest friends. It was Romani who brought Ponselle and Stracciari together at Columbia in 1920 to sing "Mira d'acerbe lagrime," the electrifying soprano-baritone duet from the last act of *Trovatore*.

Later in the spring of 1919 she and Carmela returned to Meriden for a long visit, during which they sang a single concert at Poli's Theatre. As always, they stayed with their parents. Ponselle later remembered that they also went back to their parish church on Goodwill Avenue and sang there. In town the parishioners and neighbors learned at first hand how little their success had affected the Ponzillo girls. Not even their clothes distinguished them much from what their friends remembered, for Carmela had always dressed well and Rosa had followed her in that. In memoirs and early newspaper interviews both sisters mention dozens of details about their wardrobes, from dresses and suit fabrics to hats to small touches like headbands and hairbows, shoes and belts. They created a fashionable image for themselves early in their lives and remained intent on improving it. Carmela's homemade skirts had been replaced by gowns from Bendel's.

In a full-length photograph in the *New York Sun* in May we see Ponselle as her colleagues and public did: tall and slender, with graceful arms and a beautiful face. The loss of weight shows. Her long hair, which she let down over her shoulders at home and when she was studying in the summer, is tucked under in a kind of pageboy coiffure, the "Ponselle bob." Seeing it, no one could doubt that she possessed a luminous, intense Mediterranean beauty.

THE CARUSO ERA ENDS ～

With her first season behind her, Ponselle had to prepare the new assignments Gatti had given to his loyal and now popular artist. Her first opera for 1919–20 was Jacques Fromental Halévy's *La juive,* one of the most difficult works she attempted in the early years of her career. It would be given in French, a language she barely knew, with Caruso singing his first Eleazar, and conducted by Bodanzky, who would also repeat *Oberon* with her and Martinelli. Gatti's concerns about her were expressed on July 17, 1919, when he wrote to her from Milan, saying, "I wish to especially recommend you to be quite ready before the beginning of the season for the part of Rachel in *La Juive.* My kind regards and best wishes for a pleasant summer to you, to your sister and to Maestro Romano [*sic*]." Also on her calendar were several performances of *Forza* with Caruso. Gatti then scheduled the first *Aida* of Ponselle's career and added two sacred works, Rossini's Stabat Mater and *Petite messe solennelle.* Although she was booked for twenty-eight performances, four more than in the previous season, eight of these were galas or concerts, which were far less taxing for a singer than complete operas.

Preparing to add two new works to her repertory, Ponselle rented a summer house on Lake Placid in upstate New York and coached with Romani. Wilfrid Pelletier, who was then a coach on the Metropolitan staff and joined the company roster in 1918, taught her *La juive.* When she returned to New York Gatti informed her that her first performance of the season would be on October 25, for the unofficial opening night. An out-of-schedule gala for King Albert I and Queen Elizabeth of Belgium, it began with the opera house orchestra playing "Pomp and Circumstance," then continued with Ponselle, Mardones, and Andres De Segurola performing act 2, scene 2, of *Forza*. The program that followed featured Jascha Heifetz playing works by Chopin, Dvořák, and other composers.

Not until mid-November did the Metropolitan audience finally hear *La juive*. For Ponselle, at least, it proved no triumph, although she thought she sang it well. In the *Times* Richard Aldrich dismissed her with a withering sentence: "Miss Ponselle is also given opportunities to sing well, some of which she accepts." Henderson, following on his earlier analysis of her singing, wrote that she did not "fulfill the promise" of her debut season because her voice sounded "more constrained and less noble in tone, while her action was primitive indeed." Huneker remarked that she was an artist who was still developing and that she "easily encompassed" the role. Most of the space in every review was devoted to Caruso's stunning portrayal of Eleazar, which Ponselle considered the "finest characterization that anybody could have done." In a 1973 article by her, written to commemorate the hundredth anniversary of the tenor's birth, she described Caruso's voice. She said that it

> had then reached full maturity, darkness and size. It was not as lyric as it had been when he started, I was told; but he could lighten it whenever he had to, as when he sang in *Martha* or *Elisir d'amore*. This remarkable agility was one of the things that made him such a great singer. His voice was actually at its peak [between 1918 and the beginning of the 1920–21 season]. As for his acting, he naturally and instinctively did just the amount of acting that the piece required. He could act because he loved his roles so much, no matter what he [sang]. No one can tell me that he could not act. . . . That pantomine he did when he finished his aria "Ridi, Pagliaccio" was terrific! He would run up those stairs as he made his exit in a convulsion of rage and jealousy bordering on insanity. It was magnificent acting!

In addition to *La juive*, Caruso and Ponselle sang *Forza* together that year and again in 1920–21. In them Gatti had found an almost ideal team—the veteran tenor, who had celebrated his twenty-fifth anniversary with a Metropolitan gala in March 1919, and the partner he had discovered. Many who heard him through the autumn of 1919 and into the early months of 1920 described some of the best singing he had ever done. Among them was his son Enrico Caruso Jr., who later recalled a recording session of Neapolitan songs in September 1919 when Caruso left everyone overcome at the sheer beauty and size of his voice. The tenor was filled with joy and understandable paternal pride in December that year when his wife gave birth to their first child, Gloria, who was also the tenor's only daughter. (Ada Giachetti, a soprano, was the mother of his two sons.) In general the critics had only good to say about him that season, although Caruso, like every other singer, had good evenings and bad.

Ponselle's assignments in 1919–20 and 1920–21 kept her booked with him in *Forza* and *La juive;* she also had to learn *Aida*—with "too little time for study," she said. Gatti, who followed rehearsals carefully, scheduled her first performance of that opera in March 1920, not in the opera house but in the Brooklyn Academy. Her Radamès was Giulio Crimi; Amneris, the vain American mezzo Jeanne Gordon, who had just joined the company; Ramfis, Giovanni Martino, who was by then recognized as a member of Ponselle's inner circle of friends; and Pasquale Amato as Amonasro. In her autobiography Ponselle recalled the many times she discussed the challenge of this role with other sopranos and remarked that Aida lay perfectly within her voice but that she panicked before "O patria mia" and broke off the high C the first time she sang it in full performance. This left her with "an ungodly fear" of singing it in the opera house. Although Destinn had left the company in 1916, her departure had been much lamented by the critics, so Gatti called her back from the autumn of 1919 to the spring of 1921 and used her in *Aida.* Muzio also sang the role in New York City. Ponselle did not appear as Aida in the Metropolitan Opera House until 1924, although she sang it in Brooklyn, Cleveland, Atlanta, Washington, Baltimore, and Richmond on the company's tours until April 1930.

Her concert schedule of 1920 marked a significant step upward in prestige for anyone so young. On February 1 and 8 she sang "Ocean, thou mighty monster" from *Oberon* and Muzio's trademark "L'altra notte in fondo al mare" from Arrigo Boito's *Mefistofele* with the New York Philharmonic. The newspaper coverage of this important engagement praised her "opulent voice" and "full, lovely voice," while Herbert Peyser, writing in *Musical America*, congratulated her on conquering her audience and being "tumultuously applauded." In April Ponselle gave a recital at Yale University's Woolsey Hall, singing songs and arias from *Forza, Butterfly, La Gioconda*, and *Vespri siciliani*. Her appearance at Carnegie Hall in May was followed by an important concert in Cleveland. Finally, on June 27, 1920, Ponselle sang before ten thousand people in Lewisohn Stadium in New York City as soloist with the National Symphony Orchestra, over which Mrs. Minnie Guggenheimer presided for many years. The soprano was introduced by a proud Fiorello La Guardia, who was then the president of the board of aldermen and later became the mayor of the city. This marked Ponselle's second appearance in the huge arena, for exactly one year earlier she had launched the 1919 season of popular "Stadium Concerts" with the Volpe Symphony Orchestra, conducted by Arnold Volpe. The founder of this series, whom the Ponzillo sisters had first met in 1917 in Thorner's studio, had been one of Rosa's earliest enthusiasts. His concerts, begun in June 1918 with the help of the Lewisohns, quickly became a beloved New York City summer institution in the years after the war. The program for Ponselle's 1919 appearance, which is in the collection of Ginger Dreyfus Karren, Volpe's granddaughter, included arias from *Forza* and *Gioconda*; the "Easter Prayer" from *Cavalleria* was backed by the Metropolitan Opera chorus.

At the end of her run of concerts, Ponselle retired again to Lake Placid to learn new roles, for Gatti had renewed her contract on April 15, 1920, at eight hundred dollars a week for the coming season. Thoroughly suited to her voice was Elisabetta di Valois in Verdi's *Don Carlos*, to be given in Italian, a role she learned with Romani's coaching. The opera, which she first sang on December 23, 1920, had a superb cast. Martinelli as Don Carlo was paired with De Luca as Rodrigo; Matzenauer sang Eboli; the aging Didur, who had been with the Metropolitan since 1908, was Filippo. The Grand Inquisitor's terrible scene with the king was cut for this production, but the rarely heard act 1 scene in the forest of Fontainebleau was staged. In a single performance in Atlanta in 1922 Feodor Chaliapin sang Filippo, while Jeanne Gordon and the American Marion Telva alternated with Matzenauer as Eboli. In 1922 and 1923 the first act was cut so the action could begin and end in Spain. Gatti also restored the ballet, "La peregrina," and had it choreographed by his second wife, Rosina Galli, the prima ballerina. As with his productions of *Ballo* and *Forza*, Gatti took a considerable risk by presenting this long-forgotten Verdi work, but he obviously was intent in bringing these operas to the New York audience. Having Ponselle for the soprano roles was one considerable asset on the roster. In a concert that year he also programmed the trio from Verdi's *I lombardi alla prima crociata* for Ponselle, Beniamino Gigli, and Mardones, with Gino Nastrucci playing the violin solo. As one might expect, *Don Carlos* got a mixed reception from some baffled critics, particularly from a disgruntled Henderson, who also took Ponselle to task. Other critics liked the singers and praised her but found the opera long and boring. Much to Gatti's credit, it remained on his schedules until the spring of 1923.

As every historian of the Metropolitan has observed, Gatti's successes in those years left an enduring legacy for the company, which was his in every real sense. The directors and particularly Otto Kahn remained loyal to him while the United States roared through the 1920s. Money appeared not to be a problem. Just as that decade began, however, Gatti's chief concern was Caruso's failing health. The 1920–21 season opened with *La juive*, again with Ponselle, Caruso, and Rothier. A repeat in Philadelphia at the end of November was followed by *Forza* in New York with Giuseppe Danise as Don Carlo, again with Caruso. These went as planned, but the tenor seemed ill in *L'elisir d'amore* and *Samson et Dalila*, both of which preceded the December 13 *Forza*.

On December 8 in *Pagliacci*, Caruso's upper register failed him during his signature aria, "Vesti la giubba." As he stumbled into the wings, he complained of pain in his side. Enrico Caruso Jr. wrote that his father had also been injured onstage at the Metropolitan during the December 3 *Samson* and that he had actually lost consciousness briefly during the episode in *Pagliacci*. After a delay he finished the performance, but his illness could no longer be hidden from the public. At a performance of *Elisir* at the Brooklyn

Academy Caruso suffered a hemorrhage of the throat and could be seen wiping blood from his mouth during the first act.

Gatti, in his *Memories of the Opera*, left a harrowing account of one of the worst nights in Metropolitan history, December 11, 1920. "I did not go to Brooklyn," Gatti recalled.

> My musical secretary, Giuseppe Bamboschek, had gone to Brooklyn for me. In the middle of the first act he called me on the telephone. He was very excited.
>
> "Mr. Gatti," he said, "they are singing the duet of the first act now. Caruso cannot sing and he is bleeding. I don't know whether it's the mouth or the nose. What shall we do? Everyone in the audience sees it. Everyone's excited!"
>
> "Phone me as soon as the duet is over," I said, "and give me the details."
>
> In ten minutes they called me. "Mr. Gatti," they said, "Caruso has had a hemorrhage in the mouth. He is bleeding a lot. He does not know what to do. He asks you what to do."
>
> "End the performance," I replied, "return the money to those who bought tickets for this performance and tell them that for the subscribers there will be another performance. Suspend everything tonight."
>
> At that very moment I had a fleeting premonition that Caruso was lost. . . . His last performance was *La juive* on Christmas Eve. He had insisted on singing. He sang during this performance with great difficulty. He did it, however, without complaining.

Bodanzky suggested they cut part of the opera, Gatti added, but Caruso would not hear of it. "After the performance Toscanini came to my office. He was in the country at the time on a tour with the orchestra of La Scala. . . . After the performance he said to me, 'What is wrong with Caruso? The man must be sick. He looks very bad. I am very anxious about him.' "

Caruso had an operation to relieve an abscess and other complications of pleurisy two days later. One of his doctors told Gatti that the tenor would never sing again.

Ponselle left her own accounts of the December 13 *Forza*, Caruso's last performance with her. After what had happened two days earlier, no one expected his fine Don Alvaro, which found him singing "with no apparent unusual effort" and finishing the evening in grand style. Florence Easton sang Rachel on Christmas Eve because Ponselle was scheduled for a rehearsal the next morning. Many accounts credited Caruso with one of the greatest performances of his life, in spite of his illness.

Ponselle's recollection of that period began in one interview with "Thank God I wasn't on stage with Caruso that terrible night." He had another hemorrhage on Christmas Eve; a few months later he was seemingly cured but was advised not to leave the country so he could remain under observation.

> The doctors here wanted to make sure that he was cured once and for all. But he was fed up with it. He said, "I'm fine. I'm going home. If I'm going to die, then I want to die in my Naples."
>
> He returned to Italy with his wife, Dorothy, in May 1921; and in July he wrote to Gatti: "Feeling fine. Expect to be over the top soon. I have a voice that will last twenty years. Whatever I want to do, I do with great vigor." The next day he collapsed in great pain. On August 2, he was dead.

Ponselle was in New Haven when she learned of his death. "It was devastating," she said.

> He was so young, and had given so much to the world. I remembered something he had told me when his wife was expecting. "You know," he said, "I hope it's a girl. I'd like a girl so that when I retire, I'll have my little girl to be my companion. I'm just looking forward to living for my wife and daughter." And I said, "Well, I hope it's a girl, too." And he got a girl and said, "Wonderful!" and he named her Gloria. That poor, dear man! That poor dear man! If anyone ever deserved

a long life, it was he. To me his untimely death will always be the greatest tragedy of this century.

Caruso left Ponselle a precious personal gift in memory of their collaboration. In 1920 he signed a photograph of himself with her in *La juive*:

> To my adored daughter
> to dear Rachel
> to Rosa Rosella
> called Ponsella
> I wish a long life and a beautiful career.
> Enrico Caruso (Eleazar)

His original lines are in rhyming Italian:

> A mia figlia diletta
> a Rachel chérie
> a Rosa Rosella
> nominata Ponsella
> auguro per lunga vita carriera bella.
> Enrico Caruso (Eleazer).

CHAPTER 6

1921–SPRING 1924

The loss of such a powerful sponsor and mentor as Caruso might have proved devastating to a career less well grounded than Ponselle's, for in terms of her repertory and of the sheer number of performances she had sung, her destiny had been significantly tied to his. When Caruso left the company in December 1920 Ponselle had sung fifty-seven times for the Metropolitan; of these, twenty-nine performances were with him. This means that for half of her appearances in opera she had had him at her side "to sustain" her, as he said. When the two sang together for the last time, Ponselle was twenty-three and still dangerously young for any soprano singing *Forza, La juive,* and *Aida* as standard repertory. But in addition to the handicap of her youth, she was also facing the problem of finding herself as an artist, of throwing off the appellation of "Caruso's discovery," which identified her in the press and among the public.

FTER CARUSO 〜

It is a coincidence that this crisis was thrust upon Ponselle just as Carmela returned to vaudeville with a new operatic program and was also emerging as a concert artist in her own right and undertaking her first radio commitments. She created what she called her "tabloid opera" productions, a series of condensed opera scenes; with a new agent, she tapped into what one reporter called "the current vogue for opera stars as movie and radio attractions." Farrar, who made ten films, had set singers on the path to motion pictures; others, including Carmela, were instrumental in introducing opera to radio. Perhaps the most important of the early broadcasts of music featured Carmela as Amneris in the landmark *Aida* broadcast of Armistice Day 1922 on WEAF in New York, said to be the first complete opera broadcast in the history of radio. It reached radios within a radius of one thousand miles and, Ponselle said in her autobiography, was heard by six hundred thousand people. Anna Roselle, another of Thorner's students, was the Aida, Dimitri Dobkin the Radamès, and Léon Rothier the Ramfis. Giuseppe Bamboschek conducted. A clipping from an unidentified newspaper in Ponselle's earliest scrapbook praises Carmela's inventiveness as the creator of her cameo operas and a pioneer in bringing classical music to radio. One of her most frequently used publicity photos shows her at a microphone, wearing a tailored suit and stylish hat.

Carmela's success may have been partly responsible for Tony Ponzillo's brief return to the vaudeville stage in the early 1920s. Surprisingly, after appearing in smaller houses, he was able to secure one engagement at the important Riverside Theatre in New York, where Romani had first heard Rosa and Carmela. According to Ponselle, he was able to find about seven months of work before he had to admit to himself that he would never have the major career his sisters both desired for him. Like Carmela, Tony was billed as "Ponselle" in his professional ventures in the early 1920s. Like her, he lived in New York, where his wife, Lydia, a wholesale grocer's daughter, had been born and raised. There can be little doubt of her affection for Tony's family; she was the godmother of Tony and Lydia's son, Anthony Gerard Ponzillo, born in 1923. Tony took his family back to Meriden, where he became his father's partner in the coal business and lived with his wife and baby. Ponselle's financial records show that from 1921, if not before, she lent money to Tony; in that year the loan amounted to sixteen hundred dollars.

These two career initiatives on the part of her sister and brother meant that Rosa Ponselle faced her new challenges without their daily support. She then relied on her mother, to whom she wrote often between their visits, on Prilik, her secretary, and Anna Ryan. The soprano's contract status at the Metropolitan was secure through April 1922; on April 10 that year she was reengaged for seventeen weeks in 1922–23, from December 15 (the beginning of rehearsals) through April 22, with the company retaining its option for the tour. Concerts and recitals filled out her schedule.

HE PONSELLE-MILLER LETTERS ～

Just as she was facing these changes in her life, Ponselle found a new friend and colleague in Kenneth E. Miller, a young violinist from Wathena, Kansas, whom she may have met in Saint Louis or in Hays, Kansas, in 1921 but much more likely met in Kansas City on November 30, 1922, when she appeared there with the Saint Louis Symphony. Her program, which Miller kept, included "Pleurez, pleurez, mes yeux" from Massenet's *Le Cid* and "Ernani, involami" from Verdi's *Ernani*. A snapshot of Ponselle with Miller, dated March 1925, has the caption "Ken and Rosa" on the back. It was taken when one of her concert tours took her and Prilik to the Muehlebach Hotel in Kansas City. The soprano is bundled up against the chilly midwestern spring while he wears a simply cut, light-colored suit. Peering earnestly through his glasses, with his hair parted straight down the middle and plastered flat on both sides of his head, Miller is the very image of plains rectitude. One other photograph of him shows him playing the violin in "Langworthy's K.U. Band" in his college days; the other instruments were a saxophone, piano, trombone, banjo, cornet, and drums.

She called him "Ken" and he called her "Mel," perhaps from Melba, the name she had wished to use in her confirmation. Ponselle and Miller rarely met, not more than once or twice a year when she came to Kansas. Her first letter to him dates from early December 1922, and in 1925 the correspondence appears to end; Miller also telephoned when the tenuous connections could be made, by reservation only and after long delays. He also corresponded with Carmela in that period. His and Ponselle's trust in each other makes her letters to him invaluable to a biographer because she is so frank about the responsibilities laid upon her by the Metropolitan management. These letters, when set beside Ponselle's schedule and her financial records, offer a complete picture of the struggling singer's life. As Farrar put it, "It's a dog's life." That was something Ponselle was finding out as she fought her way through the early 1920s.

Because Miller was younger than she by several years, the soprano often reminded him that "you are a school boy still" and urged him not to leave college. By 1923 she was writing "You are going to be a big Wall Street banker some day, aren't you?" But at least at the beginning of his acquaintance with her he cherished the futile hope that one day they might marry. With both her feet solidly planted on New York City soil, Ponselle disabused him of that idea, saying that "by destiny" she had to continue in her career; in one letter she recalled him again to reality by reminding him of her age: she was, she said, "going on in years" (although she was just twenty-five), and her profession made such demands on her that he would face "endless waiting." Ponselle never really let herself think of marriage to Miller; once, when Tony and Lydia Ponzillo's baby was born, she wrote wistfully of longing to have a child of her own. But whenever these issues came up, common sense ruled. She could not give up her career, she said. This was clearly a friendship based on youthful affection; two young musicians who barely knew each other exchanged confidences as he dreamed in vain of a long-term relationship with the great star. Though she kept his photograph in the drawer of her bedside table and, she said, "talked to it" and "kissed it" at night, she never lost sight of the true situation.

Of greatest interest are Ponselle's observations about her career. In December 1922, writing to Miller from the Hotel Windsor in Jacksonville, Florida, she complained about having to spend time with local journalists: "A reporter is waiting for an interview downstairs, and I (very much against my wish) must grant her one, for it is my initial appearance in Jack. and I must make good."

Two weeks later she was "depressed . . . rushed these days, and I am so nervous. . . . I rehearse every evening and all day, so you can imagine how exhausted [I am]." In an undated letter from the same period she declared that she was "back in the big city, resuming all my responsibilities, rather nervous and fidgety. Between rehearsals, costumes, performances, trying to study and memorizing new roles, [it is] some task. . . . [I have to] get up at 7:30 A.M. to get to rehearsals in time, [so I] can scarcely wait all evening [for a telephone call from Miller]."

After singing *Ernani* on Christmas night in 1922, she went home exhausted and did not celebrate the holiday until the following Sunday, six days later. "I gave an *immense* dinner," she wrote. "I also have an Xmas tree now. Santa Claus was exceptionally nice to me. . . . After my rehearsal [today, Thursday], I must go to the doctor's office for my throat is bothering me these days."

"Discouraged" a few days later, on January 2, 1923, she wrote of herself in the third person: "How lonesome Mel is for Ken." She was rehearsing from ten-thirty in the morning to five in the afternoon as a regular schedule and had "an early rehearsal Wednesday morning" for *William Tell*, as she called the opera. "Wish me luck. Then I start rehearsing another new role [for an opera] that takes place on the 20th of this month, *Andrea Chénier*." Her workload doubled as her household expenses soared.

"I am simply worked to death these days," she wrote on January 15, "and not up to my usual standard physically, together with nervousness. . . . I am simply not myself. I am singing [*Guillaume Tell*] tonight. I am taking medicine for my nerves daily and it seemed slow to take effect." And on January 30 she was "on my way to Brooklyn, where I perform [*Guillaume Tell*] this evening. I was 24 last Thursday." Lying about her age, she sent Miller snapshots of her birthday party. Carmela teased her about robbing the cradle.

During the first week in February, on a Sunday night, she wrote, "I just arrived home from a strenuous day's work. . . . I can scarcely hold my eyes open for fatigue." Even in circumstances like these she reminded him not to neglect his studies, but then went on:

You know how busy and nervous I am and how impossible it is for me to relax during this terrible, strenuous season; and how bad I feel lately, just a bundle of nerves. . . . I am a very tired and depressed girl. I am going through the tortures of hell from nervousness this season; and no one but my immediate family and my doctor knows what a mental strain I am working under; and still I must go on and on. I cannot wait for the spring to arrive, when I will go to the [West] Coast for the month of May on my concert tour. And then I do not know whether I will remain here or go to Europe this summer. I would much prefer playing golf on American soil this year . . . but I must go [abroad] sooner or later. Such is life with a career. . . . I am dead to the world. I'm lonesome.

As we shall see, she was facing a major crisis because the Metropolitan was not offering her a new three-year contract; instead, it engaged her for one season only, 1923–24. She got no higher fee and remained on the hated weekly salary, instead of getting a leading singer's performance fee. She signed the new contract on February 15.

As the season wore on, Ponselle became more desperate and weary at meeting the Metropolitan's tight schedules. On the afternoon of March 3, 1923, she wrote to Miller saying, "I am simply out of my mind with work, and now I am to create a new role, [Sélika in Meyerbeer's *L'africaine*], which means constant work and worry. I do not feel well." She described "grippe" and her "several nervous conditions" before concluding: "I must make it downtown in 10 minutes." As we can see from Ponselle's account book, taxis ate up a large part of her income, both in New York and on tour.

Exactly one week later her condition had worsened: "Thursday. Good bye child. Dear you, I'm feeling all wrong, am working myself to distraction and laid up with a cold again. . . . I am so dizzy that I can scarcely see [and] all bandaged up with plasters right now." She had sung Santuzza in *Cavalleria* the night before, with Beniamino Gigli as her tenor. *L'africaine* was twelve days later, on March 21.

One day after the Meyerbeer spectacular, Ponselle stayed in bed until evening. "Last night was the big night," she wrote to Miller, "the premiere performance of *L'Africana* [*sic*], it was quite a hit; but poor me! I am so tired after all that work that I have had within the last few weeks! . . . [Now I have to] prepare myself for my trip to the Coast. . . . I just feel like fleeing from the city into the wilds, but with you on the golf course." On April 8 the Metropolitan, in a letter signed by Gatti's aide, Edward Ziegler, engaged Ponselle for three performances at the end of the season and for the tour to Atlanta and Cleveland.

After a performance of *Cavalleria* on April 8, 1923, Ponselle wrote to her young confidant at two-thirty in the morning, describing "the trying ordeals of the past few weeks" and adding "my responsibility as an artist is tremendous. . . . I don't feel tranquil enough to sleep. . . . Addio, Mel."

Her next letter was written on the Sunset Limited as she and Edith Prilik were rolling through Louisiana en route from Atlanta to the West Coast. She was fighting motion sickness and trying to get to sleep, remembering her incredible feat of singing three operas on three consecutive days on the Metropolitan tour. "[We are] on our way to the Coast. Poor us! In Atlanta we had the time of our lives the whole week long, oh! completely grand! All we did was play, play, play! . . . Of course, I worked too, three roles in three days. Think of it!" The three operas were *Don Carlos* on April 26, *L'africaine* on the twenty-seventh, and *Guillaume Tell* on the twenty-eighth. She expressed no criticism of the management for assigning her such a dreadful schedule, just acceptance.

After she reached the West Coast, Ponselle wrote to Miller again, on May 14, from the Fairmont Hotel in San Francisco. Her first concert, on the thirteenth, had been a "huge success." She loved California—"Some beautiful country!"—and was about to play nine holes of golf. Her next stop was Los Angeles.

From Fort Worth on November 15 she said that she had just left Denver and faced a two-day train ride to Houston. That letter was followed by a Christmas card, signed "Mel."

A gap of almost one year in the collection, as it is preserved, has no record of the soprano's activity in that period. But on December 6, 1924, she wrote, "Hello, Ken," and said that she was "back on the job once more and mighty nervous, due to sing my first *Gioconda,* and don't forget me in your prayers, will you, good Pal?" By this time Miller was dating a local girl, Jeanette.

Ponselle and Miller met again in the spring of 1925, when the soprano's tour took her to Kansas City. But even before arriving there she had taken to heart the problems Miller was having with his new woman friend. "Should you change your mind and decide to marry," she wrote, "don't fail to let me know, or rather, get my advice. Au revoir, Ken, old dear, [from] Mel."

While Ponselle was in Kansas City, Stuart Ross, her accompanist, and Miller handled personal chores such as the delivery of the soprano's dresses from the dry cleaners. After leaving there, she continued to write him fairly regularly, although there were some lapses on both sides of the correspondence. "We are going to Lake Placid for the summer," she said in June 1925. And by October, writing from the Hotel Kimball in Springfield, Massachusetts, she was considering his decision to take over his father's business: "This pal wishes you the best that life has to offer."

Over the years, Ponselle sent Miller several photographs of herself, autographed to him, and kept him informed about news of such family events as the birth of Lydia's and Tony's baby, for whom she served as godmother. Miller could be trusted because he asked nothing of her, save affection, for he soon gave up his boyish dreams of marrying her. Apart from him and a few other friends outside the music business, she remained very much the favored child of her family. Outside their circle, and apart from Romani, Ryan, and Prilik, Ponselle was close to Gennaro Papi, Giovanni Martino, Giovanni Martinelli, and young singers such as Yvonne D'Arle, a Thorner student who joined the Metropolitan in 1921 and remained on the roster until the spring of 1926, singing Musettas and being kept on the reserve list of lyric sopranos.

THE FIFTH-YEAR MILESTONE AND BEYOND ～

Certainly the years after December 1920 found Ponselle at one of the most critical junctures of her professional life, as she established an adult identity for herself and became an independent artist, separate from the image of Caruso. In an interview in May 1922 she spoke of her life in bleak terms: "The story is just a record of a poor girl reaching her goal by a different route than the accepted one." These words do describe Ponselle's problems as she graphically wrote of them in her letters to Kenneth Miller from 1922 to the end of 1925. Her struggle was considerably more difficult than that of a conventionally trained singer; she had indeed taken a "different route" and was finding it exhausting. Yet no matter how frightening the challenge, she persevered and became an idol while keeping all the traits that endeared people to the young Ponselle. Her accomplishments from 1920 to 1937, from her last performance with Caruso through her Norma, the stunning *Don Giovanni*, and finally *La traviata* and *Carmen*, mark a remarkable progress through the repertory. From competence and occasions when she rose to brilliance, she acquired mastery, then artistry and genius.

ONSELLE'S TECHNIQUE AND STUDY METHODS ~

Although Ponselle said little before her retirement about how she sang or how she got into the anatomy of her roles, she was interviewed on these matters later, particularly after she began to coach young singers from the Baltimore Civic Opera. In an interview with Metropolitan Opera bass Jerome Hines, who was writing his book *Great Singers on Great Singing*, Ponselle, who was then ill, let two trusted colleagues help her describe her vocal technique by saying that she kept "a square throat," something Caruso had taught her. "He kept a little stretch in the back of the throat to keep it open, open in the back and relaxed. It feels like a square, but only on the high notes. . . . The palate is high and the back of the tongue flat. This [makes] the square."

When Hines asked specifically about keeping an open throat and asked how she applied this idea to the whole range rather than just to the high notes, as she had mentioned, he was told, "Keep the tone dark." From Romani, who "insisted on the school of Ruffo and Stracciari," she learned to keep a cover on the tone. "I used *moo* in the lower register, pure *moo*, then gradually [went to] *mah*," which she pronounced as *maw*. She added that these tones should be sung "with a slight smile" so that no tension would arise from pursed lips. Hines said that this was not a real smile, not "toothy," but the hint of a smile. "It's a low, round sensation, the *oo*, and all the vowels are based on it." Hines repeated her formula for "the basis of the open throat: the tongue flat in the back, which drops the larynx a bit, and a raised palate. If you cannot sing the *oo* with a slight smile, then the *oo* is wrong."

She emphasized breathing through the nose and mouth, not through nose alone, and relaxing the shoulders. "You widen your chest, upper part of the body relaxed, straight spine, abdomen expanded, back included, all around." The purpose of this support was "to maintain the even flow [of breath], to *appoggiare*, lean on it." She advised leaning into the sound by leaning on the diaphragm. "Push out with the stomach and abdomen during the phrase, not in."

About the placement, she said, "You use the mask, forward. You get the feeling your face is going to come off" from the vibrations. She added that she used chest voice "only when necessary but always in the mask." As she went up the scale, she kept her "mouth more open, jaw dropped, relaxed." When Hines asked her about her beautiful *pianissimo*, he was told that she had always had it, but singers could acquire it by "imagery." "You almost feel as if you're pulling a thread through your nose, and don't ever let it stop."

About vocalizing, she had said that she vocalized in the shower, or "whenever she felt like it," testing her *pianissimo* and "doing a scale or two to see if the voice was there." But she did little vocalizing, save for the "*moo, moo*" and the other vowels that followed it. She also said that she vocalized scales on the word "*addio*."

Igor Chichagov recalled, in a 1997 interview, his many sessions of accompanying her, particularly for her 1954 recordings, and of accompanying her coaching sessions. He said that she had "ultimate freedom of emission, an open throat, without any restrictions. The air was just flowing out, in an unlimited flow, without any obstruction of any kind." He added that she "liked the dark sound" and always began to vocalize with *oo* in the middle register, then moved up until she got to A above the staff, changing the *oo* vowel to *awe* or *maw* as she moved upward. "But she always kept that open throat and that dark sound," he said.

Asked about how she got into the anatomy of her roles, Ponselle said that she learned every note and every line, from the first bar to the last. Chichagov said that when she began to study a new work herself or was coaching young singers, she first read the original source of the plot, if it was available. Notably, she said that when she was studying *Carmen*, she read Prosper Merimée's novella of 1845 "over and over, getting all her ideas from it." "She did a very thorough job of preparing it histrionically," Chichagov said, adding that *Carmen* is the only one of her marked scores that has survived. "*Ernani* is blank; *Tosca* [which she prepared for the Metropolitan but never sang] "has some marks; but her other scores do not have any markings. In her music for her concert repertory, there are marks for breathing." About her pitch, Chichagov said that it was "perfect" and that he occasionally would try to throw her off pitch by moving from one key to another as he accompanied her. "She never budged," he said, "but always remained true to the original and correct pitch. It was almost uncanny."

Ponselle's *Carmen* score, which Chichagov has, includes her written instructions for movement and interpretation on every page. Although it is impossible to include many of her notes here, it is worth mentioning that in the Card Scene, she wrote: "Still impressed by fatal cards, pick up cards and place back in pocket," at the line "*Eh bien? Eh bien, nous essayerons de passer, et nous passerons.*" As Frasquita asks whether the way is clear, Ponselle wrote: "Go get gun. Place on shoulder." She later has "look in daze at cards on table" and "more and more startled." At the words "*La carte impitoyable répétera: 'la mort! Encor! Encor! Toujours la mort!'* " her instructions to herself are: "Throwing down [cards], look into [the] open. [With] both hands, turn card slowly. Creep down slowly, down on floor, throw body way back, stretch right arm with hand pointing to fatal card at the words '*la mort.*' " She also has a note to herself that reads, "Tremolo. 7th chord," then, "F-major."

Because Ponselle was consistent throughout her own career and even in her later career as a coach and teacher, these notes and the interview with Hines may be said to represent her basic understanding of her method. They provide a kind of primer on her technique and artistry.

ℋENDERSON'S VIEWS ✑

In those years, as Ponselle was proving her mettle, the course of her professional development was followed by all the critics, but none was more assiduous than W. J. Henderson of the *New York Sun* in his analysis of her growth as an artist. For nearly two decades he advised, coaxed, praised, threatened, and criticized her and countless other important singers in his columns, monitoring their work like a fond uncle or grandparent. Other critics often took positions directly opposed to Henderson's; this was the case with Ponselle, who sometimes received very favorable reviews from Huneker or Aldrich or, later, Downes that contrasted with Henderson's more severe ones. But the aged Henderson left a detailed record of how she appeared to this dean of New York critics. Henderson, who had known Patti, Tamagno, Maurel, Lilli Lehmann, and the De Reszkes and was reviewing the Metropolitan in the early 1880s, covered Ponselle's debut, lived to see her *Carmen*, and left the *Sun* just as she retired from opera. And while Downes also covered the entire reach of Ponselle's career, first from Boston and then for the *New York Times*, his understanding of the effect of historic voices in nineteenth-century opera could not match Henderson's. It is impossible not to see in this elder among reviewers a strong influence in Ponselle's development, particularly because she paid attention to what he wrote.

Year after year her strengths and weaknesses were the subject of his columns; he was among those who, like Gatti, Romani, and (after 1924) the conductor Tullio Serafin, guided her along a frightening and arduous path. Although Ponselle found Henderson the most intimidating and severest of her critics, he was also the most careful and helpful.

On the occasion of her unprecedented debut he had written:

If Miss Ponselle never sang opera before last night, she must have been born with a ready-made routine. However that may be, she is the possessor of one of the most voluptuous dramatic soprano voices that present-day opera-goers have heard. Some day, doubtless Miss Ponselle will learn how to sing; and then she will be an artist. At this moment, she is almost naive in method. But she has the precious gift of voice; and she has real temperament, not the kind that drives people into acrobatic excursions all over the stage and to wild shrieks of vocal anguish, but the kind that makes itself felt in the eloquent quality of tones and the accentuation of melody. Her debut was very interesting, and, we hope, an incident of the evening having permanent importance.

The relationship between the young Ponselle and the aging Henderson continued as she struggled to master her profession and, as she said, become an "artist" rather than a "performer." His criticisms of her hurt; that she admitted. When he praised her, she welcomed his words with enormous satisfaction. It was clear that he was more concerned over her future than any of the other critics. He followed what he called "her descent" in the early 1920s because, as he said, "she had everything but a sound and resourceful vocal technique," although he swore that he had "never detected anything approaching loss of voice in this singer. [But] she simply did not know how to get her tones out or how to join them together in long, fluent phrases."

Henderson lamented her exploitation by the Metropolitan management and worried at the toll her schedule was taking on her. When "her singing deteriorated" in her third and fourth seasons, he announced that "thousands of opera-goers supposed that something had happened to her great voice. Miss Ponselle one day awakened to a realization of her own condition; and from that time her ascent was steady from the valley into which she had descended from the clouds of glory."

It was perhaps those admonitions that led her to insist on a fairer schedule of rehearsals and performances at the Metropolitan and to find a better balance between work and rest, so she would not find herself exhausted by the demands of opera, concerts, recitals, and recordings, to which she had to add the work of learning the new roles Gatti continually assigned to her.

Glorious indeed were the days after her Gioconda when Henderson began to notice that she was being "restored to the pristine state" of her voice, returning to the level that had captivated her audience in 1918. She was, he noted, an excellent student, fulfilling the maxim "There are no good teachers, only good pupils." Curiously, this was also how Serafin described Ponselle in 1956 in an interview in Florence, when, recalling his own role as her mentor and coach, he said, "Ponselle was an ideal pupil."

Henderson complimented the soprano on having been the first to assess her own needs. "If she had not had the good sense to see her own deficiencies and to set about improving her art, she would have sunk into comparative insignificance in spite of the exceptional voice which nature bestowed upon her."

He also remarked on her wisdom in not attempting to sing the German repertory. "She is without doubt the foremost dramatic soprano of Italian opera. She does not sing German operas, and very wisely. Her artistic bent, her mind and her feeling do not run in their channels.—That is, so far as we can judge from observing her from our age-long aerie at the left end of a certain orchestra row."

After her first performances in Spontini's *La vestale* and in Bellini's *Norma* he stopped writing of "Ponselle, the singer" and began to expand on his opinion of "the artist." "Nor does this watcher of the stars believe that Miss Ponselle's Norma has yet reached its limit. The artist will surely confess to herself that she had not yet penetrated fully the secret of the classic recitative, which, when superficially sung, seems to be a heavy deterrent to the progress of an opera. Recitatives are almost uniformly badly sung at the Metropolitan. Miss Ponselle's best achievement in this misunderstood department of lyric drama was not in Norma but in her Donna Anna." Then he stepped back a pace: "But who cares? As long as Miss Ponselle can sing her arias with all the opulence of that gorgeous voice, she need not concern herself with the matters which the artists of [Giuditta] Pasta's day took so seriously."

Although Henderson later took Ponselle to task for her Violetta in *La traviata* and reviewed her Carmen, she said that his most important review of her was of *Norma*, "one of the finest reviews I ever received." He wrote that she had created a characterization "which will increase her fame and which deepens the impression created in recent seasons that the ripening of her talent has been the result of a growing sincerity of purpose and earnest study. . . . The 'Casta Diva' was a genuinely beautiful piece of singing."

This from Henderson, who had, in a sense, walked beside her from *Forza* to this *Norma*. Ponselle said that after she read this review, "at last I felt that I'd made the transition from a singer to an artist."

In 1930, again in the *Sun*, Henderson summed up her achievement in overcoming the obstacles to her growth and becoming an incomparable artist: "No doubt someone helped her. . . . But Rosa Ponselle's attainment of the level she carved out [for] her Giulia in *La vestale* and her *Norma* is due first and last to Rosa Ponselle."

Henderson's sensitive analysis of the many years of this career, as Ponselle battled for her place at the Metropolitan, fought to preserve her voice, and pushed her repertory outward in such unexpected directions that even hardened critics were stunned at her daring, portrays her struggle far more accurately than all her admirers did by laying their encomiums upon her.

Ponselle, evaluating her own situation at the time of Caruso's retirement, said that she "had a great voice" but that her "artistic growth" was still in doubt. In the backstage world of hyperbole and self-deception, such a level-headed and honest assessment is extraordinary, particularly in a young person whose fame had been trumpeted from the pages of large and small newspapers across this country. No small debt was owed to Gatti and to Romani throughout her career and to Serafin after 1924, but Ponselle, as Henderson correctly observed, created herself.

BROADENING THE REPERTORY ⁓

Even before Caruso's death, Ponselle had sung her first Maddalena, in *Andrea Chénier* on April 25 in Atlanta on the 1921 tour. When asked, she said later that she believed that Gatti had not originally intended to produce it for Caruso with her in the leading soprano role. In any case, its Metropolitan premiere came in March 1921 with Danise, Muzio, and Gigli, who had made his debut as Faust in Boito's *Mefistofele* the previous November. Ponselle's tenor in Atlanta was Crimi; Danise repeated his Gérard. She also sang the second Aida of her career in that city with Crimi, Claussen, and Danise. By relying on Martinelli, a Metropolitan veteran, Crimi, who had made his debut just before Ponselle, and Gigli, Gatti sought to fill the void left by Caruso. Later he added Toscanini's favorite, Aureliano Pertile, to the Metropolitan's tenor roster. Several American singers also took over some of the dead star's assignments, but none of these men ever equaled or surpassed Caruso, whose memory remained sacrosanct.

Ponselle was by this time comfortably situated in her large new apartment, number 7-C at 260 Riverside Drive. On the south side of a building that still faces Ninety-eighth Street and the park, the flat has a long balcony and a view of the Hudson River. Anna Ryan, whom Ponselle helped with monetary gifts, was also still teaching her prize pupil and receiving fifty-two dollars a month for the music lessons. Ponselle also gave Ryan a gift of one hundred dollars in January 1921 and seventy dollars a month for "house" in February. Prilik and Romani were always nearby, while Ponselle's mother became an ever more frequent visitor in New York. Freed by having Tony and Lydia living in Meriden, she could be nearer to her daughter than she had been in the earlier years of Ponselle's career. They all spent some summers at Lake Placid and in returns to the New Haven area and Pine Orchard. As always, the soprano's "vacations" were dedicated to study and athletics.

For 1921–22 Gatti had assigned her the new production of *Ernani,* thus continuing his program of offering the Metropolitan audience many of the Verdi operas that were half forgotten or altogether unknown in North America. Another work on Ponselle's calendar was the Metropolitan Opera premiere of Edouard Lalo's *Le roi d'Ys,* composed in 1888. Romani coached her for both works. In the September recording sessions with him as conductor, the first of which took place just one month after Caruso's death, Ponselle recorded, among other numbers, Romani's arrangement of "The

Rosa Ponselle in a publicity photograph taken about 1918, when she was twenty-one, preparing for her Metropolitan Opera debut.

(Credit: Robert Tollett)

The Ponzillo family in their backyard in Meriden, Connecticut.
FRONT ROW: *Ben Ponzillo, his wife, Maddalena Conte Ponzillo, and their daughter Rosa.*
BACK ROW: *Their son, Anthony (Tony), and oldest child, Carmela.*
The pet dogs were Bessie (left), who remained in Meriden, and Bush (center),
brought to New York by Carmela and Rosa.
(Credit: James A. Drake)

Anna M. Ryan (1874-1943), organist and
choir director in the Ponzillo's parish
church, Our Lady of Mount Carmel in
Meriden. Teacher of all three Ponzillo
children, she helped Carmela as she was
studying voice and launching her career
in New York, then lived with both sisters
until 1936, when Rosa married. Anna
Ryan then remained with Carmela until
1941, when she was placed in a nursing
home with Rosa paying her expenses.
(Credit: Anna M. Ryan–James Edgar Ryan
Scrapbook II, courtesy of James Ryan Mulvey)

ABOVE LEFT
Carmela (left) *and Rosa Ponzillo in vaudeville days.*
(Credit: Robert Tollett)

ABOVE RIGHT
Carmela Ponzillo as she appeared in vaudeville. As early as 1905 she was advertising herself as a "vocalist" in the Meriden city directory.
(Credit: Metropolitan Opera Archives and Robert Tuggle)

LEFT
Young Rosa Ponselle on vacation, where she spent some summers preparing her roles with Romano Romani.
(Credit: Metropolitan Opera Archives and Robert Tuggle)

The Ponzillo Sisters, with (left) *Carmela, who designed their headbands for their first appearance at the Palace Theater in 1916, and* (right) *Rosa.*

(Credit: The Rosa Ponselle Museum, Meriden, Conn., and Robert Cyr)

FACING PAGE
Ponselle in the second act of her debut role, Leonora in Verdi's La Forza del destino, *Metropolitan Opera, November 1918.*

(Credit: Metropolitan Opera Archives)

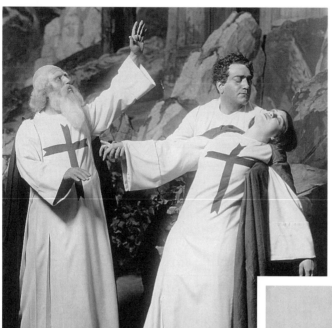

The last act of La forza del destino *at the Metropolitan, with Adamo Didur, Enrico Caruso, and Ponselle.*

(Credit: Metropolitan Opera Archives)

RIGHT

Ponselle's second role at the Met: Santuzza in Mascagni's Cavalleria rusticana, *which she sang in December 1918, in a Metropolitan Opera performance in Philadelphia. After repeating it in Atlanta on the spring tour of 1919, she first sang it in the opera house in New York in 1921.*

(Credit: Metropolitan Opera Archives)

Rachel in Halévy's La juive *was the second of Ponselle's roles with Caruso, who sang Eléazar in this 1919 production.*

(Credit: Metropolitan Opera Archives)

Ponselle, her brother, Tony, and their mother in the kitchen in Rosa and Carmela's apartment at 260 Riverside Drive in New York. In the early 1920s they often invited friends to dinner and also celebrated Rosa's January birthdays with spaghetti dinners.
(Credit: *Opera News*)

Ponselle with Giacomo Puccini in Viareggio, summer 1924. The composer died in November that year.
(Credit: *Opera News*)

FACING PAGE
Ponselle as Elvira in Verdi's Ernani, *which she first performed at the Metropolitan in December 1921.*
(Credit: Metropolitan Opera Archives)

Antonio Puccini, the composer's son, photographed with Ponselle and Romano Romani, Viareggio, 1924. In her arms Ponselle has the little fox that she later succeeded in smuggling through customs in New York.

(Credit: Metropolitan Opera Archives)

As Giulia in La Vestale, *which
Ponselle sang at the Metropolitan
in 1925 and, in 1933, in Florence for
the first Maggio Musicale
Fiorentino.*
(Credit: *Opera News*)

RIGHT, BELOW
Ponselle in a concert gown, 1925.
(Credit: *Opera News*)

ABOVE LEFT
Ponselle at Lake Placid, where she studied
Norma *in the summer of 1927 with Romani
and Marion Telva, her Adalgisa.*
(Credit: Metropolitan Opera Archives and Robert
Tuggle)

ABOVE RIGHT
*Ponselle with a friend, Helen Podeska
Freman, 1931.*
(Credit: Metropolitan Opera Archives)

RIGHT & FACING PAGE
Ponselle as Violetta in Verdi's La traviata,
*which she first sang in the Royal Opera House
at Covent Garden, London, and then brought
to the Metropolitan in January 1931. She is
seen here in act 2* (facing page) *and act 3*
(right).
(Credit: *Opera News*)

ABOVE LEFT
Ponselle in the title role of Ponchielli's La
Gioconda, *which she first sang at the
Metropolitan Opera in December 1924.*
(Credit: Metropolitan Opera Archives)

ABOVE RIGHT
Carmela Ponselle as Laura in La Gioconda
at the Metropolitan Opera, 1932.
(Credit: *Opera News*)

RIGHT
*Ponselle with tenor Giovanni Martinelli dur-
ing a benefit for the Italian Welfare League
on board the liner* Il Conte di Savoia, *1932.*
(Credit: Metropolitan Opera Archives)

Composite publicity photograph of Ponselle as Carmen, which she performed at the Metropolitan in 1935-1936 and 1936-1937.

(Credit: Robert Tollett)

Ponselle at her home, Villa Pace, near Baltimore. After her last performance with the Metropolitan in April 1937, she moved to Maryland with her husband and remained there after their divorce. She was Artistic Director of the Baltimore Civic Opera for nearly 30 years.

(Credit: Robert Tollett)

Beautiful Blue Danube." Hearing it, no one could doubt her ability to dispatch the planned *Ernani* with ease. Because she had convinced the powers at Columbia Records to let Carmela replace Barbara Maurel as the mezzo-soprano in some of her sessions, we also have the sisters' marvelously unaffected and heartfelt version of " 'O Sole Mio." On it, as Ponselle and many others have said, it is almost impossible to distinguish one sister's voice from the other's, and it is easy to see how Carmela could include soprano arias from *Tosca* and other operas in her own concerts. Like Rosa's earlier recording of "Maria, Marì," this " 'O Sole Mio" is authentic Neapolitan popular music at its consecrated best.

A much more serious commitment was made in November 1921, when President Warren G. Harding asked Ponselle to sing at the dedication of the Tomb of the Unknown Soldier, the official commemoration of the close of World War I. Held in Arlington National Cemetery on Armistice Day, the program also included Louise Homer and Morgan Kingston. Because newspapers often headlined Ponselle as "Miss Columbia," America's darling, she was a natural choice as the featured soprano. Homer, who had joined the Metropolitan in 1900, had long since become an American favorite. Ponselle's solo on that day was "I Know That My Redeemer Liveth" from Handel's *Messiah*. Recalling that moment in a later interview, she said that she was so overcome with emotion that she could barely get through it. Metropolitan audiences were already familiar with her in other sacred works, Verdi's Requiem and Rossini's Stabat Mater and Messe solennelle, but this was Ponselle's emergence as something greater, the voice of faith and promise for her country in a national commemorative event.

One week later, again in the Metropolitan's Brooklyn Academy productions, she sang *Aida*. Her first Santuzza in the opera house had come in January 1921, with Gigli as her Turiddu. They repeated *Cavalleria* in Brooklyn later that season and again in New York in November. Of Santuzza, Ponselle said that it and Carmen were the two easiest roles for her to sing, the former because it lay squarely in the middle of her voice. She also was quoted in *Opera Quarterly* in the autumn of 1993 as saying that *Ernani* was easy for her, although she found no dramatic challenge in it. "Just stock

stuff" like *Luisa Miller*, she said. "Ernani, involami" was "almost like a vo-
calise" because it, like *Cavalleria*, lay perfectly for her. As Elvira to Martinelli's Ernani in Gatti's new production of the opera on December 8, 1921, she
found herself in confident company, for this had been the role of the tenor's
debut in opera, in 1910 at the Teatro dal Verme in Milan. As Puccini's choice
for Dick Johnson in the European premiere of *La fanciulla del West* in Rome
one year later, he had won a reputation that carried him to Covent Garden
in 1912 and to the Metropolitan in 1913. Steadfast beyond any impresario's
hope for him, Martinelli became the rock on which countless productions
were founded. In the course of his four-decade career he kept his stentorian
voice and sound technique in fine condition and survived to master Otello,
the pinnacle of his last years on the stage. He also conquered Tristan, which
he sang to Flagstad's Isolde in 1939, but his true genius lay in the Italian
tenor repertory.

After the successful run of *Don Carlos*, which had its Metropolitan premiere on December 23, 1920, Gatti cast Ponselle and Martinelli in *Ernani*
with Mardones as Silva and Danise as Don Carlo, soon to be replaced by
Titta Ruffo, who had been scheduled to sing the premiere but was ill and
did not appear until later. Gennaro Papi, who loved Ponselle and respected
her musicianship, conducted *Ernani*, letting her make a veritable star turn
out of "Ernani, involami." She later recalled how he gave her free rein in
the aria, waiting for her to give him the cues. Her 1922 Columbia recording
of it was later judged to be one of her finest, while a 1927 Victor issue of it
displays the supple, pliant voice with a slightly darker hue. Even though she
said she found *Ernani* easy, her reviews in 1921 were not particularly good.
Aldrich of the *Times* faulted her for not understanding Verdi's style and
neglecting legato singing. She "dismembered" the aria in an attempt to dra-
matize it. Not surprisingly, this same criticism had been made about many
sopranos of Verdi's own day, as they sang in his "new and unfamiliar style,"
and it was made again later when Ponselle sang Violetta in *Traviata* in 1931.
Aldrich, like Krehbiel, Huneker, and Henderson, had heard such sopranos
as Patti, Sembrich, and Melba in Verdi scores that demanded florid singing
and seemed not to understand how a heavier and more dramatic singer
could do justice to them.

Early and late in the 1921–22 season Gatti returned *Forza* to the repertory, first with Crimi and Manuel Salazar and later with Martinelli singing
Caruso's role, Don Alvaro; Danise sang Don Carlo; Mardones repeated his
classical Padre Guardiano, while Raymonde Delaunois and Jeanne Gordon
were cast as Preziosilla for the two performances. In all, the season brought
Ponselle the relief of a light schedule in opera, for she sang only twenty-
three times for the Metropolitan that year, and four of those were opera
house concerts, in which she was responsible for only one or two numbers.
She also sang fourteen concerts outside New York in 1921.

Ponselle's account book, which is in the Special Collections of the Music
Division of the New York Public Library for the Performing Arts, is rich in
details about her life. It begins in 1921. In January and February that year
her salary from the Metropolitan was $1,714.28 every fortnight until February
28. Thorner was paid $139.28 each time the Metropolitan paid her. The Met-
ropolitan also paid her a flat fee of $800 for the "Atlanta Georgia season"; of
that, Thorner got $65. Her standard concert fee was $800. She sang fourteen
concerts at this fee between March 11 and April 21, covering the country
from Georgia and Alabama to Massachusetts, upstate New York, Rhode Island, North Carolina, and Washington, D.C. These concerts seem to have
been under Ponselle's old contract with Thorner. In that same period, however, Samuel Geneen of National Concerts secured an engagement at the
prestigious Rubinstein Club in New York City for $1,500, out of which she
paid him $375 as a commission. When she sang a recital under National's
management in New Haven in April, her fee was an astonishing $2,000, but
again she paid 25 percent to National Concerts. A recital in Bridgeport, also
in April and also under National, again carried a fee of $2,000 and a com-
mission of $500 to National. Her extremely complex relationship with Na-
tional and Geneen is discussed in some detail later; here it is enough to note
that Ponselle was certainly being booked by Geneen as early as March 19,
1921. For each recital she had to pay her own accompanist: $110 for Mont-
gomery, Alabama, $50 for each of the two Connecticut engagements.

The soprano returned to the concert and recital circuit in May, after the
Metropolitan tour, when she appeared in Houston, Denver, Yonkers, and

Hays, Kansas. Again in the fall before the 1921–22 Metropolitan season she sang in Maine, Massachusetts, Pennsylvania, New Jersey, Ohio, and North Carolina, being paid a fee of $1,000 for each concert. Again, these were evidently booked by Thorner, because her total commissions paid to National that year were $1,375 for the three recitals in the spring. The total fees paid to Thorner were $1,202.46.

Ponselle had fourteen bills for "gowns and wraps," including several that are easily identifiable in the Mishkin photographs of that period. "Fans, shoes and hosiery" cost her $703.50 that year, while "tights, wigs and make-up" were listed separately and totaled $660.50. Personal items such as a "negligée for dressing room" and a "negligée for concert tour" were also listed separately. Her total expense for "gowns" was $5,356. She was paying for "coaching lessons, French lessons, Italian lessons and music lessons"; later Russian and Hebrew were also added. The language lessons coast $1,100 in 1921. Edith Prilik got $400 for her services between January and June, then was not paid for the summer. For the period October–December she was paid $150; Ponselle also provided her room and board for nine months a year. Maids in the Metropolitan dressing rooms got about $100 a month; maids in hotels during the concert tour were paid a total of $350 in tips for two months. "Travel for two people" on the concert tour cost $2,052.45. Ponselle's taxi fares in New York City ran about $150 a month during the opera season and $500 for the four months of concerts and recitals. "Music for professional use" cost the soprano $450 for just one year, but "sheet music" cost $300. Her "professional entertaining" cost about $1,500 a year. "Gifts" were $1,390.63.

Among the professionals whose services Ponselle used were "throat specialists," paid $600 between January and May 1921. "Medicine for throat" cost $180 in September alone. A "musical coach for opera" got $1,200, while her "coach for concert programs" cost $900; she was also paying for "drama coaching." Her professional dry cleaning and laundry cost $300 a year. Advertising in *Musical America*, the *Musical Courier*, and other trade periodicals cost a total of $6,082.70; photographs came to $1,053.70. She made substantial payments, as much as $70 or $80 a month, for "Metropolitan tickets." On January 31, 1922, Romani was paid $2,100 for his 1921 coaching. Ponselle also had a publicity agent named Mr. Dunn. In 1921 none of her personal expenses are listed, though they do appear in later years. From later entries we learn that her apartment cost her $262.59 a month for rent, with payments of about $5 to $7 to the Consolidated Gas Company and upward of $21 to New York Telephone. One entry appears in 1921 for "bad debts" at $2,000. The money was apparently lent to a colleague and not to Tony Ponzillo, whose entries are separate.

At the end of the 1921 entries the figures are given for Ponselle's income: $13,460.67 from the Metropolitan Opera and $9,157.16 from the Columbia Graphophone Company. Curiously, her concert and recital fees are not individually given in this accounting; but when they are added up, they come to $8,000 for ten concerts, $4,000 for the two recitals in Connecticut, and $1,015 for the single New York recital. The autumn recitals and concerts totaled $9,000.

By 1922 the account book shows that the Metropolitan was paying her $2,142.85 on the fifteenth of every month and a similar sum on the last day of the month for January and February. Again Thorner was assigned his commission: $214.85 out of every paycheck. Ponselle also paid income tax in 1919 and 1920. It is clear that she had saved enough to make some investments because she received interest in 1921 from Canadian Grand Trunk Railroad, several oil companies, New York Telephone, and several banks. This said, one must add that her expenses were high and that only her careful management permitted her to make any profit at all in these early years. It is also to her credit that there are entries for "charity," including payments of $100 to Anna Ryan and $50 to anonymous beneficiaries.

The account record for 1922 shows that Ponselle received $10,633.95 from the Metropolitan, $12,487.50 from Columbia Graphophone, $44,866.72 from concerts, and $1,475 interest on investments, for a total of $69,463.17. Her professional expenses totaled $54,532.16, and her household and personal expenses were $10,490.99. She paid $617 for income tax and actually cleared only about $3,800 for the entire year. Seeing these figures, one realizes that she lived as she did because she could not afford a grander lifestyle at that time; because her modesty and simplicity were then her most appealing traits, her way of living and her character made an attractive match.

Ponselle's Italian-American household is very much in evidence in snapshots taken over the years. A fine example of how she entertained is seen at her party of 1922, when she celebrated her twenty-fifth birthday at home, cooking spaghetti at her mother's side in the kitchen at 260 Riverside. Carmela helped to entertain the guests; among them were Romani, Martinelli, De Luca, Ruffo, Martino, the stage director and singer Armando Agnini, Papi, Moranzoni, and the only woman guest in evidence, Yvonne D'Arle. Simplicity set the tone; these people were obviously comfortable with each other at this family-style dinner. The Metropolitan season was in full swing, with Ponselle singing *Aida* in Brooklyn, *Cavalleria*, *Ernani*, *Le roi d'Ys*, and *Don Carlos* in the weeks before she turned twenty-five. By the last week in April she had added her twentieth performance of *Forza*, this time with Martinelli. The season was ending with *Ernani*, scheduled for the Metropolitan tour. The empty days on Ponselle's calendar were filled with concerts, recitals, and recordings.

Gatti, ever on the search for talent, had presented two sopranos in their Met debuts in 1921–22: Amelita Galli-Curci, who was already famous in America, and Maria Jeritza, Otto Kahn's favorite, a lyric-dramatic soprano. Both took column inches away from Ponselle in newspapers all over America, although their Metropolitan debuts received surprisingly compromised reviews. Richard Aldrich wrote in the *New York Times* that Galli-Curci "was not one who could be compared with some of the great singers who have been heard in the years gone by." Another reviewer described her performance as "not that of a great operatic star." As assessments of a Metropolitan Opera opening-night *Traviata* by an already celebrated singer, these could hardly have been worse.

American knew Galli-Curci from her Victor records, which spun on old, wind-up Victrolas everywhere; New York remembered her from her appearances at the Lexington Avenue Theatre during the Chicago company's tenure there. The journalist Mabel Wagnalls wrote of her suite, an aerie on the twentieth floor of the Hotel Ambassador, where photographers were taking "flash-light photos" and the soprano's evening gowns were spilling out of suitcases, "bursting forth" in an "upheaval of flaming colors; creations in yellow, orange and rose, with comet-like trains trailing over the parapets [and] whole cloud banks of chiffon and tossed-up tulle." She said that Thorner had saved Galli-Curci from oblivion, "piloting her at once to Campanini, who was then directing the Chicago Opera."

Maria Jeritza fared much better with the critics but was still criticized for a voice that "degenerated unpleasantly into stridency." She was also faulted for her tendency to "scoop" her tones. The critics did praise her brilliant characterization of Marietta in Erich Korngold's *Die Tote Stadt*, while praising her bold, blonde beauty. Quaintance Eaton marked Jeritza's debut as a signal that "*echt deutsche* opera had at last penetrated the censorship" imposed on German works. If Galli-Curci was no threat to Ponselle, Jeritza surely was, because of the sensation she created and because she claimed so many works as her own. In her first three seasons at the Metropolitan, Jeritza sang more than ten roles. In her first season she sang her first Santuzza in *Cavalleria*, a part on which Ponselle had set her own seal. Although it seemed she could never steal *Forza*, *Don Carlos*, or *Ernani*, with Jeritza one could never predict how far she might go.

In her style of living and relentless self-promotion she was utterly unlike Ponselle. Wagnalls described the glamorous Jeritza treating the Hotel Saint Regis as her private fief. Royally ensconced on the fourteenth floor, she used most of the hall to store her twelve "huge, stout wardrobe trunks" with the initials "MPJ" emblazoned in red on each. "She is the Dawn, Aurora herself," Wagnalls gushed. The soprano described her daily lessons from Giorgio Polacco, who was then an assistant at the Metropolitan, and with Marcella Sembrich. "Of course I take lessons," Jeritza said, adding that she was also studying English three times a week. Much of the interview was about Wagner and concert tours, but Jeritza also spoke of her revolutionary approach to the second act of *Tosca*, where she "cast caution and coiffure to the winds—diamonds, too. Her hair tumbled to her waist; her tiara fell to the floor." This was an actress who sang "Vissi d'arte" lying flat on the stage, a seasoned navigator on the operatic seas.

The support of Otto Kahn, who sponsored both Jeritza and Korngold, seemed to bode ill for the Italian wing at the Metropolitan. Kahn had for years urged Gatti to feature Mozart and the French repertory and had backed many American composers; now he turned his energies toward German opera. As early as 1919 he had prodded Gatti to secure the rights to the best modern works by Slavic and German composers; with the war over and a warmer reception being given to Wagner, he redoubled his efforts. Kahn's devotion to Jeritza led not just to this first production of the work of Korngold, whom Kahn had been promoting since 1916, but also to a number of large-scale productions staged for her or featuring her in a leading role. They included *Die Walküre, Lohengrin, Der Rosenkavalier* and *Tannhäuser.* Jeritza also sang the title role in *Fedora* and added other operas as the decade progressed. Her opening nights were 1922, 1923 and 1927: *Tosca, Thaïs* and *Turandot.*

Ponselle, in one interview about her life published in *Opera Quarterly,* denied that she and Jeritza were ever rivals and said that they had spent time together at Villa Pace, long after both were retired; but she admitted that they had had "a run-in or two" during Jeritza's tenure at the Metropolitan. In fact, the presence of the glamorous Czech soprano loomed large in the first years of Ponselle's career, especially in the early 1920s. Jeritza, whom Gatti had first met at the Hotel Excelsior in Rome in 1914, lived in a style that Ponselle's salary did not permit. She had had a career in Europe and let it be known that she had sung one of Ponselle's best roles, Rachel in *La juive,* with Leo Slezak. But she clearly looked down on the young Italian-American soprano. Although Jeritza mentioned Alda, Garden, and Farrar in the first edition of *Sunlight and Song,* the autobiography she published in 1924, she said nothing of Ponselle, even though she referred somewhat dismissively to "American girl singers."

In 1922–23 Gatti also brought Elisabeth Rethberg, a German soprano who had made her debut in Dresden in 1915 and had come to the Metropolitan fully prepared to sing German and Italian roles. Although she and Ponselle became fast friends, she also proved to be something of a menace to the American soprano's career, showing at the start that she could dispatch *Aida* without a qualm. She later added *Guillaume Tell* and *Andrea Chénier* to her repertory. Ponselle was never jealous of Rethberg. On the contrary, she said, when Rethberg was onstage she sometimes stood in the wings, reveling in the sheer beauty of her voice.

All three of these new additions to the roster carried considerable weight because they came with extensive European experience and were older than Ponselle; Galli-Curci had been born in 1882, Jeritza in 1887, and Rethberg in 1894. Although Ponselle had sung almost a hundred times for the Metropolitan by the end of the 1921–22 season and had been given only major roles, she remained at risk in this period, when she might easily have slipped in the presence of such sophisticated artists. Apart from the sacred works such as Verdi's Requiem and Rossini's Stabat Mater, she remained in the realm of songs and arias, ensembles and scenes for many of her Metropolitan Opera House concert appearances, and not until the 1930s did Ponselle undertake "Glück das mir verlieb" from *Die Tote Stadt*, Jeritza's private domain, "Divinités du Styx" from Gluck's *Alceste*, and "Prosteétye vi kholmí" from Tchaikovsky's *Orleanskaya deva*. Her caution was surely her greatest asset at this time, as she held to her philosophy of using her voice in what she called "a measured way" and resisted the temptation to push. By not overreaching she could be confident of success in each professional step, while protecting herself from failure and from being let go under the "fortnight-to-fortnight" renewal clauses in her contract.

The proof that Gatti and his young soprano acted wisely in the early 1920s is found in his choice for the opening night assignments: 1921 went to Galli-Curci, who sang *Traviata*, 1922 to Jeritza's sensational Tosca, 1923 to her Thaïs, and 1924 to Rethberg's Aida. Everyone knew how important it was to singers to secure the opening nights for themselves; that Ponselle did not attain this honor from 1920, when she sang *La juive* with Caruso, until 1925 shows how she was seen—as a developing singer being eased upward by Gatti in a way that might give her a long career. As she perhaps realized, this was an advantage, not a handicap. Any dangerous forcing of her voice would have proved ruinous, particularly when she was overburdened with learning, rehearsing, and performing so many roles.

In her own words, it was "a long, uphill journey." Much to her credit, she did mature at a steady pace as a singer and actress. The measure of her growth can be better taken in the seasons when Gatti finally assigned her the opening nights, in 1925, 1926, 1928, and 1931. With them Ponselle set a Metropolitan record for the decade. In these seasons and those that followed she showed that her family's and her mentors' hopes for her were fully realized; in the winter of 1922–23, however, she had to face the possibility that the Metropolitan might not keep her under contract. As mentioned in the context of Ponselle's letters to Kenneth Miller, when the negotiations were concluded, the best she could get from the Met was a one-year contract, not the three-year commitment that was customary for leading singers. This was particularly disappointing because her old contract of April 15, 1920, had been for three seasons. But now, in February 1923, she settled for a one-season commitment, and even it covered only fifteen performances in a two-month period, from December 17, 1923, until February 16, 1924. She was to report for rehearsals on December 10. Her fee was twelve hundred dollars per week, to be paid fortnightly.

This contract has a strange "open renewal clause" under a typed insert numbered 26: "The Company reserves the right to prolong the term of this engagement in each season for one or two additional weeks, either at the end of the period of engagement of the Artist, or for the last two weeks of the opera season, upon the same terms, by giving written notice to the Artist on or before January 15th." This clause meant in effect that the singer could not accept concert and recital engagements for those two periods; if the Metropolitan did not pick up its option, fees would be lost and income seriously reduced.

The next clause reads: "It is especially agreed that the Artist shall not sing in opera with any other opera company, in the territory covered by this agreement, from the date of signing of this agreement [February 15, 1923] until May 1, 1926, in case the Artist is re-engaged for the season 1925–1926, or until May 1, 1927, in case the Artist is re-engaged for the season 1926–1927, without the written consent of the Company."

The words "in case the Artist is re-engaged" read like a potential threat, particularly to a singer who had been so widely publicized as the next great dramatic soprano and the "nation's new star." The Metropolitan clearly had reservations about Ponselle, for had the company been convinced that she had a future with it, she would have been offered another three-year contract like her first one. What she got instead was something provisional. According to Robert Tuggle, archivist of the Metropolitan Opera, "It was almost as if they were putting her on probation. Her fee was not raised, nor was she given the prestigious per-performance rate." While we may never know why Gatti seemed not to want to keep her on the roster for more than one season, it is possible that the presence of Maria Jeritza, Elisabeth Rethberg, Frances Peralta, and others led the management to conclude that they did not need Ponselle any longer. Nonetheless, she was asked to prepare nineteen roles in three languages and three sacred works in Latin. These were Sélika in *L'africaine*, the title roles in *Aida* and *Tosca*, Amelia in *Un ballo in maschera*, Santuzza in *Cavalleria*, the Leonoras of *Forza* and *Trovatore*, Elisabetta in *Don Carlos*, Maddalena de Coigny in *Andrea Chénier*, Fiora in *L'amore dei tre re*, Elvira in *Ernani*, Margherita and Elena in *Mefistofele*, Mathilde in *Guillaume Tell*, Rachel in *La juive*, Margared in *Le roi d'Ys*, and Rezia in *Oberon*. *La Gioconda*, an opera she had had to prepare years before but had never sung, was planned for the upcoming season and listed in her new contract. The sacred works were Verdi's Requiem and Rossini's Stabat Mater and mass.

Before Ponselle's return, on December 17, 1923, in *Chénier*, Rethberg took over Aida and Mathilde in *Tell*; Easton sang Maddalena in *Chénier*, Peralta became the *Forza* Leonora and Elena in *Mefistofele*, Alda continued as Margherita in *Mefistofele*, Marcella Roessler sang *Cavalleria*, and Jeritza continued as Tosca. She also made her mark in Giordano's *Fedora*.

In the very time that Ponselle faced these more experienced rivals, her own personal expenses soared, from an average of about $500 a month in 1921 to $1,108 in 1922 and between $1,700 and $2,040 in 1924. She seems to have paid Romani in lump sums of $2,100 (on January 31, 1921) or $300 (in the spring of 1924) and in individual payments for his coaching sessions, on one occasion $45 and on another, $10. Wilfrid Pelletier was paid $20 for each coaching session in the French repertory; another coach, K. Faith, or Fain, was paid $17; and Anna Ryan, as we have seen, was paid $52 "for coaching." Evening and concert gowns from Bendel's and Milgrim's, street clothes made by a Mrs. Pottish, and shoes from I. Miller were other necessary expenses in 1922.

$\mathscr{M}$ANAGEMENT ～

Between 1921 and 1924, years when Ponselle's career hung in the balance, her relationship with Thorner deteriorated as Samuel Geneen and other agents courted her. As we shall see, she was also reconsidering her first recording contract with Columbia and hoping to move to Victor. Financial burdens already mentioned weighed heavily on all decisions then, for her income fell from a gross of $69,463.17 in 1922 to $66,618 in 1923. While her expenses dropped for some items, because she had invested so heavily in gowns, wigs, and other theatrical gear in 1922, she had yet another commission to pay: $10,547.88 to National Concerts. By this time Ponselle had also decided to have her own costumes made whenever she wished to replace the unbecoming ones the Metropolitan offered her. Ponselle's battle to control her weight meant that costly alterations to costumes had to be made almost every year. She bought her own stage jewelry as needed and paid travel expenses when she took her mother or sister on tour. The costs mounted: for Romani, Pelletier, the language and dramatic coaches; for the publicity agent, Dunn; for the doctors and, sometimes, the opera house nurse; for her secretary and accompanists; and for the various tips, gifts, and small purchases, as well as her personal expenses, which grew larger each year. So did the agent's percentages paid to Thorner, for although Ponselle's contract with him expired in September 1922, he went on acting as her manager for some of her bookings, even into 1924.

The complete record in the New York Supreme Court appellate division from 1928 reveals the friction and open warfare that gradually poisoned the soprano's relationship to Thorner from about 1923 onward. In her oral and written agreements with him, dating from December 1917 and early June

1918, she promised to pay him 10 percent of her fees for "acting as her representative and manager." As we have seen, she authorized the Metropolitan to set aside a percentage of all her fees there for Thorner; inexplicably, he actually received a smaller percentage than the 10 percent agreed upon.

Later, on September 30, 1918, she sent Thorner a formal letter that begins with this: "I hereby retain you as my exclusive manager and representative for a term of four years, to arrange for me with managers of grand opera, concerts, recitals and phonograph or speaking machine companies."

The opening of the second paragraph—"As compensation for your work and lessons you have given and shall continue to give me"—implies that she had not paid Thorner for his sessions in 1917 and 1918. There is nothing unusual about this situation. Every teacher and coach who helps a promising young singer without being paid for the lessons and who then succeeds in finding work for that pupil believes that he or she has "created" the performer in question; Thorner was no different from the hundreds of others who have, over the centuries, acted first as voice teachers or coaches and then as managers for their discoveries. Galli-Curci, who said in many early interviews that Thorner had raised her from oblivion in Italy to celebrity and thanked him for getting her into the Chicago Opera, became furious with him when he advertised himself in trade magazines as her "voice teacher" and later sued him to prevent him from publicizing himself in this way. Ponselle later denied unequivocally that he had ever given her voice lessons or coaching sessions; she said that she and Carmela had used him as a conduit to get to the Metropolitan.

At the beginning of their relationship, though, in her contractual letters to him, Ponselle agreed to pay him 20 percent on all concert engagements "out of the gross receipts by me for each concert, recital or oratorio. I agree to pay you on opera engagements ten per cent of my gross earnings. I also agree to pay you ten per cent on all phonograph recordings [of] my gross earnings." She and Thorner had agreed on a minimum price of $350 for her concert engagements in or near New York; $400 for engagements at about twelve hours' distance from New York City; and $500 for a pair of orchestral engagements in or near New York City. The price of other engagements was to be agreed upon mutually. She had also agreed to pay for her own accompanist and advertising material—window cards, circulars, photographs, three-sheet posters, and all printing and express or postage charges. Finally, the contract stipulated that she would pay "to furnish all orchestral music whenever needed." After September 1919 her fees were to be automatically increased by $100 on each engagement, with a similar incremental increase each of the following years.

For his part, Thorner was to arrange all her travel, including train schedules and hotels, keep a stock book showing the amount of advertising material he sent out, arrange with the local manager for a tuned piano and "use your best efforts to secure for me as many engagements as possible."

Crucial to Thorner's claims upon Ponselle was the fact that he had negotiated the Metropolitan contract. He was present at its execution and was familiar with its terms: he had been her sole agent and manager. Her original contract with the Metropolitan had been for one season only, from November 11, 1918, to April 20, 1919; it included a clause allowing the opera management to extend the term for an additional week and to renew it for 1919–20 and 1920–21 if it wished to do so. But the killer clause in the contract provided that the Metropolitan could limit the 1920–21 season to three months of Ponselle's services or prolong her engagement from "fortnight to fortnight for up to five and one-half months." In other words, Ponselle had been on trial, with a compensation that Thorner negotiated upward to $650 a week for the 1920–21 season, from the $300 she had been paid in 1919–20. This "fortnight to fortnight" meant that the company was keeping her in reserve at the beginning of her Metropolitan career.

As the court documents show, the Metropolitan wished to continue her on the roster from "the moment her drawing powers as a box office attraction were established." On April 15, 1920, she had been given a new contract covering the seasons 1920–21, 1921–22 and 1922–23. Thorner also got the opera management to increase her salary for 1920–21 from the $650 originally stipulated to $800 a week. Five months later, on September 30, 1920, even before the season began, she signed a second agreement with Thorner, stipulating that he would remain her manager until September 30, 1922. She would continue at $800 a week; unless something changed, however, her employment by the Metropolitan was entirely at the management's discretion and was to be terminated in the spring of 1923 unless some new arrangement was made.

Through these years, as Thorner testified in two lawsuits that followed, he received "his compensation, computed upon the basis of the changed salary," but he also wished to be paid something more out of the escrow account that Ponselle had authorized the Metropolitan to hold for his use and at his discretion. Then came the day when she wanted that money. He claimed that it was his because he had placed her at "the Metropolitan, the greatest opera company in the world," and because it was supposedly held in escrow for him. As tension grew between singer and manager, he attempted to get the additional sum of $3,045; she refused to allow the Metropolitan to pay it to him. Further complications arose when the treasurer of the Metropolitan Opera Company declared on April 17, 1924, that the Metropolitan was holding $3,225 in the escrow account and that he believed it was owed to Thorner. His letter to Alfred Seligsberg, a Wall Street attorney, reads: "Judging from these letters [from Ponselle to Thorner of June 4, 1918, and from Ponselle to the Metropolitan on that same day], apparently Miss Ponselle is obligated to pay 10% commission to Mr. William Thorner indefinitely, at least that is the way I look at it." And that is exactly what Ponselle's letter to the Metropolitan said.

The situation exploded just as the Metropolitan engaged her for the last week of the New York season, asking her on April 3, 1924, to sing *L'africaine* on April 16, *Cavalleria* on the seventeenth, and *Trovatore* on the nineteenth. She was also engaged for the full week in Atlanta, beginning April 21, and to appear in *Aida* and *Trovatore* in Cleveland at the end of the spring tour. She had concerts on her own in Chattanooga on April 23 (an interruption to her Atlanta engagement that the Metropolitan allowed her) and Philadelphia on May 1.

Incredibly, Ponselle sued the Metropolitan Opera Company itself to get the money. As for the company, it was "holding" the funds until "the parties arrive at some sort of understanding."

There can be little doubt that in 1917 and 1918 Ponselle used Thorner to get her the auditions and her first contracts at the Metropolitan. His contract stipulated that he also get her recital and concert dates, and this he did, save for those engagements credited to National in 1921. He also represented her at the Metropolitan in 1920, 1921, 1922, and 1923. That much is clear from sworn testimony; but it is equally clear that by 1922 she wished to get another manager. Eventually the Metropolitan deposited $3,045 with the city chamberlain because the matter was not settled. Ponselle then won a judgment against Thorner, which he appealed. Not until February 1, 1928, did the appellate division of the New York Supreme Court decide in her favor. The next day a summary of the five-and-a-half-year litigation appeared in *Law Journal*. The soprano's attorney was Nathan Burkan, private counsel to Victor Maurel and his wife.

On July 19, 1921, while she was still under contract to Thorner, Ponselle signed a contract with Samuel Geneen to be her "sole and exclusive manager" from September 30, 1922, until September 30, 1924. She then believed her commitment to Thorner would end in September 1922; but, as we have seen, she went on letting the Metropolitan deduct his commission from each of her fees until 1924.

Surprisingly, Ponselle made a very large payment to Geneen on August 4, 1921, when she wrote a check for $14,000 to him. It is signed "Rosa Ponzillo" and drawn on her account at the Columbia Bank at 507 Fifth Avenue. One day later, Geneen deposited it to his own account at the Empire Bank and Trust Company. Because this sum cannot be explained by unpaid commissions (since her commissions owed to National Concerts are all accounted for separately), this may have been paid to Geneen for money he had advanced to her before August 1921 to cover the huge expenses of launching her career. This sum most certainly is not an advance against any expenses National might have to incur after September 30, 1922, in the course of booking her recitals and concerts. If a manager added a young, unknown singer to his list, he might ask for an advance, but Ponselle was already a celebrity. Furthermore, this $14,000 is not listed under any rubric or heading in her account book for any year, making it all the more likely that she had had some private support from Geneen and a private agreement with him. It would have been almost impossible for any beginner in the opera business to underwrite the costs of a big career on the fees the Metropolitan was paying to Ponselle in those early years. And the size of this 1921 payment shows that she owed Geneen a large amount of money. When we consider that her entire income in 1922 was only $69,463.17, and that she paid $6,698.35 to National in commissions that year, we can see how enormous this sum was. As to their later business, she signed over stock to him on January 31, 1923, consigning 180 shares of stock in a recording company and in a "Play Finance Company."

On July 20, 1923, Geneen sent her a receipt for $1,200 for the commission she had just paid to National on dates the agency had booked for her "in California." The commission was "20% on $6,000," the statement read. One day later, on July 21, Ponselle lent Geneen $8,500. The loan was formalized with a promissory note, in which Geneen wrote, "I promise to pay Rosa Ponselle $8,500 at [my office at] 1451 Broadway, with 6% interest, on July 21, 1924." Because the note remained in the soprano's archives, one has to assume that the sum was not repaid. Had Geneen repaid it, he would surely have asked to have his note canceled or returned to him. Yet the soprano lent him money again on other occasions.

The first public suggestion of any acquaintance between Ponselle and Geneen came when, as we have seen, he honored her at an elegant dinner at the dining room of the Hotel des Artistes. Because Thorner and his wife, Tony Ponzillo and his wife, Giovanni Martino, Barbara Maurel, and several others were present, that event would appear to mark the beginning of Ponselle's affairs with National; but as the records prove, her obligation to Geneen went back at least to 1921, if not earlier. All went smoothly between the artist and her "concert and recital manager" for some time; but on January 6, 1925, Geneen, furious, wrote to accuse her of having made private arrangements with the Victor Talking Machine Company to broadcast concerts under its sponsorship. "Our contract with you is an exclusive contract," Geneen reminded her, "for throughout the world; and you have no right to negotiate directly or indirectly [with others]." He was angry that

Victor had made a public announcement in the newspapers saying that Rosa Ponselle would be "broadcasting" for them. At that time she had been a recording artist for Victor for more than a year, having made her last records for Columbia in September 1923 and her first for Victor in December.

Although she had paid Geneen $14,000 at the start of their association, and although occasional disputes did arise between them, Ponselle seemed well served by National. In 1923 she earned $36,303 just from the agency's bookings; in 1924 that figure rose to $38,380. Her income from recordings almost tripled, from $6,750 paid to her in 1923 by Columbia to $20,000 paid by Victor in 1924. She was obviously making wise investments, which yielded $6,195 in dividends in 1924. Among these were her holdings in several railroads, including Union Pacific, New York Central, Pennsylvania Railroad, Southern Pacific, and Northern Pacific. Given Otto Kahn's railroad interests and his relationship to E. H. Harriman, he may have been counseling her in these matters. She also owned stock in New York Telephone, Vacuum Oil, Standard Oil, American Telephone and Telegraph, and several small corporations, including the recording company and theatrical production companies that she made over to Geneen. Edith Prilik recorded her income for 1924 as $81,645; her expenses in the United States that year were $41,591.35. Although we do not know how much she spent on her trip to Europe that year because the figures are not in her account book, it is clear that she had improved her situation considerably between 1921 and 1924. From her letters we see how she looked forward to the concert and recital tours National booked for her, particularly those that took her to the West Coast. During one tour in 1923 she was entertained by Mary Pickford and Douglas Fairbanks, Charlie Chaplin, Gloria Swanson, and Pola Negri, some of whom she met again later. In Hollywood she was treated like the celebrity she had become.

THE ARTIST'S GROWTH IN CRITICAL YEARS ~

Ponselle's twenty-three appearances for the Met in 1921–22 included not just the featured new production of *Ernani*, Martinelli's old favorite, but reprises of *Forza* and *Don Carlos* as well. With these she established herself more firmly as "a Verdi soprano," also singing arias from *Les vêpres siciliennes* and the trio from *I lombardi alla prima crociata* in the Metropolitan's concerts. She also kept *Cavalleria rusticana* largely for herself, singing it to the Turiddus of Althouse, Gigli, Giacomo Lauri-Volpi, and, in 1923, Mario Chamlee, another of Thorner's singers.

Ponselle's career turned in another, serious direction in 1922–23, when Gatti decided to produce *Guillaume Tell*, which he described in his autobiography as "very great." He said, "I consider this work one of the great monuments of music . . . [and] one of the most admirable things that exist. . . . All the choral writing in [it], the entire second act, the air of the woman, [Mathilde], the trio of the conspiracy, all these things I consider marvellous." The music, as he said, "is in a classical vein," and he paid great homage to Ponselle when he cast her in it. Martinelli, who had already sung it, was Arnold; Didur was Gessler; Mardones, Walter; and Danise, William Tell. The opera was sung in Italian and conducted by Papi.

Although Ponselle said she thought of it as "a man's opera" and found her role as Mathilde "not very demanding," it remains one of the noblest of women's parts. Rossini considered Mathilde so important that he postponed the world premiere at the Paris Opéra twice until he could give it with Laure Cinti-Damoreau, who had sung in his premieres of *Le siège de Corinthe*, *Moïse et Pharaon* and *Le comte Ory* before appearing as his Mathilde. Ponselle's "Selva opaca" from *Guillaume Tell*, made in 1923 for Columbia, remains one of her great early recordings, foreshadowing her later performances in *La vestale* and *Norma*.

In interviews and in her autobiography, the soprano said that in spite of her reservations about the Rossini role, she preferred Mathilde to Sélika in Meyerbeer's *L'africaine*, her next role at the Metropolitan; she said that it took discipline to master the latter. Gatti assigned the opera to her in the spring of 1922 so she could study it with Romani in Pine Orchard that summer. The first performance was not scheduled until March 1923. Because *L'africaine* had held the Metropolitan stage so often between 1888 and 1907, many critics and members of the 1923 audience could remember casts with such giants as Nordica, Jean Lassalle, both De Reszkes, Fremstad, Stracciari, and Caruso in its broadly drawn roles. From the beginning the colossal work had drawn stars of the first magnitude. Its widely publicized premiere in 1865 at the Paris Opéra, after Meyerbeer's death, had featured as Sélika the great Belgian soprano Marie Sass, who had sung Elisabeth in the Paris premiere of *Tannhäuser.* She then sang the first Elisabeth in Verdi's *Don Carlos.* The Vasco da Gama in the world premiere of *L'africaine* was Emilio Naudin, Parma-born and Milan-trained; Nelusko was Jean-Baptiste Faure, a leading baritone in Paris for seventeen years, who also sang the first Posa in *Don Carlos.*

Just as Ponselle began to rehearse it, the Met gave her a new letter contract for three performances at the end of the season and for the tour.

Because of its illustrious precedents, *L'africaine* presented a substantial challenge to Ponselle, whose colleagues were Gigli as Vasco da Gama and Danise as Nelusko. Ines was sung by Queena Mario, Pelletier's first wife. Léon Rothier sang both the Grand Inquisitor and the High Priest, while Bodanzky conducted. One critic thought that it was Ponselle's greatest musical and dramatic achievement, even though she thought it took her years to master it. She continued to sing Sélika until January 1934, for a total of thirty-five performances. In the early 1920s she alternated in the role with Rethberg, who, as we have seen, also sang several Mathildes.

The sure sign that Ponselle was rising toward an absolute understanding of her physical powers came in the spring of 1923, when, as we have seen, she successfully performed three operas in three days in Atlanta on the Metropolitan tour. These were Elisabetta in *Don Carlos* for the matinee of April 26, Sélika for the evening performance of *L'africaine* on April 27, and Mathilde one day later in the evening's *Guillaume Tell.* Only a soprano with a sure command of her resources could have accepted such an assignment. That she was even asked to do this may reflect the confidence Gatti had in Ponselle; it certainly shows what an astonishing range of assets she had at her disposition, although she was still only twenty-six. As we read in Ponselle's letter to Kenneth Miller immediately after the Atlanta week, she understood that her accomplishment was extraordinary but wrote not a word of self-congratulation for having done it. As her financial records show, the Metropolitan Opera paid her $1,250 "for three performances in Atlanta" in 1923.

For the season of 1923–24, National Concerts was able to fill the gaps in Ponselle's schedule left by the peculiar Metropolitan Opera contract of February 1923. The agency booked so many concerts and recitals that in the end Ponselle sang for the Metropolitan only twenty-five times. Five of these were opera house concerts; in one of them she sang "Vissi d'arte" from Tosca, ranging into Jeritza's territory. At the end of the season, Gatti finally assigned her Leonora in Trovatore, which he had had her learn so many years before. It became one of her finest roles. She sang it that season in the opera house in April and, as we have seen, in Atlanta and Cleveland on the tour. Martinelli was her Manrico, Danise the De Luna, with Karen Branzell and Marion Telva alternating as Azucena. Ponselle spoke of Leonora as she rarely did about other operatic characters, and her love for this work is felt throughout her recordings from it for Columbia in 1918, 1920, and 1922 and for Victor in 1928.

As Ponselle had grown into the styles of Weber, Rossini, early and late Verdi, Meyerbeer, Boito, Lalo, Mascagni, Puccini, Giordano, and even contemporaries such as Breil (no matter how much she despised his work) and Montemezzi, she then prepared to restudy another composer, Amilcare Ponchielli, whose La Gioconda Gatti had asked her to prepare year after year. Finally he promised her performances of it in the autumn of 1924. With her new three-year contract, her future with the Met seemed assured.

Again she agreed to be ready with her other standard repertory works: L'africaine, Aida, Ballo, Cavalleria, Forza, Il tabarro, Tosca, Trovatore, Don Carlos, Chénier, L'amore dei tre re, Ernani, Mefistofele, Guillaume Tell, La juive, Roi d'Ys, and Oberon, as well as the three sacred pieces in Latin. With her new three-year contract with the Metropolitan, which Ponselle signed on January 30, 1924, her future was reasonably secure. Unlike the compromised one-season contract of 1923–24, this provided for a fee of $1,250 per week for 1924–25, $1,400 per week for 1925–26, and $1,500 per week for 1926–27, provided the management offered her renewals.

After her birthday that year, while negotiations with the Metropolitan were about to end with the signing of this new contract, Ponselle had expressed particular satisfaction with her own success. In fact, her growth was reflected to the reviews she got in 1923, after two difficult seasons.

In 1921 and 1922 several critics expressed regret at what they called "a deterioration" of her voice. Not that they doubted her natural gifts: they felt she was using them wrong and cited problems of pitch, shrillness, and breath control when she had difficulty sustaining the tone. Not all these reviewers were in New York, for some of the wisest among them were in Philadelphia and Atlanta; and while they were still generous in their praise of her accomplishments, they did send up warning flares in those years.

By March 1923 it seemed that they were hearing an improvement. The reviews of *L'africaine* were critical of Ponselle's makeup, which two called "coppery" and "copperish." One, the *New York Sun*, said that although she was "a handsome Indian, her make-up puts a new complexion on the legend [of Sélika]; for we saw Pocahontas and John Rolfe." But "she sang with young and voluptuous prodigality." In another article in the same paper the reviewer praised her "opulent voice" and said "she accomplished a good deal with the prison 'Lullaby' of the second act and even more with the Didoan lament of the last."

The *Telegram* critic wrote: "Rosa Ponselle's voice was very beautiful [but] her Ethiopian make-up and New York manner were somewhat incongruous. Vocally she was a miracle." Another writer said her Sélika was "wonderfully sung and acted," while the Italian critic of *La Voce della Colonia* in Philadelphia described "a singer who is an absolute marvel, given her age."

When the soprano went to Atlanta for the 1923 tour in April, the *Constitution* critic wrote of "the Ponselle of last year, who scored heavily in several roles but then seemed to have reached the peak of her art. . . . [But now in *Don Carlos* we hear] the easy volume of the tone she called into play, without effort, the extreme clarity and the sweetness of every note she sang." The *Journal*, too, had nothing but praise: "She sang splendidly and proved again that she is one of the greatest artists in the Metropolitan Opera Company."

Of her *Guillaume Tell*, sung with Martinelli, Danise, and Mardones, an

Atlanta critic wrote: "Rosa Ponselle again proved that she is a vastly improved performer over the Ponselle who first came here with the Metropolitan. Her voice is peculiarly adapted to Rossini's music . . . [and has] voluptuous fullness and rounded clarity of tone."

In mid-December of 1923 several critics praised her for losing so much weight. Writing of *Andrea Chénier*, Henderson found her "unusually well made up and bewigged . . . [and] of considerable pictorial value. Her naturally beautiful voice was fresh, vibrant, at times brilliant. She sang with freedom and temperament but always with finished technique." From him, this was the highest possible praise.

Deems Taylor, "Mr. Deemus," as Gatti called him, reviewing that same *Chénier* for the *New York World*, said that Ponselle

> cast a much diminished shadow and . . . acted with considerable spirit. Her voice had all of its wonted, opulent beauty of tone but suffered occasional lapses in intonation, the result of doubtful vocal methods. . . . She sang carefully. There was a refinement in her singing and in her acting. She sang without effort, and her voice was warm and true, though we missed those luscious low notes.

A second reviewer in the *Sun* found her "thinner and more sedate, [an artist who sang] copiously [with a] voluptuously colored voice." He found fault, though, with her tendency to "go sharp" in the third act. Given these remarks about Ponselle's problems with pitch, it is important to note that her pitch seems so true on her recordings that it is hard to imagine her having "lapses of intonation" in the theater. Also, of course, these are but a handful of criticisms out of thousands of favorable reviews.

When *Ernani* returned to the Brooklyn Academy of Music on Christmas night in 1923 with Ponselle, Martinelli, and Ruffo, the reviewer of the *Brooklyn Daily Times* praised her but voiced fears for her future: "Her characterization of Elvira was drawn with bold strokes, and her acting was vigorous to a fault. Her enormous voice completely filled the [theatre] and at times it overshadowed Martinelli's. One wonders how long an artist can give of herself so generously, both vocally and emotionally, before wearing out."

The critic of the *Brooklyn Daily Eagle* praised Ponselle's "magnificent voice, which came across the footlights with a power that carried it to the last row of the balcony. . . . She has acquired good artistic routine."

Although she had sung *Cavalleria* nine times before her April 9 performance of it in 1924, all the critics found something different about the soprano that evening. "Miss Ponselle registered her greatest operatic success," wrote the *New York American* critic. "This music might have been specially written for her voice of golden velvet. She lives the part." In the *Sun* she was praised in "one of her finest parts. She is keenly alive in her interpretation of the ill-fated maiden and won the house again and again."

Finally her Atlanta *Trovatore* came, also in April. She was "Rosa Ponselle of the majestic stature and the God-given power of song [who] sang into Leonora the warmth of her personality and the richness of her equally dominant voice."

From these reviews it is clear that Ponselle was maturing as a singer and actress; but she never lost sight of the need to grow, making one decision that year that affected the rest of her professional life: she would go abroad for the first time and study with a new conductor, Serafin, who had just been engaged by the Metropolitan. The European trip, which she had considered and decided against in 1923, changed her outlook and the direction of her career, so that most of the important choices Ponselle made after that summer were influenced to some extent by Serafin and her first experience of Italian culture on Italian soil.

CHAPTER 7

The Singing Actress

SUMMER 1924–SPRING 1925

After a short concert and recital tour and her well-reviewed *Trovatore* in Atlanta, Ponselle also sang *Cavalleria* with Gigli there. Near the season's end she passed a landmark: the *Aida* that was her one hundred and fiftieth performance with the Metropolitan, sung on April 28, 1924, in Cleveland. She was partnered by the Radamès of Martinelli, who was also her Manrico in *Trovatore* there. With that last performance of the tour, the soprano's obligation to the company ended for the year, leaving her free to sail for Europe, as she had planned. The "poor girl," the Italian-American vaudevillian, had won a certain financial stability from investments, recordings, and out-of-town engagements booked by National Concerts and now could afford to travel and finally claim as her own some of the experiences that had so long been denied to her by the circumstances of her background, education, character, and professional choices.

EUROPE AND TULLIO SERAFIN

As Ponselle had admitted to Kenneth Miller in 1923, she felt obliged to go to Europe sooner or later. Now that long-postponed moment had come. Sailing from New York in first class on the *Leviathan*, accompanied by Romani and Prilik, she was half diva and half homespun American woman. After the ship docked in Southampton, Ponselle and her companions crossed the Channel. They toured in grand style, guided by the loyal Romani, who was returning to the world of his birth. From Paris to Italy they traveled by train. In Rome Ponselle had an audience with the pope; from Naples she and Prilik took a day trip to Caserta and to a country village outside the city, where Ponselle visited her aunt, her mother's sister. There she had firsthand experience of how farm women lived in the Terra di Lavoro; she found the primitive conditions shocking. Her base of operations that summer was far to the north, in a rented villa in Leghorn, where Romani had been born and still owned a house.

The most important purpose of Ponselle's trip was study, not travel, as we learn from Serafin's memoirs. As always, the soprano spent the summer brushing up on the operas her Metropolitan contracts stipulated she had to have ready at all times, in case she was called to cover for another singer. Those she surely worked on with Romani; but beyond them was *La Gioconda*, which had to be mastered if she were to sing it the following winter, as Gatti had promised her. Ponselle's account books show that she paid $935 that year "for coaching new role"; although that fee may have been Romani's, the true source of her inspiration was Serafin, who exerted an enormous influence on every aspect of her vocal and artistic development in 1924 and through the next ten years and beyond.

Tullio Serafin, one of the greatest and most respected conductors of this century, was a native of the province of Venice, having been born in 1878 in Rottanova, a hamlet just behind the levee of the Adige River, near the market town of Cavarzere. When Serafin was a youth in this agricultural community, the only language spoken or taught was Venetian dialect, the only roads were dirt tracks, the fields were crisscrossed with irrigation canals, and the weekly market in Cavarzere was the big weekly social event. In his memoirs, edited by Giuseppe Pugliese and Teodoro Celli and published under the title *Tullio Serafin*, the conductor describes the marginal conditions in which his family lived. "To tell the truth," he wrote, "in my time there were only farm laborers there, but they were always busy and they loved good times." Nervous and unsettled as a child, he found his best moments came with concerts in the piazza by the town musicians from nearby Adria, who held him spellbound for "three or four hours" on Sunday afternoons.

In spite of the family's dire poverty, Serafin's parents bought musical instruments for their children, who accompanied the father, an amateur flautist. Tullio Serafin began his studies with the violin, first in Rottanova and then in Adria, where his teacher was the bandmaster; at the same time he learned to play the piano, using an instrument his parents had rented for his older sister. Eventually he was sent to study music in Milan, where his career began. He was engaged as a violinist in the orchestra of the Teatro alla Scala, where Gatti-Casazza and Toscanini held forth until the day in 1908 when both left for New York and the Metropolitan.

Serafin's conducting career began in Ferrara in 1900; by 1903 he was engaged in Turin; in 1907 he was at Covent Garden in London, a theater to which he returned for several seasons over the next forty-three years; and in 1909 he returned to La Scala. Serafin took part in a historic opera event in Milan in 1918, when he conducted the world premiere of *La nave*, collaborating with its composer, Montemezzi. World War I was then about to end, and Italy was celebrating the victories of its forces in Trent and Trieste. During that performance Tito Ricordi, the music publisher who had inherited his family's vast interests, came before the curtain during the intermissions to announce the Italian army's progress; after every announcement Serafin ordered his musicians to play the Royal March while members of the audience "waved handkerchiefs, laughed, and cried." Because of the "tremendous joy" of that evening, he and his wife, Elena Rakowska, named their daughter Vittoria. Theirs was a musical family, for Rakowska sang at La Scala and at the Metropolitan, while Vittoria later became the first wife of Nicola Rossi-Lemeni, a world-famous bass from the 1940s through the 1960s.

After the war Serafin conducted all over Italy and in France and South America, winning fame chiefly at the Teatro Colòn in Buenos Aires and the Teatro Municipal in Rio. Gatti-Casazza, who had been searching for years for a worthy successor to Toscanini, engaged Serafin as "conductor for Italian, Russian, French, Spanish, and English operas." Promised the opening night of the 1924–25 season at the Metropolitan, November 3, Serafin was assigned *Aida* because, as he recalled Gatti telling him, "*Aida* always brings good luck."

Gatti charged Serafin with another, very specific duty: to coach Ponselle in Italy for the planned new production of *La Gioconda*. The conductor's recollection of the American soprano begins with what he had heard about her from others.

In those years there was a girl who was singing at the Metropolitan: her name was Rosa Ponselle (her real name was Ponzillo); she was the daughter of Italians from Campania. She had been discovered by Caruso, who had heard her in several concerts in churches [*sic*], where she was singing with her sister. Caruso called her to the attention of Gatti-Casazza, who was very impressed with her statuesque appearance and her voice, which was rich and equal from top to bottom—so much that he immediately gave her a contract with the Metropolitan, having her sing in *La forza del destino* with Caruso himself and De Luca and Mardones. This was in 1918, and she was a huge success; Rosa was then twenty-one.

Then, just before I began to work under my contract with the Metropolitan, Gatti-Casazza brought her to me in Italy and had me hear her, warning me, "She has a stupendous voice! What a pity she has absolutely no fire!" But I understood right away that it was not "fire" that was missing but rather preparation. It was a matter of teaching her how to bring forth her fire from the cinders and how to make herself more expansive.

But this was not an easy job. It was a matter not only of making that voice catch fire but also of teaching her all the typical ways of dramatic bel canto; but she was used to singing with tight, compact phrasing, cold and like a statue, bogged down in a quagmire and rather conventional.

Nothing in Ponselle's life became more important to her professional development than Serafin's guidance over the next decade as he directed her career and taught her *Gioconda*, *La vestale*, *Luisa Miller*, *Don Giovanni*, *Norma*, *La traviata*, and Montemezzi's *L'amore dei tre re* and *La notte di*

Zoraima. He also rehearsed and conducted her in almost every opera of her established repertory and Verdi's Requiem as well.

His success depended in part on his own character. Unlike Toscanini, who was known and feared for his rigor, Serafin was a gentle, kindly, lovable man who coddled his musicians and drew the best from them. Selfless in the extreme, he succeeded with Ponselle as a more authoritarian mentor might not have done. He could barely manage what he called "her nerves." In writing about the prima donnas he had worked with, he named some "angelic," such as Bori, and some "capricious" and indeed "impossible," such as Jeritza. But Ponselle was something else, he said: "Rosa Ponselle belonged to another category: the group of terrified prima donnas. She suffered from a terrible, uncontrollable panic. Every time she had to face a performance, she was possessed by a mortal fear, so much so that for days and days before performances she simply could not eat anything. Gatti-Casazza knew all about this, because more than once he literally had to throw her out onto the stage."

After Gatti brought Ponselle and Serafin together in Italy, Serafin insisted that she accompany him and his wife to Venice, where she could see the original buildings from which scenic designers sketched the settings for *La Gioconda.* At the Metropolitan, as at La Scala, the opera was always staged splendidly, with the company seizing every opportunity to show Venice in its glory: the Doge's Palace, Enzo's ship at its moorings on an island near Fusina, the justly celebrated and magnificent Ca d'Oro, and the ruined palace on the Giudecca Canal, where the last act takes place. All of this Ponselle saw at first hand with Serafin, who had often conducted in Venice, as her guide.

Ponselle's own account of her first encounter with Serafin described "the summer of 1924, when I went to Italy to study *Gioconda.* Gatti-Casazza had sent me to him; and I am proud to recall that when Serafin first heard me, he said, '*Here* is material with which I can do something!' " (The italics are hers.)

"Any artist who looks back on a successful career will admit, if he or she is honest, that—though God gave the material, and the artist strove unceasingly to perfect it—there was also someone at certain crucial points who provided the inspiration, the support, and guiding hand that directed and sustained the artist on the right road.

"When I look back on my nineteen years at the Metropolitan, I know that the man to whom I owe the most in this respect is Maestro Serafin." She went on to say that she owed a "lifelong debt" to him, a "true 'singers' conductor,' " one who taught her and others "what it means to be helped, guided, sustained and coaxed into giving something even better than you ever thought you could do yourself. . . . I would like to call Maestro Serafin the 'singers' conductor' par excellence. He knows the tasks and the difficulties of any singer just as though they were his own. We always used to say that he not only sang with us, he breathed with us. And only when you have a man like that in command [may] you expect what we call 'a great performance.' "

In a taped interview with a Mrs. Howard, who represented a music club in Washington, Ponselle said something that may illuminate further her remarks about Serafin. She was speaking of herself and Carmela at the time:

> The technique was there [from the start]. We both had a natural, God-given technique; all we needed to do was polish it, naturally, with experience and a proper coach to guide you. That's what a singer needs—a real musician, a real musician to guide her, to listen to her, so she does not deviate [from what is correct], because you can't always hear your own faults. But I was very fortunate, and Sister was, to have had a natural technique, coloratura, staccatos, as my early recordings will tell you—the Columbia I recorded, [I had hardly] made my debut when I recorded those. . . . I felt instinctively [about the music]. . . . No conductor ever stopped me. No conductor, in fact, has ever given me any tempi; I took my own tempi. I am a fairly good musician, and they respected that. I just did things intuitively, instinctively; I have a musicality, they say, that is quite sensitive. . . . The meaning [of a given piece is] prompted by the

words. The words, the text, controlled or guided my coloring of the voice, the shading, the decrescendo, the crescendo. That was all guided by the text; and in other words, [if] you live your text and suffer with your text, you will get the vocal coloring.

Part of the mastery Serafin taught her was this thorough understanding of the text. As Gatti and he both knew, she had a magnificent natural voice that she used "intuitively, instinctively." But to become an artist, she had to learn how to marry the voice to the drama in the libretto, to bring the work to life. Without that union of voice and text, there is no opera. Ponselle was fortunate indeed to have become Serafin's favorite singer when she was twenty-seven years old, with so much of her career ahead of her.

Ponselle said that it was Serafin who,

when he came to New York in the 1924–1925 season, declared to Gatti, "This will eventually be a *Norma* voice." I think I am right in saying that Gatti was skeptical at first. . . . But Serafin said, "We will bring her to it gradually; the material is there. Let her prepare *La vestale* in the coming year; and then we will see."

How lucky we were, we young singers who worked under a musical director who knew how to develop and not exploit a voice! It was never a question of how we could be used to bring an audience into the house. It was simply this: How can we bring this talent to full flower?

Remarking further on her experience with Serafin, she said:

He was always the great maestro, and when he stood at the desk and took his baton, there was always that intangible something which makes a performance take fire and glow with the genius that was there. But he was also so kind and almost fatherly, too. I always think of him as the "Father of Lyric Drama" in the interpretive sense, because [in addition to] the knowledge and authority behind it all, there was always that sense of kindly guidance, that almost affectionate determination that those in his care (and I use the word "care" deliberately) should give their best.

Of all the people who led her down what she called "the right road" toward maturity as an interpretive singer, pride of place must go to Serafin, as she freely acknowledged. After 1924, she said in one interview, she continued to study "musically with my dear and valued coach, Romano Romani," and turned to Serafin for "what I might call the final, refining process." Clearly she had made a value judgment; it proved to be the one that led her toward greatness.

A VISIT WITH PUCCINI ～

While Ponselle was in Italy she also met Giacomo Puccini, who was willing to receive her because of Romani's old acquaintance with him. After she and Prilik returned from Rome, Naples, and Caserta they stayed in Leghorn, near Romani and only a short drive along the coast from Puccini's villa at Viareggio. She remembered that it was August when they arrived there. Puccini had lived in his new house at Viale Buonarroti 76 for less than three years, having reluctantly left his refuge at Torre del Lago after industrial development on the formerly unspoiled Lake Massaciuccoli ruined it for him. He was past sixty, with his long career behind him. The *Trittico* had been premiered at the Metropolitan in December 1918, but without young Ponselle, for although Gatti asked her to prepare the role of Giorgetta in *Il tabarro*, she had never performed it. Nonetheless, it remained on her list of operas in her 1920–21 contract, as did *Tosca*, which had been the only Puccini work in her original 1918 contract.

As for the composer, he had begun to consider composing *Turandot* in 1920 and had been working on it ever since. By the spring of 1924 he had been writing without interruption for four months on what he called "the grand finale of the third act" of that opera. Thin and ill with his long-seated diabetes and with what was eventually diagnosed as cancer, he had suffered from a severe sore throat that spring and had gone in June to the spa at

Salsomaggiore, near Fidenza, to take the cure. Nothing helped; discouraged, he returned to Viareggio for the summer.

Ponselle's own experience of Puccini's work extended to the operas of her Metropolitan assignments and her Columbia recordings of "Vissi d'arte" from *Tosca* and "Un bel dì" from *Madama Butterfly*, both recorded in 1919; "In quelle trine morbide" from *Manon Lescaut*, recorded in 1921 and again in 1923; and "Sì, mi chiamano Mimi" from *La bohème*, also recorded in 1923. At that point in Ponselle's career, Gatti might perhaps have assigned a Puccini opera to Ponselle at any time, for she was vocally right, as her recordings prove. But, as she said, her physical appearance seemed unsuited to *Manon Lescaut*, *Bohème*, and *Butterfly*, for which she was too tall and too heavy. Bori, in any case, was always welcome as a diminutive Mimi; Alda had claimed Manon; after Farrar's retirement, Easton had been cast as Butterfly; and so long as Jeritza had a grip on Tosca, that would probably not fall to Ponselle either.

Her visit to Puccini began, as Father Dante Del Fiorentino remembered, with a joke that Ponselle, perhaps out of respect for Puccini and for her own reputation, seems never to have told anyone. Del Fiorentino, or "Father Dante," as everyone called him, held the title of monsignor when he lived in Glen Cove, on Long Island, and in New York City in the 1940s and 1950s. But he had grown up on Puccini's native soil and had first watched the composer from afar, as a boy studying for the priesthood and as a teenage seminarian, spending the summers with his family in the hamlet of Quiesa, just across the lake from Torre del Lago. A pesky youth, he finally met his idol but so annoyed him that Puccini dubbed him "Gonnellone," or "Big Skirt," making fun of the long, black cassock that Italian clergymen wore. Eventually young Del Fiorentino was ordained in the Cathedral of San Martino in Lucca, where generations of Puccinis had played the organ and composed. He celebrated his first mass in the parish church in Quiesa, with his aged great-uncle, also a priest, as his organist for the occasion. Because both loved Puccini, the music chosen for the ceremony was an "Ecce sacerdos" by him, a work that the composer had given to the venerable older man. During the banquet given in honor of Del Fiorentino, the local band played numbers from *Tosca*, including the Te Deum from the first act; later a chorus of amateurs from Quiesa sang "Giovinezza è il mio nome" from *Manon Lescaut* and other favorites from the Puccini repertory.

As he grew older and more serious, Del Fiorentino became Puccini's acquaintance. They had one visit together at Torre del Lago as World War I began, just because the priest was being sent to the Alpine front as a chaplain. On that day Puccini looked like "an old man, grey, taciturn, plunged in thought and prey to sorrows," walking through his garden at Torre and looking "as lonely as a grave." On a short leave, Del Fiorentino was able to see Puccini again, that time in Pisa.

More than two years passed before they met again. After the war ended Del Fiorentino was named assistant curate in the parish church of Torre del Lago. This made Puccini his parishioner, and from then on, the two men met frequently, chatted about music and local affairs, and sometimes exchanged confidences. Once the priest even wrote a libretto, which he offered to Puccini, hoping he would choose it as the text for a new opera. He not only refused but even threw the manuscript onto the fire as the two were sitting together in the composer's study. Del Fiorentino, undaunted, went on to write another, using a subject from Dante's *Inferno*, the story of Count Ugolino of Pisa. It was Puccini who provided the money and contacts to permit Del Fiorentino to leave Torre del Lago for New York; but the separation was not permanent, for the priest returned home each summer. After Puccini moved to Viareggio, Del Fiorentino visited him in the new villa, but sometimes they took coffee together in the elegant Caffè Gianni Schicchi, on one of the main shopping streets of the city.

Thus it happened that Puccini and Del Fiorentino were sitting together outside the café, sipping a cool drink when, as the priest recalled in his book *Immortal Bohemian*, "a young woman came and sat down unannounced at our table."

This is Del Fiorentino's account of their meeting with Rosa Ponselle:

"I am Pellerossa from New York," she said simply. "Pellerossa" means "Redskin." It was evident that the young lady, though she was tanned, had no Red Indian blood. "My father is a Red Indian chief," she went on, with mock seriousness.

"That's fine," Giacomo murmured, without enthusiasm.

"I am Pellerossa," she repeated. "I am making my debut in one of your operas. I can't remember the title!"

"Let's hope you will remember the music," Giacomo said dryly.

"Thank you, Maestro, for your deep interest. I am Pellerossa . . ."

It went on indefinitely. Giacomo was unimpressed, bored, incredulous. Who was this person who kept talking about Redskins? She was certainly beautiful. Also, he had the curious feeling that he had seen her before. Suddenly he realized that she was playing with him, as a fisherman plays with a fish.

"Who the devil are you?" he demanded at last.

She said that she was Rosa Ponselle; and he was immediately captivated. His son Tonio arrived at that moment.

"Tonio can smell the presence of a woman the way a hunter smells game," Giacomo said. "He's a good boy, though. I don't know what he is going to do to earn a living."

The conversation then turned to Puccini's royalty statements and to performances of his operas abroad. He began to make fun of Tonio's ignorance of geography.

"To think of all the money I spent on Tonio's education!"

At that point he turned sharply to Tonio and said, "You're no good at geography. Then what the devil are you good at? Pretty girls, I suppose."

"Like father, like son," Tonio said softly.

This incident, more than perhaps any other recounted about Ponselle, shows a playful side of her character; she loved playing jokes on people. Here is the same young woman who made flippant remarks to Caruso on the first day they met. One other anecdote she told about herself concerns a day when she came upon Gatti-Casazza in his office at the Metropolitan. As he was looking in the mirror and adjusting his tie, he asked her whether it was straight.

"Oh, yes," Ponselle assured him. "The tie's all right; but it's your nose that's crooked."

Reading this, one can easily believe that the young, irrepressible woman who had made Caruso laugh with her irreverent send-ups of opera scenes would sit down, uninvited, at Puccini's table in a café in Viareggio and introduce herself with silly banter about American Indians.

She was utterly serious, though, when she, Prilik, and Romani were invited to Puccini's villa for dinner. The composer asked her to sing for him and accompanied her as she ran through "Vissi d'arte" several times. After she sang, he complimented her, suggesting that she had sung it perfectly. During this visit Prilik took a snapshot of Puccini and Ponselle on a rustic path in the pine woods that surrounded the house. Another photograph shows the soprano with Romani and Tonio Puccini, and a third shows all four with the composer's wife on the terrace of Puccini's house.

Del Fiorentino, who had been in New York that year and had been corresponding with Puccini, found him "terribly changed" that summer of 1924, complaining of his failing eyesight. Tonio confided to the priest that Puccini was plagued with coughing and recurring throat problems. Once when Puccini and Del Fiorentino met that year in front of the post office in Torre del Lago, the composer took a scrap of paper, leaned against a tree trunk, and made a sketch of his throat to show just where it hurt. In later meetings he spoke frankly about the seriousness of his illness; Del Fiorentino was among the friends who wished Puccini well as he and Tonio boarded the Rome–Paris train on their way to Brussels, where the composer was to receive radium treatments for what had finally been identified as cancer. Puccini died on November 29, 1924, in the clinic where he was being treated.

For Ponselle, this meeting with the world's most celebrated living composer of opera added yet another dimension to her musical understanding. In a certain sense, a Great Chain of Operatic Being had been forged: Amilcare Ponchielli, born near Cremona in 1834, had composed *La Gioconda* and had become Puccini's teacher and mentor at the Milan Conservatory in the 1880s. Puccini, in turn, had helped Romano Romani through his student days at the conservatory and as he began working for Columbia in Milan. Romani had coached Ponselle and accompanied her on this visit to his old friend. Now, with Puccini's blessing, she and her coach were on their way back to New York City, where, Gatti had assured her, she would sing Gioconda for the first time.

THE NEW YORK SEASON AND *LA GIOCONDA* ⁓

By 1924 Ponselle had a regularly scheduled concert tour each fall; that year she also had her recording dates with Columbia in September. Although she was studying for the Metropolitan, she began her tour, only to have to end it in Kansas City in the first week of October, when she fell ill with pyelitis, a kidney infection. She returned to New York, where her doctor, Antonio Stella, confined her to bed and advised Gatti that she also had "a mild pharyngitis" and "an arthritis of long standing." She required rest and continuing care.

The opening night at the Metropolitan, November 3, featured Rethberg, Matzenauer, Martinelli, and Danise in *Aida* under the baton of Serafin, whose debut it was. The event, as Gatti had predicted, was a huge success; it brought the conductor "good luck," so that he remained with the company for ten consecutive seasons.

Still ill, Ponselle lost a *Tell* to Rethberg and *Chénier* to Easton. Jeritza's Tosca on November 7 preceded by one day the season's first performance of the *Gioconda* revival, which Gatti assigned to Easton. This opera had had a brief run at the Metropolitan in the 1880s with Christine Nilsson in the title role but had soon disappeared from the repertory. Not until Caruso came did it return, with him, Lillian Nordica, and Eugenio Giraldoni as its leads. In the 1909–10 season, Gatti's second at the Metropolitan, he staged it with Destinn, Caruso, Homer, and Amato, a cast that he rarely changed through its many performances between then and 1915. Toscanini conducted it for the opening nights of 1909 and 1913 and on other occasions; his alternate was Giorgio Polacco, who had joined the Metropolitan roster in the autumn of 1912 and had conducted an astonishing 342 performances before leaving in 1917 for Chicago. In this period the hardy Destinn became so identified with the role of the Venetian street singer that she sang it forty-two times from the opening in 1909 until 1915. It was then again removed from the program, in the same season that Toscanini left the company.

In the 1924 production of *Gioconda* Gatti gave the first performance to Gigli, who had sung Enzo at his debut in Rovigo in 1914. Easton was Gioconda, Matzenauer was Laura, Mardones sang Alvise, and Danise was the villainous Barnaba; Serafin conducted. Ponselle rejoined the company with *Andrea Chénier*, which she had sung six times before, in 1921 and 1923. Her first appearance came on November 29 with Gigli and Danise. Lawrence Tibbett, who had come to the Metropolitan in the 1923–24 season after meeting the soprano in California one year earlier and auditioning for her, sang the minor role of Fléville. This was the first performance Serafin ever conducted for Ponselle. Her next assignment was the Puccini Memorial Concert of December 7, in which Serafin conducted her "Un bel dì" from *Butterfly*. Other major artists on the program were Bori, De Luca, Danise, the tenor Miguel Fleta, Alda, Jeritza, Gigli, Telva, and Martinelli. Because Puccini had come twice to the Metropolitan and because so many of these singers had known him personally or even sung under his direction in premieres of his works, this concert, only a week after Puccini's death, proved to be a particularly dramatic and serious event.

Ponselle had been rehearsing in the opera house since mid-November, after spending more than a month in bed. For perhaps the first time in her career she was thoroughly prepared to face a risky, demanding work. Her first performance of *La Gioconda* came in Philadelphia on December 9. Cast with her were Gigli, Danise, and Mardones, with Jeanne Gordon as Laura and the American Merle Alcock as La Cieca.

Speaking of the opera years later, Ponselle reflected on the Wagnerian dimensions of its music and, in an interview with Boris Goldovsky broadcast as a Texaco Metropolitan Opera intermission feature on March 17, 1954, said that *Norma* and *Gioconda* were the two most difficult operas she ever sang.

"Gioconda is a savage part, full of violence," she observed. Interviewed by Tom Villella on another occasion, she recalled the support she had from Serafin as she left the stage between her mother and Enzo during act 1. She was referring to performances of *Gioconda* that she had sung with Carmela, who finally joined the Metropolitan roster in January 1925:

> Carmela and I sang the *Gioconda* together. Serafin conducted a number of those performances, and when it came to the high B flat of "Enzo adorato! Oh, come t'amo!" Tullio Serafin had a way of knowing whether I was in fine fettle or not that night. And he set that pace so slow! He could tell by how long it took me to start walking off with [my] mother and Enzo. And when I took my time, to take that first step, and [my] pace was very slow, he'd just broaden that whole phrase out as long as Rosa could hold onto the note. He instinctively knew how long I could hold it; he had a way of knowing by the pace of my walking.

Three years after her initial interview with Goldovsky, on April 20, 1957, in another broadcast intermission feature with him, she said:

> It's a kind of Italian *Elektra*, with an intensity that never lets up. [In the last act] comes that sombre recitativo, when the street singers appear with the body of Laura and hide her behind the screen. Then Gioconda is alone, and her unhappiness [and] her longing come out in an aria that stirs your soul, ["Suicidio"]. You'd think this would be the climax of the act, but no! It's only the beginning. And those conflicting moods—here is Gioconda with her rival, Laura, in her power. At one terrible moment, when the moon is covered by clouds and there is no one to [see her], she thinks of murdering this woman, of dropping her body into the canal. . . . Here is a woman with a volcano inside her, looking across the lagoon at the lights of Venice. Their splendor only heightens her loneliness. And in a moment of total despair, she sings that wonderful melody from the first act— "Cuore! dono funesto!" "Oh, heart, fatal gift!"—sweeping everything before it, like an avalanche.

At that point in the interview, Goldovsky began to play from a piano-vocal score, and Ponselle went on at full power, half-speaking and half-singing the words of the scene and ending with a wrenching sob: "In core mi si ridesta, si ridesta la mia tempesta! Immane! Immane! O furibonda! O amore! Amore!! Ah, Enzo, pietà! Enzo, pietà di me! Enzo! Enzo! Pietà! Enzo! Pietà di me!"

Remarking on the rest of the scene, she recalled the final encounter between Gioconda and Enzo, when he, believing that she has stolen Laura's body from the catafalque, threatens to kill her. He then realizes that Laura is not dead but alive, lying on the bed behind the screen. Gioconda unites the two lovers." Ponselle said, "and I'll never forget the moment when Gioconda lifts her cloak [and covers her eyes], so as not to see the happiness of their embrace." Utterly carried away by the music, she stopped speaking her lines altogether and began to sing, delivering "Nascondili, o tenebra" in a full, voluptuous, and emotion-riven voice.

Hearing her, even within the rigid frame of a formal broadcast intermission feature, even tape recorded, as this one was, in the music room of Villa Pace about twenty years after she left the Metropolitan Opera, one cannot help being moved by the raw and shattering power behind her interpretation. We understand how, as an artist, she was positively transported by the music. Her passion was authentic, not contrived. It is also easy to understand how *La Gioconda* became "her" opera, the work Gatti assigned to her thirty-six times between 1924 and 1935. Thirty-one of those performances were conducted by Serafin, who showed her how to acquire a perfect command of the drama, the music, and the idea of singer as artist.

It is clear from the reviews that the critics discerned "a new Ponselle" in this opera. After her first performance in Philadelphia on December 9, the *Bulletin* carried a long article mentioning her recent recovery "from a long illness that prevented her appearance with the company as early this season as expected. But there was little trace of the indisposition noticeable. At times, [the voice] may have lacked some of its accustomed lustre, but so glorious were her full, rich tones, her luscious mezza voce and [her] rising to such splendid heights with the dramatic climax of her interpretation of this difficult [opera] that it veritably was a triumph."

Ponselle returned to New York in a familiar role, Santuzza in *Cavalleria*, four days after her first *Gioconda*. In this new production she was partnered by Armand Tokatyan, who often sang with her or with Carmela in recitals and concerts outside of the city. This and *Pagliacci*, also on the bill, were directed by the Ponselles' friend Armando Agnini. Papi conducted. Ponselle did not sing *Gioconda* in the opera house until December 19; and when she read her New York reviews she understood how far her effort had taken her.

The *New York Times* critic wrote: "Rosa Ponselle was new to *La Gioconda* [and was] a direct and vital singer of Venetian tragedy, fairly superb in the last, famous 'Suicidio' air."

Significantly, the *World* said: "Rosa Ponselle restored *La Gioconda* to her place in the spotlight yesterday at the Metropolitan. Her lavish voice and personality swept through this excessively grand opera with a delight and a [sense of] triumph that was infectious. This Gioconda dominated not just the cast but her own destiny as well."

From the *Sun* came nothing but praise: Ponselle was "a striking heroine, in excellent voice; and [she] gave a dramatic and vigorous portrayal. . . . Vocally she gave her best, which is very good indeed; and her upper register disclosed a wealth of golden tone."

"*La Gioconda* was thoroughly suited to her talents, having much in which her vocal vigor and strong top notes could be used to her advantage," wrote the critic of the *Tribune*.

Ponselle's further growth was on display six days later, when she sang her first *Aida* in the opera house. This was only her fifth performance of the role she had once considered something of a threat because of the high tessitura of the Nile scene. Serafin conducted her in this opera for the first time on Christmas Day, with Fleta as her Radamès and De Luca as Amonasro. On December 26 almost all the critics praised her Aida in glowing terms.

"She looked well and sang admirably in a role which is well suited to her," wrote the *New York Times* critic. "Miss Ponselle is advancing as a dramatic singer and knows how to modulate her voice according to the sentiments required of her [character]."

In the *Evening Post* she was described as being "particularly fitted to the role, with the opulence of her wonderful voice; and [she is] physically perfect in its delineation."

Only the *Sun* reviewer expressed reservations, finding her "not convincing, a superficially emotional creature with a striking figure and often with a wealth of golden tone."

Earlier in the month Ponselle had begun her first recordings for Victor, hoping for better reproduction than she had had from Columbia, although she said she had been fond of her colleagues there. Victor also offered her more freedom to choose her music, she said in her autobiography. Beyond that, Victor had a far wider market than Columbia as well. As we see from her account books, her income from recording soared after she moved to Victor; some of their payments of ten thousand and twenty thousand dollars enabled her to add premium stocks to her investment portfolio.

L'africaine followed *Aida* by only two days. The soprano did not sing in *Gioconda* again until the first week in January; by then dozens of news and feature stories in papers all over the country were announcing an event that soon turned into a public relations blitz: a Metropolitan Opera concert, scheduled for January 11, 1925, in which Carmela and Rosa would sing together for the first time on that stage. Most articles ran blazing headlines across two or three columns with pictures of both sisters and accompanying copy that tugged at the heartstrings with anecdotes about their family's poverty in Meriden, the sister act in vaudeville, and the sacrifices Carmela had made to help her parents and launch Rosa's career. Even in interviews when she was only a solo act in "vaude" Carmela had spoken of her efforts on her sister's behalf, but this was surely the first time the subject had been mentioned in such important spreads. The advance publicity was astounding.

Although Ponselle herself may have helped to get Carmela a chance to sing at the Metropolitan, it is far more likely, as has been reported, that Otto Kahn heard her at the Catholic Actors Guild annual benefit concert in New York and asked Gatti to add her to the list of artists for the Sunday night concerts at the Metropolitan. Kahn was the foremost patron of the Guild; he had heard Carmela before, when she and Rosa had first auditioned for Gatti. Quite beyond that, he attended the benefits of many other charitable organizations for which Carmela regularly sang in New York and on Long Island. Whatever else she was, she was positively inexhaustible in donating her services to the Milk Fund, the Children's Health Fund, the Italian Welfare League, orphanages, hospitals, and other good causes.

The possibility of Kahn's intervention and Gatti's later acceptance of Carmela is made all the more believable because in her scrapbook she kept two identical copies of the concert program from that sensational event at the Metropolitan. In pencil she wrote "audition night" on one of them and "debut" on the other. It is hard not to believe that one of these notes was scribbled before the well-publicized concert and the other after she was told that she would indeed get a full contract with the Metropolitan.

Carmela Ponselle made her Metropolitan Opera debut that January, singing "O don fatale" from *Don Carlos*. This was her first official act in the opera house, on a program that was shared with her former teacher Giovanni Martino, who opened the evening with "Il lacerato spirito" from *Simon Boccanegra*. Rosa then sang "Tacea la notte" and "D'amor sull'ali rosee" from *Trovatore*. Then the two sisters sang the duet "Fu la sorte" from the second act of *Aida*. Lawrence Tibbett offered "Eri tu" from *Un ballo in maschera*; other young artists completed the program. Giuseppe Bamboschek, a close friend of all, was the conductor.

Because there had been so much advance coverage, the New York press could report the next day that the concert was "a gala occasion" with "the house packed from floor to ceiling with a huge, enthusiastic audience." Two hundred people came from Meriden alone. The *Tribune* reported that the sisters' "appeal sold out the house, even with extra chairs in the orchestra pit [*sic*] and crowds of standees, until the doors bulged," and recalled Carmela's 1923 recital at Town Hall in New York and her Amneris in *Aida* at the Polo Grounds. Describing the Metropolitan Opera event, the critic wrote that Carmela had "a voice of considerable depth and richness, with full and soaring high notes."

The *World* noted that there had been "applause for ten minutes after the *Aida* duet," while the *Sun* said that Carmela's "O don fatale" was "enthusiastically applauded." The *Telegram* offered a fair and more extended review of her: "When Miss Carmela Ponselle made her appearance, she was warmly received and made a most favorable impression in 'O don fatale' from *Don Carlos*. Here is a voice which, though not great, is very good. There are no holes in it; its steady legato travels from the lowest note to the highest in one unbroken flow of sound. It is full, round and musical and well trained in the operatic style. At the conclusion of her air, she was re-called three times." About the *Aida* duet the reviewer said, "The two [voices] blended in a most attractive manner. From every point of view, this was one of the most telling moments of the evening; and the sisters were recalled again and again."

Carmela must have been told at once that she would be given a contract with the Metropolitan after her "audition" in the concert, for she signed with the company on January 23, 1925, for the following season, engaged from December 20 to April 18, 1926. Notwithstanding the date that was sup-posed to mark her first service with the Met, Carmela's first operatic per-formance in the opera house took place on December 5, two days before she was to have reported for her first rehearsals and fifteen days before she offi-cially became a contracted member of the company. The opera was the mati-nee *Aida* with Rethberg, Martinelli, De Luca, and Mardones under Serafin's baton. This strongly suggests that Carmela was called upon to substitute for another Amneris, perhaps Telva, who had sung the role earlier, and may account for the nervousness that at least one reviewer noticed in the experi-enced and stagewise mezzo. She repeated Amneris on Christmas afternoon, five days after her contract really began. This was undoubtedly her first scheduled performance. Two days later she returned to the Metropolitan concert program with Rosa, the baritone Mario Basiola, Mardones, Cham-lee, Ralph Errolle, and Tibbett, among other singers. The sisters sang the duet from the second act of *La Gioconda*; Rosa sang "Pace, pace, mio Dio," and Carmela sang "Mon coeur s'ouvre à ta voix" from *Samson et Dalila*. At thirty-seven she had reached her goal at last.

Although she arrived late at the Metropolitan, Carmela stayed remark-ably on course. On the day after her debut in the Sunday night concert, the *New York Times* ran its leading editorial with the headline CHEERS IN THE

THEATRE saying, "On Sunday night a Metropolitan audience hailed Carmela Ponselle. In her case, it was a heart-throb in the genuine sense." Over the years to come she often got excellent reviews; the *New York World* critic called her Santuzza "one of the most vital impersonations the Metropolitan [audience] has ever witnessed."

From that moment until the mid-1930s there were two artists from the Ponzillo-become-Ponselle family in almost every Metropolitan season. The sisters continued to live together at 260 and later at 90 Riverside Drive, and while Rosa remained the celebrity, Carmela pursued a serious career in opera, concerts, recitals, and above all radio, for which she became a major spokeswoman and promoter. At her recitals she was accompanied often by Romani or Stuart Ross and occasionally by Willard Sektberg, who later accompanied Leonard Warren. She continued performing and, after she left the stage, she taught voice in New York.

It was Rosa, though, whose "grand career" was about to begin under Serafin's watchful eye. In the seven years after Ponselle's debut in *Forza* she was never once awarded the Metropolitan's signal honor: an opening night with her as the star. But with the conductor's continuing support and the huge success of *La Gioconda*, that plum was hers at last, when Gatti told her that she would open the Metropolitan's next season.

CHAPTER 8

The Grand Career

The grandiose *La Gioconda* that opened the Metropolitan's 1925–26 season was always thought of as "Ponselle's opera" because she was as successful in it that night as she had been the year before; but part of the glory was owed to a cast that could hardly have been improved upon, for it included Gigli, Matzenauer, Danise, Mardones, and Telva, with Serafin conducting. On a personal level the event itself represented a victory over Jeritza, who had opened the 1922–23 season with *Tosca* and the following season with *Thaïs* and had also had important revivals and new productions mounted for her. Relations between her and Ponselle remained cool at best and were to boil over in a backstage dispute later. The season that began in the autumn of 1925 mattered not for intramural quarrels, however, but for the stunning artistic steps that measured Ponselle's progress with Serafin as her mentor. For the first time in several years she was focusing on opera instead of out-of-town appearances, and just in terms of scheduling she had taken a meaningful change of direction with her greater commitment to the Metropolitan. Between November 2 and May 5 of the next year Ponselle was to sing twenty-nine times, as opposed to the eighteen she had sung in 1924–25. The extended concert and recital tours of earlier seasons were replaced by brief ones, limited to the period before October 15 and to less than two months in the spring.

Early in 1925 Ponselle agreed with Gatti and Serafin that she should undertake something entirely new to her, a rarely produced opera written in an unfamiliar style by a virtually forgotten composer: *La vestale* by Gaspare Luigi Spontini. Born in 1774, Spontini had been the favorite of the Neapolitan court and had produced several operas before moving to Paris just after 1800. The protégé of the Empress Josephine, he composed a successful *Milton* in 1804 and followed it in 1807 with *La vestale,* the landmark of Spontini's career. The elevated libretto, by Etienne de Jouy, tells the story of a Roman captain who returns from war to find that the young woman he loves has been forced to become a vestal virgin. Produced first at the Paris Opéra, *La vestale* was followed by the wildly extravagant *Fernand Cortez* of 1809. Both had their premieres during the reign of Napoleon and virtually fell out of the repertory after Waterloo. Later Spontini moved to Berlin and eventually returned to Italy, where he died in 1851.

La vestale had been given in the United States in 1828 and at Covent Garden in 1842 and had been a vehicle for Jenny Lind. A production of it for the carnival season in Rome in 1875 encouraged some to believe that it might return to the repertory. Exaggerated claims for it were put forth, leading to a public dispute over its merits in 1877, when the critic d'Arcais began to praise it and even tried to push it onto the schedule in several Italian opera houses. Verdi, in a letter to Giuseppe Piroli, wrote, "D'Arcais is truly wrong to 'force,' as people say, the hand of these impresarios, poor devils, who will end up by being utterly ruined financially. I think I told you when we met that *La vestale* is an opera that was enormously valuable as a response to the demands and needs of that period [the early 1800s], but it is no masterpiece."

Not until December 1908 did *La vestale* appear on the stage at La Scala. Its star, Ester Mazzoleni, repeated the work in Paris one year later. Although we do not know whether Serafin heard it, he was conducting at the Teatro dal Verme in Milan from September through December 1908 and had every chance to see a rehearsal or performance at La Scala. He is much less likely to have seen the 1923–24 revival at the Teatro Costanzi in Rome.

That the opera could not win the favor of the Metropolitan Opera audience was a lesson Gatti was about to learn, but *La vestale* did not ruin him, and the role of Giulia did prove to be a perfect vehicle for the voice that

Serafin believed he had discovered in Ponselle: a voice suited to the technically difficult works of composers such as Spontini and Bellini.

Serafin wrote of his choice:

> I took [Ponselle] under my protective care. I first made her sing *La
> vestale* in November 1925 as a way of bringing her close to Bellini's
> style, and she was a huge success. Then we began to prepare *Norma*,
> working virtually every day on it. Vocal exercises; then the music of
> Bellini; then more vocal exercises. Gradually I began to be aware that
> a fire was rising up from beneath the ashes, and that the figure of
> that unhappy priestess [Norma] was matched precisely to [Pon-
> selle's] voice, which was austere and passionate, in all its tragic
> quality.

The conductor and soprano clearly perceived *La vestale* as a prelude to
Norma. In one interview Ponselle said that she worked for about eighteen
months "on *Norma*," but on another occasion she said "two years." *Vestale*
fell in that period. And while it is true that Ponselle believed that Gatti-
Casazza had always intended for her to sing *Norma*, because he had asked
her to prepare "Casta diva" for her second audition at the Metropolitan in
1918, it is beyond dispute that he did little in the years that followed to bring
her into the classical repertory. It was Serafin who did. In her autobiography
she said that Gatti approached her in 1925 when "Serafin had already assured
him that I was ready for *Norma*; and to Gatti, Serafin's word was law."

Ponselle added her recollection of the approach to *La vestale* in her
tribute to Serafin. She said, "I prepared *La vestale* during the summer of
1925, musically with my dear and valued coach Romano Romani and then,
in what I might call the final refining process, with Maestro Serafin. [Giulia
in] *La vestale* is a strictly classic role. You achieve your applause on the
singing—or you don't achieve it at all! No dramatic quick or cheap results
there! And during the 1925–1926 season, of course under the baton of Maestro Serafin, I sang *Vestale* and began to know what it was like to taste the
fruits of success in great classic singing."

That Ponselle might learn to lighten her voice for these roles, Romani followed Serafin's orders by using sections of *Vestale* as vocalises. Serafin also taught her restraint to prevent her from resorting to "volume and intensity" as she was doing in *Gioconda*. The conductor "was instrumental in the shaping of many careers, mine especially. The Normas and Vestales were all shaped and coached by that marvelous man, in conspiracy with Romani and Gatti. I didn't think I'd ever sing *Norma*; and they had a way of getting around that. *La vestale* was the forerunner of *Norma*. But I didn't know that they were planning to produce either *Vestale* or *Norma*. It was all a plot."

The first performance of *La vestale* in Metropolitan history took place on November 12, 1925, with Ponselle as Giulia, the Canadian tenor Edward Johnson as Licinio, Matzenauer as the High Priestess, De Luca as Cinna, and Mardones as the Pontiff, with Serafin conducting. The critics' response was overwhelmingly positive.

"In splendor and massiveness [the production] would have rejoiced [Spontini's] megalomaniac soul," wrote Lawrence Gilman in the *Herald Tribune.*

> First of all there was the Vestal herself, Rosa Ponselle; for here was a "youngest Vestal" who was obviously young. Here was a singer who could sing Spontini's long, gravely sculptured melodies with the required sense of line and dignity of style, and with the formal and somewhat stilted pathos that is their quaint and special mark—as in her second act aria "Tu che invoco con orrore"—for Miss Ponselle sang these passages of cantilena with admirable phrasing, with loveliness of tone and severity of style; and she was no less admirable in those moments of true dramatic expression with which the score abounds.

Gilman had equally kind words for Matzenauer, Johnson, and De Luca but had reservations about the opera itself: it was "worth doing," as Gatti was claiming, but its composer was "not quite a genius," nor was there "much to be said for his melodic invention, nor for his harmonic resourcefulness." Gilman ended his review with faint praise for Spontini's orchestration.

W. J. Henderson, whose opinion Ponselle respected, wrote glowingly of her, saying that she had "ceased to content herself with splitting the ears and had gone in for real singing" and commenting on her acquired ability to lighten her voice. She possessed "one of the most beautiful organs of tone that the Metropolitan has ever known."

Ponselle said in her autobiography that these words "practically made my whole year."

Harold C. Schonberg, the veteran critic who served the *New York Times* for many years, spoke in an interview in 1996 about his early experience, saying that Ponselle's *La vestale* was "sublime." As a boy he heard the soprano in this and other works, he said. "Her voice hit little Harold on the head and went around my shoulders and down my back. She had the greatest voice I ever heard, the greatest single voice in any category. She had a quality, a color of sound that no one else ever had."

Much of that quality can be heard in Giulia's two great arias from *La vestale*, which Ponselle recorded in May 1926 for Victor with Rosario Bourdon as her conductor. Both reveal a reserved and perfectly controlled classical artist of great sophistication. In "Tu che invoco con orrore" Ponselle makes believable the confusion and fear of the young vestal, while "O nume tutelar" shows a masterly command of dynamics and phrasing that sets it quite apart from almost everything she had recorded up to that time. Remembering the observations of the critic who said that her huge voice completely filled the auditorium of the Brooklyn Academy and threatened to drown out even Giovanni Martinelli's robust tenor, one can only stand in awe at Ponselle's refinement and control in "O nume tutelar." The recording is simply beautiful. The high notes are securely in place; when volume is demanded, she has it ready; and she can spin her *pianissimi* down to a thread without once overrefining her sound, running out of breath, or vitiating the sustained dramatic power of the scene.

Because *La vestale* did not prove popular, the soprano sang it only nine times for the Metropolitan, eight in New York and one in Philadelphia. After her first appearance in it she returned to her old repertory and went back to *La juive*, which she had not sung since 1920. In its 1925–26 revival Martinelli took Caruso's old role and Rothier returned as Brogni. Louis Hasselmans

replaced Artur Bodanzky on the podium for all performances of it that season. Ponselle also sang in three important concerts. The first commemorated the centenary of Italian opera in New York. The second, in January,
marked the twenty-fifth anniversary of Verdi's death. His Requiem was offered with Ponselle, Gigli, Alcock, and Mardones. In the third concert, already mentioned, she and Carmela sang the duet "E un anatèma" from
Gioconda.

During the first months of 1926 Ponselle's contracts and managerial
arrangements were all under review. At that time she was still singing at the
Metropolitan under her old contract, which she and Gatti had signed in
January 1924. It provided for her employment each year "for a period of
two-and-a-half months, between the beginning of November and about the
beginning of May." Her fee of $1,250 a week for 1924–25 had been raised to
$1,400 a week for 1925–26. In the 1926–27 season she was to receive $1,550 a
week.

With her engagement through the spring of 1927 covered under her
previous three-year contract with the company, Ponselle and Gatti had obviously been negotiating again, for on January 7, 1926, they signed a new agreement, also for three years, that would cover her from the autumn of 1927 to
the spring of 1930, if the company exercised its annual renewal option.
Again, as in 1925–26, she was to be available in the fall from the first week
in November and make herself available for the tour, if needed; but the new
contract guaranteed her three months of work for the Metropolitan each
year, two weeks more than her earlier agreement had done. This new contract also reflected her significantly improved status with the Metropolitan:
for the first time she won the consideration of being paid as the stars were,
at a per-appearance rate rather than by the week. For the season of 1927–28
her fee would be $1,150 "for each performance or concert." In 1928–29 she
would get $1,250 for each, as she also would in 1929–30.

Ponselle was guaranteed no fewer than twenty-one "performances or
concerts" each season. The list of her operas, as given in the contract, reads:
"In Italian: *Africana, Norma, Ballo in Maschera, Cavalleria Rusticana, Forza
del Destino, Gioconda, Tabarro, Tosca, Trovatore, Don Carlos, Andrea Chénier,*

Amore dei Tre Re, Ernani, Mefistofele (Margherita and Elena), *Guglielmo Tell, Vestale.* In French: *Juive, Roi d'Ys.* In English: *Oberon.* In Latin: Verdi's *Requiem*, Rossini's *Missa Solemnis*, Rossini's *Stabat Mater.*"

Gatti gave Ponselle a great deal of time to prepare *Norma*, from January 1926 until October 1927, when the first rehearsals got under way—a vast difference from 1918, when she had had to prepare *Aida, Trovatore, Cavalleria, Forza,* and the Verdi Requiem in about five months, with no fund of experience to draw on. If it is true that her assignment in *Vestale* came as a surprise and that Gatti left her only a short time to learn it, it is now clear that he gave her all the time she needed to prepare Norma, a much more demanding role. He also promised Ponselle her second consecutive opening night: *La vestale* for the 1926–27 season.

Less than one month after signing her new contract with the Metropolitan, Ponselle changed managements, leaving National Concerts, Inc., and Samuel Geneen. Her personal manager, Libbie Miller, an employee of National, went over to the new management the soprano chose. She later would set up her own business and handle Ponselle's affairs for many years to come. But beginning in 1926 the soprano's new agency was the Metropolitan Music Bureau of New York City, Inc., a firm of some distinction that, notwithstanding its name, had no connection to the Metropolitan Opera Company. Ponselle's manager at the Metropolitan Music Bureau was F. C. Coppicus. Their agreement, dated February 3, 1926, stipulated that he would negotiate concerts and grand operas and that Ponselle would be paid no less than $2,000 for each concert. For 1926–27 only, she would receive "65% or 70% of the gross receipts" of five concerts. Coppicus also had the right only in 1926–27 to book certain other engagements at $1,850 and two "musicales" in New York City or Washington for $1,500 each. Ponselle was guaranteed absolute and sole control over the programs she would sing and could stipulate the order in which her numbers would be performed. As in all such contracts, she had to cover her traveling expenses as well as her accompanist's fees and traveling expenses, including hotels and rail fares. She also had to pay all costs of advertising material and publicity, which were a large expense each year for Ponselle, as she also kept her own press agent, Mr.

Dunn, and a clipping service. The contract with Coppicus reads: "To induce her to execute [this agreement] Coppicus agrees to pay to Ponselle the sum of $6,500 on the execution of this agreement and an additional sum of $6,500 [plus interest, later]." She signed, giving her address as 260 Riverside. Coppicus's office was in the old Aeolian Building on Forty-second Street.

With the Metropolitan Opera contract settled and a new manager in place in 1926, Ponselle also renegotiated her recording contract with the Victor Talking Machine Company. Her original agreement dated from March 1923 and had been modified by a supplemental contract of September 1924. As we have seen, the former month marked her last Columbia recordings, while December 1923 brought her to Victor's studios for the first time.

Ponselle's first records for Victor, made on December 5, 1923, at the old studios in Camden, New Jersey, were "O patria mia" and "Ritorna vincitor" from *Aida.* Decisions about what to record were almost exclusively Ponselle's; her first wish was apparently to reissue important numbers that she felt could be improved upon. Later, knowing that her first contract with Victor was about to expire, she arranged a renewal that would continue her guaranteed control over her recording career. Her attempt to negotiate on her own for a Victor radio concert, which had so angered Geneen, resulted finally in her debut on the Victor Talking Machine Hour on New Year's Day 1927. She was also the guest artist on that program exactly one year later. At that time the Metropolitan's regular Saturday matinee broadcasts were still in the future, but many classical artists had already won wide audiences on the air, and Ponselle would follow.

Her 1926–27 season at the Metropolitan was one of the easiest she ever had, for although she sang thirty-one times, Gatti required only one new role of her: Fiora in Montemezzi's *L'amore dei tre re.* As he had promised, Gatti gave Ponselle the opening-night *Vestale* of November 1. She had a new Licinio, Giacomo Lauri-Volpi, replacing Armand Tokatyan, who had been alternating with Edward Johnson in this role. Lawrence Gilman of the *New York Herald Tribune* compared Lauri-Volpi, "the new Italian," with Johnson, observing that he sang much louder than the Canadian tenor "with a voice that was sometimes as hard and smiting as his early Roman sword." Five years Ponselle's senior, the sturdy tenor had made his debut in Italy in 1919 and joined the Metropolitan roster for the 1923–24 season. Matzenauer and De Luca remained in place from the original cast, while Ezio Pinza made his debut on that opening night in Mardones's old role, the Pontiff. Also from Rome and also Lauri-Volpi's age, Pinza made an impression at once. Gilman saw in him "an imposing figure" with "an excellent voice; and he sings with brains and discretion. High Priests are usually the dullest animals in the operatic herd. Mr. Pinza made this one much more than tolerable." The critic had nothing but praise for Ponselle. "As before," he wrote, she "sang Giulia; and if anyone could impart an accent of poignant verisimilitude to the music, this admirable artist surely could." Pinza, writing of his debut years later, recalled "the dark splendor of [Ponselle's] voice" in *La vestale*.

One highly publicized event at the Metropolitan followed in November: the American premiere of *Turandot* with Jeritza as the protagonist and Lauri-Volpi as Calaf. Left unfinished when Puccini died in 1924, the work had been completed by Franco Alfano and given its world premiere, directed by Toscanini, at La Scala in April 1926 with Raisa and Fleta. At the Metropolitan it, like *Vestale*, was conducted by Serafin, who recalled the problems he had with Jeritza while it was in rehearsal. He described his "memorable arguments" with her:

> She had a beautiful figure for the Princess Turandot, a face that was hieratic and sensual at the same time; but her voice, even though it was pure and rich, was a little short [on top]. The piano rehearsals all ended up in confrontations between her and me [because] she expected me to change or transpose down Turandot's music, something I would not allow. At a certain point I shouted at her. . . . That infernal creature, who spoke Italian very badly, said with a little smile, "Serafin is gentleman and lets ladies get away with their little whims." And I: "Ladies, yes. But prima donnas, no!" And I added, "You're nothing but a bluff: you claim that the role of Turandot is written perfectly for you. Raisa claims that, too. But Raisa can sing it as it is written, and you can't." She shut up and blushed, as if I

had slapped her. But she worked hard, got the top notes, and sang the role exactly as it is written, note for note. Just one more thing about *Turandot:* I have to add that Giacomo Lauri-Volpi was a marvelous Calaf, who, from that night on, made that role his own in all the great theaters in the world."

Fortunately, Serafin had no similar problems with Ponselle, who, after the undisputed success of *Vestale,* went on with the Metropolitan season. This marked the return of *Forza* to the repertory for the first time in four years. In the cast were Ponselle, Martinelli, Danise (with Mario Basiola as his alternate), Pinza as the Padre Guardiano, Telva as Preziosilla, and Tibbett (who quickly became a star in his own right) as Fra Melitone. After Caruso's death Gatti had treated *Forza* somewhat warily, casting first Crimi then Salazar as Don Alvaro. Finally Gatti chose Martinelli, who settled into the role and continued to sing it through the 1926–27 season with Ponselle as his partner in New York. It then became a tour staple, heard with them in Atlanta, Cleveland, and Rochester that spring. Again the following year *Forza* came back, in November 1927, as popular as it had been earlier. Ponselle sang Leonora a total of thirty-five times in her career at the Metropolitan; after 1922 all but one of these performances was with Martinelli, and many were with Pinza.

On December 29, 1926, Ponselle sang her first Fiora in *L'amore dei tre re,* a work with which she was thoroughly familiar. It was, after all, one of the first two operas she said she had seen at the Metropolitan, years before she first stood on its stage. The work had also been in her list of "operas the artist is required to prepare" for several seasons, all the while being sung mostly by Bori and Muzio. One year after its world premiere at La Scala in 1913, *L'amore dei tre re* reached the Metropolitan, where it proved to be remarkably successful. Ponselle, who said she prepared it with Serafin, called it one of her favorite roles. The 1926 version was billed as a "revised production" with a new set for act 2 designed by Joseph Novak. In Ponselle's first performances of it in 1926 and 1927 the opera was played on a double bill, first opposite John Alden Carpenter's *Skyscraper,* then with *Gianni Schicchi.*

Finally it was given a whole evening to itself, which it surely deserved. On October 29, 1928, Ponselle sang Fiora in New York, marking the fourth time in her career that she appeared in the Metropolitan's opening night. Her 1929 appearance in it came in Philadelphia, and it was her last. She sang opposite four different tenors cast as Prince Avito, one in each of her four performances: Gigli, Tokatyan, Martinelli, and Johnson. In her performances Ponselle had the blind King Archibaldo sung twice by Didur, who was by then a veteran bass, having joined the company in 1908, and twice by the newcomer, Pinza.

The rest of Ponselle's schedule that 1926–27 season included two performances of *La juive,* her fifteenth and sixteenth, again with Martinelli and Rothier. Hasselmans conducted both. She also repeated other, more familiar operas: *L'africaine, Gioconda,* and *Cavalleria* in New York: *Trovatore* in Baltimore, Washington, Cleveland, and Atlanta; and *Aida* in Cleveland. A hint of things to come might have been detected in her choice of "Morgen" by Strauss and "Träume" by Wagner for one of the Sunday evening concerts. What had by 1926 become a Metropolitan standard for her was the trio from Verdi's *I lombardi alla prima crociata,* "Qual voluttà trascorrere," which she had been singing for years. In a November concert she sang it with Tokatyan and Pinza. Similarly, she sang the trio "Non imprecare, umiliati" from *Forza* in a January 1927 concert with Vittorio Fullin, the husband of Marù Castagna (stage name, Maria Falliani), as her tenor. In an earlier event that same month, Carmela made one of her many concert appearances, singing "Vissi d'arte"; Rosa followed with "Tacea la notte" from *Trovatore.* For the first time at the Metropolitan the two Ponselles sang the Norma-Adalgisa duet, "Mira o Norma." It gave the first hint to the audience of what would later become Rosa's greatest role.

In his autobiography Gatti set forth his cogent reasons for returning *Norma* to the Metropolitan's program and added a few words about his satisfaction with the outcome:

> Sometimes one age forgets the greatness of the art of another because
> of the differences between old and new styles, or, in some cases,

because the artists of a young generation are ignorant of the effect of the proper interpretation. One of our most interesting and important revivals, which took place in the season of [1927–28], was that of Bellini's *Norma,* an opera which I was very proud to be able to present with adequate interpreters to the Metropolitan public. In this noble masterpiece, so difficult for singers that few opera houses can present it today, Ponselle was magnificent. With her were Marion Telva, Lauri-Volpi and Pinza. Serafin did a masterly job. I think I can say that the opera, especially for a generation unfamiliar with its beauties, proved a revelation.

Ponselle, though she was far too young to have seen Lilli Lehmann in *Norma* at the Metropolitan before the turn of the century, had heard Rosa Raisa sing it in New York at the old Manhattan Opera House. In 1921 Gabriella Besanzoni sang Adalgisa. Of that first experience of seeing *Norma* onstage, Ponselle later recalled that she thought she would never sing it because the tessitura of the role lay too high for her voice. Nevertheless, that performance by one of the greatest sopranos of the age had given Ponselle a considerable grasp of its style, costumes, and staging. Now that Gatti had assigned it to her, she had to master it for herself. She prepared for *Norma* by spending the summer at Lake Placid with her mother, Prilik, and Romani, whom she paid fifteen hundred dollars for coaching her in the opera and some additions to her concert repertory. Marion Telva, who would sing Adalgisa, also studied with her that summer.

Recalling how she prepared for the role, she said:

In the summer of 1927 I was put to work in earnest on *Norma.* Before this I had been encouraged to study the "Casta diva" and other outstanding numbers [from it] "as an exercise," [as I was told]. "No, no," I was assured, "there is no need to be afraid." No one was talking of my doing the role, just a question of "a superb exercise for developing the voice," and so on. Gradually, of course, I lost my heart to *Norma,* and then I found that Serafin, Gatti, and Romani, too, had fully intended for me to do it for years.

How we worked that summer! And how Serafin supervised, with loving care and supreme genius, the smallest detail of the most minor character in that [production]. That was one of the most wonderful things about working with him. No one and nothing was too insignificant for his meticulous but ever kindly guidance [of us]. If things went wrong, he joked and made us feel that we could put it all right again. And we did.

What "went wrong" we learn from an affectionate memoir that Serafin left of these events. Discussing his role in persuading Ponselle to sing it, he said that he had first made her learn Spontini's *Vestale* in 1925 just as a way of getting her to begin to understand a composer close to Bellini's style. Although some of his account has been cited earlier, it is worth recalling that he said that he coached Ponselle for *Norma* "almost on an every-day basis, and that went on for a year and a half: vocal exercises, then Bellini's music, then more exercises" until her "fire" was lit, so that she and her voice and the character of the priestess became one.

Norma was not Ponselle's first opera in 1927–28: Gatti was far too wise to schedule something so frightening at the start of her season; instead, she was called to begin her work with rehearsals in the opera house in mid-October that year. Her first assignment was *Gioconda* in Philadelphia, followed by a repeat of the previous season's *Forza* in New York on November 4. This was her 230th performance with the Metropolitan. Twelve days lay between it and the premiere of *Norma*.

Serafin left a vivid account of Ponselle's emotional state in that period:

We got to the day of the last rehearsal before the final dress rehearsal; it went very, very well. It was November 1927. But at the end of the rehearsal I was called into Gatti-Casazza's office. Ponselle was there, half hidden, curled up in a big armchair. She was sobbing as if her heart would break.

Seeing me, she attacked me: "You're the person who has ruined me! You've destroyed my voice! Are you willing to admit that you are responsible for wrecking my career? Are you willing to accept the consequences of that ?"

And she went on crying, absolutely desolate.

"Stop that," I said, in a tough but affectionate tone of voice. "I take full responsibility for it. But now go get something to eat."

Who knows how long it had been since she had eaten?

He was all too aware of how nervous Ponselle was and knew that she had to force herself to get food down "for days and days" (as he said) before the last rehearsals of an opera. After he calmed her down, Ponselle went home, ate properly, rested, and got ready for the dress rehearsal. As Serafin had imagined, it went well.

The cast for *Norma* included Lauri-Volpi as Pollione, Telva as Adalgisa, and Pinza as Oroveso. Gatti presented it as a magnificent new production. Serafin recalled the first night: "*Norma* went onstage on November 16. It was a triumph; but not just any ordinary triumph. People discovered that *Norma* is a masterpiece; people were talking about 'a miracle' that they had discovered in an opera that no one knew. Bellini's genius exploded from it. And for Ponselle, it was the most complete revelation imaginable."

At the time Ponselle first sang *Norma* the work had not been heard at the Metropolitan for decades, and consequently few members of the audience were familiar with what Krehbiel, writing for the *Tribune* in 1890, had called "the old domain of beautiful singing" when he reviewed Lilli Lehmann's single benefit performance of it that year. She repeated the opera in the 1891–92 season, singing it twice, but after that it was heard no more; thus a "revelation" was indeed visited upon the Metropolitan audience in November 1927. It heard Bellini's bel canto performed by singers who could rise to all its challenges, commanding the techniques of breath control and support, to say nothing of the agility to negotiate extremely difficult *fioritura* passages, all the while maintaining the dignity and elevated style that the librettist and composer demand.

W. J. Henderson, who had often heard Lehmann, was never reluctant to criticize. Reviewing *Norma* in the *New York Sun*, he deplored some "pitiably cheap and commonplace stuff in the melodic content of the work" and wrote devastatingly about the Druids' march, which, he said, John Philip Sousa "would have been ashamed to father." But "Casta diva" was another matter, an aria "with its deep breathed phrases and its mellifluous suavity." He went on: "The opera depends heavily on what the artists put into it. If it cannot be proclaimed that Miss Rosa Ponselle reached [the highest] level last evening, it can at least be said that she added to her repertoire an embodiment which will increase her fame and which deepens the impression created in recent seasons that the ripening of her talent has been the result of growing sincerity of purpose and earnest study. Her 'Casta diva' was a genuinely beautiful piece of singing."

The "earnest study" had meant absorbing all of Serafin's instruction and several hours of coaching with Romani every day the previous summer, then dozens more hours alone at home at night with the score, as she described her work in her autobiography.

Olin Downes, writing in the *Times* of the "admirable performance" of *Norma,* said that the evening's success was "due largely to the singing of Rosa Ponselle, who has probably the most beautiful voice of any soprano of her generation and who has advanced remarkably as an artist in late years. . . . The performance was halted for minutes after Miss Ponselle's 'Casta diva' and after each act; and especially after the final scenes the audience singled her out for attention."

Ponselle had so far surpassed anything else she had done that one may truly say that she had reached down within herself to find reserves of power and artistry that she herself was not sure she had. The musician and the artist were one, and the image of her sublime Norma became an operatic icon. That accounts for the statue of her in the Druid robe that still stands today on the façade of the I. Miller Building in New York City, just as it accounts for the representation of her as Norma that appears now on a United States postage stamp.

When Ponselle was asked to discuss her achievement many years later in an interview with Tom Villella, she said of it: "Not bad! I appreciate my effort now more than I did at the time. When I was singing it, I was too much engrossed in conscientiously trying to perfect my interpretation. I was never pleased with myself—always grateful, mind you, but never pleased. But today I realize that I did a pretty good job." Further on in the interview she said, "I worked hard. I was a dedicated person."

By perfecting her interpretation while never moving down from musical and stylistic high ground, Ponselle joined a drastically short list of definitive Normas that included Giuditta Pasta, who created the role in the world premiere of *Norma* at La Scala in 1831; Giulia Grisi, the first Adalgisa, who also added the title role to her repertory; Maria Malibran, whose Norma is commemorated in a statue showing her as the Druid priestess; and Lilli Lehmann, the only soprano who could compare singing it to singing Brünnhilde. Audiences of the decade of the 1920s and 1930s were fortunate indeed to have both Raisa and Ponselle accept the daunting role.

After her triumph as Norma, almost everything Ponselle sang was weighed against it. Although she had achieved the benchmark performance of her career, there was no time for resting on her laurels: just three days after the *Norma* premiere she was back on the Metropolitan stage as Santuzza in *Cavalleria rusticana,* which was paired with Martinelli's Canio in *Pagliacci.* On November 23 she returned as Sélika in *L'africaine;* and after another *Norma* in Brooklyn, she came back to the opera house stage as Leonora in *Forza.* That was followed by *Trovatore* on December 7. All this in a month and three days! By the end of December she was again singing in *Gioconda,* while January 1928 brought her back as Maddalena in *Andrea Chénier.* When the tour got under way she was cast in *Forza, Norma, Trovatore, Aida,* and *L'africaine.* She closed her season in Rochester with *Norma.* She had sung twenty-nine performances for the Metropolitan that season and had managed two recital tours, one in the fall and one in the late winter and early spring.

As her fame grew, so did her income. In 1927 she earned $140,404 from the Metropolitan, concerts and recitals, recordings, an endorsement for Knabe pianos, and interest on her investments. In 1928 she earned $155,765.

This was a year that saw her honored once more with the opening night of the Metropolitan 1928–29 season. The opera was *L'amore dei tre re,* on

October 29, with Pinza as Archibaldo, Danise as Manfredo, and Martinelli as Prince Avito. It was followed by a season in which Ponselle had no new roles to learn but got to repeat many of her favorite standards. *Ernani* returned to the repertory, with Pinza as Silva, a role that he mastered so completely that one critic wrote of that evening that he "clearly outsang Miss Ponselle, Martinelli and Ruffo." As casting, this was nearly ideal. Titta Ruffo, who had joined the Metropolitan in 1922, had appeared in *Ernani* that year in the role of Carlo with Mardones as Silva and had sung Gérard to Ponselle's Maddalena in *Chénier* and Barnaba to her *Gioconda;* but the combination of his baritone to her soprano, Martinelli's neat tenor, and Pinza's seductive bass brought Verdi to the highest level imaginable at the Metropolitan. Ruffo was almost twenty years older than Ponselle, at the peak of a long career when this *Ernani* reached the opera house stage, and it was a great loss to the company when he left it in 1929.

After *Norma* Ponselle naturally had to consider what professional options were most attractive to her. Again she considered the German repertory, from which she knew virtually nothing, although she had mastered several songs, some of which she had sung in concerts or recorded. From the French and Italian repertory, what was there to choose? Jeritza had already claimed much of that territory for her own. But after 1927 and 1928 both sopranos were facing the same dilemma: How to surpass such significant characterizations as Norma and Turandot? How to recreate themselves with new images? Turandot and Norma, particularly when they are interpreted by women as imposing as Jeritza and Ponselle, both statuesque, make many other roles seem insignificant. They solved their problems in different ways, as one would expect from women so different in background and training.

After its premiere created such a sensation, Gatti chose *Turandot* to open the 1927–28 season; later that year Jeritza forged a new identity for herself by singing the title role in the first American performance of Korngold's *Violanta;* in 1928 she added Strauss's *Die Aegyptische Helena*, where again she was the protagonist. In 1929 she revealed her idiosyncratic Carmen and, finally, her boisterous and sensuous Minnie in *La fanciulla del West.* Each of these put a "new Jeritza" before the public.

After *Norma,* of which Ponselle said it was "simply the most difficult opera ever written," anything else was bound to be less of a challenge and to hold less promise. Her first foray into *L'amore dei tre re* provided nothing so spectacular as Jeritza's choices, although Ponselle favored the role of Fiora and was successful in it. But she was thinking of singing abroad, rather than simply introducing a new role in the United States. The major influence behind this change of course was Serafin, whose experience in Europe and South America encouraged the soprano and gave moral support and direction when she most needed it.

Ponselle, the child of the United States and daughter of the Metropolitan, had never shown the slightest inclination to risk her career on foreign soil, although she said she had had offers from theaters outside this country; but with Serafin to strengthen her resolve, she felt somewhat safer. Having first conducted in Buenos Aires in 1914, he had gone to Havana, where Ponselle sang concerts in 1923, then to Rio de Janeiro and, in 1928, São Paolo. His engagement at the Teatro Colón in Buenos Aires in July and August 1925 had surely led Ottavio Scotto, its impresario, to send Ponselle a blank contract in February 1926 inviting her to join the Colón company that summer. It had very favorable terms, with a guarantee of forty-five hundred dollars paid into a New York bank before the season and fifteen hundred dollars for each of fifteen performances. There was nothing new to learn, for the operas were *Gioconda, Ernani, Cavalleria rusticana,* and *L'africaine;* the schedule was easy, with no more than two appearances per week and a guarantee of no performances on consecutive nights. Although this would have been an easy way to earn money during a summer when Ponselle normally had no income, she did not accept; when Serafin conducted *Norma* at the Colón in 1928, it was without her.

Fear of foreign audiences probably prompted her refusal. She admitted that she was terrified at the idea of becoming the target of angry or disappointed opera fans in South America and in Europe. In the music business stories of furious demonstrations during performances were often the stuff of after-dinner conversations, and they were not imagined or invented but were easily confirmed by those who had survived them. In Parma many singers had been driven from the stage and one or two even from the Teatro Regio itself, fleeing to the station while still in costume and boarding the first train out. Once during *Il barbiere di Siviglia* the curtain had to be brought down and the performance stopped when enraged patrons hurled some of the first-row seats onto the stage. Every singer dreaded hearing "the Parma groan" as it rose from the throats of people in the audience; others feared hearing shouts of derision from the last balcony. "Hey, Campanèn, this is how it goes!" the public had shouted when the famous tenor Italo Campanini once forgot his lines. People in the audience had then begun to sing along with him, word for word. Nor was Parma the only city where such demonstrations were commonplace. The memory of the fiasco of Puccini's world premiere of *Madama Butterfly* at La Scala was still fresh in everyone's mind. If a great soprano like Rosina Storchio could be hooted and whistled at, with such a fury unleashed in the theater that she could not even hear the orchestra, a young, vulnerable American singer might expect something far worse. With her chronic stage fright and her "nerves," Ponselle admitted that she could never run the risk of being attacked in such a demonstration.

Serafin, who had conducted at Covent Garden many years before, then convinced Ponselle to make her European debut in London, where decorous behavior was obligatory. She would be protected there and guaranteed a serious hearing in a landmark theater. So the momentous decision was taken. Ponselle, who had spent the summer of 1928 in a log cabin in Pine Orchard, working on *L'amore dei tre re* for the Metropolitan's opening, would cross the Atlantic in 1929, not as a tourist, but as a working artist on her way to her first engagement abroad.

CHAPTER 9

Closing the Circle

SPRING 1929–AUTUMN 1938

Ponselle's Metropolitan Opera season of 1928–29 ended with her and Gatti-Casazza signing on April 13 a lucrative new four-season contract that would reach from the autumn of 1930 through the spring of 1934, with a guarantee of three months' work and no fewer than twenty-one opera or concert performances each season. Within days she was on the tour, which ended for her with two engagements in Cleveland, where she sang in *Norma* on April 29 and *Gioconda* on May 1, both to extraordinarily good reviews. She left at once for New York, then sailed for England in first class, as always, accompanied by Edith Prilik, the dancer Antonia Merce, known as La Argentina, and Libbie Miller, who was by then free to call herself the soprano's personal manager, under Coppicus and Frederick Schang of the Metropolitan Music Bureau, who officially handled most of the soprano's bookings and continued to list her on their roster. Also with them was Lena Tamborini, Ponselle's childhood friend.

 EUROPEAN DEBUT ❧

In London Ponselle followed the custom of other famous singers by staying at the Savoy, a few blocks down the hill from the Royal Opera House at Covent Garden. Then, as now, it was an expensive hotel, which meant a large outlay for her. But whatever else London meant for Ponselle, earning high fees and turning a profit were not foremost among her motives. Prilik, under the rubric "1929," listed Ponselle's income for some but not all of her Covent Garden appearances: $2,800 for two performances of *Norma* in 1929, $2,800 for two performances of *L'amore dei tre re* in 1930, and $4,200 for three of *La traviata,* for a total of $9,800 for seven performances. These figures appear to reflect her net return; there is no note of how much she was paid for *Gioconda* in 1929 or for other work in 1930 and 1931.

Letters written between January and September 1930 from Colonel Eustace Blois, the director of Covent Garden, to Ponselle and Prilik reveal a clearer picture. The terms of her first contract, for 1929, were in dollars; the contracts for 1930 and 1931 were in English pounds. For 1931 she was to be paid the equivalent of $2,200 a performance for a minimum of ten performances, plus $1,500 toward her transportation from New York to London. Blois wrote to Ponselle personally in December 1930, saying, "I am sure, dear Rosa, that we are paying you more than we ever paid anybody, except Chaliapin; but I know the expense you are put to in coming here."

They were both well repaid for the investment, for Ponselle created a sensation in London in each of the three seasons she sang there. Settled in at the Savoy, she soon found a way to continue her long, routine walks, striding along the Embankment and through the park that lies beside the Thames and on Savoy Place behind the hotel, then making her way on the Strand and up Bow Street to the opera house. The English author Ida Cook, who, like her sister Louise, was an admirer of Ponselle, recalled in conversation her surprise at seeing the soprano pushing along crowded Floral Street toward the stage door in an era when other celebrities arrived at the theater in limousines.

Frederick Gaisberg, the representative of the Victor Talking Machine Company who was then living in London, recalled her visits in *The Music Goes Round* and *A Voice in Time,* describing her "dark, swarthy complexion" and athleticism. In *The Music Goes Round* he wrote: "Here comes Rosa Ponselle. Tall, with a graceful carriage and finely cut features, she sweeps along. So striking is her appearance that you could never miss her in a crowd." He went on to define her voice as "perhaps the most perfect *lirico spinto* soprano that ever lived" and added that at the time Ponselle was in

London "her gramophone contract alone was worth £7,000 a year." He said that "of her portrayals of Violetta, Norma, Luisa Miller, Giulia in *La Vestale,* Leonora and Gioconda, she has no equal. I will go further than this and hail her as the greatest actress singer of our time." Quite beyond her artistry, the diva also showed her human side during an elegant supper party at the Savoy that Gaisberg recalled. She, hating overheated rooms, "escaped" from the dining salon and walked with him and his guest along the Embankment. When the guest felt ill, Ponselle seated him on the base of Cleopatra's Needle and "bathed his head and soothed him until he recovered. There was an air of tender solicitude and pity in her nursing that I shall never forget," Gaisberg wrote.

Ponselle and Tamborini went sightseeing together. Like Carmela and Rosa, Tamborini looked back to their school days in Meriden's West Side and the simple life of its Italian-American colony; in 1929 she was a housewife. Tamborini's presence, Ponselle said, reassured her. Opera fans soon learned that these American women had unpretentious ways, even when they were living at the Savoy; and everyone could see how different they were from the extravagant Jeritza, who had arrived with an entourage of servants and pets four years earlier. The Czech soprano had been set quite apart from other singers by her own fame, her title, Baroness Popper, and the reputation of her mother-in-law, Blanche Marchesi, one of the world's greatest singing teachers. Ponselle arrived with none of these endowments. Instead, she came with her handsome presence, stylish wardrobe, and modern way of thinking, along with her stagecraft, musicality, and voice. She utterly conquered London, garnering two- and three-line headlines in major papers and winning the audience as well.

In 1929 the soprano's choice of operas proved wise, for *Norma* and *Gioconda,* the two works that had closed her tour season in Cleveland, were the two that she offered at Covent Garden in May and June. As Blois had hoped, they were fresh in her mind and in her voice, so that little was required in the way of preparation beyond becoming familiar with the physical layout of the theater and testing its acoustics. She rehearsed with the cast of *Norma,* which included Irene Minghini-Cattaneo as Adalgisa, chosen, said the critic Harold Rosenfeld, because her "rich, mellow tones could both contrast and combine with Ponselle's." The "competent" Oroveso was Luigi Manfrini. But the cast had one serious liability, an undistinguished Pollione, Nicola Fusati, for whom Blois later apologized. Fusati had originally been engaged for this role and Otello, but his performance in the Bellini work was so poor that the Covent Garden management canceled the second opera, making 1929 the first summer season in nearly forty years with no Verdi on the program.

Although Vincenzo Bellezza conducted *Norma,* Ponselle's musical and dramatic characterization, in London as in New York, had been developed with Serafin, who said of the opera:

> In my opinion [*Norma*] was the most important event of my years at the Metropolitan. I had sworn that it would be my sacred duty to present Bellini's masterpiece, which . . . was considered by most people to be an old opera of no value whatsoever. But it was exactly for this reason that I wanted to present it with dignity and honor and with perfect style. . . . I decided that Rosa Ponselle must be Norma, but must be the Norma that I wanted: that is to say, she must sing it without using the standard compromises to manage the difficulties of the score (as even the admirable Muzio did), but rather note for note, with the trills, the *fioriture,* all the embellishments, but all understood in the dramatic sense, with florid or sustained singing that was always full of fire.

His and Ponselle's effort was rewarded, perhaps even more in London than it had been in New York. Of it Harold Rosenthal said, "The fabulous American soprano's reputation, which had preceded her, was fully justified, and she was acclaimed as being in the true line of great bel canto singers." Writing in the *London Times,* Ernest Newman said of her, "Here is that rarity of the operatic stage, an artist who can not only sing but create a character." In the *Times* she was also praised for a voice "as remarkable for its purity in the big dramatic passages as in the quiet phrases of the 'Casta diva,' and a really finished style alike in the long-sustained notes and in the coloratura passages." The normally restrained audience, which customarily applauded only at the ends of the acts, burst out with a huge ovation after "Casta diva."

Ponselle's second opera at Covent Garden in 1929 was *Gioconda*, which had its first performance on June 3. The first mezzo was Minghini-Cattaneo, whom Ponselle did not particularly like. The Milanese tenor Francesco Merli, who was exactly Ponselle's age, made a heroic Enzo. Giovanni Inghilleri, a regular at Covent Garden, sang Barnaba; and La Cieca was Marù Castagna, the wife of Vittorio Fullin, singing as Maria Falliani, with whom Carmela and Rosa had both sung at the Metropolitan. Fernando Autori was Alvise.

At the end of this enormously successful engagement Ponselle and Prilik left for Italy, where the soprano had to study for her scheduled new operas for the Metropolitan. They were the title role in *Luisa Miller* and Donna Anna in *Don Giovanni*, which she prepared with Romani, who summered in Leghorn, as always, and Serafin, who had finished his Paris engagement in June and was not due in New York until October. He had two villas, one near Florence and another at Bosco Chiesanuova, just north of Verona. On different occasions he had Ponselle as his summer guest while she studied with him.

When Ponselle returned to New York, the most important nonmusical event on her schedule was "a halcyon day" in October that was set aside for the dedication of her statue and those of Mary Pickford, Marilyn Miller, and Ethel Barrymore on the facade of the I. Miller Building at 1552 Broadway. The police department of New York City closed Forty-sixth Street for the day so a stage and chairs could be set up for dignitaries, and the whole block was "overflowing with people eager to catch a glimpse of [these stars]," one officer of the I. Miller firm later recalled.

Beneath a grand, scrolled pediment stood the statue of Ponselle as Norma, in her full, hieratic stance, the very image of power, with her hair streaming over her shoulders and the train of her gown sweeping to the bottom of the marble frame that enclosed the niche. During the ceremony the soprano spoke simply about her life. Whatever else it did, this dedication elevated Ponselle far above almost all her colleagues, past and contemporary. Not since the days of Caruso had any opera singer been tendered such honors.

This public celebration came as the soprano was mastering difficult scores that were new to her and was seeking ways to broaden her repertory still further. Yet it seemed that although she was sometimes advised to try the German operas, she would be forever identified with Italian works. In London Blois had already decided that Ponselle would prove to be his most valuable energy source in the revival of Italian opera in England, while at home Gatti-Casazza was hoping to seize upon her *Traviata* to carry the 1930–31 season at the Metropolitan. With luck, they might even be able to present her Violetta in 1929–30, the memory of her Norma adding stature to any new characterization.

*P*ONSELLE'S INTERNATIONAL CAREER CONTINUES ∾

To be fought over by opera company managements on two sides of the Atlantic was something new for Ponselle. In London Blois was putting up fierce defense of his terrain, writing to her on January 16, 1930, to say that he did not want her to sing *Traviata* in New York before presenting it in London. "The original idea that you should sing *Traviata* was mine; I had this idea fixed in my head both before I ever saw you and after I had heard you sing; and I want the first time you do it to be on *this* stage." He got his way. She was also offered other performances of *Norma*, with a replacement for Fusati. The new Pollione would be Renato Zanelli, whom Blois described as having had "a great success here in 1928 as Otello. Chilean, a very nice fellow, big man and a fine actor." Blois had decided "to drop *Forza*—too many scenes and [intermissions]. I do not think it would go over so well with our public." Instead he offered her Fiora in *L'amore dei tre re*, promising that Montemezzi would come for the premiere. Archibaldo, the bass Autori, whom Ponselle knew from the previous year, would be "a splendid old man, and he has promised me to carry you very carefully at the end of Act I." He closed his letter with "God bless you!"

As Blois was writing this, at the beginning of 1930, the United States and Europe had already begun to fall into the trough of the Great Depression, which affected the theatrical and music business just as it did every other aspect of life. Throughout the 1920s many important singers had fared well in their earnings; and some, notably Farrar, Bori, Jeritza, and even Tibbett, had amassed significant wealth. While few of them would ever match the earnings of a Gershwin or a Jolson, many, like Ponselle, had done very well indeed. She was rich by any standard before 1929, with a substantial, steady income from concerts, recitals, recording, and radio and an occasional fee from an endorsement. To put this in context, when her career began and World War I ended, most American workers were earning something between $1,500 and $2,500 a year from an average work week of fifty hours; many laborers worked sixty and seventy hours a week. Although significant gains were made during the 1920s, no "common man" of that era could hope to reach the $40,000 level, as Ponselle soon did, nor to approach her highest level of income, from $141,404 in 1927 to around $150,000 toward the end of the decade. The years from 1923 to 1929, when her earnings were at their peak, had been termed the "New Era of Prosperity"; but some people were clearly more prosperous than others, with the profits of the wealthy increasing more rapidly than the incomes of the middle class and the poor.

The worst effects of the stock market crash were not felt at once, though no one remained unaffected by it, even at the start of the Great Depression. But over time five-sixths of the value of the market of September 1929 simply vanished. In her biography of Bernard Baruch, Margaret Coit said that the "very rich" became "merely rich," while the "rich became comfortably off." Ponselle falls into the latter category. She had probably been following the counsel of Otto Kahn in investing heavily in utilities and railroads, so she quite naturally suffered from the collapse of the market after October 1929. Gaisberg, who knew quite a bit about her affairs, wrote: "Of course she made money, plenty of it; but then she was a definite draw. Unhappily, a large percentage of her profits was lost [after] the Crash in Wall Street in

1930–1931." She said, speaking of her own situation, that she had acted on sound advice, moving out of stocks and into bonds; but even those were affected.

Through most of 1930 Ponselle and Carmela remained in their old apartment at 260 Riverside, with Romani conveniently down the drive. During the winters the sisters spent much of their time at the Metropolitan, but both also performed in concerts and recitals, sometimes together, in the autumn and spring. Both sisters had important radio concert careers, Carmela's having been launched early and Rosa's beginning in 1927 and lasting for more than ten years. Rosa's *Forza* of June 1 and her *Traviata* of June 9 at the Royal Opera House in Covent Garden were both broadcast in 1931. After the New York season Carmela would stay in the States, singing concerts, while Rosa divided several summers between study in Tuscany or the Veneto with either Romani or Serafin, then would go to Saint-Moritz, as she did from 1930 to 1933. In Italy she would visit Venice and the Lido and move to a house she leased, Villa Platani on Lake Como, where she summered in the early years of the decade, making brief visits to Gatti-Casazza in his villa on Lake Orta or meeting friends such as Eustace Blois for lunch at the elegant Ristorante Campari near La Scala in Milan.

Villa Platani was at Brienno, north of the city of Como and Villa d'Este, where Ponselle was photographed amid the flowering trees. She had chosen the most picturesque retreat imaginable, where many famous people vacationed. Brienno, with its mysterious cave, the Grotto dei Platani, had attracted visitors from the late 1500s onward; the place commanded a splendid view of the water and and the Alps. Lake Como itself, so near Milan, had always attracted musicians. Bellini had often been a summer guest on Como, sometimes in the home of Giuditta Pasta, his first Norma. At nearby Cadenabbia was Villa Ricordi, which belonged to the famous dynasty of music publishers G. Ricordi and Company. There Verdi, Puccini, and many other favored Ricordi composers had spent long visits in the summers. Liszt, Rossini, Byron, and Stendhal had vacationed at Villa La Pliniana, which was directly across the arm of Como from Ponselle's villa.

When Gaisberg was Ponselle's guest in 1931 he said, "I observed the very clever way she mapped out her day to concentrate on her studies. Her recreation was cycling through the Italian countryside and generally 'going native,' dressed in shorts and with a bandanna around her head. . . . She was indistinguishable from the peasants of the country. A good meal is a gift from the gods, not to mention the divas, and I recall . . . that savory dinner of pasta al sugo, a macaroni preparation, and lake trout, which she set before me that day." He added that Ponselle had made it herself. "Cooking is the glory of every Italian girl; they are so practical in the kitchen, and how they enjoy it!"

But it was her career, and not the kitchen, that commanded Ponselle's full attention after the stock market crash. She was facing the Metropolitan Opera House premiere of Verdi's *Luisa Miller* and the controversial revival of *Don Giovanni* at the Metropolitan, both scheduled for the autumn of 1929, as well as one of the most challenging assignments of her career, Violetta in *La traviata,* which Blois had finally convinced her to learn. As we know, Gatti endorsed the idea. When we consider what Ponselle said about her own study techniques, we realize how remarkable her achievement was, for she learned every score from the first note to the last, one line at a time, memorizing the entire text and every singer's music and familiarizing herself fully with the orchestral score as well. As she remarked, at least two of her famous colleagues, Gigli and Pinza, said that they could not read music and learned their roles by rote repetition. Ponselle, in contrast, had a far more profound understanding of her art.

She left Italy through the port of Genoa, staying briefly at the Hotel Miramare e de la Ville before embarking for New York. After her usual concert and recital tour she began her 1929–30 opera season at the Metropolitan on December 21 with *Luisa Miller,* given at the Metropolitan for the first time in its history. This opera, like *Ernani,* which she had sung at the end of the previous season, lay perfectly for her voice at that time. Conducted by Serafin, she was partnered by Lauri-Volpi as Rodolfo, De Luca as Miller, Pasero as Walter, and Pavel Ludikar as Wurm. Not even this excellent cast could make the audience like this work; and after six performances Ponselle never sang it again.

Don Giovanni was another matter. Pinza, in his autobiography, wrote of the personal and professional crises that threatened to ruin his career and bring down the new production with it. His marriage was troubled. Ponselle was ill. A rivalry with Ludikar and a spate of anonymous letters left him unsettled about his future. Nor was he certain of being assigned the all-important title role of the opera. Gatti had told Serafin and another coach to help Pinza learn the music, then several times had had Pinza sing the "Serenade" and other numbers from it for members of the staff, in a kind of "room audition." Not once had Gatti told him that he would in fact sing the Don. Finally came the day when Il Direttore gave Pinza that assignment; but that was kept a secret for many months. When the news broke, Ludikar, De Luca, and even the aged Scotti were angry at the idea that they, baritones all, would not get the role and that a bass would sing it. As he had done with Ponselle, Gatti ordered Pinza to study with Serafin and packed both off to Europe.

As Pinza recalled, "everything went wrong" from the start of rehearsals because the cast failed to "find the key" to Mozart's music. Like the rest of the cast, Ponselle, who despite a throat infection continued to attend rehearsals, was affected by the tension. Pinza, in one infamous incident, got his coat and started to leave the rehearsal hall. When Gatti tried to stop him, the bass shouted, "What are you doing on the stage? Go back to the office, where you belong!" It was unthinkable that anyone would speak to the impresario like that; everyone was stunned. Gatti walked out without saying a word; a stage director then took Pinza's coat and laid it on a chair, and as the bass remembered, "the rehearsal was resumed." The next morning, Pinza apologized to Gatti, who laughed and told him to get back to *Don Giovanni*.

The crisis did not end there. After such a disruption, everyone in the cast was edgy. Pinza remembered Ponselle's "war with steam heat": her dressing room radiator was never turned on and all the pipes onstage had to be kept cold "from early morning on" whenever she had a rehearsal or performance. She went around and touched each one, he remembered, to be sure that no heat was on. Francis Robinson once went beyond that and said in a personal conversation that Ponselle sometimes even asked the stagehands to open the huge doors onto Seventh Avenue to cool the house for her. But as she faced her first *Don Giovanni* her nerves and her sore throat took their toll. The soprano was so ill that on the evening before the first performance she had to be replaced by Leonora Corona, who, Pinza said, had the part of Donna Anna thrust upon her with "too little rehearsal time to do justice to the role." Although Corona had joined the company two seasons before and had a good reputation, the critics were not kind to her.

When Ponselle returned, Pinza said, everyone was grateful for "the miraculous warmth of [her] voice." They were good colleagues; in 1953 she invited him to visit her at Villa Pace, where they were photographed together. In the cast of *Don Giovanni* they were perfectly matched. Gigli sang Don Ottavio; Rethberg was Donna Elvira; the miscreant Ludikar was Leporello; and Editha Fleischer sang a fine Zerlina. Ponselle, when she returned to the cast on January 2, 1930, was widely credited with the enthusiasm the American public began to show for Mozart from that moment on. Olin Downes wrote in his *New York Times* review:

> Rosa Ponselle added another opera portrait to her list of notable achievements when, as Donna Anna . . . she roused her audience to demonstrations of enthusiasm which recalled the legendary days of the opera gods of a past generation. Such singing as she accomplished in a role far removed from the vocal and dramatic style to which she is accustomed was something of a revelation, even to her most ardent admirers. In the typical Italian roles with which Miss Ponselle has been identified, she has often—legitimately, perhaps—employed her unique voice in a style occasionally mannered, toying with the grandiloquent phrases and reveling in the sheer beauty of a mellow flood of tone. Last night she consecrated herself wholeheartedly to the very essence of the Mozartean tradition, never projecting herself out of the picture, always maintaining an aristocratic elegance of line, an aloof distinction and a careful coordination of vocal and dramatic elements with the performances of her associates.

Ponselle sang Donna Anna fifteen times in all; these included the Metropolitan Opera broadcasts of December 1932 and February 1935.

In reviews of the first night of this *Don Giovanni* revival, Gigli and Rethberg were praised for their style, although she had been in poor voice that evening. Ludikar, Editha Fleischer, and Rothier came off badly. Pinza, in the title role, was roundly criticized, particularly by Gilman in the *Herald Tribune;* but gradually he mastered the role, making it one of his greatest characterizations. Serafin got the most credit, for preserving "the long breath and continuity of design" essential to any Mozart production.

At the same time that Ponselle was heralded in the United States for her Donna Anna, the critics and audiences in London were crediting her for kindling another passion at Covent Garden. "Italian Opera in the Ascendancy" is the title Harold Rosenthal chose for a chapter in his history of that theater, in which he wrote, "The debut of Ponselle and the success of *Norma* and *Gioconda* . . . resulted in Blois embarking on a more adventurous Italian policy for 1930 and 1931." These were her last two seasons there.

She sailed from New York on the liner *Roma* on May 10, 1930, and returned to the Savoy, then opened the season at Covent Garden on May 16 with a reprise of *Norma*, again with Minghini-Cattaneo as Adalgisa and again to the same wildly enthusiastic reception she had had the year before. Because Zanelli had not been engaged, her Pollione was Tullio Verona, "hardly any improvement over Fusati," Rosenthal remarked. Ponselle later would work with Zanelli's brother, Carlo Morelli, when he joined the Metropolitan roster in 1935 and, later, in Baltimore. Oroveso in this London production was Pinza, who was by then on his way to becoming a star in his own right. He was also Ponselle's Archibaldo in the second *L'amore dei tre re*, when Blois honored its composer, Montemezzi. As Blois had promised, the first Archibaldo was Autori. Prince Avito was sung by the Milanese tenor Francesco Merli. All were again under the baton of Vincenzo Bellezza.

Ponselle's first Violetta in *La traviata*, sung at Covent Carden on June 13 with Gigli as her Alfredo, was hailed as one of the most original character interpretations of her entire career. After first studying the role with Romani and Serafin, she had prepared it with Gemma Bellincioni, one of the most celebrated Italian sopranos of the previous generation. Born in Monza near Milan in 1864, the retired star was past sixty when Ponselle sought her out. After an early career singing the standard repertory, Bellincioni had emerged as the definitive singing actress of the verismo movement, appearing as Santuzza in the world premiere of *Cavalleria rusticana* in 1890, then as the leading soprano in Giordano's premieres of *Mala vita* in 1891 and *Fedora* in 1898. Frequently she was partnered by the tenor Roberto Stagno, her teacher and husband, who was the first Turiddu. Verdi had been urged to give Bellincioni the role of Desdemona in the world premiere of *Otello;* when Boito, his librettist, first heard her in 1886, he reported to Verdi about her gifts:

> If I were ten years younger, I would already have fallen in love with her. She is so pretty; she is tall, thin, young, elegant, dark-haired, and lithe; and with blond hair [as Desdemona] she would be even prettier, because there is a great deal of sweetness in her face, and she exudes the aura of being loveable. . . . At the end of the scene I became aware that I always was *watching her sing:* that proves how lovely her face and whole being are, and how white her teeth are— but nothing more. Too bad!—but I do not think that Bellincioni was born to be strangled on the island of Cyprus. Too bad!

Verdi then heard her and agreed with Boito. Later, when she was considered for a role in *Falstaff,* he found her unsuitable because she was "very, very intelligent but [invests her roles with] too much emotion." That very quality of heightened emotion was taught to Ponselle as she was studying *Traviata.*

For Ponselle this investment in theater craft returned huge dividends in London. Ernest Newman, one of the world's most respected musicologists and critics, wrote of her Violetta, "It was difficult to believe that she was singing the role for the first time. In the great scene at the end of the first act, she repeats the [phrase] 'E strano'; each time it was different because the mental image at the back of the note was different." Francis Toye, the author of one of the finest biographies of Verdi, said that Ponselle's Violetta was an example of the "alliance between first-class singing and first-class intelligence. I do not think I have ever heard anything to surpass or perhaps even to equal it."

When she sang Fiora in the Montemezzi work, the *London Times* lamented that she was in only the first two acts of the opera: "It was a pity that Fiora's death should occur at the end of the second act, for she had given a performance of great visual and aural beauty." Giovanni Inghilleri, who had sung Germont in *Traviata*, was Manfredo.

For the first time in her life Ponselle showed a romantic interest in a fellow singer when she and Merli, the Prince Avito of the Covent Garden *L'amore dei tre re*, became emotionally aroused during one of the rehearsals. Nothing came of this, however, because by then the soprano had begun a serious relationship with an Italian-American, Giuseppe Russo, whom she had met in New York City (possibly as early as 1915, when he lived next door to Mary Marino's nickelodeon, where the Ponzillo sisters had made their unofficial debut in vaudeville). Heading the dealership for a luxury automobile, the Isotta-Fraschini, he was also well situated in Italian society and had introduced the soprano to Toti Fraschini, the Italian golf champion, and his wife. They were the heads of the automobile manufacturing enterprise, which counted Ponselle among its clients after she bought a sedan from Russo. She spent part of her vacations with the Fraschinis, meeting them in Milan and hosting a luncheon for them, the Milanese attorney Icilio Foligno, Gatti-Casazza, Rosina Galli, Gatti's second wife, and the Metropolitan's Earle Lewis and his wife and family. Toti Fraschini proved his expertise in golf matches with Ponselle. While in Italy she again stayed at Villa Platani on Como. With Richard Crooks she took fishing trips in the Alps at Saint-Moritz, where she also went mountain climbing every summer.

Because of her established popularity in London, Blois wanted to plan for 1931 at once and again feature Ponselle, who had opened and closed his 1930 season. Having reconsidered *Forza*, he wrote to the soprano even as early as September, while she was still at the Hotel Miramare in Genoa, en route back to New York. Her fee would be twenty-two hundred dollars for each performance, with a guaranteed minimum of ten performances, plus fifteen hundred dollars toward her transportation. Negotiations went forward through September. In October, when Ponselle's opera season began in Philadelphia and in New York, Prilik wrote to Blois, saying, "Rosa sang her first performance last night, *'La Giaconda'* [sic], which was a huge success, and she sings again Friday in the *'African'* [sic]. . . . [These] keep her out of mischief and are helping her forget 'the Husband Complex.' " Here for the first time since the early 1920s one sees a mention of the soprano's hopes for marriage. Given her involvement with Russo, she may have thought of becoming his wife, for she was thirty-three and beginning her thirteenth year at the opera house and her sixteenth on the stage. Her first performance that season marked 307 times she had performed for the Met.

Her commitments to the Metropolitan that year were among the heaviest she had ever had, with a total of twenty-seven appearances in opera and concerts. Apart from the operas mentioned in Prilik's letter to Blois, Ponselle sang *Trovatore, Don Giovanni, Norma, Forza, Andrea Chénier, Luisa Miller,* and in what she believed would be a kind of epiphany, *La traviata,* the matinee performance of January 16, 1931. She had Lauri-Volpi as her Alfredo, De Luca as Germont, and as her conductor Serafin, who considered this one of his finest achievements.

Surprisingly, Ponselle's interpretation of Violetta, which had had such success in London, received mixed reviews from the New York critics. Most centered on her intense dramatic approach to the character and the music, for they were all accustomed to Galli-Curci and Bori, while some, like Henderson, even looked back to Patti, Melba, and Nordica. Clearly they expected more lyricism and could not comprehend a heroine who owed anything to verismo or fitted the mold of Eleonora Duse. The American conductor and musicologist Will Crutchfield, writing of Ponselle's recorded *Traviata* duet with Tibbett, as it was released by the Metropolitan Opera Guild in the 1980s for the Centennial Collection, said that if every other Violetta earned a grade of three or four, Ponselle got a perfect ten.

Even greater praise came from one colleague who sang with Ponselle from the 1927–28 season until the end of her Metropolitan career. First in the casts of *Chénier,* then in *Africaine, Traviata,* and *Carmen,* George Cehanovsky had a chance to judge her. Interviewed by George Jellinek much later, Cehanovsky simply said of Ponselle's voice, "It was like a volcano."

In view of this, one has to issue caveats about the American critics' occasional bad reviews of Ponselle. But if the New York critics of her own era sometimes had doubts, London did not. Covent Garden wanted her to return, and wanted her badly. Even though the Great Depression had Europe in its clutch, what Blois offered the soprano for another season was substantial, given the financial pinch that threatened his and all theatrical enterprises. In October 1930 he wrote guaranteeing a fee of £440 per performance and £300 toward Ponselle's transportation, something far more secure than the faltering dollar, at a time when the exchange rates were fluctuating daily, leaving everyone to worry about the future of the American currency. As he had done before, Blois asked Ponselle about repertory for her 1931 season at Covent Garden but requested *Traviata* and *Forza,* which he had finally decided to risk. Having replaced the unpopular Bellezza with Serafin, he felt more confident about his season, in spite of the Depression. Sometime that autumn Ponselle put forth a request of her own, asking Blois to schedule a new production for her: Romani's *Fedra.*

Disheartened, Blois answered her, saying that he was having "considerable difficulty about the scenery, costuming and other matters." These "matters" concerned the box office, at a time when every impresario was having trouble filling the theaters. Still, he said, he hoped "to overcome these and write favorably to Romani soon." But if he could not manage *Fedra,* Blois wished to have Ponselle sing *Norma,* chiefly because he did not think he could produce *Trovatore,* which would be paired with *Forza.* By December, though, he had settled on *Fedra.* "Please tell Romani." Blois, like Gatti-Casazza and many local concert managers, was concerned about Ponselle's health and possible cancelations. "I hope you did not get a cold this year," he wrote, recalling the problems she had had in the 1929–30 season.

By the end of 1930 Ponselle, Carmela, Anna Ryan, and Edith Prilik had moved from 260 Riverside Drive to a penthouse at 90 Riverside, at a much more fashionable address and in a more modern building than the old one they had lived in for the twelve previous years. With its terrace facing the Hudson River, this elegant apartment gave the prima donna a more appropriate setting for the guests she entertained and the few journalists she allowed in during the last years of her opera career.

At the end of her 1930–31 Metropolitan Opera season, which she concluded on tour in Baltimore, White Plains, New York, and Cleveland, Ponselle sailed for England on May 11 on the liner *Aquitania,* with Franklin Delano Roosevelt on board. Not yet president, he was nevertheless a celebrity and was photographed at the captain's table with Ponselle at his side. She went directly to Covent Garden, where she opened a Royal Opera House season that was "more ambitious than the previous years," as Rosenthal remarked. Blois had prepared the way for the unfamiliar and ponderous *Forza* by circulating a great deal of publicity about it and having Toye, "the Verdi expert," give a public lecture about the opera in the foyer of the theater. Despite his best efforts, the opera, which opened on June 1, did not fare well. Although Ponselle was "not quite in her best form" in the first act, she quickly recovered, giving the audience "some beautiful moments" in her scene with the Padre Guardiano, Pasero. Aureliano Pertile, her Alvaro, and Benvenuto Franci, the Don Carlo, were hailed by the audience for their "eternal friendship" duet. Rosenthal remarked that Serafin, who had conducted in London in 1907 and again in 1912, proved to be the surprise of the night and "a revelation," as one can easily believe.

On June 4 the *New York Times* reported that King George V and Queen Mary had "paid a surprise visit to Covent Garden" for the *Forza* and, arriving after the opera had begun, sat in the royal box, "unrecognized, until the lights went up at the end of the first act. The Queen wore a tiara of diamonds and sapphires and a gown of mauve and silver." After they met Ponselle, she was invited to the royal enclosure at Ascot for the races, "something unprecedented for an American" and "seldom before extended to a performing artist," the *Times* observed on June 19.

Romani's almost-forgotten *Fedra* was offered on a double bill with *Gianni Schicchi,* also under Serafin's baton. In the cast were Cesare Formichi, who had sung in the work at its world premiere, and the Spanish tenor Antonio Cortis, who had sung Calaf in Covent Garden's *Turandot* earlier. Ponselle, singing the title role in *Fedra,* was consoled by the *London Times* review, which said that she held her audience "by means of her voice, her gestures, her costumes, all her arts, in fact." But the music, even though

Romani had added a new aria, "O divina Afrodite," expressly for Ponselle, did not fare well. The score was "devoid of any individual character," the *Times* critic said. Much better was Ponselle's popular *Traviata,* which had its first performance on June 9. Dino Borgioli and Dennis Noble were her Alfredo and Germont, respectively, while Serafin again conducted.

Ponselle, who had been scheduled to open and close the season, was ill with laryngitis for the last *Forza* and had to be replaced by Iva Pacetti. Having leased Villa Platani on Lake Como again, the soprano left for Italy with Prilik and Romani, for she needed to recover and prepare to open the next Metropolitan Opera season, 1931–32. The opera Gatti chose for her was *La traviata.*

"AFTER THAT CAME THE DELUGE" ~

Anyone as stagewise as Ponselle would have seen the harbingers for the future of the music business in the half-empty houses at Covent Garden, which Rosenthal judged to be filled at no more than 58 percent of capacity during that summer season of 1931. It was Ponselle's last in London. But perhaps nothing could have prepared her for what awaited the members of the Metropolitan Opera company in New York that autumn and winter. A few days before the 1931–32 season was to open, Otto Kahn resigned from his two posts as president and chairman of the company and was replaced on the board by his attorney, Paul D. Cravath. Gatti recalled that the opening night, "when we presented *La traviata* with Ponselle in the role of Violetta, . . . gave us no indication of the reefs that lay ahead. There were the usual excitement, the usual brilliancy and the usual crowd." But, he recalled, "the first few weeks of the season were extremely difficult. I do not say that this was due to Mr. Kahn's resignation in any way; it was just the natural concomitant of a period of depression that was becoming progressively more severe and reaching out to affect more and more interests." Quaintance Eaton described the Met as being "at the top of a steep, swift slide into real trouble," for Kahn's departure left a void, in spite of what Gatti said.

Kahn had supported the opera company with financial contributions for many projects, running into the millions of dollars over a period of almost thirty years beginning in 1903. It had been Kahn's backing of Gatti that had let him build up the huge reserve fund of one million dollars that sustained the opera company through the 1920s. But the four years from 1929 to 1933 were the worst of Kahn's life, for he was ill and suffering from what his daughter, Margaret Kahn Ryan, called "private despair." Writing in 1930 to the president of the Pennsylvania Railroad, Kahn lamented conditions in "this wretched year." Despite his sadness he went abroad in 1931, as he had always done, and it was certainly his visit to Villa d'Este that drew Ponselle there that year, as Villa Platani was only a few miles up the shore. But Kahn's retirement from the Metropolitan caused a huge disruption, both emotional and financial, because the mainstay of the board's support system was gone at a time when the reserve fund was rapidly being eroded. For three decades Kahn had discovered singers and composers, suggested repertory, and sponsored productions, whole tours, and even the building of the New Theatre; he had given Gatti wide-ranging backing and openly expressed, unfailing affection. The loss of Gatti's partner shook him and the entire company, with which Kahn had been so closely identified that journalists, playing on his familiar "O.H.K." signature, had dubbed him "Opera House Kahn."

"After that came the deluge," Gatti wrote. "Rumor and tales concerning the Metropolitan were rife on every hand." Some said that the company would close altogether; others feared that the season would be cut to a few weeks. "It was said that I imposed a compulsory [salary] cut [on everyone]. There were tales of rivalry and dissension in the company. There was talk of [moving to] Radio City, bankruptcy. . . . All this had its effect, and although we gave excellent performances throughout the season, there was an air of mistrust on the part of a small portion of the public."

Gatti went on to describe the faltering subscriptions, which always provided the essential base of any major opera company's income. In the three years after the stock market crash, the Metropolitan lost more than 30 percent of its regular subscribers, most of them in high-priced orchestra seats. The empty places left by nonrenewing patrons made the house look spotty and a lot like Covent Garden, with its scattered and uneasy audience. This naturally demoralized the singers. Plans for most new productions were canceled, and only a few exciting, fresh voices were brought in. One of the most promising of these was Lily Pons, who, living in Paris, had signed her first American contract with Anthony Stivanello; his father, Agostino Stivanello; and their partner, Philip Culcasi. On the letterhead of their Standard Lyric Agency and dated February 4, 1930, the contract guaranteed Pons's round trip from Paris to New York and a salary of seventy-five dollars per week for "repertoire: standard, old and new." The engagement was for the spring season of the G. Magni Operetta Company; but Pons, who made her Metropolitan Opera debut in January 1931, became famous for her Lucias and Lakmés, not for operetta.

By and large, the Italian repertory was falling out of favor. As Gatti recalled, the benefits and the Wagner performances were his chief successes in this period. This is virtually the worst thing any impresario could say about the theater that, under his hand, had become the foremost presenter of Italian opera in America. The German repertory, bolstered by the successes of Jeritza, Rudolf Laubenthal, Gertrude Kappel, Lauritz Melchior (who had joined the company in the late 1920s), and Kirsten Flagstad, who came in 1934, naturally affected Italian productions. In this deleterious process, diminishing input yielded diminishing returns that threatened to relegate Italian operas to their old status as "hack" works, fodder for organ-grinders and not worthy of genuine respect.

Ponselle, like everyone else in the company, found herself coping with a situation that had no precedent in her lifetime, although at the start the 1931–32 season seemed almost normal. After her opening-night *Traviata* on November 2, she returned to familiar territory: *Forza, Gioconda, Don Giovanni, L'africaine, Norma,* and *Trovatore.* The sole new work scheduled for her that season was Montemezzi's *La notte di Zoraïma.* It got devastating reviews. In one of them the composer was accused of "shilling melodrama" and writing music that was a "distant echo" of *L'amore dei tre re.* In spite of the continuing popularity of his earlier opera and Serafin's enthusiasm for Montemezzi, his close friend, the opera proved a failure. "It is hard to exon-

erate the composer, for he has exchanged his birthright for a mess of pot-
tage," Downes wrote. Ponselle sang it only five times and disliked it.

One disappointment like this cannot seriously harm an established career, but Downes's review of Ponselle's *Il trovatore* was a different matter. In
the *New York Times* of January 16, 1932, he criticized her for not studying
"the music of Leonora with the same care and assiduity that she would
bestow on Bellini's *Norma*. The music of Leonora has more in it than Miss
Ponselle gave it yesterday. . . . The natural beauty and opulence of the diva's
voice delighted the audience [but] in point of style and technical impeccabil-
ity this performance left considerable to be desired." Nor did Downes give
much credit to the others in the cast: Danise's Count Di Luna was "workmanlike," while Lauri-Volpi had "a notable disregard for pitch." Only the
Azucena of Faina Petrova was spared.

At the same time, Ponselle's income began to fall. Early in the season
Gatti had begun his campaign to persuade his company to accept modest
salary cuts. Although, as he said, he did not "order" these cuts, the pressure
put on singers to agree to his demands hurt morale in the company. On
November 30, 1931, he wrote to Ponselle to outline two modifications to her
contract. The second of these read: "Your remuneration from and after the
30th day of November 1931, during the season 1931–1932, is hereby reduced
by ten percent (10%)."

This Ponselle accepted, but it came as Gatti was also planning to shorten
his seasons. The concert and recital market, which supplemented the singers'
income from opera, was also threatened at all levels, from community concerts in small cities up to Town Hall and Carnegie Hall. And soon Gatti was
forced to ask even greater concessions. On January 29, 1932, he wrote to
Ponselle to say that her period of engagement with the Metropolitan for
1932–33 would be in the first part of the season. "It is not definitely settled
yet on which date the Metropolitan season will begin, but as soon as this is
settled, we will notify you." His letter was written thirteen days after the bad
Trovatore review came out, and while no one can say that Gatti based any
major decision on a critic's column, he certainly cannot have been happy
with an unfavorable opinion about one of his leading artists, especially in
such precarious times.

In real terms this meant that in a year when she had not been engaged to return to London that summer, Ponselle also could not authorize the Metropolitan Music Bureau, her management agency, to make firm bookings for anything beyond September 30, because she did not know when she would be called for rehearsals at the opera house or whether she might be assigned another opening night there. At one point it was even rumored that the Metropolitan might close. Eventually Tibbett opened the 1932–33 season with *Simon Boccanegra*, while *Hansel and Gretel* opened the following season on Christmas Day.

Although Ponselle was covered by contract through these seasons, her status, like that of every other member of the company, was uncertain, because of the Met's standard renewal clauses. When Gatti asked Ponselle to accept a further salary reduction, as other singers had done, she refused at first. Negotiations went on into spring, with her appearing on the tour in Baltimore and Cleveland without knowing what her arrangements with the Metropolitan would be.

Soon the newspapers began to air the soprano's problems in their news and tattle columns, identifying her with a group of uncooperative singers. Gigli was "out of the opera," balking at his pay cut, the *New York Times* reported on April 30, 1932, while Ponselle was "still negotiating for her salary. Opera officials are still confronted with the question of whether or not Rosa Ponselle, soprano, will be willing to agree, as other stars have done, to a salary reduction." She capitulated finally in 1932 but, as we will see, became identified with the rebel "Big Four" of 1935, when the Metropolitan management demanded further cuts as a condition of issuing new contracts to its leading artists. The other three, as Quaintance Eaton described them, were Pons, Tibbett, and Lotte Lehmann. "Finally the Big Four were reinstated," Eaton wrote; but by then a great deal of hostility had built up between the opera company and these stars.

They were "just trying to make a living," they said. As Libbie Miller's letters to Ponselle of March 1934 prove, some of these same singers were also willing to make significant concessions to get concert and recital bookings, but not Ponselle. Pons, Tibbett, Fritz Kreisler, and Yehudi Menuhin were among those accepting "straight percentage dates and dates with minimum [fees]." But Ponselle continued to ask for fees between two thousand and three thousand dollars, depending on the engagement. She also refused to sing in some benefits at the height of the Depression, when other colleagues were being praised in the newspapers for such appearances. Her decisions about fees, more than any other, slowed the pace of her career outside opera, for American concert audiences from one coast to another had fallen off to such an extent that local presenters could no longer afford to pay artists as they had once done, knowing that even a handful of failed events might bankrupt them. The figures on one Ponselle concert show how much they were at risk. On November 8, 1934, a Cleveland paper (unidentified, because part of the clipping is missing) ran an article under the headline PAYING THE PIPER, attacking "a certain diva" who "received $3,000 for a single performance . . . and actually drew less than $700 at the box office. . . . It is doubtful whether there is an artist in the world worth $3,000 a night."

In January 1934 Miller had urged Ponselle to set a fee schedule for the future at $2,000, $2,250, and $2,500 but to sing at least some dates on a percentage. Thus income was still further reduced. Two months later the soprano asked to postpone an important concert in New Orleans, although the local booking office was begging her not to "disappoint people from four states who have bought tickets." In that same month one local manager reported that his total box office on one of Ponselle's engagements was $922. By 1937 another manager reported "very slow single sales" and an advance sale of "only $450" in Washington, D.C.

Most of these problems could be traced to the Depression itself, for the concert business had fallen off to a shadow of its 1920s prosperity. But the course of Ponselle's career was particularly affected by a change of management at this critical juncture, when she was harmed by the decision of Coppicus and Schang to drop her from the roster of their powerful Metropolitan Music Bureau, which was then about to become the Columbia Concerts Corporation. This led Libbie Miller to leave that firm and set up her own small agency with Ponselle as (she said) her only star. Although Miller had long been an effective saleswoman-negotiator in the concert division of

America's largest management company, she soon found that she had only limited power as the head of her own business. Hers was the kind of office the big agencies tried to crush. No longer able to use the standard big-management strategy of offering local presenters several artists as a package or using one artist as bait to secure an engagement for another, Miller was handicapped from the start and worked for the next four years in an ever deteriorating situation.

All this came as Ponselle learned that her first attempt to get a film contract in Hollywood had come to naught because of "your type, size, age, etc.," as Miller wrote in January 1934, when the Metropolitan Opera crisis was also about to come to a head. The soprano's twenty-seven appearances with the Met in 1930–31 had been cut to twenty-three in 1931–32, then eleven each in 1932–33, 1933–34, and 1934–35. Her three-year guarantees, as we shall see, were cut back to one-year contracts, granted on demeaning terms.

To all these problems were added the higher monthly running costs the soprano had to cover for her new apartment, her household, and her Isotta-Fraschini sedan. Loans to help Russo through the Depression had cut into her reserves. In this period she also suffered several short bouts of incapacitating illness that were amply covered in newspapers across the country, fed, as they were, by the wire services. The first two of these cost her the first night of *Don Giovanni* at the Metropolitan and the closing *Forza* on the last night of the Royal Opera season. Once a picture of her in bed in Saint Raphael's Hospital in New Haven was circulated by a photo service. In the spring of 1932 she had to postpone her sailing on the liner *Saturnia*, leading the press to note that she could not leave "for her vacation abroad . . . because she was ill with a severe attack of grippe."

She also was roundly criticized in the press for canceling a Metropolitan Opera tour performance in Boston, leaving Gatti to call Rethberg from New York to cover for her. This event led three local papers to write critical articles implying that sheer whim or bad temper had been the true cause of her default and that Ponselle frequently canceled, which was not the case. Singers often had to miss performances, then as now, and opera company managers almost always had someone else ready to step in at the last minute. But Ponselle's cancelations were treated as something out of the ordinary. They were not. The tone of several of these pieces about her was strangely hostile, with journalists even inviting audiences to boycott her appearances. One castigated her for accepting a concert fee of three thousand dollars at a time when millions of people were having a hard time putting food on their tables. Reading these barrages, one has the sense that at the height of the Depression, she—of all people, for she had been the darling of the press for fifteen years—was singled out for harmful criticism. This surely hurt Ponselle, who had always been emotional and sensitive about other people's feelings and was always well liked by most of her colleagues. After all, this was the woman of whom Gaisberg said she had not one enemy in the whole world.

Because she had long had the habit of studying in the summer in Europe, where she had access to Romani and Serafin, Ponselle spent her delayed vacation of 1932 at Lake Como, visiting Saint-Moritz briefly. She then returned to a much-reduced recital and concert tour. But just as it was about to end and she was to sign in for rehearsals at the Metropolitan, her mother died, on November 5. Shattered, Ponselle collapsed at the graveside in Sacred Heart cemetery in Meriden. When she returned to the Metropolitan, it was to sing works from her standard repertory: *Gioconda, Andrea Chénier, Traviata, Don Giovanni,* and one *Cavalleria.* In a 1997 interview Rose Bampton recalled Ponselle's grief and her kindness on the evening of her own Metropolitan debut, November 22, 1932, when she appeared with Ponselle as Laura in *Gioconda.* In 1932 and the years that followed, the Metropolitan always called on Ponselle to star in the gala concerts that were good box office for the company. For the 1933 event celebrating Gatti-Casazza's twenty-fifth anniversary, she was Elvira, with Frederick Jagel, De Luca, and Pinza in "O sommo Carlo" from *Ernani,* but she also improvised in a comic scene with Bori, Moore, Pons, Carmela, Melchior, Schipa, and others. This February concert, which was broadcast and billed as "A Grand Operatic Surprise Party," preceded one of the most successful and satisfying engagements of Ponselle's career: her Italian debut.

𝒯HE MAGGIO MUSICALE FIORENTINO ∽

Again, as in the past, it was Serafin who convinced the soprano to risk her reputation abroad, this time in the important new festival that the Italian government inaugurated in Florence in the spring of 1933. Ponselle said that she went there to fulfill her mother's request that she sing at least once on Italian soil. The Maggio Musicale Fiorentino owed its launching to the determination of Vittorio Gui, the Roman conductor who had founded the Florence Orchestra five years earlier. The site chosen for Ponselle's production was the old Teatro Politeama Vittorio Emanuele, which had been renamed the Teatro Comunale in 1932.

Gui, who was to conduct her two performances of *La vestale*, had Serafin at his side, having entrusted the scheduled May productions of *La Cenerentola* and *I puritani* to him. Hans Busch was the assistant stage director. Ponselle spent almost all of April with Serafin and his family at Bosco Chiesanuova near Verona, brushing up the score with him, then moved to Florence for her first rehearsals. With her in the cast were the tenor Alessandro Dolci, the great Italian mezzo-soprano Ebe Stignani, and Tancredi Pasero.

Because this historic event was broadcast in Italy on EIAR, the predecessor of RAI, and carried on shortwave outside the country, a wide-ranging opera public in the theater and far away heard Ponselle's unforgettable Giulia. After the aria "O nume tutelar" such a swell of applause and shouting arose from the audience that Gui, who was absolutely opposed to letting singers give encores, could not resist this hysterical outpouring of enthusiasm. He raised his baton, and repeated the aria. Pandemonium followed.

A magnificent review in *La tribuna* hailed the American dramatic soprano who "deserved the greatest honors that can be offered her." She possessed an "authoritative and absolute talent" and was "vigorously dramatic" in the role, all the while preserving its flawless classical beauty. With her "full and perfect timbre," she was also "flexible," with a "voice like a silken ribbon. Madame Ponselle can work every imaginable kind of virtuoso miracle."

In a later interview Ponselle recalled her joy at such a reception and remarked on her own satisfaction with her performance at "the international festival in Florence." She said, "I sang a command performance at the Royal Palace before the Crown Prince and Princess of Italy [and] was also entertained on a number of other occasions." Among her fans was the affectionate Princess Mafalda of Savoy. Benito Mussolini, who had either heard Ponselle or heard about her success, granted her an audience in Rome.

As Ponselle soon discovered, her performances in Florence had become a kind of benchmark of operatic achievement. Ida Cook, the English writer who, with her sister Louise, often visited New York and the offices of the Metropolitan Opera Guild and *Opera News* after 1950, heard the first *Vestale* in the theater in Florence and said of the soprano's performance that it was "faultless classical singing." Will Crutchfield, in a 1996 telephone conversation, said that her rendition of "Tu che invoco con orrore" from *Vestale* was one of his three favorite Ponselle recordings. The others were her *Forza* and the song "Amuri, amuri." Asked to describe her voice, he burst out, saying, "Fabulous! Fantastic! I don't have enough words to describe it."

THE CAREER ENDS: 1933–1938 ∽

As one looks back on Ponselle's achievement in Florence, it becomes ever more difficult to understand why she declined Serafin's invitation to return to the Maggio in 1934 for *Forza* and *Don Giovanni* or why she refused offers from Buenos Aires that August or, in 1937, from the Royal Opera in London. Although she said in her autobiography that she feared becoming the target of hostile demonstrations at La Scala, she must have understood that after her success in *Vestale,* Florence would treat her well, and she surely knew that London audiences were never rude. Whatever her reasons, she never sang abroad again.

Nor can one imagine why the Metropolitan did not make a greater effort to follow Ponselle's triumph in Florence with some special event for her. No one would have dreamed of suggesting a new production or a revival of something that was bad box office, as *Vestale* was. (It had not even sold well when Gatti first produced it.) But surely some extraordinary use could have been made of her voice at a time when, by all accounts, she was singing better than she ever had. She remarked of her second *Vestale* in Florence that it "rivaled the best that I had ever done." Perhaps if Gatti had not been exhausted by the Depression and battles with deficits, Paul Cravath, and the other directors, if he had not been discouraged about his advanced age and thinking of retirement, he might have changed the course of Ponselle's career by finding some appropriate vehicle for her. This Serafin might have done, but he was also about to leave the Metropolitan. Responding to one of the many offers he regularly received, he agreed to become the director of the Teatro Reale dell'Opera in Rome, where he would assume his new post in the summer of 1934. Thus he was no longer in a position to dictate repertory in New York.

After Florence, Ponselle returned to the Metropolitan with *L'africaine* in December, with Serafin conducting, Martinelli taking Gigli's place as Vasco, and Armando Borgioli singing Nélusko. *Don Giovanni, Cavalleria, Traviata,* and one *Gioconda* followed, with Ponselle singing only eleven performances for the company that season. On March 11, 1934, she sang and clowned in another "Grand Operatic Surprise Party" concert, which celebrated the fiftieth anniversary of the founding of the Metropolitan Opera. She did a Gay Nineties skit, an "audition" farce, and a boisterous "Hail, Hail, the Gang's All Here" with more than fifty other company members.

Whatever the good humor of the "party," Ponselle's position at the Metropolitan was far from settled that spring. Ironically, she was beset by problems when she had a complete mastery of her voice, for in this period her most loyal supporters in the company could do little or nothing to help her. Otto Kahn died unexpectedly on March 29, 1934, immaculately dressed, with his boutonniere in place, as he rose from the luncheon table in the partners' dining room of his Wall Street firm. Serafin left the Metropolitan twelve days later. With Gatti's retirement imminent, the company could barely afford to operate at a minimum pace.

For the 1934–35 season Ponselle again was assigned only eleven performances, beginning with a December 27 *Gioconda.* This alternated with *Traviata* and *Don Giovanni,* while one *Cavalleria* was added in February. A hint of things to come can be found in the *Carmen* trio, "Les tringles des sistres tintaient," which she sang in a concert in the opera house. The saddest event of the year was the gala that honored Gatti-Casazza on March 19, 1935, and marked the occasion of his retirement, which would come at the end of the season. In that gala Ponselle sang the act 3 scene from *Norma,* the most appropriate music imaginable, with Gladys Swarthout as Adalgisa and Phi-line Falco as Clotilde. Ettore Panizza conducted. Ponselle had not sung the complete opera since December 1931 and was never again to sing any of its score in the opera house. In a sense, this was the only fitting farewell to this opera and to Gatti, who, more than anyone else, had taken direct responsi-bility for guiding her toward it. This was her last event for the company that year.

Ponselle, seated on Gatti's left, was one of his three guests of honor at the farewell luncheon offered for him in the opera house's Louis Sherry restaurant. The others were Geraldine Farrar, seated on his right, and Arturo Toscanini, who had been conducting the New York Philharmonic since Jan-uary and was about to leave for Italy. The two men ended their long es-trangement that day. When a toast was proposed, Gatti rose and said, in his halting English, "Long life to the Metropolitan Opera." He then reached over to clink glasses with his successor, Herbert Witherspoon, and—acting on impulse—leaned forward and kissed Toscanini on the forehead. As the *New York Times* reported, everyone was stunned because Gatti had been so angry over Toscanini's precipitous abandonment of the Met in 1915. For a moment the guests were silent, and many sat with their heads bowed and tears in their eyes. Suddenly Farrar, always cool, no matter what the situa-tion, recovered herself and, without a word, went to the piano and began to play "The Beautiful Blue Danube." Seeing her, Lucrezia Bori and Edward Johnson, who had been sitting together, walked to the center of the room and began to waltz. Within moments Toscanini and Gatti were chatting about how they would exchange visits in their villas on the Italian lakes that summer. The tension was gone.

Even at that moment Ponselle was preparing her own surprise for Gatti: a champagne farewell to him and his wife on the liner *Rex* on a Saturday at the end of April, just before sailing time. To avoid publicity the saddened and downcast Gattis had gone on board late the previous evening; but the quiet leave-taking they hoped for was interrupted by Ponselle and about two hundred guests, armed with gifts and a bright banner the soprano had designed and ordered. Even though everyone knew that Gatti would welcome many of them in his villa that summer, it was a dreadful moment for those artists whole professional destinies were so closely tied to his. Everyone cried, and the biggest stars made speeches, paying tribute to "Il Signor Direttore," then went ashore.

No one could have foreseen the events that followed. On May 10 Witherspoon, the new general manager, was preparing for a meeting with his board when, without having shown any sign of illness, he dropped dead in his new office. In this moment of reorganization of the company, no one knew just what to do. Edward Johnson, who had been chosen to manage a proposed supplementary season of opera, was on the spot and was competent, so he took Witherspoon's place. Any business enterprise that has two changes of management in less than a month is likely to have problems; the Metropolitan was no exception.

These are the circumstances that led to the strife between the "Big Four," Pons, Ponselle, Lehmann, and Tibbett, over their contracts. Bori and the board sided with management, as Johnson threatened to bring in young Americans to replace them. Several popular singers were offered single-year renewals, among them such favorites as Grace Moore, the aged Florence Easton, Mario Chamlee, Edith Mason, and John Charles Thomas.

From Ponselle's contracts with the Metropolitan, it is clear that she was facing an increasingly untenable situation. From a fee of eighteen hundred dollars for each performance in the 1931 tour, she was reduced to a compromised situation as her four-season-old contract was to expire in the spring of 1934. On June 16 of that year she signed for only eight weeks in 1934–35 at a fee of one thousand dollars per performance, with her repertory reduced to seven operas: *L'africaine, L'amore dei tre re, Andrea Chénier, Cavalleria, Don Giovanni, La Gioconda,* and *La traviata.*

On November 8, 1935, only about five weeks before the opera season was to open, Edward Johnson engaged Ponselle for just two months with not more than one performance a week, again at one thousand dollars per performance. He had assigned *Traviata* to Bori for the opening night, December 16. Ponselle's roles were *Carmen,* which she had been studying for more than a year, and "other such roles of the Artist's repertoire" as they could agree on. This contract was negotiated not by Libbie Miller but by William M. Sullivan, a powerful Wall Street attorney. He soon found out that the agreement the soprano had signed prevented her from taking the concert engagements that had been previously agreed upon; he then had to set "dear Ed" to rights on that score.

The next year, when she was again negotiating with Johnson, Ponselle found her situation no less difficult than before because nothing was concluded until autumn. As in 1935 the delay made it impossible for her manager to book concerts one year, or even months, in advance, although Miller was urging her to do just that. On October 26, 1936, Ponselle and Johnson signed another one-season contract that in effect provided only two months of work. It reduced her fees to a level she had not accepted since she was a young singer. Ponselle agreed to sing two performances of *Cavalleria* for an unbelievably low five hundred dollars each and five other works from her repertory for one thousand dollars each—this for an artist who was still hoping to get paid three thousand dollars for her concerts and was a favorite on such radio programs as the "Chesterfield Hour." The seven appearances were to take place between January 4, and March 6, 1937, and be preceded by the usual two weeks of opera house rehearsals. In a supplementary letter the two parties agreed that of her five performances, two would be *Carmen;* there were the usual options for the tour.

The reality Ponselle faced was this: Johnson was assigning all her old roles to other singers. *Cavalleria* went to Hilda Burke, Gertrude Wettergren, Elisabeth Rethberg, and Rosa Tentoni; *Gioconda* and *Norma* to Gina Cigna; *Aida* to Rethberg, Cigna, Burke, and Dusolina Giannini; *Traviata* to Vera Bovy and Bidú Sayao, after Bori retired; and *Trovatore* to Cigna, Rethberg, and Rose Bampton. Ponselle's alternates in *Carmen* were Wettergren and Bruna Castagna.

In these parlous years between 1933 and 1937 Ponselle conducted herself with great dignity, remaining a radio star and continuing her concerts and recitals. In March 1935 President and Mrs. Roosevelt invited her to the Mayflower Hotel for a dinner in the Chinese Room to celebrate Roosevelt's third year in the White House. With them were their "unofficial family," the members of the cabinet, and Mrs. James Roosevelt, the President's mother. After dinner Ponselle sang a short program. This was only one of many events at which she was honored. And in spite of being handicapped by an ineffective manager and the breakdown of the concert market, she managed to get some engagements.

She also learned and sang Carmen, the last opera role of her career, and resolved a host of personal problems as well. Foremost among these was her relationship with Giuseppe Russo, whom Carmela (still living with her at 90 Riverside) disliked and suspected of having ties to organized crime.

When Russo followed Ponselle to Italy in 1933, she did not feel comfortable having him in Florence but kept in touch so they could meet later. In July she picked up her mail at Thomas Cook's in Milan and found a letter from her father, the only one from him that has survived. Apologizing for not having been able to "get a man to write" correct English for him, Ben Ponzillo sent her a report on where he and Tony had spent the money she gave them; interest payments and repairs to the house on Springdale Avenue had taken it all, for he had shingled the house and painted the porch. On the front steps new rubber mats with brass edging made the "house look fine." Crushed by the Depression, Carmela had run out of funds, and Tony had very little "coming in." But their father's main worry was Russo. "Rose, Pop don't like them people very much; and when he comes to see you, don't believe everything he says to you." He went on to remind her that her first cousin had also married "the same kind of people, and she had enough trouble. You are not a baby, so look out for yourself," he warned, thinking of Russo's presumed ties to the Camorra. Proud of his daughter, the elder Ponzillo had collected newspaper accounts of her success in the Maggio Musicale and had cut out photographs of her "in Fiorenze," where she had made "good sucseses in front of 5,000 people." He added that he had gone to the judge of the probate court in Meriden and made his will, naming his heirs as "you, Tony [and] Carmel." The letter ends with "I send you love and kissis, Pop."

In spite of her father's sound instincts about Russo, Ponselle continued to see him, spending part of the summer of 1933 with him in Saint-Moritz. They did not break off their association until some three years later, after she had lent him a considerable amount of money, which, she said, he did not repay.

As early as 1932 Ponselle had been considering adding *Carmen* to her repertory. In 1935 in Saint-Moritz she began studying it with Albert Carré, the nephew of the French librettist Michel Carré, author of librettos for Meyerbeer, Gounod, Bizet, Thomas, and Offenbach, including such staples of the French repertory as *Dinorah, Faust, Roméo et Juliette, Les pêcheurs des perles, Hamlet, Mignon,* and *Les contes d'Hoffmann.* Albert Carré had been the director of the Opéra Comique in Paris. His wife, Marguerite Giraud, was the daughter of the director of the opera house in Nantes. A celebrated soprano, she had created the leading roles in fifteen works at the Comique and sung the first Cio-Cio-San in *Madama Butterfly* in Paris. She had also won fame for her interpretations of Louise, Manon, and Mélisande. In the hands of the Carrés Ponselle was sure to be coached in the most solid inter-pretation possible—not just of her role, but of the whole score of *Carmen.*

Ponselle may have decided to work with them because, as she said in her autobiography, Gatti-Casazza had been somewhat skeptical and Romani outspokenly disapproving when she first said that she wanted to sing the role. That it lay right for her voice no one could dispute, for she had sung arias from it on concert and radio programs; but their reservations con-cerned her characterization and height. By her own account, she paid the Carrés for two months of coaching and invested further effort and money on her costumes, attempting to make them modern rather than use, for example, the traditional hoop skirt in the last act.

Fully prepared musically and dramatically by the Carrés and Romani, three of the most experienced professionals in the business, Ponselle had learned not just her role but the whole opera, as she always did. She had been coached in dance by La Argentina and had had her costumes made by Valentina, a well-known designer. Her rehearsals at the Metropolitan began in early December 1935 with Martinelli as Don José, Pinza as Escamillo, and Hilda Burke, the wife of stage director Désiré Defrère, as Micaela. Louis Hasselmans conducted. Although Ponselle had influenza just as the final rehearsals were scheduled, no one in the company suspected that the production would not be well received. It opened on December 27, 1935.

Because there has probably been more discussion about Ponselle's *Carmen* than any other work she sang after her debut *Forza,* it is important to see it in perspective. She performed *Carmen* fifteen times in two consecutive seasons at the Metropolitan to enthusiastic audiences; that alone means that it passed one test of success. Because several critics wrote unfavorably about the first night, "Ponselle's Carmen" became fodder for columnists, "letters to the editor" compilers, people in the music business, and lay partisans pro and con.

Apart from all the chatter and gossip, the box office figures, preserved in the Metropolitan Opera Archive, tell the story of a financial success, because in many weeks—right up to the last performance of Ponselle's career—"her" *Carmen* almost always outsold all the other operas on the program and did well even when it did not bring in the highest weekly box office:

Week of December 23, 1935: *Carmen,* $12,673.25, followed by *Rigoletto* ($12,313.25) and Pons's *Lakmé* ($9,064.25).

Week of January 6, 1936: *Carmen,* $11,611.00, followed by *Götterdämmerung* ($9,670.50) and Bori's *Manon* ($9,245.50).

Week of January 13: *Carmen,* sold on a straight fee to the Bushnell Memorial Auditorium in Hartford, $12,000. The presenter kept all the profits, which are not recorded. It was followed by *Tannhäuser* in New York ($12,408.50).

Week of January 20: *Carmen,* sold on a straight fee to the French Hospital Benevolent Society, $8,500. As in Hartford, the sponsor kept the profits. It was followed by the disappointing *Juive* revival with Rethberg ($9,489.25) and *Aida* ($9,432.25).

Week of January 27: *Carmen*, $12,682, followed by *Carmen* in Philadelphia ($12,187) and Lehmann's *Tosca* ($10,108.75).

In the week of February 10 *Carmen* was outsold by *Tristan und Isolde* with Flagstad and Melchior and *Trovatore* with Rethberg and Martinelli.

In the week of February 24 *Carmen* drew $6,077.25 at the Brooklyn Academy of Music; Pons's *Lucia di Lammermoor* drew $6,004.75. This was always "a $6,000 house" for the Metropolitan, and finally the management secured a guarantee to cover it.

In the week of March 9 *Carmen* was outsold by *Tristan* and *Bohème* in New York.

Week of March 29: *Carmen*, on the tour in Baltimore, brought in an astonishing $15,994. *Bohème* with Bori outsold it by only about $600.

Week of March 23: *Carmen*, on the tour in Boston, tied for top box office with *Fidelio* at $13,137.50.

Week of January 4, 1937: *Carmen*, $12,110, followed by *Samson et Dalila* in Philadelphia ($11,319).

In the week of January 18 *Carmen* was outsold by *Rigoletto* in Hartford and *Contes d'Hoffmann* in New York.

In the week of February 15 *Carmen* was outsold by *Tristan und Isolde* and by the revival of *Norma* with Cigna, Castagna, Martinelli, and Pinza.

Week of April 12: *Carmen*, on tour in Cleveland, had exactly the same box office returns ($13,500) as all other tour operas there, because of the Metropolitan's arrangement with the presenter. This was Rosa Ponselle's last performance with the Metropolitan, where she sang 407 times in all. Here her career in opera ended.

The double bill of *Cavalleria* and *Pagliacci* in Baltimore on March 31, 1937, with Ponselle as Santuzza and Martinelli as Canio brought in the highest single box office return for any opera of the entire season: $17,122. Ponselle's *Cavalleria* in Cleveland, her penultimate performance with the

Metropolitan, brought in $13,500. Only Bori's farewell in March, 1936 outdid these, with $20,204 in receipts.

As all this proves, Ponselle's much discussed *Carmen* was a success on purely financial terms. The critics were another matter. Several but not all opening-night reviews were unfavorable; others praised Ponselle for either her voice or her characterization or both. Because of the controversy over her interpretation, scores of letters flooded the reviewers' desks; some of those were printed a week or more after the first night. Lawrence Gilman in the *Tribune* hailed her "intelligent and workmanlike" performance in "the baffling role." He complimented her for being "a serious and thoughtful artist" who had delivered a Carmen that was "vividly conceived, alive at every moment." The chief fault he found was in her "toughness," something that other writers also found dismaying, because, as one writer observed, the critics were accustomed to seeing her as Norma or Vestale or Donna Anna. Gilman's review was more than favorable, although he believed that she had "undertaken a role for which Nature did not fit her." Still he thought she would grow more comfortable with it as the season went on.

Henderson, the oldest and most respected New York critic, reviewed it after the opening and again on January 7, 1936, in the *Sun*, after the second performance. The latter headline reads: ROSA PONSELLE ESSAYS CARMEN— AND METROPOLITAN OPERA HOUSE AUDIENCE VOICES ITS AUGUST APPROVAL. In his first sentence Henderson praised her because she cherished "the spirit of adventure" in attempting Carmen and said that she had "bravely grappled with it on [the first night] when she was not entirely recovered" from her illness. Seeing it the second time, he observed that "Miss Ponselle cannot be bound by the authorities or hampered by traditions, for [as Merimée wrote,] 'Carmen will always be free.' Miss Ponselle knew that." He found that her Carmen was "presented a little more discreetly" on the second night than at the opening but felt that it would not be likely to secure a place among the immortal interpretations of the role. That said, he also remarked on some vocal problems that were perhaps attributable to illness and said that she had "moderated some of the musical exaggerations which marred her first interpretation."

Pitts Sanborn, another respected writer, published his commentary after the first night and noted with some fairness that there had been so many Carmens emphatically different from one another that "the part is without type or tradition. . . . Miss Ponselle . . . depicted the gypsy baggage in terms of the Tough Girl of old-fashioned vaudeville. The brazen air, the killing glances, the arms akimbo were all here." He thought it lay badly for her voice and remarked on her "startling costumes, which . . . are bound to be talked about."

Leonard Liebling, writing in the *Daily American* after the second performance, headed his article with HEARERS ENTHUSE OVER PONSELLE'S GLOWING CARMEN. He said that the opera house was packed, with even standing room completely sold out. Liebling believed that she had fallen afoul of some of the critics, "even though there could be no doubt of her striking success," because she had taken liberties with the music and added "unconventional touches" to the character. "Both as a singer and as an actress Miss Ponselle . . . was far more sure of herself [than on the first night]. She balanced her points logically and put reserve and some subtlety in place of physical exactitude." He felt it was only a matter of time before she "settled firmly into the role and made it into a complete characterization. There can be no fault-finding with the spirit and the glow that animate her portrayal even now, not with the enthusiasm that enlivens her singing." He, too, reminded readers that she was still recovering from illness and had some vocal problems that were attributable to laryngitis. "The audience extended fervent applause and recalled Miss Ponselle repeatedly afterward." The many curtain calls showed how much the audience appreciated her. Other critics remarked on Ponselle's Latin beauty and slim figure—she was the thinnest she had been since she was a girl, she said—and reported that the opera house was "jammed to the doors."

One thoroughly bad review in the *World Telegram* faulted her acting and said she lacked both color and style. "Her voice had little of its once lovely quality," although in "Là-bas, là-bas dans la montagne" "the luscious roundness emerged." Others remarked on vocal problems they felt they had detected; but again they wrote these off to illness. Yet it was Olin Downes's long, unfavorable review in the *New York Times* that set off such a storm of support for Ponselle that the newspaper was obligated to publish almost an entire half page of letters to the editor about it on January 5 and 12, 1936. Downes's original article, which appeared after the opening night, included a fairly favorable assessment of her first act, in spite of his reservations about her musical style. The rest of the piece denounced her interpretation as an unredeemable failure. He said that he had never heard her sing so badly and had "seldom seen the part enacted in such an artificial and generally unconvincing manner." This was a prelude to unkind remarks about her musicianship, "time, rhythm, . . . tone, pitch, vocal style," and "dancing," as well as acting that was "affected, overdrawn, often inept." To sum it up: "There was bad vocal style, carelessness of execution, inaccurate intonation."

This barrage brought Downes a "desk full" of letters in Ponselle's defense, and of them the *Times* published four, all thoughtful and worthy of consideration. The first appeared on January 5 and referred only to the opening night. Its writer, who had seen the first night, accused Downes of being "strangely prejudiced" against the soprano. She had a voice "particularly fitted to the music of *Carmen*" and "gave that music life and color and vivacity; and every nuance of her phrasing was remarkably emphasized by the most realistic acting I had ever seen on the opera stage." The writer also defended her dancing—"truly atmospheric and graceful." She was a "vivid and engrossing Carmen . . . with a lusciousness of voice that is Miss Ponselles's own particular virtue. The three qualities must certainly bring before us a superb Carmen; and it indeed seemed superb to those whom I heard discussing the performance as they left the Opera House on Friday night."

For the *Times* to dedicate nineteen column inches to a reader's letter and to give that letter a headline two columns wide, there must have been an extraordinary outcry over Downes's devastating review. And indeed on January 12 he had to publish three more letters—two against Ponselle and one in her favor. But the controversy did not end there. Many other critics in New York and in the tour cities gave her Carmen favorable reviews. For the *Baltimore Sun* critic she was "a huge success," while the *Baltimore Ameri-*

can review mentioned her "dramatic sense . . . humor . . . passion and caprice." In Boston she brought down the house. The *Philadelphia Record* reviewer found her "dramatically excellent and vocally superb," while the *Philadelphia Evening Ledger* reviewer compared her interpretation to that of the original Carmen, Célestine Galli-Marié, adding that Ponselle also brought to the role "her lower notes [which had] the color of a real mezzo-soprano, while she retained her glorious high notes." In the the *New York Evening Post* Samuel Chotzinoff congratulated "the celebrated singer [who] scored a definite success."

All things said, Ponselle created a sensation with this role, the last of her repertory, and brought a vociferous and enthusiastic public into the opera house and the tour theaters. For once, one writer said, no claque had to be hired: the applause rang from all parts of the house and was genuine.

Because Ponselle's *Carmen* was broadcast four times by the Metropolitan and has been released on LP and CD recordings, it is available to all and bears witness to her modern and theatrical conception of a difficult role. More than "workmanlike," as Gilman described it, it has a substantial dramatic heft, at least as one hears it on CD.

When Ponselle returned to the Metropolitan in January 1937 a heartening review appeared in the *New York Sun,* where W. J. Henderson was about to end a fifty-year career in journalism. His article opened with questions about her future: Would she sing only Carmen, as she had done the previous season, or would she add her other familiar roles?

> A demonstrative audience welcomed the soprano when she made her first entrance and called her before the curtain many times, alone and in company with other members of the cast. . . . [Her] characterization appeared to have been subjected to some moderating second thoughts, and there was an added fidelity to the notes as written. There remained much of the original self-consciousness and over-elaboration of studied detail, tending steadily to externalize the role. As at last year's performances, the singer was more convincing in those parts of the opera calling for dramatic vehemence than she was

in moments of swagger and insolence. In design an animal Carmen, this impersonation scores its points bluntly, directly, literally and often effectively. But it can boast little of the sensual appeal or the seductiveness that presumably is the end sought in much of the stage business. The dark lower voice of the soprano was satisfactorily adjusted to the mystic [parts of the score] though without any such beauty of sound as has been Miss Ponselle's in pure soprano roles.

This balanced review by Henderson, who had covered every one of Ponselle's opera roles and many of her concerts, served as a counterweight to some of the virulent articles of the previous year and attested to the star's undiminished popularity. In his conservatism, Henderson also gave voice to what older patrons felt. The younger generation—the generation raised on "picture shows"—was a different matter. One savant said that Ponselle conceived Carmen as she did because she was determined to break into motion pictures and make the kind of Hollywood career that Tibbett and others had: hers was a cinematic Carmen rather than an operatic one. She had evidently decided to eliminate, so far as possible, the handicaps described by Libbie Miller—her "type, size, age, etc."—that would keep her out of films. By the time she had perfected the role, she had solved many of those problems by creating a Carmen that may have been meant to catch the eye of film company magnates and directors rather than the general opera audience; after all, the soprano had lost a great deal of weight and had chosen a new hairdresser and a Hollywood costumer. With the highly dramatic gestures that so offended the conservative New York critics, she presented herself more as a "film gypsy" than as a successor to Emma Calvé. Her stage business actually worked very well, as one can see in surviving screen tests, and she had a chance of being hired for motion pictures, for her trips to Hollywood in the 1920s and 1930s brought her into the orbit of film stars and had a professional purpose.

From her accounts of the years from 1930 to 1936 one learns that the first person who contacted Ponselle about a screen test was none other than Carmela's old nemesis Edward Valentine Darling, a veteran of the Keith vaudeville circuit booking office. Having known both Ponzillo sisters from about 1915 on, he had a good idea of what Rosa could do, even though the young girl from "vaude" had become the celebrated opera star. The Ponselle of the 1936 screen tests looks like a sleek *Vogue* model in designer street clothes, while her gorgeously costumed Carmen in the same test is utterly convincing. Whether she was singing the "Chanson bohème" for motion picture cameras or being photographed in California with Shirley Temple or Joan Crawford (to whom she gave singing lessons and coaching for an unlikely lieder recital in the film star's home), Ponselle appeared every bit as glamorous as any Hollywood luminary and a good deal more lively and intelligent than most. If she did not get a screen contract, the fault was her own, as Libbie Miller lamented in one letter: the soprano asked for too much money, and Hollywood turned her down.

At this same time both Carmela and Rosa were making decisions that affected every aspect of their life. Carmela, who had lived with Rosa and Anna Ryan since 1915, announced in October 1933 that she was going to marry again—some two decades after her short-lived marriage to Henry Giamarino. As she was about to sing *Aida* in Hartford that month, she told the Associated Press representative that her fiancé was "a New York businessman, 45 years old, a bachelor." She also said she had three suitors. As newspaper reports of February 1934 reveal, one of these—the one she finally chose—was Francis X. Bushman, the matinee idol of silent films. On February 7 Bushman got a marriage license in Chicago and awaited Carmela, who was then singing in Boston. "He's marvelous, the grandest person in the world," Carmela declared as she boarded the Chicago-bound train. For Bushman, who was then a partner in a retail liquor firm, this would be his third marriage. But something went drastically wrong after Carmela's arrival, even though Bushman had called in reporters to announce that he and Carmela would marry. By February 17 the wedding was off; Bushman said he was going to remarry his first wife, from whom he had been divorced for more than sixteen years. The reason: his children had intervened and begged him not to marry again. "Carmela and I talked it over," Bushman said. "She is big and fine, and she decided for the sake of the children, we had better call if off." Thus their "engagement" ended in amicable renunciation, and Carmela returned to New York, Rosa, Edith Prilik, and Anna Ryan.

Rosa was rethinking her own life. Early in 1936 she ended her relationship with Russo because they argued, because he did not repay the $13,000 or more than she had lent him, and because Carmela and their father distrusted him. When the Metropolitan Opera tour took her to Baltimore in *Carmen* that spring, she met Carle A. Jackson, the mayor's son. Their romance, covered in articles in the Baltimore papers that survive in the clipping files of the public libraries in Baltimore and New York, quite naturally attracted the attention of the press. "Opera star" meets "prominent socialite" at "Bori's farewell performance at the Lyric Theatre in Baltimore," as the papers described it. But they tell only a part of the story, for Jackson was the headstrong thirty-year-old divorced father of a child, while Ponselle, who had turned thirty-nine the previous January, was facing personal and career challenges that were no less daunting than those of her earliest years at the Metropolitan. Whatever else it was, this was not "love's young dream" but rather the free association of sophisticated adults.

According to all accounts the two fell in love almost on sight and, after a courtship that lasted through that summer, were married on December 13, 1936, in Ponselle's penthouse at 90 Riverside Drive. The man who officiated was New York State Supreme Court Justice Salvatore A. Cotillo, who knew both Rosa and Carmela well, for in November 1934 they had sung at the wedding of his daughter Helen to Carlo Paterno, another of the Ponselle sisters' circle. That ceremony, at "The Castle," the Cotillo mansion overlooking the Hudson River in Westchester County, had been amply covered by reporters. Now they were back in force for Ponselle's wedding.

She wore "a gray crushed velvet gown with a cowl and carried a muff of lavender orchids" because lavender was "her favorite color," she said. The soprano was given away by "her father, Benjamin Ponzillo of Meriden, Connecticut." Carmela was the maid of honor, while Riall Jackson, the groom's brother, served as best man. The Metropolitan Opera tenor Richard Crooks sang "Oh, Promise Me." Among the invited guests were Rosa and Carmela's brother, Tony, and his wife; Jackson's parents; and Frederick

Huber, the "director of municipal music of the city of Baltimore." Edward Johnson and Earle Lewis, with his wife and daughter, represented the Metropolitan Opera.

After a short honeymoon in Canada the couple returned to New York, where Ponselle's next engagement was the Metropolitan *Carmen* of January 7, 1937. She appeared on the Met's stage for the last time in the March 14 concert, then sang three times on the tour, ending her season in Cleveland with the *Carmen* broadcast mentioned earlier. The first months of this marriage were fraught with problems as the couple divided their lives between Ponselle's New York apartment and the house Jackson had rented for them in Baltimore. Ponselle also had recital and concert dates to keep, even as Libbie Miller was pressing her to accept a full schedule of bookings for the 1937–38 season. The soprano herself fully expected to return to the Metropolitan in either December or January, as we shall see.

At a personal level other unresolved issues brought new aggravations and unprecedented uncertainty to Ponselle, who had lived her entire adult life—about twenty years—with a fixed routine and with the full support of the same three people—Carmela and Prilik, who lived in the soprano's apartment, and Anna Ryan, for whom they always kept one bedroom free because she so often stayed there. This was their home: here, according to the U.S. Census, Carmela was the head of household. They all kept "opera singers' hours," sleeping late whenever the rehearsal schedule permitted it, vocalizing and practicing their scores in the living room, serving dinner at eight or nine, and going to bed late. But Jackson's schedule was that of an athlete, a polo player, an early riser. At his insistence these three women moved out, and he soon took over many of Prilik's responsibilities, acting as his wife's personal manager and financial representative. Carmela, harboring a great deal of anger, went back to the sisters' old neighborhood and rented apartment 9-K in the building at 230 Riverside Drive, near Romani. Carmela shared the apartment with Anna Ryan. With several different accompanists Carmela continued to sing concerts and recitals and did many benefits and radio broadcasts, as she had in the past. Beyond that she taught voice in New York for many years. One of her closest friends for several more decades was Bamboschek, who had lived in the next apartment to the Ponzillo sisters at 260 Riverside from 1920 to 1930 with William Tyroler, their close friend, who had often coached and accompanied them.

Although Jackson was able to move these women a certain distance away from his wife, he had a far more difficult time with Libbie Miller, who, although she never actually lived with her famous client, had worked hard for more than ten years to advance her career and did not intend to let a small event like a marriage stand in her way. In the correspondence between Jackson and Miller one can sense a certain hostility and, more than anything else, their conflicting interests. As an independent manager, Miller had to keep her clients busy in order to survive, but often she was frustrated by Jackson's interference—sometimes he merely wanted his wife to stay at home—and Ponselle's cancelations of important, announced engagements such as the "General Motors Hour" radio dates of 1936–37 and a Town Hall recital of 1938. Miller continued as the soprano's manager at least until 1938, but the situation became ever more unsatisfactory, with Ponselle caught in the middle. The deterioration in their relationship is felt in Miller's letters, which also contain some surprising information about the end of the soprano's career. The letters reveal that Ponselle could easily have returned to the Metropolitan Opera for the 1938–39 season if she had chosen to do so and could have pursued her career in recitals, concerts, and radio for many years to come.

Above all, there were the impressive Metropolitan box office figures from *Carmen* and *Cavalleria*. Just the surprising amount of money Ponselle had earned for the company ought to have guaranteed her return. Singers know what they are worth; she, seeing how many seats were sold for *Carmen*, would have been certain to be reengaged. Indeed, Ponselle told Tom Villella that she had no idea that her last performance in Cleveland in the spring of 1937 would be her last with the company. "I went home with every intention of returning that next year," she recalled. When the moment came for writing new contracts the Metropolitan still had Ponselle's name on its roster, and Miller was writing to Jackson, begging him, "Do not let Rosa speak [in public] about the Met until after November 23." Negotiations were still in progress.

Far more troubling were the "most distressing and most damaging [articles being circulated] about Rosa. . . . [She will ruin everything] by not going back and putting over some performances in great style; she will do irreparable damage to a career that, up to a few years ago, has been one of the most glorious in musical history." She was rumored in newspaper articles to be about to cancel a benefit for crippled children in Boston. She also canceled Town Hall in New York and concerts in Columbus, Charleston, and other cities. In January 1938 Miller, desperate, wrote to Ponselle to say that she was "not willing to go on for next season" as her manager because the soprano had delayed so long in accepting bookings for the period from October 1938 to June 1939. In November 1938 the soprano was "terribly ill" and was refusing to postpone yet another Town Hall appearance, ordering Miller to "cancel outright." Miller's letter to Ponselle goes on: "The fact that you do not wish to sing at the Metropolitan this season has given new impetus to the rumor that you are 'through' and has depressed your concert and radio markets to the point where I feel I cannot . . . get sufficient business to make it worth while, until you agree to a [new] fee schedule of $2,000 to $2,500 and some dates at 60%-40%, with a minimum [fee] of $1,500 and a radio fee of $3,000."

Miller confided to Jackson that "the Paramount *Carmen* deal fell through because of Rosa . . . [and we have] lost a really very wonderful offer." She also mentioned an article in the *Tribune* saying that Ponselle was "retiring."

The unresolved situation at the Metropolitan distressed all parties and remained an issue for two years. Ponselle said, "When it was time to talk about contracts [in 1937] I told them I would return if they would give me a new role. I'd sung *Carmen* for three years, and I wanted to appear in public in something new." Ponselle went on: "Maestro Toscanini had revived an opera in Europe, and it was all the rage! And what a part for a singing actress! The opera? Francesco Cilea's *Adriana Lecouvreur!*"

It is true that Toscanini had conducted this opera shortly after the turn of the century in Buenos Aires with a company that included Ericlea Darclée, Caruso, and De Luca, but it was surely Serafin who suggested it to Ponselle in 1936. He had conducted it many times, first in 1903 at the Pergola in Florence, then at the Teatro Comunale in Bologna. In 1904 he had taken it to the Teatro Vittorio Emanuele in Turin, in 1907 to La Fenice in Venice, and in 1923 to the San Carlo in Naples. Finally on January 14, 1936, Serafin revived *Adriana Lecouvreur* at the Teatro Reale dell'Opera in Rome, in the same season that opened with the *Forza* he had asked Ponselle to sing. Writing of Cilea, Serafin said, "What a dear, sweet creature! . . . He had come to Florence [in 1903] to oversee his *Adriana.* He was present as I was preparing the production; he explained his intentions to me, point by point; I listened; I took notes; and, knowing the opera from memory, I found it easy to translate the wishes of the composer into reality." More than anyone else, Serafin was qualified to coach the role of Adriana with Ponselle.

She persisted in her campaign to return to the Metropolitan with it.

I told them I would sing in *Don Giovanni, Gioconda, Carmen* and [even] four or five operas for nothing, if they would only give me *Adriana.* They refused. What hurt me more—it was the first time in my career that I asked them for something! . . . So the next season [1937–38] the Met opened without me. They did not believe that I was not returning, so they kept my name on the roster. I insisted that they remove it, but they never did. The following year [1938–39] they came to me with a "let bygones be bygones" story and offered me not only *Adriana* but any other operas I wanted. But by then it was too late. I had begun a new life and no longer wanted to return to the rigors of an operatic career.

Although Ponselle could have continued singing in New York, London, Rome, Florence, or Buenos Aires, fulfilling her professional commitments with dignity and honor, she chose not to do so. In the autumn of 1939 she made her last recordings with Victor, with Romani as her accompanist. She also sang her last concerts that year. With them her stage career ended.

CHAPTER 10

1938–1981

One problem every opera singer has to face after retirement is this: how to fill the empty days when there are no more rehearsal calls, no more performances. Many teach or coach young singers. Farrar continued singing concerts and recitals, produced her own touring company of *Carmen,* served as mistress of ceremonies for Metropolitan Opera broadcasts, wrote her autobiography, and lived in dignified old age in Ridgefield, Connecticut.

Lucrezia Bori, after her farewell in 1936, continued to live at 1 East Sixty-sixth Street and remained active in Metropolitan Opera and Metropolitan Opera Guild affairs for almost a quarter century, until the end of her life. Even before her retirement Bori had played an effective political role with the company, first as the general chair of the Executive Committee to Save the Metropolitan. Then, with Eleanor Robson Belmont, Bori organized the Opera Ball of 1933, in which Mrs. Belmont appeared as the Empress Eugénie and Bori played Patti. She had also been the co-founder of the Musicians Emergency Fund in 1932. As an elected member of the Opera Management Committee from 1935 and, later, on the board of directors, she wielded considerable power at the Met, long after she might have been expected to withdraw.

Both Farrar and Bori had made a clean break with the Metropolitan Opera stage yet managed to remain active with the company. But, as David Hamilton wrote in his notes for the CD *Rosa Ponselle: Portraits in Memory,* Ponselle's situation was different, her leave-taking ragged. "Faced with so many uncertainties and transitions, [Ponselle] evaded decisions, set impossible conditions and let things slide. There were no films, no return to the Met, no public appearances at all, only an abortive visit to the recording studios [in 1939]—and Rosa Ponselle settled into married life."

ℛETIREMENT ~

Ponselle's withdrawal from Metropolitan affairs was not total, for her support of the new Metropolitan Opera Guild led her to appear as an honored guest at its second membership meeting, where Lily Pons was seated to Mrs. Belmont's right at the luncheon and Ponselle was seated to her left. This photograph, in the second Ryan scrapbook, shows "Mrs. B" at her noble best, Pons looking composed and fashionable, and Ponselle as a dashing woman with a brilliant, unforced smile. In spite of her activity on behalf of the Guild, about thirteen years were to pass before Ponselle returned to a life in the theater, becoming, as we shall see, the artistic director of the Baltimore Civic Opera.

Her recording session in the RCA studios on October 31, 1939, produced "The Nightingale and the Rose," Tosti's "Si tu le voulais," and the song "A l'aimé," all sung to Romani's accompaniment. All three display her velvet sound and the "gold" of earlier years, together with brilliance, when needed, and superb control. The last of these three songs surpasses many of her other recordings in its depth of feeling and artistry. Widely acknowledged by critics to be one of her most perfect achievements, it profoundly affected Harold Schonberg, who speaks even today of its power to demonstrate the artist's "range and incredible control." On that same day she also recorded "When I Have Sung My Songs to You," one of her signature pieces, again of the highest quality. One day later she and Romani were back in the studio with the violinist Mischa Schmidt to record Schubert's "Ave Maria," which they recorded on November 7. Hearing them, one might think that Ponselle would have continued her recording career for years, perhaps also singing an occasional concert, even though she was to give up grander events. But nothing followed.

Her renewed hope for a film career was pursued for the third time in five years when Ponselle and her husband spent part of the autumn of 1938 in Hollywood. Believing perhaps that she would have better luck in direct negotiations than she had had using Libbie Miller, she rented a house and renewed old friendships with such stars as Joan Crawford and Gloria Swanson. Still nothing came of her negotiations with the studios' representatives, perhaps because she was intent on filming *Carmen,* about which they had many doubts. No satisfactory script could be found for it. While she and Jackson were caught up in the West Coast professional and social scene, Ponselle had one final communication from the Metropolitan, asking her to decide whether she would return. After some consideration she answered, telling Edward Johnson to remove her name from the roster. Then that door, too, closed behind her, although for more than a decade "Ponselle's return to the Met" was regularly and inaccurately reported in the newspapers.

In Hollywood Ponselle had constant moral support from Romani, who, recently married, moved there from New York in 1938 after she persuaded Metro Goldwyn Mayer to hire him as a vocal coach to the stars. Among many others, he taught Ann Sothern, Joan Crawford, Ilona Massey, Deanna Durbin, Eleanor Powell, and Tibbett's baritone protégé Douglas McPhail. Although Romani did not remain in Hollywood long, he won a fine reputation there. After another brief stint in New York he lived during World War II in a guest house on the estate of Ponselle and Jackson. With him then were Ruth, his wife, and their infant son, Romano Romani Jr., who was Ponselle's godson. After the war ended Romani and his family moved back to Santa Monica, where he resumed his work with the studios. He also kept a home in Tuscany.

The course of Ponselle's life changed suddenly late in 1938 when steady pressure from Jackson's father, the mayor of Baltimore, took her and her husband back to the East Coast. Since their marriage they had been living in Ponselle's penthouse at 90 Riverside Drive and socializing with film people and her colleagues from the music business. Some of her friendships with them dated back more than twenty years. Now circumstances demanded that they move to Baltimore. This they did on November 1, 1939. There for the first time in her life Ponselle had no day-to-day contact with Carmela, nor could she visit her former colleagues from the Metropolitan. Her trips to New York were few. Although she had broken with Edith Prilik in 1937, they were reconciled one year later, when Prilik married Albert Sania, although they saw each other rarely after that. Prilik did visit Ponselle in Baltimore in the mid-1960s and telephoned her occasionally. Libbie Miller ended her professional and personal association with her celebrated client in 1939, threatening to sue her for breach of contract.

After Ponselle and Jackson settled in Maryland, he worked in his family's insurance business. He and his secretary received all correspondence addressed to Ponselle and answered it, sometimes with her knowledge and sometimes without it. Jackson also managed his wife's business affairs, including the administration of her considerable fortune. Ponselle, ever the celebrity, was sought out by friends and acquaintances she had met in Baltimore during her many professional appearances there. The most recent of those, the Metropolitan's hugely successful *Cavalleria* of March 1937 and Ponselle's last recitals, remained vivid in her fans' memory. William Weaver, the Verdi and Puccini scholar, prize-winning translator of Umberto Eco's works, and featured speaker on the Metropolitan's Saturday afternoon intermission features, remembers hearing the soprano in Baltimore in "about 1936," when he was a twelve- or thirteen-year-old student in boarding school there. It was her "farewell recital," he says. "At the end the accompanist stayed backstage, and she came out and sat down at the piano. She played and sang 'Home, Sweet Home.' I adored her. I was fascinated by her. I remember we went backstage afterwards." Weaver also saw his first opera in Baltimore at about that same time, produced by a small company that had as its stage director Edward Bagarozy, who was then touring in the States with his wife, the mezzo Louise Caselotti. This was nearly a decade before the Bagarozy-Caselotti couple "discovered" Maria Callas. Their company and the De Feo, the San Carlo, and other small touring companies were typical of Baltimore's winter opera fare in the years before the Baltimore Civic Opera was founded. Spring brought the Metropolitan Opera tour.

Because Ponselle was so well known in Baltimore, renewing her old friendships there proved easy, and she rarely returned to New York in those early years. Her first visit to the Metropolitan Opera House after her retirement came in 1940 when she attended De Luca's farewell *Barbiere di Siviglia*. Sitting in a box with Edith Prilik, the popular soprano was recognized, applauded, and cheered by the audience. What might have been a joyful occasion for reminiscence was marred by a bitter backstage argument with Edward Johnson, over their failed negotiations for her return; but before the evening ended, the two were reconciled.

Ponselle went back to Baltimore the next day, to what she called her "new life" as Carle Jackson's wife. The social events she attended were regularly covered by the Baltimore papers, simply because she was Rosa Ponselle. This was a world of teas, dinner parties, country club and Hunt Club dances, horse races, polo matches, charity benefits, and attendance at concerts, recitals, plays, and opera performances. Because she did not like card games, Jackson hosted his evening poker and bridge sessions with his old friends while his wife sat at the piano in another room and sang for herself. Family events with Jackson's relatives also helped to fill their calendar, although, as Ponselle said, she missed the excitement of Hollywood just as she missed the intimacy of her old associations in New York. But she and Jackson were very much in love. Soon they were thinking of building a new home. For Ponselle, this was something she had done before, although not for herself: Anthony and Lydia Ponzillo's big house on Bradley Avenue in Meriden was built with money Ponselle gave the couple and was planned by her. Later she bought both it and her parents' old house on Springdale Avenue. Clearly she cared a great deal for the idea of what Carmela and she had once called "the family homestead." Now, in Baltimore, Ponselle was about to have one of her own.

On January 21, 1940, the Baltimore papers ran long news stories about Carle and Rosa Jackson's purchase of "a portion of the 'Nacirema' property, 155 acres in the Green Spring Valley," north of the city in Stevenson, Maryland. They planned to build a mansion there, one reporter wrote, adding that it would cost seventy-five thousand dollars. By the first week in February the couple's domestic life in "a small, white and blue farmhouse" in the Valley was also being covered. They could not wait to move into the grand residence on a nearby hilltop.

Villa Pace, the Villa of Peace, was named after Ponselle's great aria from the last act of her debut opera, *La forza del destino*. As Francis Robinson once said in conversation the villa was "Rosa's Buckingham Palace," for no air of simple country style intruded on its urban magnificence. Villa Pace was truly a setting for royalty. Describing the house, Ponselle once said that it was a Tuscan villa affected by American taste. That it was, at least on the outside, for it had walls of white stucco and a red tile roof. But the interior looked more like a Venetian palazzo on the Grand Canal than a rural retreat near Florence. Surrounded by a grove of trees and acres of grass extending in all directions, the house and its outbuildings were reached by a long driveway that wound up the hill. Its elaborate gateway was decorated by a stave of music where the first notes of "Pace, pace" were set in stone, with a rose for each of the notes.

Ponselle had the mansion designed on a cross plan, in which four arms reach out from a center crossing. There she located the entryway, with its cathedral ceiling and ornate, sweeping staircase. Perfectly polished brass Venetian lions' heads—the lions of San Marco—supported swags of silk rope that provided a banister. As in her New York penthouse, wrought iron gates provided their scrolled accents. (Some of these, in fact, were brought from her old apartment.) Spacious and airy, the house had high ceilings and floor-to-ceiling French doors and windows, all decorated with expensive silk valances and draperies. With its painted rafters, extraordinary coffered ceilings, sumptuous fabrics and expensive carpets, polished wood doors, paneling, gold-framed mirrors, fine antiques, paintings, wall sconces, and carved marble fireplace mantels, the utterly Italianate house provided the proper setting for a retired diva. It is to Ponselle's credit that she furnished it herself. Outside were a guest house, a huge swimming pool, and tennis courts where many home movies of Ponselle and her guests were filmed. Later, when she entertained Swanson, Jeritza, Raisa, Albanese, and other goddesses of the period, all felt right at home. At first, though, her guests were mostly from Baltimore, where she quickly became the center of a circle of trusted friends.

Had World War II not caused such disruptions in her personal life, Ponselle might have remained for decades just what she was in 1940 and 1941: a celebrated artist in retirement who sang only for herself and for friends at impromptu after-dinner programs. She was the wife of a socially prominent man whose position in Baltimore was secure. From his security came her own. After more than twenty years of hectic striving on the stage, she had indeed found such peace that nothing, it seemed, could draw her back into her old theatrical world, although she was besieged by impresarios and managers with offers. The Washington critic Paul Hume even wrote during these years of rumors that Ponselle would return to the Metropolitan.

Among the wrenching changes brought on by the war was the absence of her husband, for Jackson enrolled in the navy and was sent off to sea. At that same time Romani and his wife and baby then came to live at Villa Pace, using the guest house during the war and after. They had moved from New York to California and back to New York before the rigors of wartime rationing brought them finally to Villa Pace. Bolstered by Ponselle's generosity and kindness, they weathered the conflict in comfort and safety, which they would surely not have been able to do in Italy, where Romani hoped to settle. It was during the period of Jackson's absence and Romani's stay at the villa that Ponselle came out of retirement, very briefly, in 1943 or 1944. The event that took her back to the stage was Jackson's graduation from officers' indoctrination school. Also present that day was George Bernard, then an eighteen-year-old ensign, who was a musician himself, having studied trumpet with a member of the Cleveland Symphony Orchestra. In a 1995 interview he remembered the conductor, Officer Sugden, the chief bandmaster of the U.S. Coast Guard. Ponselle sang "Ave Maria" and one or two other pieces, "wearing a long white dress and looking absolutely radiant and beautiful. She had a star quality and presence," Bernard recalled. "The 'Ave' was sung with great feeling." She also sang at Fort Matanzas, he said. But appearances like these and later ones at official programs connected to government events remained isolated occurrences and were never followed by any real professional commitments.

For nearly five years, from the outbreak of war until 1946, Ponselle waited for Jackson's return; yet when he did come home, their marriage began to show signs of strain. According to her own account of these difficult postwar months, her husband seemed more interested in parties and hunting than in being alone with her. This came at a time when she was less interested in most social affairs than she had ever been. "I felt like a stranger in my own home," she said. Nevertheless, she often attended musical events such as symphony concerts and opera performances in Baltimore. When she entered her box in the theater, the audience always greeted her with an ovation, during which she would lean over the parapet, waving and smiling. Always dressed in expensive gowns, she was perfectly groomed and made up, with the broad Ponselle smile firmly in place. In 1946 I first met her after a concert in Baltimore. I was leaning against the left wall of the auditorium, waiting for friends, when a mutual acquaintance introduced us. I had, of course, bought many of her records and told her so. We then exchanged simple greetings and nothing more. On another occasion we met again, just as the Baltimore Civic Opera was being organized by Mary Martinet with the help of the stage director and costumer Anthony Stivanello. At a post-performance cast party Ponselle presided at dinner, gorgeously dressed in a dark evening gown and bursting with enthusiasm, telling funny stories about singers who had once been her colleagues. I saw her at other Baltimore events, and then interviewed her for *Opera News* in 1952.

This was the public Ponselle just before and during her divorce; but these were also several years marked by private suffering and anguish as her marriage was failing and despair brought her down. Depression and her correct perception that she was being neglected were accompanied by bouts of edginess and insomnia. These her doctor treated with tranquilizers. According to her own account in her autobiography, shortly after Thanksgiving in 1946 she accidentally took an overdose of these prescribed medications. Like many others, she forgot exactly what she had already taken; soon she fell into deep, dangerous sleep, from which her husband and Romani later shook her. Under the care of her personal physician, she spent four months in a psychiatric hospital after that. This was not the first time she had gone completely to pieces. Once, because Carmela had become ill, both sisters were hospitalized at once, one for physical reasons, the other for what was then called "nervous collapse."

Although Ponselle's highly sensitive nature had stood up to the buffeting and bruising endemic to theatrical life, troubling family or personal matters left her emotionally shattered, as she herself was the first to admit. The steady deterioration of her relationship with her husband led to their having fewer and fewer shared interests between 1946 and 1949. Perhaps this led her to make a crucial decision after she left the hospital: she left Villa Pace to visit old friends in New York. During her stay she, De Luca, and Martinelli were guests at a party in March 1947. There the two men persuaded her to sing with them. With little ado they launched into the duets and trio from the Nile scene in *Aida* and brought their voices together again for the first time since her retirement. At a similar event several weeks later, recently recalled by the mezzo-soprano Blanche Thebom, Carle Jackson and Ponselle were among the guests. Ponselle sang "Ritorna vincitor" from *Aida,* then sang duets with Robert Merrill and Thebom, with the young Leonard Bernstein at the piano. At some point in the evening, one guest remembers, Jackson turned to a guest and asked, "Won't someone get that Wop away from the piano?" Although Ponselle never referred publicly to his insulting words, she did say that these impromptu living room concerts with her old colleagues gave her back the strength she believed she had lost. Encouragement from Ida and Louise Cook also helped. To Ponselle's credit, she began to practice and, as she said, "sing again."

The dramatic finale to her marriage came on January 9, 1949, when Jackson invited four of their closest friends for dinner. Articles in the *Baltimore Sun* and on the Associated Press wire service include direct transcriptions from court testimony that leave no doubt about how he treated his wife in front of their guests, Ruth and Romano Romani and Sonia Parr and her husband. The Parrs were later called as witnesses in court hearings held over the next eighteen months. Before dinner, while the Jacksons, the Romanis, and the Parrs were sitting in the library of Villa Pace having a glass of wine, Jackson turned to his wife and said, without any preliminaries,

"Rosa, I have very unpleasant news for you. I have apparently failed you as a husband, and as of six-twenty I am leaving you." Stunned and humiliated, Ponselle protested, then listened as he went on: "My bags are already in the car." When he rose to leave the room, she reacted at last, smashing the wine glass he still held and cutting his lip. At exactly 6:20, without another word, he left. As she collapsed in near hysteria, Romani and the Parrs called her physician, who reassured her and gave her a sedative.

It would be almost impossible to overstate the shock that the failure of their marriage dealt to Ponselle, who had given up so much for it. She had waited almost twenty years to marry, having turned her back on suitors such as Dr. William Verdi and James Ceriani in her teen years and having discouraged young Kenneth Miller when he courted her in the early 1920s. As a busy professional in New York and Hollywood she had turned down offers of marriage from celebrities such as the aviation executive Glenn Martin and had not married Giuseppe Russo, as her father and Carmela feared she might do. The mature woman, the artist Rosa Ponselle, had abandoned one of the greatest stage careers of this century to marry Jackson. Raised as a strict Catholic, she had been unable to marry in a church rite because Jackson was a divorcé when they met; nevertheless, like all Catholic women of her time, she believed that marriage ought to be conventional and enduring. It is clear that Ponselle was swept away from the start by her love for Jackson. According to her own statement in her autobiography, she believed even after he left her that they still "loved each other." Hearing of his behavior, anyone would be skeptical about his love for her, but Ponselle still clung to this hope. She had perhaps never anticipated that her marriage would end in this way or that anyone would abuse her emotionally as her husband did. It is safe to say that without the support of Romani and other friends, Ponselle could never have survived a life crisis on this scale.

Quite beyond the emotional issues, there was money. Ponselle had brought to her marriage a large fortune that she alone had earned. Huge sums drawn from her accounts had paid for the house and furnishings at Villa Pace, although the land itself had been bought by a four-person partnership that had invested together to acquire it. After she and Jackson separated, their attorneys had to work out the details of the settlement. These also were reported in the *Baltimore Sun,* which quoted court records. Her lawyers and Jackson's arranged a bizarre settlement agreement that left Ponselle all the real estate and personal property "except for the books and one dozen highball glasses." Her petition for divorce was filed on July 17, 1950. On August 17, 1950, by order of Circuit Court Number 2, she was granted the right to resume her maiden name and become Rosa Ponselle once more. Her divorce became final in February 1951.

Ponselle was helped through these difficult years by old friends and new. Among the latter was Dr. James H. Bailey, who met her late in 1949, when he was a graduate student at George Washington University and she was separated from her husband. At the reception after a wedding in Washington, she sang Schubert's "Ave Maria" "as a blessing for the just-married couple," accompanying herself at the piano, Dr. Bailey recalls. As the guests were leaving, he says, "I was on the portico of the house when she came out. We talked. I then asked her, 'Would you like to go to the Shoreham and dance?' The hotel then had a summer terrace for dancing. She accepted." Dr. Bailey says he was surprised at what a "marvelous dancer" she was, "very light on her feet." Because he "liked her as a person," he and Ponselle kept in touch. After Margaret Truman's first recital in Washington, Dr. Bailey met Ponselle with Anna Case Mackay. When Ponselle was asked, "Do you think Truman can sing very well?" she answered, "I *know* that she cannot sing very well."

Ponselle invited Bailey to Villa Pace and asked guests to a pool party in his honor. This, he says, was the first of many visits there. She would call him to come for Sunday dinner or Thanksgiving; he responded by inviting her out for dinner and dancing at fine restaurants near Baltimore. She spoke about her failed marriage and said that she had given Jackson a string of polo horses when they married. She mentioned her fondness for Jackson's father. When Ponselle was in very good humor, she would sing for her new friend. "I remember her sitting on the piano bench while she played and sang the 'Habañera,'" Dr. Bailey recalls. "On one occasion I asked her, 'Why did you give up your career?' She said, 'I wanted them to remember me at my peak.'"

𝒯HE BALTIMORE CIVIC OPERA ～

All through the 1940s the demand for opera in Baltimore had been growing steadily, fed in part by the interest generated by the Metropolitan tour performances. Other enterprises were the old opera company headed by George De Feo and supported by the Stivanello family and Fortune Gallo's touring San Carlo Opera Company. Both offered standard repertory. The local impresarios behind these efforts were Eugene and Mary Martinet, who eventually launched a program of their own. The "Eugene Martinet Presents" rubric covered concerts and a 1946 *HMS Pinafore* with John Charles Thomas. Martinelli came with the San Carlo, again under the Martinet banner. Baltimoreans applauded when Ponselle appeared in a box seat for one of the San Carlo performances, wearing a draped green gown with four or five showy, gold bracelets on her arms, looking every inch the prima donna. After the death of Mr. Martinet in 1947 his wife and their son Leigh continued as presenters, again with Stivanello as costumer and stage director. They founded the Baltimore Civic Opera, which put on its first productions in the old Maryland Casualty Insurance Company auditorium.

It was quite natural at that point for them to turn to Ponselle for support, although perhaps at the outset it was not certain what kind of support might be forthcoming. Mary Martinet had first met the soprano in Baltimore in 1936 and had often entertained her in their home. During these informal evening gatherings the soprano sang for them and their guests, accompanying herself at the piano. Over more than a decade a deep friendship and sense of trust had grown between her and this family, chiefly because of her support for the arts in their city. As it happened, the birth of the new opera company coincided more or less with serious signs of trouble in the Ponselle-Jackson marriage.

When Stivanello, who had known Ponselle for years, suggested to the Martinets that they present *Aida,* he agreed to provide scenery, costumes, and stage direction. They then engaged Maud Key Shelton, a young soprano from the south, to sing the leading role. Mrs. Martinet asked Ponselle to coach her. So far as is known, this was Ponselle's first contribution to this company, making Shelton the first of a long line of "Ponselle's chicks," as she called the young people she worked with. While she remained the grand prima donna and never became a mother hen, it is surely not wrong to say that Villa Pace became an incubator for Ponselle's flock and that she poured out her artistry and affectionate care for them. Beyond the coaching sessions, her kindness extended to after-rehearsal buffets and meals and lodging for those who came from out of town.

Among dozens of other singers she helped were Beverly Sills, whom Ponselle coached for *Manon;* Shakeh Vartenissian, for *Bohème;* Sherill Milnes, for Gérard in *Chénier;* Raina Kabaivanska, for *Forza* and *Gioconda;* Plácido Domingo, for *Les contes d'Hoffmann;* and Joshua Hecht, for *Aida.* Lili Chookasian, William Warfield, Raina Kabaivanska, and James Morris were "regulars," seeking Ponselle's coaching over long periods of time, while Leontyne Price was an occasional visitor, though not in a formal coaching situation.

One of the people closest to Ponselle in this period was the pianist, conductor, and coach Igor Chichagov. He shared his recollections for this book in a 1997 interview and in earlier conversations about his mentor. Born in Irkutsk, Siberia, he had moved with his family to Saint Petersburg and trained there before emigrating to East Germany and then to the United States. Chichagov came to Baltimore in 1950 with the soprano Kyra Baklanova, who was later coached by Ponselle at Villa Pace. He first met Ponselle in the spring of 1951, when she asked him to help prepare the Baltimore Civic Opera's *Carmen,* scheduled for December that year. Asked about her methods as a coach, Chichagov said, "She was always putting life into everything, putting excitement into it. She would work for *hours* on one phrase. 'I'm not getting from you what I want,' she would say to a singer. She was fanatical over details. Time never mattered to her. When she was satisfied, she would say, 'Now we've got it!' " He also confirmed that she began with the first note of the score and went straight through to the end, as she said she had done all her life. "She was an excellent pianist, and nothing was beyond her."

Ponselle's work with the Baltimore Civic Opera "revived her," Chichagov said. "It gave her a new lease on life." He particularly remembered three incidents in his thirty-year friendship with Ponselle.

> She spent the whole summer in the swimming pool in icy water. Just as she hated hot air, she hated warm-water pools. And she also slept all winter long with the air conditioning on. She would come in from the pool in her swimming suit and sit at the piano and begin to play and sing. When you looked at her you saw an old lady in a swimming suit, sitting on the piano bench. But as she sang, that old lady disappeared and she absolutely became the character that she found in the music. She was transformed before your eyes from the old lady into the character. It was a transformation. No other word describes it.

Chichagov went on. "One afternoon as I was preparing a mezzo for Amneris in *Aida,* this young woman got to the lines 'Ah, vieni! Vieni, amor mio m'inebria' and 'Vieni, amor mio, ravvivami.' Ponselle came in and began to sing the scene. She *was* Aida. She was suffering, regal and beautiful." On another occasion she was running through *Norma* in a coaching session. "There is the scene where Norma learns from Adalgisa that she has been unfaithful to her vows. Norma does not know that her own lover, Pollione, has betrayed her and fallen in love with Adalgisa. When he enters and Ponselle realizes what has happened, she would confront him, singing, 'Costui!'—'*He* is the one!' She could kill him. Watching Ponselle, you could die of fear. She made a horrible sound! But it was a beautiful horrible sound, like nothing else you ever heard in your life."

Chichagov also recalls one of the greatest events of the last years of Ponselle's life: her recording sessions of 1954 at Villa Pace, when she was almost fifty-eight years old. Geraldine Souvaine, who produced the Metropolitan Opera broadcasts, heard Ponselle singing at Villa Pace in the early 1950s and begged her to record again. Ponselle refused. But later, when George Marek came down, he began the campaign again, asking her to go to the old Victor studios at Camden, New Jersey. That Ponselle would not do; so the Victor representatives came to Villa Pace with the soprano's former engineer, who had overseen her last recordings in 1939. He brought aides, all his equipment, and a Steinway piano. Chichagov said that the Victor team stayed at the villa for a week. He accompanied her on many of the songs recorded, with her standing in the middle of the grand foyer of the house, directly under the chandelier, with a twenty-eight-foot ceiling overhead. He sat at the piano in the next room. Chichagov said that they used all the pieces that had been agreed upon, "then Rosa got out her old concert songbook, and we recorded things we had not even rehearsed. She also played her own accompaniment for some songs." Among these is "Amuri, amuri," which Crutchfield values so highly. Others are Tosti's "Vorrei," which Ponselle sang in English as "Could I?," and "Fa la nana, bambin."

These recording sessions came soon after Ponselle began to play a full and active role with the Baltimore Civic Opera and served as a lesson and example to the young people she was coaching. Although the soprano modestly claimed later that a *Traviata* of 1951 was the first opera she could say was "her own" with the company, the truth is that she influenced its direction from the moment of its founding. For the Martinets' second work, *Carmen,* which followed the initial *Aida,* Ponselle was more qualified than anyone else to oversee it; this was every inch "her production," although she was still not officially connected to the company. Leigh Martinet said that he insisted on an official announcement of her position in 1949 because from the beginning she played a major role in the organization, helping to plan repertory, coaching young artists at Villa Pace, supervising auditions, and overseeing rehearsals. When the company was later renamed the Baltimore Opera Company, Ponselle still held the title of artistic director. In addition to three productions of *Aida,* she oversaw three of *Bohème* and two each of *Faust, Forza, Manon Lescaut, Tosca,* and *Traviata. Chénier, Boris Godunov, Cavalleria* and *Pagliacci, Le nozze di Figaro, Die Fledermaus, Lucia, Butterfly, Otello, Rigoletto, Thaïs, Tosca, Trovatore,* and *Turandot* were given one production each. In spite of the wide sweep of her philanthropy, Ponselle's energy was chiefly spent on the Baltimore Civic Opera. She did not resign until 1979, when she was ill and past eighty.

Always a volunteer, Ponselle also became more and more steadily involved with fund-raising for the Baltimore Symphony Orchestra. Newspaper coverage of her effort describes the open houses at Villa Pace, particularly at Christmas. She led the effort in a project to record and sell an LP that features her, Carmela, and other professionals and amateurs on carols and other pieces. Over the years Ponselle presided at countless opera balls and benefits and persuaded contributors large and small to help the cause of the arts in her adopted city. No one could have made a greater effort on their behalf.

Her commitment to these organizations did not prevent her from making a large number of appearances at grand public events where she sang. In September 1952 General Dwight D. Eisenhower was running for the presidency. Having met Ponselle earlier, he asked her to appear with him and his wife at a rally in the Fifth Regiment Armory in Baltimore. The official soloist was John Charles Thomas, but soon Ponselle was called onstage. There she and Thomas sang together before the general and his wife arrived. Then Ponselle sang "Ave Maria" and "Some Enchanted Evening." After the general completed his nationwide telecast, she sat at the piano and accompanied her own singing, as she had so often done at concerts. At the end of the program General Eisenhower kissed the soprano on the cheek, and Mrs. Eisenhower embraced her while the general expressed to the audience his appreciation of her great art. This event was widely covered by the wire services and the *New York Herald Tribune*.

She gave *Opera News* her interview of 1952 that same fall, as she was preparing the young singers for *La bohème,* which the Baltimore Civic Opera had announced for October and November that year. After I interviewed Ponselle at Villa Pace, she had several members of the *Bohème* cast there for a rehearsal in the great music room of her home. I saw how her magisterial oversight created a coherent ensemble out of a group of well-meaning but unpolished singers. More than anything else, Ponselle acted like a drill sergeant. She focused on the details because she was ever the perfectionist.

ℋONORS, DECORATIONS, AND LOSSES ∿

Through the final decades of her life Ponselle was often recognized for her contributions to music and to civic affairs. Year after year, *Opera News* and the major newspapers and wire services carried interviews and feature stories about her. She and Luciano Pavarotti were shown together at the keyboard of her Knabe piano at Villa Pace, in full color on the cover of a Sunday supplement magazine. On two occasions Boris Goldovsky let her tell of her career on the Texaco Metropolitan Opera Saturday broadcast intermission features, and Francis Robinson created a long biographical study of her for television, fully documented. In October 1957 she became the first woman to receive the Colombo Award from the Italian-American Civic Club in Baltimore. The Italian government in Rome awarded her the citation Commendatore al Merito della Repubblica Italiana in January 1969 and decorated her with it in February. A postage stamp honoring her was issued by the government of Colombia in 1975, the forerunner of the U.S. postage stamp celebrating her, scheduled to be issued in 1997. Ponselle also received honorary doctorates from the Peabody Conservatory in Baltimore in 1965, that city's College of Our Lady of Notre Dame, and the University of Maryland. Several birthdays of her later life provided occasions for huge parties drawing celebrities from the world of music to Villa Pace, where photographs of her taken during the festivities show a remarkably beautiful woman of sixty-five, seventy, seventy-five, and eighty.

Quite naturally Ponselle's last years were marked by personal loss. Anna Ryan, the former organist in the parish of Our Lady of Mount Carmel in Meriden, died in New York on February 6, 1943, after almost forty years of association with Carmela and Rosa. Even in 1937, after Rosa was married to Carle Jackson, one bedroom in her penthouse was kept free for Anna Ryan, who as we have seen, later shared Carmela's apartment at 230 Riverside until 1940, when, old and crippled with arthritis, she moved to a New York City nursing home, where Rosa paid the bills. It is no exaggeration to say that this humble organist from a tiny parish was responsible—more than any other single person—for getting the Ponzillos out of Meriden and setting them on the road to success.

Dr. William Verdi, who had been Ponselle's personal physician from her earliest days in New Haven, died in that city in 1957, at the age of eighty-five. A graduate of Yale University, where he was also on the faculty of obstetrics and gynecology, he had been a leader in his native city for decades and had also served as president of the Connecticut State Medical Association. Having met young Rosa Ponzillo just before he went to Europe in the army medical corps, he had her as his patient for many years, so long as she lived in Connecticut or New York.

A shattering loss was that of Romani, who had coached Ponselle from 1918, saw her fairly frequently after her marriage, and kept in touch all the time with "mia cara Rosina" through his and his wife's letters to her. After they left Villa Pace, the Romanis divided their time between Santa Monica and New York City, then vacationed in a home he bought near Leghorn, his Italian birthplace. Ponselle helped him in every imaginable way, even pulling strings at the State Department in Washington in 1955 to get him a new passport when he found his had expired, leaving him caught in the web of bureaucracy. Through Romani Ponselle kept up with the music business as she would never have been able to do without his stream of information. It was from him and his wife, Ruth Brown, that she first heard news in 1950 of a promising new soprano in Italy: "There is a young singer here by the name of Callas that imitates you in singing. I understand that she is in the hands of Serafin. There is a record of *Puritani* with her."

Romani had remained in Italy from 1952 to 1955, although he had become an American citizen in 1942. He urged, even begged Ponselle to come over, but she, secure at Villa Pace, did not budge. As a result, when he returned to the States he spent time at the villa. Romani was on his way back to Italy in 1958 when he decided to stop for a visit. He and his sixteen-year-old son got to the house on the last day of June. As usual, coaching sessions with young singers took up the afternoons, and Romani offered to help out with one of these. A few days after he arrived, Ponselle was on the terrace while Romani sat at her piano, teaching. Suddenly, without any warning of any kind, he fell over the keyboard. Twenty minutes later he died in the guest room bed. It was July 4. His funeral was celebrated in a requiem high mass at the Church of Saint Charles Borromeo in Pikesville, Maryland, on July 9. After the rites he was buried in Baltimore's Druid Ridge Cemetery.

The obituaries emphasized Romani's forty-year-long friendship with

Ponselle and his dedication to Puccini, his studies at the royal conservatories in Naples and Milan, his early tenure as the musical director for Columbia Graphophone in New York, his record as a composer, and his coaching of Zinka Milanov, Vivian Della Chiesa, Riccardo Stracciari, Maria Barrientos, Marion Telva, Giacomo Rimini, Giulio Crimi, Rosa Raisa, Hipólito Lázaro, and Cesare Formichi.

If the shock of Romani's death and the way he died were devastating to the seventy-year-old Ponselle, the aftermath proved difficult for her. She and members of her household had to care for his son and notify his wife and sister, Lola Romani Savazzini, who was living in Italy. Matters relating to his estate were also of concern. Quite naturally, it was some time before some semblance of normal life could be resumed. Ponselle was aided in these difficult moments by Carmela and by Celina Sanchez, the young singer Romani was coaching when he collapsed. Sanchez, along with the Ponzillo sisters' old friends Giuseppe Bamboschek and his wife, also cared for Carmela after she returned to New York.

Through all these years Ponselle and her sister remained close; after Jackson left Villa Pace, Carmela came to visit, particularly at Christmas and during the summer. Winters found Carmela in New York, where she taught voice and entertained friends in her modestly furnished apartment. She made her last professional appearance in April 1951 at Madison Square Garden, when, at the age of sixty-three, she sang "O don fatale" from *Don Carlos*. After that, Carmela dedicated much of her life to helping the handicapped and the underprivileged, especially children. Her profound religious convictions sustained her through some difficult times when she depended on "the Heavenly Spirit"—as she referred to God—to see her through.

When Carmela wrote her memoir in the 1930s she left a precious record of life in the Ponzillo family and her own and Rosa's first years on the stage. Several years later, on November 24, 1940, Carmela began a typed revision of the first pages of that memoir. She signed herself Carmela Anna Ponselle. Dedicated "in memory of my beloved Mother and best friend, Madeline [*sic*] Conte Ponzillo," it acknowledges the help of Anna Ryan, "who really brought to light my musical talent;" Rosa Ponselle, "my younger sister, whose great talent has been an inspiration;" Romani, "for his coaching;" the late Giulio Gatti-Casazza, "for giving me my great opportunity at the Metropolitan Opera Company;" Tullio Serafin, "for his support;" Martinelli, "for his encouragement in my debut as Amneris in *Aida;*" Rethberg, "for her tenderness and friendship at my debut" and the "entire staff of the Metropolitan Opera Company, for their assistance." "Last but not least, to my great and wide American public, which followed my career from its early beginnings." So far as we know, Carmela never completed this personal account of her career, but it remains a document full of invaluable insight into the Ponzillo sisters' lives and their careers as the Ponselles.

At the end of their days, the two women had shared concerns that could not be neglected, for both were involved in matters relating to their brother, Tony, and to their father's estate. Benjamin Ponzillo died in the Meriden Hospital on April 25, 1952, having fallen at home and broken his hip two days earlier. His death certificate lists him as "coal merchant, retired," a description provided by Tony, who went to the city clerk to declare the death. Carmela, always close to her father and brother, attended the requiem mass at their parish, the Church of Our Lady of Mount Carmel, and the interment in Sacred Heart Cemetery, where Maddalena Conte Ponzillo had been buried twenty years earlier. Rosa Ponselle, the youngest of his children, remained in Baltimore, unable to travel.

After each of these events, though, Ponselle soon returned to her Baltimore Civic Opera projects at full speed. In her last years she received unfailing support from Miss Elayne Duke, a close family friend who was also her personal representative. After each visit with Rosa, Carmela returned to her flat on Riverside Drive, where she lived to be eighty-nine. Like her sister, Carmela had invested her earnings wisely in General Motors and Pan-American Airlines, among other stocks, even though she told interviewers that she "always spent more than she had." In fact, Carmela's holdings at the end of her life were valued at $43,941.88. It remained for Elayne Duke to make arrangements for the oversight of her affairs. Like her father, Carmela suffered the consequences of a broken hip after a fall. She died on June 13, 1977, in Montefiore Hospital in New York City. At her own request she was laid to rest in Baltimore, in the same cemetery where Romani's grave was. Carmela is buried above the ground in a chapel where a burial place was also acquired for Rosa. At the time of her sister's death, Ponselle, in a state of emotional collapse, asked to have the wall between her own cubicle and Carmela's removed, so that the two could be as close together in death as possible. Ponselle's attorney, Michael J. Abromaitis, also wrote to Tony Ponzillo in September 1977 to say that "Rosa is still distraught over the death of Carmela. She has been in the hospital several times since the funeral."

Ponselle resigned in 1979 from her post as artistic director of the Baltimore Opera. The last years of her life were marked by illness, as multiple myeloma, a plasma cell disease, took its toll. It had first shown its symptoms in the mid-1970s, even before Carmela's death. Weakened by it, Rosa Ponselle died in her own room in Villa Pace on May 25, 1981. The funeral mass for her was offered at the Church of Saint Charles Borromeo in Pikesville, from which Romani had been buried earlier. Vocal music during the rite was provided by William Warfield and Kyra Baklanova. At the end of the service Ponselle was buried beside Carmela. Like her, she had dedicated her life to singing; now, with Rosa's death, their era ended. If ever lives had fitting closures, those of Romani, Carmela, and Rosa did, for they were united in death as in life, in the solitude of Druid Ridge.

Notes

CHAPTER 1

Important sources of information on the Terra di Lavoro are *Campania,* published by the Banca Nazionale di Lavoro; the Italian Touring Club *Guide to Campania; La mia Italia,* a publication of the Italian Government Travel Office; and the books on Caserta and its territory cited in the bibliography. Roberto Mainardi's essay "Historical and Environmental Determinants and the Hard Quest for a Regional Equilibrium," (in *Campania,* pages 7–20), is particularly valuable. The Italian Cultural Institute and the Italian Government Travel Office, both in New York, provided detailed information on the history of the area and its culture. All maps consulted are in the libraries of these two institutions and in the New York Public Library.

Social issues, the conditions of the working class, and the problems of rural communities and emigration are described in *Ideology, Economic Change, and the Working Classes: The Case of Italy,* by Samuel Surace; *A Traveler's History of Italy,* by Valerio Lintner; Count Stefano Jacini's *Inchiesta agraria* of 1883; *La storia,* by Jerre Mangione and Ben Morreale; Gay Talese's *Unto the Sons;* and in dozens of letters in the published correspondence and public statements of figures such as Cavour, D'Azeglio, Garibaldi, Verdi, Count Opprandino Arrivabene, and other Risorgimento figures. Denis Mack Smith's *Italy: A Modern History* and *Cavour and Garibaldi, 1860* are particularly valuable in illuminating the Italian situation in the nineteenth century. George Martin's *Verdi: His Music, Life and Times* describes the war in the Terra di Lavoro on page 374.

All vital records and parish register entries from Caiazzo were provided by the parish priests of that town, through the courtesy of Enrico Caruso of Piedimonte d'Alife and Cav. Aldo Mancusi, founder of the Enrico Caruso Museum of America. The history of the Caruso family appears in *Enrico Caruso: My Father and My Family,* by Enrico Caruso Jr. and Andrew Farkas.

Much information on the emigrants is found in the National Archives in New York City and the New York Public Library. Apart from the passenger lists, which are on microfilm, an important research tool is the compilation of emigrants' records for the years 1880 through December 1891 in *Italians to America,* edited by Ira A. Glazier and P. William Filby.

The Federal Censuses of 1880 and 1900 provide further data on dates of arrival and age; they can often be used to clarify incorrect data found elsewhere. They were especially important in the search for information on the Ponzillos' and Contes' arrival in America and on Filomena and Maddalena Conte. Despite the Ponselle family tradition that Maddalena Conte and Bernardino Ponzillo came to America together in 1885, accompanied by her mother's parents, no one from those families came that year; the passenger list of the *Burgundia* shows that Filomena Conte and Bernardino Ponzillo arrived in 1886, accompanied by Alfonso Faraone. Maddalena and her mother followed one year later.

CHAPTER 2

Joel H. Monroe's *Schenectady, Ancient and Modern* and A. A. Yates's *Schenectady County, New York* are the main sources for the history of the city and Italian-American life there. A map and atlas of 1900 shows Myers Alley, Gleason's Alley, the Locomotive Works, and the downtown area. Because the Federal Census of 1890 has been lost, the Schenectady city directories of 1888 and 1890 helped to fill in missing information.

Other data on New York State and New York City come from the Federal Censuses of 1900 and 1910, the passenger lists cited in the notes to chapter 1, contemporary newspapers, the Social Security Death Index and computerized Phone Search diskettes, and Trow's New York City Directories for 1910–11 and 1915.

Connecticut city directories and the censuses for Meriden and New Haven (1900 and 1910) supplemented documents in the city and county records collections, especially the civil birth, death, and marriage records and the Registry of Deeds and Probate Registry. Rosa Ponzillo's baptism record of 1898 [*sic*] is in the archive of the Church of Our Lady of Mount Carmel in Meriden. The Ponselle folders in the Meriden Public Library proved helpful in this research, as did Carmela Ponselle's 1933 memoir and scrapbook, which are in the Rosa Ponselle Collection in the New York Public Library for the Performing Arts at Lincoln Center. Carmela's account of her marriage to Dr. Henry J. Giamarino is found in her memoir. Louis Snyder contributed the information about Frederick Grannis.

Rosa Ponselle's direct quotations are from her 1952 *Opera News* interview, the Ithaca College Oral History Project interview, conducted by James A. Drake, and the Radio Free Europe program interview. Anthony (Tony) Ponzillo's remarks about his mother and older sister are in James A. Drake's biographical study of Carmela, published in the *Meriden Morning Record and Journal* on July 16, 1977. The original clipping is in the Meriden Public Library.

Peter Salwan's *Upper West Side Story* is the source of the historical information on the Ponzillos' New York City neighborhood. The correct records of the households of Paul Savage, Carmela Ponzillo's teacher, and of Margaret and Mary McCabe, the Irish women who operated the rooming house where the Ponzillos and Anna Ryan lived, are found in the U.S. Censuses of 1900 and 1910 in the National

Archive, Varick Street, New York City, and in city directories and maps in the New York Public Library Local History and Genealogy Division and in the Map Division.

Two of the most valuable research resources for this biography, the Anna Ryan–James E. Ryan scrapbooks, are described in the front of this book.

CHAPTER 3

Carmela Ponselle's scrapbooks and 1933 memoir (in the Rosa Ponselle Collection), the Anna Ryan–James E. Ryan scrapbooks, and Rosa Ponselle's many taped and live interviews about this period are the chief sources for this chapter. Details about the appearance and careers of Gene Hughes, Edward Valentine Darling, and Edward Albee, together with a rich history of "vaude" and its stars, are found in *Vaudeville: From the Honky Tonks to the Palace,* by Joe Laurie Jr., who knew the Ponzillo sisters well and had nothing but praise for them. Douglas Gilbert's history of vaudeville provided the general background for this overview of the period. The career of Sylvester Poli is described in Anthony Slade's *Encyclopedia of Vaudeville.*

All street addresses and correct names for theaters, restaurants, apartment buildings, hotels, private residences, and small places of business are found in city directories, particularly Trow's and Polk's for the period 1915–20, real estate registers, *Bromley's Atlas of New York City, 1915,* with its block and lot numbers, and the later Reverse Address Directories.

Although Rosa Ponselle stated in interviews that she and Carmela made their debut at the "Star Theatre in the Bronx," Carmela more correctly identifies the site of their tryout appearance as a theater at First Avenue and 110th Street. This is in fact described in city and real estate directories as the small "moving picture house" owned by Mrs. Mary Marino. It occupied the lot at 2157 First Avenue, between 111th and 112th Streets, according to Bromley's 1915 *Atlas of New York City.* Just a few feet to the south were two huge Consolidated Gas tanks, a lime shed, and a coal yard belonging to the Standard Gas and Light Company. The building that housed Mrs. Marino's motion picture theater soon became a carpenter's shop, with grocery storage and a dress contractor upstairs. Although closed, it is still there, in good repair. Next door, at 2159, is Giuseppe Russo's home, also still standing.

The well-documented Star Theatre at 107th Street and Lexington Avenue (later the Fox Film Corporation's Star Theatre) had fallen on bad times after a promising new beginning in 1903. It did have vaudeville, as its printed programs prove, and was within the expanding Italian enclave, the gathering place of a simple, unsophisticated "family audience." The Ponzillo sisters did play in the Bronx at the Royal Theatre, just after they launched their sister act, as Carmela's scrapbooks show. Photographs of William Thorner and his apartment are in the clipping files of Ponselle and Galli-Curci and on the microfilms of Ponselle's scrapbooks, all in the Music Division of the New York Public Library for the Performing Arts.

Emelise Aleandri's *A History of Italian-American Theatre, 1900 to 1905* is an invaluable source of information, not just for the period specified in the title but for the first quarter of the century. It covers almost every important performer and troupe active in the eastern half of the United States and is especially important for its study of Eduardo Migliaccio, called Farfariello, the friend of the Sisca family and of Caruso.

CHAPTER 4

Many of the reviews and interviews cited in this chapter are found in the Rosa Ponselle Collection and in Ponselle's clipping files in the Music Division of the New York Public Library for the Performing Arts at Lincoln Center. Where possible, I have cited the name of the journalist and publication, although these are missing from some articles. In the case of Terese Rose Nagel, who interviewed Rosa and Carmela in their Ninety-seventh Street apartment and again after they moved to Apartment 7-c at 260 Riverside Drive, the name of her newspaper, not given, may be deduced from the formatting of the photographs. Some reviews from the *New York Times, New York Sun,* and the *Tribune* are also in the first edition of *Metropolitan Opera Annals,* compiled by William H. Seltsam.

Ponselle's auditions, rehearsals, and the premiere of *La forza del destino* were described by Carmela in her memoir and by Ponselle herself in many interviews, including those with Francis Robinson, Robert Lawrence, and Thomas Villella. A transcription of an unidentified telephone interview, conducted on the occasion of the hundredth anniversary of Caruso's birth, is signed and countersigned by Ponselle; it also has her corrections in her own hand. A few sentences about Caruso taken from it appeared in the *New York Times,* in Donal Henahan's article of February 20, 1973.

In addition to *Metropolitan Opera Annals,* I also used Quaintance Eaton's *The Miracle of the Met,* Giulio Gatti-Casazza's *Memories of the Opera,* especially pp. 101–103, and my biography of Otto Kahn, as well as my interview with Ponselle for *Opera News* in 1952. Pelletier's remarks about Ponselle's first audition are from his *Une symphonie inachevée,* p. 103. The *Etude*'s Wagner essay contest was provided by William R. T. Smith of the Wagner Society, Chicago chapter. Edith Van Dyne's *The Flying Girl* was published in Chicago in 1911 by Reilly and Britton, Inc.

Analysis of the dialects of Campania in general, the Terra di Lavoro in particular, and the Veneto are found in *I dialetti delle regioni d'Italia* by Giacomo Devoto and Gabriella Giacomelli, published in Italy by Sansoni in 1972. S. Nittoli's *Vocabolario di vari dialetti del Sannio,* published in Naples in 1873, analyzes the use of language in the ancient Samnite lands.

Ponselle's earliest recordings have been reissued by Pearl on two CDs under the title *Rosa Ponselle: The Columbia Acoustic Recordings.* Although Ponselle said she did not like these, resented the pressure brought on her to keep the recordings to the four-minute time limit, and felt that she sounded as if she had been "put in a box," several of these show how Thorner, Romani, Gatti, and Caruso heard her.

CHAPTER 5

Reviews of Ponselle's performances are found in her scrapbooks, which, along with her contract with National Concerts and the photograph of her with Geneen and his guests, are in the Rosa Ponselle Collection. The photograph of her with Caruso, in costume for *La juive* and autographed by him, belongs to the Rosa Ponselle Charitable Foundation, Inc.

As in chapter 1, material on Caruso comes from the biography by Enrico Caruso Jr. and Andrew Farkas. Other information on Caruso came from Ponselle's typescript "The 100th Anniversary of the Birth of Enrico Caruso." Gatti-Casazza described Caruso's illness in *Memories of the Opera*, pp. 230–231. Caruso's letter to Gatti about his illness is quoted in Ponselle's typescript.

Records of Ponselle's Metropolitan appearances are from Gerald Fitzgerald and Jean Uppmann's *Annals of the Metropolitan* and from Geoff Peterson's *Rosa Ponselle, a Custom Chronology.*

Richard Wandel, archivist, provided the dates of the New York Philharmonic concerts in Carnegie Hall and Brooklyn.

Arnold Volpe's contributions to New York City music are documented in the collection of Ginger Dreyfus Karren, his granddaughter.

One unusual postscript to the account of Caruso's death was provided by Nino Pantano, who discovered an extraordinary expression of America's grief in a *New York Times* advertisement that appeared on Wednesday, August 3, 1921, one day after his death. It was paid for by Lord and Taylor, a department store. It reads:

～ CARUSO

We called him ours—an American, even as today Italy calls him Hers!
But more truly he was a native of all shores, more than any man of our time.
Not one nation, but a world of nations mourns his passing.
He sang, and vast audiences *hushed* before the magic of his great voice,
For it was not merely a voice singing
But a heart also.
The voice is gone; but its music will live on through the centuries,
So long as there are men and women to hear
And weep and laugh.

—Lord and Taylor

CHAPTER 6

Ponselle's contracts are housed in the Metropolitan Opera Archives, along with relevant correspondence, photographs, clippings, and press books.

The scrapbooks of Carmela and Rosa Ponselle are found in the Rosa Ponselle Collection, as are Rosa Ponselle's financial records and the files on Thorner and National Concerts, Inc. W. J. Henderson's articles are in the clipping files on Ponselle in the General Music Collection.

The letters, postcards, Christmas cards, photographs, and snapshots Ponselle sent to Kenneth E. Miller are in the collection under his name in the Special Collections of the Music Division of the New York Public Library for the Performing Arts. His files also include the note from Stuart Ross, her accompanist, and the program Miller kept of the concert she sang in Kansas City with the Saint Louis Symphony.

Mabel Wagnalls's *Opera and Its Stars* is the source for descriptions of the apartments of Galli-Curci at the Ambassador and Jeritza at the Saint Regis. Wagnalls called on Emma Eames at the Hotel Marie Antoinette, at Sixty-sixth Street and Broadway, where a "powdered and be-wigged footman in satin knee-breeches and the full court costume of [Marie Antoinettes's] period" opened the huge glass doors for her. In the lobby stood cabinets full of the guillotined queen's personal effects. "With its stained glass dome and carved oak walls," and with "soft-voiced maids" to take a guest's coat, the Marie Antoinette was the perfect setting for an opera diva. When Eames finally appeared, she was "a royal vision" in satin and pearls, "seated on a silken divan."

Lillian Nordica held forth at the Waldorf-Astoria in a suite on a high floor with thick carpets, "shaded electric lights," tall vases full of long-stemmed roses, and heavy draperies over the doors. She wore a "house-gown of pale, clinging blue silk."

Mabel Wagnalls's portraits in words cover everyone from Lilli Lehmann, Calvé, Sembrich, and Melba through Garden and Farrar, who retired when she reached forty, just as she had assured the writer she would do. Wagnalls's description of Farrar's Metropolitan Opera debut is worth the price of the book, now considered rare. Although *Opera and Its Stars* reflects Wagnalls's awe of these grand singers, it also provides fascinating glimpses of their homes, clothing, costumes, and personal habits.

Nothing could be further from those lifestyles than that of the Ponselle sisters in their modest apartment, number 7-C in the building at 260 Riverside Drive (also 319 West Ninety-eighth Street). There Rosa, Carmela, their mother, Anna Ryan, and Tony Ponzillo, who was the cook for his sister's birthday party in 1924, let guests come into the kitchen to watch them cook pasta for dinner. With Giuseppe Bamboschek and William Tyroler in the apartment across the hall, they created a little neighborhood of their own.

As in other chapters, Ponselle's remarks about her roles and colleagues are taken from direct interviews with her, from her autobiography, and from James A. Drake's autumn 1993 article in *Opera Quarterly*.

CHAPTER 7

Tullio Serafin: Il Patriara del Melodramma, edited by Giuseppe Pugliese and Teodoro Celli, contains Serafin's own recollections of his childhood and youth in "Figlio di tutto il paese," pp. 22–24, while references to the Metropolitan, Bori, Jeritza, and Ponselle are found in "Al Metropolitan," pp. 97–103.

Ponselle's own observations about Serafin and his influence on her are found in a transcript of a conversation, running to two single-spaced typewritten pages, in the Rosa Ponselle Collection. Here, too, are the financial records used in previous chapters. A taped interview with a Mrs. Howard from Washington, D.C., also contains material on Serafin and *La Gioconda*.

Dante Del Fiorentino's memoir of Puccini, *Immortal Bohemian*, is the source for the incidents of his own life and of Puccini's encounter with "the American Indian," Rosa Ponselle, in Viareggio in the summer of 1924 (pp. 201–202).

The two interviews with Boris Goldovsky were broadcast on March 7, 1954, and April 20, 1957, for Texaco Metropolitan Opera Saturday intermission features. I thank Michael Bronson, the Metropolitan Opera, and Texaco for making them available to me for use in this book.

CHAPTER 8

Verdi's letter to Giuseppe Piroli about Spontini and *La vestale* is reproduced in Franco Abbiati's *Verdi*, vol. 4, p. 25.

Pugliese and Celli's *Tullio Serafin* is the source for the conductor's personal recollections. Thomas G. Kaufman provided the dates of Ester Mazzoleni's performances at La Scala.

As in other chapters, Ponselle's contracts with the Metropolitan Opera, now in the company's archive, are the source for information on her obligations and fees. Her contract with Coppicus and the Metropolitan Music Bureau is in the Rosa Ponselle Collection, together with her financial records and correspondence with Libbie Miller. A list, compiled by Ponselle's secretary Edith Prilik, of Ponselle's Columbia recording sessions and first Victor session is in the possession of James A. Drake, who kindly sent me a copy of it.

Reviews were retrieved from the first edition of Seltsam's *Metropolitan Opera Annals* and from Ponselle's scrapbooks in the Rosa Ponselle Collection.

The exact date on which Ponselle saw Raisa in *Norma* at the Manhattan Opera House may never be known, but because she later mentioned Gabriella Besanzoni one may assume that she saw *Norma* with her on January 21, 1921.

CHAPTER 9

As in previous chapters, all information about Ponselle's contracts comes from the Metropolitan Opera Archive.

Correspondence from Eustace Blois of the Royal Opera at Covent Garden, Prilik, Libbie Miller, and Benjamin Ponzillo is in the Rosa Ponselle Collection. Also there are all the reviews and other clippings cited and correspondence with I. Miller, photographs of the Ponselle statue, and clippings about the dedication.

Lily Pons's contract with Anthony and Agostino Stivanello and Philip Culcasi is in the archives of the Stivanello Costume Company, Inc.

Verdi's and Boito's letters about Gemma Bellincioni are found in vol. 4, p. 270, of Franco Abbiati's *Verdi*. Harold Rosenthal's accounts of Ponselle at the Royal Opera appear in his *Two Centuries of Opera at Covent Garden*. Gatti's *Memoirs,* Serafin's memoirs (in Pugliese and Celli, *Tullio Serafin*), Otto Kahn's archive in the Firestone Library at Princeton University, and Quaintance Eaton's *The Miracle of the Met* are the chief sources for information about events of the 1920s and 1930s.

Florence and Ralph Postiglione identified Villa Platani on Lake Como and provided information on its history.

All street addresses and personal data are found in the U.S. Censuses of 1900, 1910, and 1920, city directories, immigration and citizenship records, and real estate registers in the New York Public Library, the Mormon Family History Center Library, and the National Archive, all in New York City.

The out-of-town reviews of *Carmen* are found in the second Ryan scrapbook, from the estate of James E. Ryan.

CHAPTER 10

The correspondence files of Carle Jackson, Libbie Miller, and Ruth and Romano Romani are in the Rosa Ponselle Collection.

Information on the Baltimore Civic Opera is drawn from the clipping files of the Baltimore Public Library and my own recollections as well of those of Igor Chichagov, Leigh Martinet, and Anthony L. Stivanello.

William Weaver recalled his first experience of hearing Ponselle in recital in a 1996 conversation; Frank Bradley, formerly of the Local History and Genealogy Division of the New York Public Library, recalled her activities at the opera. In a long telephone interview on January 18, 1995, George Bernard remembered her participation in the officers' training school graduation. The film comedian Buddy Ebsen was also there that day.

Accounts of the purchase of the Nacirema property and the construction of Villa Pace are found in the clipping files of the Baltimore Public Library, as are the *Sun* news articles covering the dissolution of Ponselle's marriage, her divorce, and the legal proceeding that allowed her to resume her maiden name. Several clippings about her separation and divorce from the United Press and Associated Press wire services are in the second James E. Ryan scrapbook. Dr. James H. Bailey shared his memoirs of Ponselle with me during a 1997 visit in Virginia.

The death certificates of Benjamin Ponzillo and his wife were provided by the City Clerk's office in Meriden, Connecticut. Carmela's death certificate is in the Carmela Ponselle Papers in the Rosa Ponselle Collection. Anna Ryan's death certificate is in the New York City Department of Records and Information Services, Municipal Archives.

Bibliography

MAPS

Campania and the Terra di Lavoro: *Campania*. Banca Nazionale del Lavoro. Martellago, Venice, 1977 (end papers).

Italia, Atlante Stradale De Agostini. Novara, 1989.

La mia Italia. Novara, 1994.

Meriden, Connecticut: Maps in the Meriden Public Library.

New York City, 5 Borough Pocket Atlas. New York, 1992.

New York City: *Bromley's Atlas of the Borough of Manhattan, 1915* and real estate records in the Map Division, New York Public Library.

Schenectady, New York: Maps and atlases in the Map Division, New York Public Library.

VITAL RECORDS, ESTATE RECORDS, PERSONAL DATA

Note about the documents: Italian civil records are found in the municipal or provincial archives, in the Stato Civile or Anagrafe; baptisms, marriages, and deaths are in the parish registers, either deposited in the parish itself (usually in the rectory) or in the diocesan archive. Some Italian parishes also have parish censuses, which give all vital record information on every person in every dwelling.

In the United States, I used birth, death, and marriage records in municipal and state archives. Locally they are often in the City Clerk's office. Wills and estate settlements are in the county probate court or surrogate court archives. City directories, immigration records, and Federal Censuses used in this book are in the National Archive branch in New York City and in the New York Public Library. City directories for Meriden are in the local public library, which also has a large Ponselle clipping file. Every Mormon Family History Center has access to these and many other records.

Caiazzo, Province of the Terra di Lavoro, Italy: Civil records and parish register entries (nineteenth century).

Meriden, New Haven County, Connecticut: Birth, marriage, and death records; reg-

istry of deeds; wills and estate settlements; parish register entries; city directories; Federal Census records of 1900, 1910, 1920.

New Haven County and Town, Connecticut: Birth, marriage, and death records;
Social Security Death Index records; city directories; Federal Census records of
1900, 1910, 1920.

New York City, New York: Death records, Federal Census records of 1900, 1910,
1920; city directories from 1900 to 1935; telephone directories; *New York Times*
obituaries.

Piedimonte d'Alife (now Piedimonte Matese), Province of the Terra di Lavoro, Italy:
Civil records and parish register entries (nineteenth century).

Schenectady City and County, New York: Birth, marriage, and death records; Federal
Census records of 1900; city directories from 1885 to 1895; Social Security Death
Index records.

State of Connecticut: Death Records, 1945–96.

METROPOLITAN OPERA ANNALS, HISTORY, AND CHRONOLOGY

Eaton, Quaintance. *The Miracle of the Met.* New York, 1968.

Fitzgerald, Gerald, and Jean Uppmann. *Annals of the Metropolitan Opera.* 2 vols.
Boston and New York, 1989.

Peterson, Geoff, ed. *Rosa Ponselle: The Complete Metropolitan Opera Performances,
1918–1937: A Custom Chronology.* New York, 1996.

Seltsam, Henry. *Metropolitan Opera Annals.* New York, 1947.

BOOKS AND ARTICLES

Abbiati, Franco. *Giuseppe Verdi.* 4 vols. Milan, 1959.

Alda, Frances. *Men, Women, and Tenors.* Boston, 1937.

Aleandri, Emelise F. *A History of Italian-American Theatre, 1900 to 1905.* Ann Arbor,
Mich., 1996.

Aloi, Enrico. *My Remembrances of Rosa Ponselle.* New York, 1994.

———. *Rosa Ponselle: A Pictorial Essay.* New York, 1996.

Barbagallo, Corrado. *L'Italia dal 1870 ad Oggi.* Milan, 1918.

Campania. Banca Nazionale del Lavoro. Martellago, Venice, 1977.

Caruso, Enrico, Jr., and Andrew Farkas. *Enrico Caruso: My Father and My Family.*
Portland, Oreg., 1990.

Del Fiorentino, Dante. *Immortal Bohemian.* New York, 1952.

Devoto, Giacomo, and Gabriella Giacomelli. *I dialetti delle Regioni d'Italia.* Milan, 1972.

Drake, James A. "Ponselle: The Seasons Abroad." *Opera Quarterly* 10, no. 4 (summer 1994); 73–90.

———. "Rosa Ponselle Recalls Roles and Colleagues, 1918–1924." *Opera Quarterly* 10, no. 1 (autumn 1993): 85–108.

"Etude Readers Decide the Case of Richard Wagner." *Etude,* July 1918, 439–440.

Gatti-Casazza, Giulio. *Memories of the Opera.* New York, 1933.

Glazier, Ira, and P. William Filby, eds. *Italians to America.* 4 vols. New York, 1992, 1993.

Hines, Jerome. *Great Singers on Great Singing.* New York, 1985.

Jacini, Count Stefano. *Frammenti dell'inchiesta agraria.* Rome, 1883.

Jeritza, Maria. *Sunlight and Song.* New York, 1924.

Laurie, Joe, Jr. *Vaudeville: From the Honky Tonk to the Palace.* New York, 1953.

Lindenberger, Harold. *Opera: The Extravagant Art.* Ithaca, N.Y., 1984.

Lintner, Valerio. *A Traveler's History of Italy.* New York, 1989

Mack Smith, Denis. *Cavour and Garibaldi, 1860.* Cambridge, Eng., 1954

Mainardi, Roberto. "Historical and Environmental Determinants and the Hard Quest for a Regional Equilibrium," in *Campania,* a publication of the Banca Nazionale di Lavoro, pp. 7–20.

Marion, John Francis. *Lucrezia Bori of the Metropolitan Opera.* New York, 1962.

Martin, George. *Verdi: His Music, Life, and Times.* New York, 1963.

Monroe, Joel H. *Schenectady.* Geneva, N.Y., 1914.

Pelletier, Wilfrid. *Une symphonie inachevée.* Ottawa, 1972.

Phillips-Matz, Mary Jane, and Charles Matz. "From the Villa Pace," interview with Ponselle in *Opera News,* November 24, 1952.

———. *The Many Lives of Otto Kahn.* New York, 1963. 2d ed. 1984.

Pinza, Ezio, with Robert Magidoff. *Ezio Pinza: An Autobiography.* New York, 1958.

Ponselle, Rosa, and James A. Drake. *Ponselle: A Singer's Life.* New York, 1982.

Pugliese, Giuseppe, and Teodoro Celli, eds. *Tullio Serafin: Il Patriarca del Melodramma.* La musica nel Veneto, vol. 1, edited by Giuseppe Pugliese. Venice, 1985.

Rosenthal, Harold. *Two Centuries of Opera at Covent Garden.* London, 1958.

Salwen, Peter. *Upper West Side Story.* New York, 1989.

Surace, Samuel J. *Ideology, Economic Change, and the Working Classes: The Case of Italy.* Berkeley and Los Angeles, 1966.

Talese, Gay. *Unto the Sons.* New York, 1992.

Van Dyne, Edith. *The Flying Girl.* Chicago, 1911.

Volpe, Marie. *Arnold Volpe: Bridge between Two Musical Worlds.* Coral Gables, Fla., 1950.

Wagnalls, Mabel, *Opera and Its Stars.* New York, 1924.

ARCHIVAL SOURCES

Rosa Ponselle Collection.

The papers of Rosa Ponselle and Carmela Ponselle, including the latter's unpublished memoir (1933). 57 boxes, plus 21 scrapbooks, photographs, and memorabilia, c. 1911–81. In the Music Division (Special Collections) of the New York Public Library for the Performing Arts at Lincoln Center.

Kenneth Miller Letters. Letters, cards, and photographs from Ponselle to Kenneth Miller. In the Music Division (Special Collections) of the New York Public Library for the Performing Arts at Lincoln Center.

Anna M. Ryan-James Edgar Ryan scrapbooks and papers. In the private collection of James Ryan Mulvey.

Clipping Files, Programs

General collection of the Music Division of the New York Public Library for the Performing Arts at Lincoln Center. Indexed by surname.

Special collections of the Baltimore Public Library. Indexed under Rosa Ponselle.

Collection of the Meriden Public Library. Indexed under Rosa Ponselle.

The New York Philharmonic Archives, Avery Fisher Hall.

The United States Army Military District of Washington, Public Affairs Office.

TAPED INTERVIEWS

Ithaca College, Oral History Project Tapes, Music Department, conducted by James A. Drake.

Texaco Metropolitan Opera Broadcast Intermission features by Boris Goldovsky (1954, 1957) and Francis Robinson (1961).

Radio Free Europe Interview, tape from the collection of Rudolph S. Rauch.

Thomas Villella tapes and transcriptions.

A Rosa Ponselle Discography

We are extremely fortunate in that almost all of the commercial recordings made by Rosa Ponselle are readily available today on compact discs. Because earlier, more complete versions of Ponselle's recorded legacy are available in libraries for the collector interested in more in-depth detail about the recordings, we have chosen here to concentrate on what is currently available. In order to identify the various "versions" of a given selection, we have chosen to list the "matrix" and "take" numbers for all selections, followed by the catalog numbers of the available compact discs. The "take" number indicates the number of times a given selection was recorded, with the published "take" shown in bold face type.

Section 1 details the first series of recordings that Ponselle made for the Columbia Graphophone Company. Section 2 lists the three series of recordings she made for RCA Victor, 1923–29, 1939, and 1954. Selections from her commercial radio broadcasts are shown in section 3, and a few of the "private" recordings (vocal and spoken) that Ponselle made at her home, Villa Pace, are listed in section 4. Section 5 lists the titles and catalog numbers of the various available compact disc collections and one videotape.

For their help and support, I wish to express appreciation to Bernadette Moore of BMG Records, Louise and Virginia Barder of Romophone, Nimbus Records, and to James A. Drake, James M. Alfonte, H. Ward Marston, Jeffrey Miller, Hugh M. Johns, Raymond Horneman, Fono Enterprise SRL, Italy, and Elayne Duke of the Rosa Ponselle Foundation.

Bill Park

Athens, Texas, 1997

COLUMBIA RECORDS

1. Abide with Me (Monk), with B.
   Maurel (orch. R. Romani)
   78557-1, -**2**
   9 July 1919

2. *L'africana* (Meyerbeer): Figlio del
   sol (orch. R. Romani)
   98059-**1,**-2   CDS 9964
   1 Feb 1923

3. *Aida* (Verdi): Ritorna vincitor
   (orch. R. Romani)
   98092-**1,** -2   CDS 9964, NI 7878
   19 Sept 1923

4. *Aida* (Verdi): O patria mia
   (orch. R. Romani)
   49557-1, -2, -3, -4, -**5**   68036D;
     8910M CDS 9964, AB 78576
   29 Nov 1918

5. *Aida* (Verdi): O terra, addio!, with
   C. Hackett (orch. R. Romani)
   49734-**1**   CDS 9964, AB 78576
   14 Jan 1920

6. Blue Danube Waltz (Strauss)
   (orch. R. Romani)
   49988-1, -2, -3, -**4**   CDS 9964,
     VA 1120, MIN 7, RY 74
   17 Sept 1921

7. *Bohème* (Puccini): Sì, mi chiamano Mimi (orch. R. Romani)
   98062-1, -**2**   CDS 9964, NI 7878
   13 Feb 1923

8. Carolina Sunshine (Hirsch-
   Schmidt), with C. Ponselle
   (orch. R. Romani)
   78927-1, -2   (unpublished)
   15 Jan 1920

9. *Cavalleria rusticana* (Mascagni):
   Ave Maria (Intermezzo)
   (orch. R. Romani)
   49556-1   (unpublished)
   29 Nov 1918

10. *Cavalleria rusticana* (Mascagni):
    Voi lo sapete (orch. R. Romani)
    49570-1, -**2**   CDS 9964, NI 7878,
      MET 218CD, AB 78576
    9 Jan 1919

11. Comin' thro' the Rye (Tradi-
    tional), with C. Ponselle (orch.
    R. Romani)
    78847-1, -2, -**3**   CDS 9964,
      MET 218CD, AB 78576
    9 Dec. 1919

12. *Ernani* (Verdi): Ernani! Ernani,
    involami (orch. R. Romani)
    98028-**1,** -2   NI 7878, CDS 9964
    9 June 1922

13. Flower of the Snow (E. Brown)
    (orch. R. Romani)
    49756-1   (unpublished)
    Between 20 and 27 February 1920

14. *La forza del destino* (Verdi): La
    Vergine degli angeli, with chorus
    (orch. R. Romani)
    49558-1, -2, -4, -5, -**6**, -7, -**8**
      CDS 9964, (-**6**), NI 7846 (-**6**),
      AB 78576
    2 December 1918

15. *La forza del destino* (Verdi): Pace,
    pace, mio Dio (pf. R. Romani)
    Test record, matrix number un-
    known   EKR CD46
    3 April 1918

16. *La forza del destino* (Verdi): Pace, pace, mio Dio (orch. R. Romani)
49859-1, -**2**   CDS 9964, AB 78576
5 July 1920

17. *La Gioconda* (Ponchielli): Suicidio! (orch. R. Romani)
49735-1, -**2**, -**3**   CDS 9964 (-**3**), MET 218CD (-**3**)
14 January 1920

18. Goodbye (Tosti) (orch. R. Romani)
49560-1, -2, -**3**   CDS 9964, NI 7846, VA 1120, MIN 7, RY 74, AB 78576
2 December 1918

19. *Guglielmo Tell* (Rossini): Selva opaca (orch. R. Romani)
98058-**1**, -2   CDS 9964, NI 7878, MET 218CD
1 February 1923

20. Home, Sweet Home (Bishop) (orch. R. Romani)
49935-**1**   CDS 9964
16 February 1921

21. *La juive* (Halévy): Il va venir (orch. R. Romani)
98096-1, -2
28 September 1923
-**3**   CDS 9964, NI 7846
11 January 1924
-4
14 January 1924

22. Keep the Home Fires Burning (Novello), with quartet: Harrison, Miller, Croxton, Sarto (orch. R. Romani)
49585-1, -2, -**3**   CDS 9964, VA 1120, MIN 7, RY 74, AB 78576
15 February 1919

23. Little Alabama Coon (Starr), with quartet: Harrison, Miller, Croxton, Sarto (orch. R. Romani)
79980-1, -2, -3
10 September 1921
4, -**5**   CDS 9964
13 April 1922

24. *Lohengrin* (Wagner): Einsam in trüben Tagen (orch. R. Romani)
98093-**1**, 2   CDS 9964, NI 7846, BIM 701-2
21 September 1923

25. *Madama Butterfly* (Puccini): Un bel dì vedremo (orch. R. Romani)
49571-1, -**2**   CDS 9964, NI 7846, NI 7802, AB 78576
9 January 1919

26. *Mademoiselle Modiste* (Herbert): Kiss Me Again (orch. R. Romani)
49869-1, -**2**   CDS 9964, NI 7846, NI 7851, MET 218CD, AB 78576
26 July 1920

27. *Manon Lescaut* (Puccini): In quelle
    trine morbide (orch. R. Romani)
    79971-1, -**2**   MET 218CD
    7 September 1921
    -**3**   (with recitative) CDS 9964,
        NI 7846
    19 September 1923
    -4
    11 October 1923

28. Maria, Marì (Di Capua)
    (orch. R. Romani)
    49870-1, -**2**   CDS 9964, VA 1120,
        NI 7878, MIN 7, RY 74, AB 78576
    26 July 1920

29. *Maritana* (Wallace): Scenes That
    Are Brightest (orch. R. Romani)
    49982-1, -**2**   CDS 9964, MET 218CD
    9 September 1921

30. *Norma* (Bellini): Casta diva
    (orch. R. Romani)
    49720-1, -2, -3, -**4**   CDS 9964,
        AB 78576
    11 December 1919

31. Oh! That We Two Were Maying
    (Nevin), with C. Ponselle
    (orch. R. Romani)
    80391-1, -2, -3   (unpublished)
    9 June 1922

32. Old Folks at Home (Foster)
    (orch. R. Romani)
    49934-**1**   CDS 9964
    15 February 1921

33. 'O Sole Mio (Capurro-Di Capua),
    with C. Ponselle (orch. R. Romani)
    49983-**1**   CDS 9964, VA 1120, MIN 7,
        RY 74
    9 September 1921

34. *Otello* (Verdi): Ave Maria
    (orch. R. Romani)
    98029-1, -**2**, 3   CDS 9964
    9 June 1922

35. I *pagliacci* (Leoncavallo): Stridono
    lassù (orch. R. Romani)
    98063-1, -2
    13 February 1923
    -3, -4, -5
    22 September 1923
    -**6**, -7   CDS 9964, NI 7878,
        MET 218CD
    11 January 1924

36. Rachem (Manna-Zucca) [Yiddish]
    (orch. R. Romani)
    49925-1, -2, -**3**   CDS 9964
    8 January 1921

37. Rose of My Heart (Löhr)
    (orch. R. Romani)
    49987-1   (unpublished)
    17 September 1921

38. Rose of My Heart (Löhr)
    (orch. R. Romani)
    80307-**1**   CDS 9964
    13 April 1922

39. *Sadko* (Rimsky-Korsakov): Song of
    India [Eng.] (orch. R. Romani)
    49920-1, -**2**   CDS 9964, NI 7846,
        AB 78576
    30 December 1920

40. *Tales of Hoffmann* (Offenbach):
    Barcarolle [Eng.], with C. Ponselle
    (orch. R. Romani)
    78846-1, -**2**, -3   CDS 9964, AB 78576
    9 December 1919

41. *Tosca* (Puccini): Vissi d'arte
(orch. R. Romani)
49569-1, -2, -3, -4, **-5** CDS 9964,
NI 7846, NI 7851, AB 78576
7 January 1919

42. *Il trovatore* (Verdi): Tacea la notte
(orch. R. Romani)
98051-**1**, -2 CDS 9964, NI 7878
16 November 1922

43. *Il trovatore* (Verdi): D'amor sull'ali
rosee (orch. R. Romani)
49559-1, -2, -3, **-4** CDS 9964, NI
7846, MET 409CD, CD MOIR 428,
AB 78576
10 December 1918

44. *Il trovatore* (Verdi): Mira d'acerbe
lagrime, with R. Stracciari
(orch. R. Romani)
49922-1, **-2** CDS 9964, MET 218CD,
CD MOIR 428, AB 78576
30 December 1920

45. Values (Vanderpool)
(orch. R. Romani)
78920-1, -2, **-3** CDS 9964, AB 78576
10 January 1920

46. *I vespri siciliani* (Verdi): Mercè, di-
lette amiche (orch. R. Romani)
49686-1, -2, **-3** CDS 9964,
MET 218CD, AB 78576
4 November 1919

47. Where My Caravan Has Rested
(Löhr), with C. Ponselle
(orch. R. Romani)
80392-1
2 June 1922
-2, **-3** CDS 9964
13 June 1922

48. Whispering Hope (Hawthorne),
with B. Maurel (orch. R. Romani)
78325-1, -2, -3
1 March 1919
-4, **-5**, **-6**
9 July 1919

VICTOR RECORDS

49. *L'africana* (Meyerbeer): Figlio del
sol (orch. R. Bourdon)
C 31710-**1** MET 218CD,
ROM 81006-2 (B)
-2 BMG 7810-2-RG,
ROM 81006-2 (B)
14 January 1925

50. Agnus Dei (Bizet) (org. I.
Chichagov)
(no matrix number as-
signed) ROM 81022-2 (C)
20 October 1954

51. *Aida* (Verdi): Ritorna vincitor
(orch. R. Bourdon)
C 29063-1, **-2** ROM 81006-2 (A)
5 December 1923
-3, **-4** ROM 81006-2 (A)
11 December 1923
CVE 29063-5, **-6** ROM 81007-2 (A)
20 MAY 1926
-7, -8
8 DECEMBER 1927
-9 NI 7846, BMG 7810-2-RG,
ROM 81007-2 (B), CD MOIR 428,
CD 9210
18 January 1928

52. *Aida* (Verdi): Qui Radamès verà
. . . O patria mia
(orch. R. Bourdon)
C 29061-1, -**2**   NI 7805, MET 218CD,
   BMG 7810-2-RG, ROM 81006-2 (A),
   CD MOIR 428
5 December 1923
-3, -4
11 December 1923
CVE 29061-5, -**6**   ROM 81007-2 (B)
20 May 1926

53. *Aida* (Verdi): Pur ti riveggo, mia
dolce Aida, with G. Martinelli
(orch. R. Bourdon)
C 29446-1, -**2**, -3   NI 7805,
   ROM 81006-2 (A), MET 706CD,
   CD MOIR 428
7 FEBRUARY 1924

54. *Aida* (Verdi): Là tra foreste ver-
gine, with G. Martinelli (orch.
R. Bourdon)
C 29447-1, -**2**   NI 7805,
   ROM 81006-2 (A), MET 706CD,
   CD MOIR 428
7 February 1924

55. *Aida* (Verdi): La fatal pietra, with
G. Martinelli (orch. R. Bourdon)
C 29451-**1**   ROM 81006-2 (A)
-**2**   ROM 81006-2(A), NI 7878
8 February 1924

56. *Aida* (Verdi): O terra, addio!, with
G. Martinelli (orch. R. Bourdon)
C 29450-**1**, -2   ROM 81006-2 (A),
   NI 7878
8 February 1924

57. *Aida* (Verdi): La fatal pietra, with
G. Martinelli (orch. R. Bourdon)
BVE 35459-1, -2, -**3**   NI 7846,
   ROM 81007-2 (A), MET 503CD,
   CD MOIR 428
17 May 1926

58. *Aida* (Verdi): Morir! si pura e
bella!, with G. Martinelli
(orch. R. Bourdon)
BVE 35460-1, -2, -**3**   NI 7846,
   ROM 81007-2 (A), MET 503CD,
   CD MOIR 428
17 May 1926

59. *Aida* (Verdi): O terra, addio! (Part
1), with G. Martinelli & chorus
(orch. R. Bourdon)
BVE 35461-**1**, -2   NI 7846,
   ROM 81007-2 (A), MET 503CD,
   CD MOIR 428
17 May 1926

60. *Aida* (Verdi): O terra, addio! (Part
2), with G. Martinelli, E. Baker &
chorus (orch. R. Bourdon)
BVE 35462-1, -**2**, -3   NI 7846,
   ROM 81007-2 (A), MET 503CD,
   CD MOIR 428
17 May 1926

61. A l'aime (de Fontenailles)
(pf. R. Romani)
PBS 042207-2, -3,-**5**   NI 7839,
   BMG 7810-2-RG, ROM 81022-2 (A)
31 October 1939

62. *Amadis* (Lully): Bois épais (pf.
I. Chichagov)
E 4-RC-0701-1, -**2**
   ROM 81022-2 (B)
16 October 1954

63. Amuri, amuri (Sadero) (pf.
    R. Ponselle)
    E 4-RC-0707-**1**, -2   BMG 7810-2-RG,
       ROM 81022-2 (B)
    17 October 1954

64. An die Musik, op. 88, no. 4
    (Schubert) (pf. I. Chichagov)
    E 4-RC 0723-**1**   ROM 81022-2 (C)
    20 October 1954

65. Aprile (Tosti) (pf. I. Chichagov)
    E 4-RC-0710-**1**   ROM 81022-2 (B)
    18 October 1954

66. Asturiana (from *Seven Popular
    Spanish Songs*) (de Falla) [Sp.] (pf.
    I. Chichagov)
    E 4-RC-0727-1, -**2**
       ROM 81022-2 (C)
    18 October 1954

67. Ave Maria (Bach-Gounod)
    (orch. R. Bourdon)
    CVE 35470-1, -**2**   NI 7846,
       BMG 7810-2-RG,
       ROM 81007-2 (A),
       CD 9210
    19 May 1926

68. Ave Maria (Kahn)
    (orch. R. Bourdon)
    BVE 38856-1
    2 June 1927
    -2, -3, -4
    13 June 1927
    -5, -**6**   ROM 81007-2 (A)
    16 June 1927

69. Ave Maria (Luzzi) (org.
    I. Chichagov)
    (no matrix number as-
       signed)   ROM 81022-2 (C)
    20 October 1954

70. Ave Maria (Millard) (org.
    I. Chichagov)
    (no matrix number as-
       signed)   ROM 81022-2 (C)
    20 October 1954

71. Ave Maria (Sandoval) (org.
    I. Chichagov)
    (no matrix number as-
       signed)   ROM 81022-2 (C)
    20 October 1954

72. Ave Maria, op. 52, no. 6 (Schubert)
    (pf. R. Romani; violin M. Schmidt)
    PCS 42212-2, -3, -**5**   NI 7861,
       ROM 81022-2 (A), MET 206CD
    1 November 1939
    -9, -**10**   ROM 81022-2 (A)
    7 November 1939

73. Ave Maria (Tosti) (pf. I. Chi-
    chagov)
    E 4-RC-0722-1   ROM 81022-2 (C)
    20 October 1954

74. 'A Vucchella (Tosti) (orch.
    R. Bourdon)
    BVE 35466-1, -**2**, -3   ROM 81007-2
       (A), MET 210CD, CD 9210
    18 May 1926

75. 'A Vucchella (Tosti) (pf. I. Chi-
    chagov)
    (no matrix number as-
       signed)   ROM 81022-2 (A)
    18 October 1954

76. I battitori di grano (Sadero) (pf.
    I. Chichagov)
    E 4-RC-0706-**1**, -2
    ROM 81022-2 (B)
    17 October 1954

77. Beau soir (Debussy) (pf. I. Chi-
    chagov)
    (no matrix number as-
    signed)   ROM 81022-2 (A)
    17 October 1954

78. Beloved (Silberta)
    (orch. J. Pasternack)
    BVE 32852-1
    1 June 1925
    -2, -3, -4
    4 June 1925
    -**5**, -6   LCD 179-1, ROM 81006-2 (B)
    5 June 1925

79. Bonjour, Suzon (Delibes) (pf.
    I. Chichagov)
    (no matrix number as-
    signed)   ROM 81022-2 (A)
    17 October 1954

80. Carmè (arr. De Curtis) (orch.
    R. Bourdon)
    B 29878-1, -**2**, -3   NI 7805,
    ROM 81006-2 (B)
    11 April 1924

81. Carmen-Carmela (arr. Ross) [Sp.]
    (pf. I. Chichagov)
    (no matrix number as-
    signed)   BMG 7810-2-RG,
    ROM 81022-2 (A)
    21 October 1954

82. Carry Me Back to Old Virginny
    (Bland) (orch. J. Pasternack)
    CVE 32856-1, -2, -**3**
    ROM 81006-2 (B),
    NI 7878, CD 9210
    2 June 1925

83. La chevelure (Debussy) (pf. I. Chi-
    chagov)
    (no matrix number as-
    signed)   ROM 81022-2 (A)
    17 October 1954

84. Colombetta (Buzzi-Peccia) (pf.
    I. Chichagov)
    E 4-RC-0725-1   ROM 81022-2 (C)
    (incomplete)
    20 October 1954

85. Could I? (Tosti) (Pf. R. Ponselle)
    (no matrix number as-
    signed)   ROM 81022-2 (A)
    21 October 1954

86. Cradle Song, op. 49, no. 4
    (Brahms) [Eng.]
    (orch. R. Bourdon)
    B 29453-**1**   ROM 81006-2 (A)
    8 February 1924

87. Cradle Song, op. 49, no. 4
    (Brahms) [Eng.] (pf. R. Bourdon)
    B 29454-1 (unpublished)
    8 February 1924

88. Dicitencello vuje (Falvo) (pf.
    R. Ponselle)
    (no matrix number as-
    signed)   ROM 81022-2 (A)
    21 October 1954

89. Drink to Me Only with Thine Eyes
   (Jonson) (pf. I. Chichagov)
   E 4-RC-0719-**1**   ROM 81022-2 (B)
   19 October 1954

90. Elégie (Massenet) (orch.
   R. Bourdon)
   CVE 35469-**1**, -2   ROM 81007-2 (A),
     NI 7846, CD 9210
   -3   ROM 81007-2 (A)
   19 May 1926

91. Der Erlkönig, op. 1 (Schubert) (pf.
   I. Chichagov)
   E 4-RC-0715-**1**, -2   ROM 81022-2 (B)
   19 October 1954

92. *Ernani* (Verdi): Surta è la notte . . .
   Ernani! Ernani, involami! (orch.
   R. Bourdon)
   C 29062-**1**   ROM 81006-2 (A)
   5 December 1923
   -2, -3
   11 December 1923
   -4   NI 7805, MET 218CD,
     ROM 81006-2 (A)
   23 January 1924
   CVE 29062-**5**   ROM 81007-2 (A),
     CD 9210
   16 June 1927
   -6   BMG 7810-2-RG,
     ROM 81007-2 (B),
     CD MOIR 428, CD 9210
   17 January 1928

93. Extase (Duparc) (pf. I. Chichagov)
   (no matrix number assigned)
   17 October 1954 (unpublished)

94. Fa la nana, bambin (Sadero) (pf.
   R. Ponselle)
   E 4-RC-0708-1, **-2**
     ROM 81022-2 (A)
   17 October 1954

95. *La forza del destino* (Verdi): La
   Vergine degli angeli, with E.
   Pinza & chorus (orch. G. Setti)
   CVE 41636-**1**   NI 7805, MET 105CD,
     CD 9351, ROM 81007-2 (B),
     CD MOIR 428
   23 January 1928

96. *La forza del destino* (Verdi): Pace,
   pace, mio Dio (orch. R. Bourdon)
   C 29060-1, -2
   5 DECEMBER 1923
   -3   ROM 81006-2 (A)
   -4   ROM 81006-2 (A), NI 7878
   11 December 1923
   -5   MET 218CD, ROM 81006-2 (A),
     BMG 0926-61580-2
   23 January 1924
   CVE 29060-6
   13 June 1927
   -7
   16 June 1927
   -8   NI 7878, BMG 7810-2-RG,
     CD 9351, ROM 81007-2 (B),
     CD MOIR 428
   -9   ROM 81007-2 (B), CD 9210
   17 January 1928

97. *La forza del destino* (Verdi): Io
muoio!, with G. Martinelli & E.
Pinza (orch. R. Bourdon)
CVE 41625-**1**   ROM 81007-2 (B)
-**2**   BMG 7810-2-RG, CD 9351, ROM
81007-2 (B), CD MOIR 428, CD
9210
18 January 1928

98. *La forza del destino* (Verdi): Non
imprecare, with G. Martinelli & E.
Pinza (orch. R. Bourdon)
CVE 41626-**1**   ROM 81007-2 (B)
-**2**   BMG 7810-2-RG, CD 9351,
ROM 81007-2 (B), CD MOIR 428,
CD 9210
18 January 1928

99. *La Gioconda* (Ponchielli): Suicidio!
(orch. R. Bourdon)
C 31709-**1**   NI 7805,
BMG 7810-2-RG, ROM 81006-2 (B)
-**2**   ROM 81006-2 (B)
14 January 1925

100. Goodbye (Tosti) (orch.
R. Bourdon)
CVE 29876-**1**   ROM 81006-2 (B)
-**2**   ROM 81006-2 (B)
11 April 1924
CVE 29876-3, -4
2 June 1927
-5, -**6**   ROM 81007-2 (A)
13 June 1927

101. Guitares et mandolines (Saint-
Saëns) (pf. I. Chichagov)
E 4-RC-0702-**1**   ROM 81022-2 (B)
20 October 1954

102. Happy Days (Strelezki) (orch.
J. Pasternack)
BVE 32839-1, -2, -3 (unpublished)
1 June 1925
-4, -5, -6
4 June 1925
-7, -8
5 June 1925

103. Home, Sweet Home (Bishop)
(orch. J. Pasternack)
CVE 32866-1, -**2**   LCD 179-1,
ROM 81006-2 (B)
3 June 1925

104. Homing (Del Riego) [Eng.] (pf.
I. Chichagov)
E 4-RC-0718-1, -**2**
ROM 81022-2 (B)
18 October 1954

105. Ideale (Tosti) (pf. I. Chichagov)
E 4-RC-0709-**1**   ROM 81022-2 (A)
18 October 1954

106. In questa tomba oscura (Beetho-
ven) (pf. I. Chichagov)
E 4-RC-0726-**1**, -2
ROM 81022-2 (B)
17 October 1954

107. In the Luxembourg Gardens
(Lockhart-Manning) (pf. I. Chichagov)
(no matrix number as-
signed)   ROM 81022-2 (C)
19 October 1954

108. L'invitation au voyage (Duparc)
(pf. I. Chichagov)
(no matrix number as-
signed)   ROM 81022-2 (C)
17 October 1954

109. Jeunes fillettes (18th-cen. Bergerette; arr J. B. Weckerlin) (pf. I. Chichagov)
     E 4-RC-0703-**1** ROM 81022-2 (A)
     17 October 1954

110. The Little Old Garden (Hewitt) (orch. J. Pasternack)
     BVE 32850-1, -**2**, -3 LCD 179-1,
       ROM 81006-2 (B), VA 1120, MIN 7,
       RY 74
     1 June 1925

111. Love's Sorrow (Shelley) (orch. R. Bourdon)
     B 29875-1, -**2** ROM 81006-2 (A)
     11 April 1924

112. Lullaby (Scott) (pf. R. Bourdon)
     B 29412-1 (unpublished)
     23 January 1924

113. Lullaby (Scott) (orch. R. Bourdon)
     B 29452-**1**, -2 MET 218CD,
       ROM 81006-2 (A)
     8 February 1924

114. Luna d'estate (Tosti) (orch. R. Bourdon)
     BVE 35467-1, -**2**, -3 MET 218CD,
       ROM 81007-2 (A), NI 7878,
       CD 9210
     18 May 1926

115. Marechiare (Tosti) (pf. I. Chichagov)
     (no matrix number assigned) ROM 81022-2 (A)
     18 October 1954

116. Maria, Marì! (Di Capua) (orch. R. Bourdon)
     B 29411-1, -2
     23 January 1924
     -3, -**4** NI 7805, ROM 81006-2 (B)
     11 April 1924

117. El Mirar de la Maja (Granados) (pf. I. Chichagov)
     (no matrix number assigned) ROM 81022-2 (A)
     18 October 1954

118. Mir träumte von einem Königskind, op. 4, no. 5 (Trunk) (pf. I. Chichagov)
     E 4-RC-0712-**1** ROM 81022-2 (B)
     18 October 1954

119. *Molinara* (Paisiello): Nel cor più non me sento (pf. I. Chichagov)
     E 4-RC-0721-**1** ROM 81022-2 (A)
     18 October 1954

120. Morgen, op. 27, no. 4 (Strauss) (pf. I. Chichagov)
     E 4-RC-0717-**1** ROM 81022-2 (C)
     19 October 1954

121. My Dearest Heart (Sullivan) (orch. J. Pasternack)
     BVE 32853-1, -2 (unpublished)
     1 June 1925
     -3, -4
     2 June 1925
     -5, -6, -7
     4 June 1925
     -8, -9, -10
     5 June 1925

122. My Lovely Celia (Higgins)
(orch. R. Bourdon)
B 29877-1, -2   ROM 81006-2 (B)
11 April 1924

123. My Lovely Celia (Munro) (pf.
I. Chichagov)
(no matrix number as-
signed)   ROM 81022-2 (C)
18 October 1954124.

124. My Old Kentucky Home (Foster)
(orch. J. Pasternack)
CVE 32857-1, -2, -3
ROM 81006-2 (B),
NI 7878, CD 9210
2 June 1925

125. Nana (from *Seven Popular Spanish
Songs*) (de Falla) [Sp.] (pf. I. Chichagov)
E 4-RC-0728-1   ROM 81022-2 (C)
18 October 1954

126. The Nightingale and the Rose
(Rimsky-Korsakov) [Eng.] (orch.
R. Bourdon; flute C. Barone)
BVE 38857-1, -2   ROM 81007-2 (A)
2 June 1927

127. The Nightingale and the Rose
(Rimsky-Korsakov) [Eng.] (pf.
R. Romani)
PBS 042208-2, -3   NI 7805,
BMG 7810-2-RG, ROM 81022-2,
VA 1120, MIN 7, RY 74
31 October 1939

128. The Night Wind (Farley) (pf.
I. Chichagov)
E 4-RC-0720-1, -2
ROM 81022-2 (B)
19 October 1954

129. *Norma* (Bellini): Sediziose voci . . .
Casta diva (Part 1) (orch. G. Setti,
with Metropolitan Opera Chorus)
CVE 49031-1
31 December 1928
-2, -3, -4   NI 7805, NI 7801,
BMG 7810-2-RG, CD 9317,
ROM 81007-2 (B), CD 9210
30 January 1929

130. *Norma* (Bellini): Ah! bello a me ri-
torna (Part 2) (orch. G. Setti, with
Metropolitan Opera Chorus)
CVE 49032-1, -2   NI 7805, NI 7801,
BMG 7810-2-RG, CD 9317,
ROM 81007-2 (B), CD 9210
31 December 1928

131. *Norma:* Mira, o Norma (Part 1),
with M. Telva (orch. G. Setti)
CVE 49703-1, -2   NI 7805,
MET 218CD, CD 9317,
ROM 81007-2 (B), CD 9210
30 January 1929

132. *Norma:* Cedi . . . deh cedi! (Part 2),
with M. Telva (orch. G. Setti)
CVE 49704-1, -2   NI 7805,
MET 218CD, CD 9317,
ROM 81007-2 (B), CD 9210
30 January 1929

133. *Le nozze di Figaro* (Mozart): Voi che sapete (pf. I. Chichagov) (no matrix number assigned) ROM 81022-2 (C) 21 October 1954

134. Nur wer die Sehnsucht kennt, op. 6, no. 6 (Tchaikovsky) (pf. I. Chichagov) (no matrix number assigned) ROM 81022-2 (C) 16 October 1954

135. O del mio amato ben (Donaudy) (pf. I. Chichagov) E 4-RC-0714-1, -**2** ROM 81022-2 (B) 19 October 1954

136. Old Folks at Home (Foster) (orch. J. Pasternack) CVE 32865-1 3 June 1925 -**2**, -**3** ROM 81006-2 (B), NI 7878 -**4** ROM 81006-2 (B) 4 June 1925

137. On Wings of Dream (Arensky) [Eng.] (pf. R. Romani; violin M. Schmidt) PCS 042213-1, -3, -**5** NI 7805, ROM 81022-2 (A), BIM 701-2, VA 1120, MIN 7, RY 74 1 November 1939

138. *Otello* (Verdi): Salce! Salce! (orch. R. Bourdon) C 29410-**1**, -2 NI 7805, BMG 7810-2-RG, ROM 81006-2 (A) 23 January 1924

139. *Otello* (Verdi): Ave Maria (double string quartet, R. Bourdon) C 29409-**1**, -2, -3 NI 7805, MET 207CD, ROM 81006-2 (A) 23 January 1924

140. Panis angelicus (Franck) (org. I. Chichagov) (no matrix number assigned) (unpublished) 20 October 1954

141. La partida (Alvarez) (pf. I. Chichagov) E 4-RC-0713-**1** ROM 81022-2 (A) 18 October 1954

142. A Perfect Day (Bond) (orch. J. Pasternack) BVE 32867-**1**, -2, -3 NI 7805, ROM 81006-2 (B) 3 June 1925

143. Plaisir d'amour (Martini) (pf. I. Chichagov) (no matrix number assigned) ROM 81022-2 (A) 17 October 1954

144. Psyché (Paladilhe) (pf. I. Chichagov) (no matrix number assigned) ROM 81022-2 (C) 21 October 1954

145. Rispetto (Wolf-Ferrari) (pf. I. Chichagov) E 4-RC-0724-1, -**2** ROM 81022-2 (B) 20 October 1954

146. The Rosary (Nevin) (orch.
   J. Pasternack)
   BVE 32864-1, -2, -3
   3 June 1925
   -4, -5, -6
   4 June 1925
   -7, -8   ROM 81006-2 (B)
   5 June 1925

147. Rosemonde (Persico) [Fr.] (pf.
   I. Chichagov)
   E 4-RC-0704-1   ROM 81022-2 (B)
   17 October 1954

148. La Rosita (Dupont, pseud.
   G. Haenschen) [Eng.] (orch.
   J. Pasternack)
   BVE 32851-1, -2, -3
   1 June 1925
   -4, -5   LCD 179-1, ROM 81006-2 (B),
   VA 1120, MIN 7, RY 74
   4 June 1925

149. Se (Denza) [It.] (pf. I. Chichagov)
   (no matrix number as-
   signed)   ROM 81022-2 (C)
   18 October 1954

150. Serenade (Tosti) [Eng.] (harp
   F. Lapitino)
   C 29879-1, -2   ROM 81006-2 (B)
   -3   ROM 81006-2 (B), NI 7878
   12 April 1924
   CVE 29879-4, -5   ROM 81007-2 (A)
   2 June 1927

151. Since First I Met Thee (Rubin-
   stein) (orch. R. Bourdon; cello
   Lennartz)
   BVE 41624-1, -2, -3
   ROM 81007-2 (B)
   17 January 1928

152. Si tu le voulais (Tosti) (pf.
   R. Romani)
   PBS 042206-2, -3, -5
   ROM 81022-2 (A), NI 7878
   31 October 1939

153. Songs My Mother Taught Me, op.
   55, no. 4 (Dvořák) [Eng.] (orch.
   R. Bourdon)
   BVE 41623-1   ROM 81007-2 (B)
   17 January 1928

154. La Spagnola (Di Chiara) [Eng.]
   (orch. J. Pasternack)
   BVE 32873-1, -2, -3   BIM 701-2,
   LCD 179-1, ROM 81006-2 (B),
   VA 1120, MIN 7, RY 74
   5 June 1925

155. Ständchen (Schubert), with C.
   Ponselle (orch. R. Bourdon)
   CVE 35471-1, -2   ROM 81007-2
   (COMPOSITE OF BOTH TAKES)
   19 May 1926

156. Star vicino (attr. Rosa) (pf. I. Chichagov)
   E 4-RC-0715-1   ROM 81022-2 (A)
   19 October 1954

157. Le temps des lilas (Chausson) (pf.
   I. Chichagov)
   E 4-RC-0705-1   ROM 81022-2 (B)
   17 October 1954

158. Der Tod und das Mädchen, op. 7,
   no. 3 (Schubert) (pf. I. Chichagov)
   (no matrix number as-
   signed)   ROM 81022-2 (C)
   18 October 1954

159. Träume (*Wesendonck Lieder,* no. 5)
(Wagner) (pf. I. Chichagov)
(no matrix number as-
signed) ROM 81022-2 (C)
19 October 1954

160. Tre giorni son che Nina (Ciampi)
(pf. I. Chichagov)
(no matrix number as-
signed) ROM 81022-2 (C)
19 October 1954

161. Tristesse éternelle (Vocal air of
Etude, op. 10, no. 3) (Chopin-
Litvinne) (pf. I. Chichagov)
(no matrix number as-
signed) ROM 81022-2 (C)
21 October 1954

162. *Il trovatore* (Verdi): Miserere, with
G. Martinelli and Metropolitan
Opera Chorus (orch. G. Setti)
CVE 41637-**1** ROM 81007-2 (B),
CD MOIR 428 (-**1**)
-2 ROM 81007-2 (B)
23 January 1928

163. *La vestale* (Spontini): Tu che in-
voco (orch. R. Bourdon)
CVE 35464-**1**, -2 NI 7805,
MET 218CD, ROM 81007-2 (A),
CD 9210
18 May 1926

164. *La vestale* (Spontini): O nume tutelar (orch. R. Bourdon)
CVE 35465-**1** NI 7805,
BMG 7810-2-RG, ROM 81007-2 (A),
CD 9210
-**2** ROM 81007-2 (A)
18 May 1926

165. Von ewiger Liebe, op. 43, no. 1
(Brahms) (pf. I. Chichagov)
E 4-RC-0711-**1** ROM 81022-2 (B)
18 October 1954

166. When I Have Sung My Songs
(Charles) (pf. R. Romani)
PBS 042209-**1** BMG 7810-2-RG,
ROM 81022-2 (A)
-2, -**3** ROM 81022-2 (A)
31 October 1939

RADIO BROADCASTS

Annie Laurie (Trad.)
General Motors Hour: 31 May
1936, orch. E. Rapée
LCD 179-1, VA 1120, MIN 7, RY74

Ave Maria (Kahn)
Cincinnati Symphony Proms
Concert: 25 April 1937, orch.
E. Goossens
EKR 51

Big Brown Bear (Manna-Zucca)
Chesterfield Hour: 3 December
1934, orch. A. Kostelanetz
RY17

Blue Danube Waltz (Strauss)
Chesterfield Hour: 15 October
1934, orch. A. Kostelanetz
LCD 179-1, RY17

Carmé (arr. De Curtis)
"Then and Now": 10 December
1936, orch. C. Kelsey
EKR 51

Carmen (Bizet) with Maison, Pinza,
Burke
    Metropolitan Opera: 28 March
    1936, orch. L. Hasselmans
    EKR CD 6
Carmen (Bizet) with Maison, Pinza,
Burke
    Metropolitan Opera: 17 April 1937,
    orch. G. Papi
    WHL 15
Carmen (Bizet): Air des cartes
    Chesterfield Hour: 26 February
    1936, orch. A. Kostelanetz
    BIM 701-2
Carmen (Bizet): Chanson bohème
    Chesterfield Hour: 4 March 1936,
    orch. A. Kostelanetz
    BIM 701-2
Carmen (Bizet): Habanera
    Chesterfield Hour: 25 March 1936,
    orch. A. Kostelanetz
    BIM 701-2
Carmen (Bizet): Seguidilla
    Chesterfield Hour: 26 February
    1936, orch. A. Kostelanetz
    BIM 701-2, RY17
Carry Me Back to Old Virginny (Bland)
    RCA Magic Key: 2 May 1937,
    orch. F. Black
    LCD 179-1, BIM 701-2, RY17
Cavalleria rusticana: Ave Maria
    Chesterfield Hour: 8 October 1934,
    orch. A. Kostelanetz
    BIM 701-2, RY17

Cavalleria rusticana: Voi lo sapete
    Chesterfield Hour: 11 March 1936,
    orch. A. Kostelanetz
    BIM 701-2
The Chocolate Soldier (Straus): My Hero
    Chesterfield Hour: 8 October 1934,
    orch. A. Kostelanetz
    BIM 701-2
The Chocolate Soldier (Straus): My
Hero, with F. Forest
    Cincinnati Symphony Proms Con-
    cert: 25 April 1937,
    orch. E. Goossens
    LCD 179-1, EKR 51, VA 1120, MIN 7,
    RY74
Comin' thro' the Rye (Trad.)
    Chesterfield Hour: 11 March 1936,
    orch. A. Kostelanetz
    BIM 701-2, LCD 179-1
The Cuckoo (Lehmann)
    Chesterfield Hour: 1 April 1936,
    orch. A. Kostelanetz
    LCD 179-1, VA 1120, MIN 7, RY74
The Cuckoo Clock (Griselle-Young)
    Chesterfield Hour: 1 October 1934,
    orch. A. Kostelanetz
    LCD 179-1, VA 1120, MIN 7, RY74
Danny Boy (Trad.)
    Chesterfield Hour: 4 March 1936,
    orch. A. Kostelanetz
    LCD 179-1, BIM 701-2
Dicitencello vuje (Falvo)
    General Motors Hour: 27 Septem-
    ber 1936, orch. E. Rapée
    BIM 701-2

Don Giovanni (Mozart): Batti, batti
Chesterfield Hour: 1 October 1934,
orch. A. Kostelanetz
BIM 701-2, RY17

A Dream (Bartlett)
Chesterfield Hour: 26 November
1934, orch. A. Kostelanetz
LCD 179-1, RY17

Fedra (Romani): O divina Afrodite
RCA Magic Key: 2 May 1937,
orch. F. Black
BIM 701-2

La forza del destino: La Vergine degli
angeli
"Then and Now": 10 December
1936, orch. C. Kelsey
EKR 51

Goodbye (Tosti)
Chesterfield Hour: 1 April 1936,
orch. A. Kostelanetz
BIM 701-2, LCD 179-1, RY17

Here's to Romance (Grosvener): I Carry
You in My Pocket
Chesterfield Hour: 26 February
1936, orch. A. Kostelanetz
LCD 179-1, VA 1120, MIN 7, RY74

Home, Sweet Home (Bishop)
RCA Magic Key: 2 May 1937,
orch. F. Black
LCD 179-1, VA 1120, MIN 7, RY74

Homing (Del Riego)
General Motors Hour: 27 September 1936, orch. E. Rapée
BIM 701-2, LCD 179-1

Humoresque (Dvořák)
Chesterfield Hour: 18 March 1936,
orch. A. Kostelanetz
BIM 701-2, LCD 179-1, VA 1120,
MIN 7, RY74

I Love You Truly (Bond)
Chesterfield Hour: 1 October 1934,
orch. A. Kostelanetz
BIM 701-2, LCD 179-1, VA 1120,
MIN 7, RY74

The Last Rose of Summer (Moore)
Chesterfield Hour: 29 October
1934, orch. A. Kostelanetz
BIM 701-2 .

Mademoiselle Modiste (Herbert): Kiss
Me Again
"Then and Now": 10 December
1936, orch. C. Kelsey
ERK 51

Mademoiselle Modiste (Herbert): Kiss
Me Again
RCA Magic Key: 2 May 1937,
orch. F. Black
LCD 179-1, VA 1120, MIN 7, RY74

Marechiare (Tosti)
General Motors Hour: 31 May
1936, orch. E. Rapée
RY17

Moonlight Bay (Madden-Wenrich)
"Then and Now": 10 December
1936, orch. C. Kelsey
EKR 51, EKR CD46

El Morenito (Buzzi-Peccia)
Chesterfield Hour: 1 April 1936,
orch. A. Kostelanetz
RY17

The Night Wind (Farley)
  Chesterfield Hour: 25 March 1936,
  orch. A. Kostelanetz
  LCD 179-1
The Night Wind (Farley)
  Cincinnati Symphony Proms Con-
  cert: 25 April 1937,
  orch. E. Goossens
  EKR 51
None but the Lonely Heart
(Tchaikovsky)
  Chesterfield Hour: 26 February
  1936, orch. A. Kostelanetz
  BIM 701-2, RY17
None but the Lonely Heart
(Tchaikovsky)
  Cincinnati Symphony Proms Con-
  cert: 25 April 1937
  EKR 51
The Old Refrain (Kreisler)
  Chesterfield Hour: 11 March 1936,
  orch. A. Kostelanetz
  BIM 701-2, LCD 179-1, VA 1120,
    MIN 7, RY74, RY17
The Old Refrain (Kreisler)
  Cincinnati Symphony Proms Con-
  cert: 25 April 1937,
  orch. E. Goossens
  EKR 51
Otello (Verdi): Ave Maria
  General Motors Hour: 27 Septem-
  ber 1936, orch. E. Rapée
  BIM 701-2, RY17
Ouvre ton coeur (Bizet)
  Chesterfield Hour: 18 March 1936,
  orch. A. Kostelanetz
  RY17

La traviata (Verdi)
  Metropolitan Opera: 5 January
  1935, orch. E. Panizza
  PEARL CD 9317, FT 1513.14, RY 10.02
L'ultima canzone (Tosti)
  Chesterfield Hour: 11 March 1936,
  orch. A. Kostelanetz
  RY17
La vestale (Spontini): Tu che invoco
  Chesterfield Hour: 1 April 1936,
  orch. A. Kostelanetz
  BIM 701-2, RY17
What Is in the Air Today (Eden)
  Chesterfield Hour: 26 November
  1934, orch. A. Kostelanetz
  RY17
When I Have Sung My Songs (Charles)
  Chesterfield Hour: 18 March 1936,
  orch. A. Kostelanetz
  LCD 179-1, BIM 701-2

17 March 1954
  Rosa Ponselle and Boris Goldovsky
  discuss Bellini's Norma
  EKR51
11 March 1960
  Rosa Ponselle and Boris Goldovsky
  discuss Verdi's La forza del destino
  EKR51

PRIVATE RECORDINGS

Adriana Lecouvreur (Cilea): Io son
l'umile
  (pf.): 5 September 1953
  BIM 701-2

Adriana Lecouvreur (Cilea): Poveri fiori
    (pf.): 5 September 1953
    BIM 701-2
L'arlisiana (Cilea): Esser madre [Fr.]
    (pf.): 5 September 1953
    BIM 701-2
Ave Maria, op. 52, no. 6 (Schubert)
    (pf.): 25 September 1952
    EKR 51
Gianni Schicchi (Puccini): O mio
babbino caro
    30 June 1952
    BIM 701-2
Home, Sweet Home (Bishop)
    January 1952
    BIM 701-2
Kiss Me Kate (Porter): So in Love
    (pf. Romani): 5 January 1950
    LCD 179-1
Old Folks at Home (Foster)
    (pf.): 25 September 1952
    EKR 51
Manon (Massenet): Adieu notre petite
table
    (pf. Ponsell): 25 November 1952
    BIM 701-2
Russian Gypsy Song (Trad.) [Rus.]
    (pf. Chichagov): 30 March 1957
    BIM 701-2
Samson et Dalila (Saint-Saëns): Amour!
viens aider ma faiblesse!
    (pf. R. Lawrence): 7 November
    1953
    BIM 701-2

Samson et Dalila (Saint-Saëns): Mon
coeur s'ouvre à ta voix
    (pf. R. Lawrence): 7 November
    1953
    BIM 701-2
Samson et Dalila (Saint-Saëns):
Printemps qui commence
    (pf. R. Lawrence): 7 November
    1953
    BIM 701-2
South Pacific (Rodgers): Some
Enchanted Evening
    (pf. Romani): 5 January 1950
    BIM 701-2, LCD 179-1
South Pacific (Rodgers): Some
Enchanted Evening with John Charles
Thomas
    (pf.): 25 September 1952
    EKR 51
The Star Spangled Banner (Key)
    (pf.): 25 September 1952
    EKR 51
Die Tote Stadt (Korngold): Glück, das
mir verblieb
    (pf. Ponselle): 27 October 1951
    BIM 701-2
Rosa Ponselle and Ruby Mercer discuss
songs contained in *Rosa Ponselle Sings
Today,* circa 1955
    ROM 81022-2 (B)

COMPACT DISC RELEASES

Label: Biographies in Music
    Catalog Number: BIM 179-1
    Title: *Rosa Ponselle: The Cross-
    Over Album*

Label: Biographies in Music
Catalog Number: BIM 701-2
Title: *Rosa Ponselle: When I Have Sung My Songs*

Label: Eklipse
Catalog Number: EKR 51
Title: *Rosa Ponselle in Concert (1936–1952)*

Label: Eklipse
Catalog Number: EKR CD46
Title: *The American Prima Donna*

Label: Eklipse
Catalog Number: EKR CD 6
Title: *Carmen (Boston, 1936)*

Label: Forties Radio
Catalog Number: FT 1513.14
Title: *La traviata (1935)*

Label: Grammofono 2000
Catalog Number: AB 78576
Title: *Rosa Ponselle: Best from Her Acoustic Records*

Label: Legato Classics
Catalog Number: LCV 017 (VIDEO)
Title: *Legends of Opera* (includes Ponselle's MGM screen test, 1936)

Label: Memoir Classics
Catalog Number: CD MOIR 428
Title: *Rosa Ponselle and Giovanni Martinelli Sing Verdi*

Label: Metropolitan Opera
Catalog Number: MET 105CD
Title: *Ezio Pinza: Great Artists at the Met*

Label: Metropolitan Opera
Catalog Number: MET 207CD
Title: *A Sunday Night Concert at the Met*

Label: Metropolitan Opera
Catalog Number: MET 210CD
Title: *Songs Our Mothers Taught Us*

Label: Metropolitan Opera
Catalog Number: MET 218CD
Title: *Rosa Ponselle: Portraits in Memory*

Label: Metropolitan Opera
Catalog Number: MET 409CD
Title: *Great Operas: Il trovatore*

Label: Metropolitan Opera
Catalog Number: MET 503CD
Title: *Great Operas: Aida*

Label: Metropolitan Opera
Catalog Number: MET 706CD
Title: *Met Centurians: Giovanni Martinelli*

Label: Minerva
Catalog Number: MINERVA 7
Title: *Rosa Ponselle—Songs and Operettas (1918–1939)*

Label: Nimbus Prima Voce
Catalog Number: NI 7801
Title: *The Great Singers (1909–1938)*

Label: Nimbus Prima Voce
Catalog Number: NI 7802
Title: *Divas*

Label: Nimbus Prima Voce
Catalog Number: NI 7805
Title: *Rosa Ponselle, Volume 1*

Label: Nimbus Prima Voce
Catalog Number: NI 7839
Title: *Prima Voce Party*

Label: Nimbus Prima Voce
Catalog Number: NI 7846
Title: *Rosa Ponselle, Volume 2*

Label: Nimbus Prima Voce
Catalog Number: NI 7851
Title: *Legendary Voices*

Label: Nimbus Prima Voce
Catalog Number: NI 7861
Title: *The Spirit of Christmas Past*

Label: Nimbus Prima Voce
Catalog Number: NI 7878
Title: *Rosa Ponselle Volume*

Label: Pearl Gemm
Catalog Number: CD 9210
Title: *Rosa Ponselle: Casta Diva*

Label: Pearl Gemm
Catalog Number: CDS 9317
Title: *Rosa Ponselle in La traviata*

Label: Pearl Gemm
Catalog Number: CD 9351
Title: *La forza del destino—
Giovanni Martinelli*

Label: Pearl Gemm
Catalog Number: CDS 9964
Title: *Rosa Ponselle: The Columbia
Acoustical Recordings*

Label: Radio Years
Catalog Number: RY 10.02
Title: *La traviata (1935)*

Label: Radio Years
Catalog Number: RY 17
Title: *Rosa Ponselle on Radio
(1934–36)*

Label: Radio Years
Catalog Number: RY 74
Title: *Rosa Ponselle: Light on Radio*

Label: RCA/BMG
Catalog Number: 7910-1-RG
Title: *Rosa Ponselle: Verdi, Bellini,
Meyerbeer, Ponchielli*

Label: RCA/MET
Catalog Number: 0926-61580-2
Title: *100 Singers, 100 Years*

Label: Romophone
Catalog Number: 81006-2
Title: *Rosa Ponselle: The Victor Re-
cordings (1923–25)*

Label: Romophone
Catalog Number: 81007-2
Title: *Rosa Ponselle: The Victor Re-
cordings (1926–29)*

Label: Romophone
Catalog Number: 81022-2
Title: *Rosa Ponselle: The Victor Re-
cordings (1939–54)*

Label: Vocal Archives
Catalog Number: VA 1120
Title: *Rosa Ponselle: Rare Songs Re-
corded (1918–1939)*

Label: Walhall
Catalog Number: WHL15
Title: *Carmen (17 April 1937)*

Index